MARX'S PHILOSOPHY OF REVOLUTION
IN PERMANENCE FOR OUR DAY

Studies in Critical Social Sciences Book Series

Haymarket Books is proud to be working with Brill Academic Publishers (www.brill.nl) to republish the *Studies in Critical Social Sciences* book series in paperback editions. This peer-reviewed book series offers insights into our current reality by exploring the content and consequences of power relationships under capitalism, and by considering the spaces of opposition and resistance to these changes that have been defining our new age. Our full catalog of *SCSS* volumes can be viewed at https://www.haymarketbooks .org/series_collections/4-studies-in-critical-social-sciences.

Marx's Philosophy of Revolution in Permanence for Our Day

Selected Writings

Raya Dunayevskaya

Edited by
Franklin Dmitryev

Haymarket Books
Chicago, IL

First published in 2018 by Brill Academic Publishers, The Netherlands.
© 2018 Koninklijke Brill NV, Leiden, The Netherlands

Published in paperback in 2019 by
Haymarket Books
P.O. Box 180165
Chicago, IL 60618
773-583-7884
www.haymarketbooks.org

ISBN: 978-1-64259-067-8

Distributed to the trade in the US through Consortium Book Sales and
Distribution (www.cbsd.com) and internationally through Ingram Publisher
Services International (www.ingramcontent.com).

This book was published with the generous support of Lannan Foundation and
Wallace Action Fund.

Special discounts are available for bulk purchases by organizations and
institutions. Please call 773-583-7884 or email info@haymarketbooks.org for
more information.

Cover design by Jamie Kerry and Ragina Johnson.

Printed in United States.

10 9 8 7 6 5 4 3 2 1

Library of Congress Cataloging-in-Publication Data is available.

Contents

PART 3
Post-Marx Marxism and the Battle of Ideas

PART 4
Marx as Philosopher of Revolution in Permanence—Reading Marx for Today

SECTION A
Marxist-Humanism

Editorial Note and Acknowledgements

Editorial Note

All footnotes outside the introduction, besides simple citations, are by Dunayevskaya unless otherwise noted. Within the text of some documents the following abbreviations are used for works by Marx and Dunayevskaya:

MCIK = *Capital*, Vol. I, Kerr edition
MCIIK = *Capital*, Vol. II, Kerr edition
MCIIIK = *Capital*, Vol. III, Kerr edition
MCIP = *Capital*, Vol. I, Penguin edition
MCIIP = *Capital*, Vol. II, Penguin edition
MCIIIP = *Capital*, Vol. III, Penguin edition
MECW x, p. y = Marx and Engels, *Collected Works,* Vol. x, p. y
RDC, p. x = *The Raya Dunayevskaya Collection* and *Supplement to the Raya Dunayevskaya Collection,* microfilm page number x.

Acknowledgements

We wish to thank the Raya Dunayevskaya Memorial Fund for giving permission to publish documents from the *Raya Dunayevskaya Collection—Marxist-Humanism: A Half Century of Its World Development* and its *Supplement,* the most complete collection of Dunayevskaya's writings. The entire Collection (except for audiotapes, videotapes, and books with marginalia), the Supplement, and Guides to the Collection and Supplement are on the Internet at www.rayadunayevskaya.org. Originals are on deposit at Wayne State University Archives of Labor and Urban Affairs, Detroit, Michigan.

We thank Eugene Gogol, Terry Moon, Bob McGuire, Fred Mecklenburg, Olga Domanski, Nigel Gibson, Mary Jo Grey, Malcolm Campbell, Ron Kelch, Susan van Gelder Stellar, Daniel Bremer, and Russell Rockwell for editorial assistance and comments on drafts. Kevin O'Brien digitized Dunayevskaya's translations of "Private Property and Communism" and "Critique of the Hegelian Dialectic" from Marx's *Economic-Philosophic Manuscripts of 1844* as published in the first edition of *Marxism and Freedom.* Chris Clayton and Damon Maxwell transcribed for the Marxists Internet Archive Chapter 3, originally titled "Marx's Humanism Today," and Chapter 26, originally titled "Negro Intellectuals in Dilemma," respectively.

We wish to thank News and Letters Committees, the Marxist-Humanist organization co-founded by Dunayevskaya and the publisher of *News & Letters,* without which this book would not have been possible. Some chapters were originally published in whole or in part in *News & Letters* (www.newsandletters .org), under Dunayevskaya's guidance. Some were excerpted in *News & Letters* after her death.

Introduction: Raya Dunayevskaya's Renewal of Karl Marx's Philosophy of Revolution in Permanence

Franklin Dmitryev
National Organizer, *News and Letters Committees*, for the
Raya Dunayevskaya Memorial Fund

First, last, and always, Raya Dunayevskaya was a revolutionary. Revolution in permanence, transforming the world to create a truly free society on new human foundations, is what her life was about. That is central to the affinity she felt with Karl Marx. He too lived for revolution, in life and in thought. Dunayevskaya's writing pulsates with the living history of freedom struggles and the ideas growing out of those struggles. That very commitment to revolution, in the face of all its contradictions, inexorably led her into an ever-deeper relationship with philosophy. Practice, revolutionary activity, is indispensable, and at the same time she held that it is not enough if it is separated from philosophy. While never retreating from the struggles going on in life, she felt compelled to dive into thought, not only the debates of contemporary theoreticians but the thought of epochal thinkers, especially Marx and the philosophy Marx was rooted in, that of the great dialectician G.W.F. Hegel. Thought to her was not limited to the great philosophers. Revolution, she insisted, is in the thinking as well as doing of those struggling for freedom, workers, women, youth, Blacks, Latinos, LGBTQ people, oppressed nations. All this led to her own original contribution with the creation of the philosophy of Marxist-Humanism. At its core is a new concept of the relationships of theory and practice, philosophy and revolution.

1 Marx and Revolution Re-emerge

Revolutions that began in North Africa in 2010 became 2011's Arab Spring, leading to a worldwide wave that returned revolution to center stage. The complications that quickly ensued underscored the unfinished nature of the revolutions and movements, and the need for what Marx called revolution in permanence. The Arab Spring, however unfinished, helped inspire revolts from the town square occupations by *indignados* in Spain to the Occupy Wall Street movement that spread across the U.S.—and, just as importantly, a resurgence of the idea of revolution. In each case demands for political freedom against the monopoly of power by a small elite were fused with a quest for fundamental changes in economic relations, in a way that brought to the fore the questions at the heart of Marx's revolutionary life.

The worldwide capitalist economic crisis that began in 2007, and which fed this new period of revolt, once again ushered Marx into the headlines. Again and again over more than a century, and especially since the fall of state-capitalist Communism in Russia and East Europe, Marx has been declared dead, only to be resurrected by world events. In the recession's aftermath, the business press revisited Marx's analysis of capitalism's tendency to lurch into crises. New discussions and study groups on Marx's *Capital* after 2008 helped set the stage for the proliferation of conferences on *Capital* on its 150th anniversary in 2017 and on Marx with the bicentenary of his birth in 2018. One commentator wrote in *Businessweek:*

> Now, once again, unbridled capitalism is threatening to undermine it-self.... It's time for another burst of enlightenment. In years past, Britain's John Maynard Keynes and America's Hyman P. Minsky (author of *Stabilizing an Unstable Economy*) did capitalism a service by diagnosing its tendency toward crisis and advising on ways to make things better. The sooner policymakers today "recognize we're facing a once-in-a-lifetime crisis of capitalism," as [George] Magnus writes, "the better equipped they will be to manage a way out of it." Grasping the ways in which Marx was right is the first step toward making sure that his predic-tions of capitalism's downfall remain wrong.[1]

It was as if the specter of capitalism's transience had frightened its boosters into dusting off the scripts from an earlier period of global economic crisis in the mid-1970s. Then too the crisis brought Marx into the headlines. The busi-ness press suddenly reversed itself and discovered that there might be some validity to Marx's theory of the rate of profit's tendency to fall. Dunayevskaya's analysis included in this collection, "Today's Epigones Who Try to Truncate Marx's *Capital*," presciently indicated a basic change in the U.S. and world economy. That analysis, which also took the measure of "Marxist epigones," continued in "Capitalist Production/Alienated Labor," and anticipated the current situation.

---

1   "Marx to Market," by Peter Coy, September 14, 2011, *Businessweek*. The article by George Magnus is "Give Karl Marx a Chance to Save the World Economy" in the August 28, 2011, *Businessweek*.

The debate over Marx's linking of economic crises to the rate of profit rages today, especially among Marxists, though almost always confined within economics.[2] Unlike most commentators who turned to Marx, but a truncated Marx, Dunayevskaya rejected any separation of his theory of crises from his philosophy of revolution. She never forgot that the fetishistic nature of capitalist economic categories is rooted in the actual reified human relations in production, and that surplus value—the basis of profit—is inherently linked to the reification and alienation expressed in the duality of concrete labor and abstract labor. It manifests the dialectical inversion of subject and object, so that the object (machines) dominates the subject (workers); yet at the same time the human being never ceases to be a subject with a quest for universality and a propensity to resist and revolt. She traced the integrality of the economic and philosophical categories in Marx's *Economic-Philosophic Manuscripts of 1844*, to which she often referred as his Humanist Essays, through *Capital* and related manuscripts, to the *Ethnological Notebooks* he wrote near the end of his life.[3]

The simultaneously economic and philosophical nature of Marx's categories is not alone for better analyzing how capitalism works but rather is needed to make our way through all the vicissitudes of revolution overturning capitalism and establishing a new society. Dunayevskaya's question of "what happens after the revolutionary conquest of power" is as urgent today as it was when the monstrosity of so-called Communist states still constituted a real and stifling presence. (Today's China is almost universally understood to be capitalist.)

Though she saw how fundamental economic relations and their needed transformation are, she left no room for economic reductionism or any deterministic search for root causes. The point was the depth and totality of revolution needed to reach the new society: the revolution in permanence.[4] That is still the point today. And she took care to point out not only capitalist crisis

---

2   See, for example, "David Harvey, monomaniacs and the rate of profit" by Michael Roberts on his blog (https://thenextrecession.wordpress.com/2014/12/17/david-harvey-monomaniacs-and-the-rate-of-profit/, accessed, Oct. 7, 2017).

3   The first edition of her book *Marxism and Freedom, from 1776 until Today* included the first publication in English of Marx's *Economic-Philosophic Manuscripts of 1844* as well as of Lenin's conspectus of Hegel's *Science of Logic*.

4   See Chapter 31 of this book, "Philosopher of Permanent Revolution and Organization Man," for Dunayevskaya's analysis of this concept of Marx's, from his use of the term in "On the Jewish Question" through his March 1850 *Address to the Communist League*, which worked out a theory of revolution in permanence, to his last decade, when she saw him deepening the theory without using the phrase. See also Chapter 11 of *Rosa Luxemburg, Women's Liberation, and Marx's Philosophy of Revolution*, "The Philosopher of Revolution in Permanence Creates New Ground for Organization."

and repression, but what she called the "passion for philosophy," of which the renewed interest in Marx is one manifestation.

Her rejection of the post-Marx Marxism that confined his thought and activity to one dimension—whether economics, politics, or sociology—is indispensable for confronting today's world, which continues to experience what she called "myriad global crises," rather than being simply determined by economic crisis alone. The inability of the capitalist system, no matter how globalized, to solve any of these crises underscores the need for revolutionary transformation. What has emerged is growing havoc wrought by climate change, the threat of nuclear war, and the resurgence of fascism.

Quintessential to Dunayevskaya's Marxist-Humanism was her confidence that the human quest for universality could not be snuffed out. New stirrings of revolt never cease to come from below. From 2008 on, the lingering economic crisis spurred not only austerity programs but strikes across Europe and factory occupations from Chicago to South Korea. Even in China, workers toiling in the world's sweatshop boldly engaged in thousands of strikes and demanded their own independent organizations. Revolts from Iran to Bosnia, Okinawa to Honduras, spilled beyond the bounds of traditional parties. Shack-dwellers in South Africa and Indigenous people in Bolivia self-organized to continue their struggles in practice and in theory, each in the face of a new national regime that spoke or had spoken of its support for socialism and its opposition to U.S. imperialism. Within the U.S., Black Lives Matter is the latest manifestation of African-American liberation movements, and the massive Women's March on Washington of January 21, 2017, revealed anew the intensity of revolt by women and others.

While none of these have burst out into the fullness of social revolution, they raise the specter and the idea of revolution, and they signal the continuation of the struggles in which Dunayevskaya found a passion for freedom, and therefore for philosophy. It is no coincidence that so many today are rediscovering Marx—and usually in explicit contrast to official Communism past and present, such as the South African shack-dwellers movement's invocation of "that philosopher called Karl Marx" in their criticism of the South African Communist Party and African National Congress.[5]

---

5   In a statement responding to attacks from the South African Communist Party, the shack-dwellers movement Abahlali baseMjondolo declared, "That philosopher called Karl Marx once wrote that communism is the real movement that abolishes the state of things. He didn't write that communism is the vanguard that disciplines and condemns the real struggles of the people.... Any party or groupuscule or NGO that declares from above that it is the vanguard of the people's struggles, and that the people must therefore accept their authority,

Resistance abounds, and the passion for philosophy is present, yet philosophy of revolution remains the unfulfilled imperative. As Dunayevskaya wrote in her second book, *Philosophy and Revolution: From Hegel to Sartre and from Marx to Mao,*

> Ours is the age that can meet the challenge of the times when we work out so new a relationship of theory to practice that the proof of the unity is in the Subject's own self-development. Philosophy and revolution will first then liberate the innate talents of men and women who will become whole. (p. 292)

2   A New Epoch, a New Philosophic Moment

Central to Dunayevskaya's thought is a penetrating insight into the nature of the age we live in, which she saw as characterized by a new stage of production, automation, and a new stage of cognition. In this new stage, the practice of masses in motion for freedom is a movement from practice that is itself a form of theory, and needs to be met with a movement from theory that is a form of philosophy and revolution. To her, this insight was essential for concretizing Marx's philosophy of revolution for our age.

The concept of the movement from practice that is a form of theory is what Richard Gilman-Opalsky describes as

> a profound understanding of the intellect of revolt. [Dunayevskaya] focused on the philosophical content of what she called "spontaneous mass action," which she argued emerges as a dialectical force within and against the capitalist lifeworld....
>
> Dunayevskaya reads the revolts of everyday people around the world, which she constantly watched with a close eye throughout her life, as both an oppositional force to, and a philosophical questioning of, the capitalist reality.
>
> ...within this milieu, only Dunayevskaya regularly insisted upon seeing revolt as a philosophical event.... Dunayevskaya articulates a distinct position that connects mass rebellion to "philosophic cognition."[6]

---

is the enemy of the people's struggles. Leadership is earned and is never permanent." See "South African Activists Slam Communist Party," November-December 2010 *News & Letters.*

6   *Specters of Revolt: On the Intellect of Insurrection and Philosophy from Below,* by Richard Gilman-Opalsky (London: Repeater Books, 2016), pp. 237–38, 240–41.

Her concept of what characterizes this epoch began to take shape as she worked out the theory of state-capitalism, responding to a counterrevolutionary change in the world that began with Stalinism. After Joseph Stalin's 1939 treaty with Hitler paved the way for World War II, she reevaluated the theory of Leon Trotsky, for whom she had been Russian secretary in Mexico. She broke with Trotsky's position that the USSR's nationalized property must be defended in the coming war. Painstakingly analyzing the USSR as not a workers' state but a state-capitalist society, she then broadened the analysis into a theory of state-capitalism as a world stage.[7]

Nor could this new stage be confined to economics alone. For one thing, it was seen in the thought of administrative Planners. Dunayevskaya worked this out in relationship to the statist socialist Ferdinand Lassalle, a contemporary of Marx, whose organizational approach has been very influential within the Marxist movement.[8] She saw Lassalle as the model of the administrative type of our day, from State Planners in Stalinist Russia to trade union bureaucrats in the West. Today it applies equally to vanguard party leaders and to anti-vanguardist designers of blueprints for the new "participatory economy" society.

Above all, she kept looking for forces of revolution that would emerge from the new stage. In the midst of World War II, she singled out strikes by miners and rebellions by African Americans, and shortly after the war she singled out women's revolt against existing relations at work, at home, and in the radical movement. When the coal miners struck against the introduction of automation, she was able to identify a new stage of production and the revolt specifically against it.[9]

In the process of working out what new stage the world faced, she turned to Marx's Humanism and the dialectic in Marx, Lenin, and Hegel. To her, the workers' state achieved by the Russian Revolution had transformed into its opposite, totalitarian state-capitalism. This raised questions about what happens after revolution and whether Marx's concept of revolution had been

---

7   See her detailed analysis in Part 4 of *Russia: From Proletarian Revolution to State-Capitalist Counter-Revolution: Selected Writings by Raya Dunayevskaya* (Leiden: Brill, 2017).

8   See Chapter 31 of this collection, "Philosopher of Permanent Revolution and Organization Man." See also *Marxism and Freedom*, Chapters 4 ("Worker, Intellectual, and the State"), 9 ("The Second International, 1889 to 1914"), and 11 ("Forms of Organization: The Relationship of the Spontaneous Self-Organization of the Proletariat to the 'Vanguard Party' "), and *Rosa Luxemburg, Women's Liberation, and Marx's Philosophy of Revolution,* Chapter 11 ("The Philosopher of Permanent Revolution Creates New Ground for Organization").

9   See Chapter 21 of this collection, "The Emergence of a New Movement from Practice that Is Itself a Form of Theory."

narrowed not only by Stalinists but by their opponents within the revolutionary movement.

Her recovery of Marx's Humanism and dialectic, and with it her appreciation of the role of philosophy for Marx and Lenin, set her apart both from "Marxist-Leninists" and from those who praised Marx's early writings but separated their Humanism from his later writings like *Capital*. The attempt to eject Humanism and Hegel from Marx is prominent in the thought of French Communist Louis Althusser, whose anti-humanist and anti-dialectical revision of Marx underlies much current Marxist and post-Marxist theory.

Dunayevskaya, however, comprehended Hegel's dialectic, including his Absolutes, as a movement of liberation, and recognized Marx's reliance on its "self-development, self-activity, self-movement."[10] Furthermore, she wrote,

> Lack of confidence in the masses is the common root of *all* objections to "idealistic, mystical Hegelianism." That includes not only outright betrayers, but also intellectuals committed to proletarian revolution; outsiders looking in; academic Marxists ... permeated to the marrow of their bones with the capitalistic concept of the backwardness of the proletariat. One and all, they are blind to the relationship of theory to history as a historical relationship *made by masses in motion.*[11]

Dunayevskaya's confidence, deeply rooted historically and philosophically, enabled her not only to see this relationship of theory and history made by masses in motion, but also to work out theory on its basis. Her theoretical and philosophical work showed a remarkable development over a period of close to half a century.

3   Dunayevskaya's Marx

At each stage of that development, Dunayevskaya discovered new aspects of Marx's thought. Overall, she gives us a deeper, expanded picture of Marx, as against the narrowed, compartmentalized understanding all too common among Marxists today. Marx's Humanism and dialectic constituted her continual point of departure and return. As the feminist poet Adrienne Rich wrote in "Raya Dunayevskaya's Marx,"

---

10   *Philosophy and Revolution,* p. 288. For an articulation of this argument, see especially Chapter 2 of *Philosophy and Revolution.*

11   *Philosophy and Revolution,* p. 288.

Dunayevskaya's way of grounding herself was to turn to Marx. Not, I should emphasize, as a *turning backward* but as rescuing for the present a legacy she saw as still unclaimed, having been diminished, distorted, and betrayed by post-Marx Marxists and the emerging "Communist" states. But she didn't simply turn to Marx, or to Hegel (whose work she saw as a living, still uncomprehended, presence in Marx's own thought), as texts. Her work ... is an explication of the fullness of Marx's thought *as she came to live it,* in living through the liberation movements of her own era. She translated Marx, interpreted Marx, fitted together fragments of Marx scattered in post-Marxist schisms, refused to leave Marx enshrined as dead text, ill read, or relegated to "the dustbin of history.".…

And, indeed, what is finally so beautiful and compelling about the Marx she shows us is his resistance to all static, stagnant ways of being, the deep apprehension of motion and transformation as principles of thought and of human process, the mind-weaving dialectical shuttle aflight in the loom of human activity.

Raya Dunayevskaya caught fire from Marx, met it with her own fire, brought to the events of her lifetime a revitalized, refocused Marxism.[12]

As a child whose family had just immigrated to Chicago from Ukraine, Raya Dunayevskaya became a committed Bolshevik revolutionary. During her teenage years she was very active, distributing Communist Party newspapers to workers at the McCormick Reaper plant and writing for and working with the *Negro Champion* newspaper issued by the American Negro Labor Congress. At 18 she was expelled from the Party's youth group, and thrown down a flight of stairs, for raising questions after Trotsky's expulsion from the Communist Party of the USSR.[13]

After many years in socialist groups, labor agitation, strikes, and African-American freedom struggles, Dunayevskaya became Russian Secretary to Trotsky in 1937, while he was in exile in Mexico, helping him respond to the outrageous slanders fabricated about him in the Moscow show trials. At the time, civil war was raging in Spain, and revolutionaries like Trotsky saw Stalin's forces destroying the Spanish revolution. To Dunayevskaya, this raised new questions, which crystallized two years later when Stalin and Hitler approved

---

12   "Raya Dunayevskaya's Marx," in *Arts of the Possible: Essays and Conversations* by Adrienne Rich (New York: W.W. Norton & Company, 2001), pp. 85–86, 95.

13   See "Dunayevskaya, Raya," by Terry Moon, in *Women Building Chicago 1790–1990: A Biographical Dictionary,* edited by Rima Lunin Schultz and Adele Hast (Bloomington: Indiana University Press, 2001).

their 1939 non-aggression treaty that gave the green light to Hitler's invasion of Poland and to World War II. She then broke with Trotsky, who called for the defense of the USSR in the imperialist war, holding to his position that it was still a "workers' state, though degenerate." This break led to her analysis of the USSR as not a workers' state but a state-capitalist society. She joined with C.L.R. James to form the Johnson-Forest Tendency on the basis of their shared position on the nature of Russian society.[14] She elaborated this as a theory of state-capitalism as a world stage, including such varied forms as Nazi Germany, Japan's Co-Prosperity Sphere, and the U.S. New Deal.

She theorized state-capitalism not as a continuous quantitative growth of monopoly capitalism but rather monopoly capitalism's transformation into opposite into a wholly new stage. Seeking the stage's dialectical opposite in forces of revolution, she carefully watched the revolt of rank-and-file workers, African Americans, and colonized peoples. From mass revolt emerged her concept of four forces of revolution in the U.S., which also included women and youth.[15]

She would later argue that the theory of state-capitalism was a necessary precursor to the philosophy of Marxist-Humanism. Unlike some later analyses of state-capitalism such as that of Tony Cliff, this theory was not limited to an economic analysis. That is seen in her emphasis on "political and social rule" by the working class in her first writing on state-capitalism, "The Union of Soviet Socialist Republics Is a Capitalist Society" (1941). Within two years, her "Labor and Society" took up alienated labor and Marx's point that the essence of private property was not its legal forms but the power of disposal over the labor of others. This was her first writing to cite Marx's then little-known

---

14   Both Dunayevskaya (Freddie Forest) and James (J.R. Johnson) went with the Workers Party when it split from the Socialist Workers Party in 1940 because the latter continued to call for "defense of the Soviet Union" even after the Hitler-Stalin Pact. Within the Workers Party they organized the Johnson-Forest Tendency, at first around the analysis of the USSR as state-capitalist rather than, as Max Shachtman and the majority held, a "bureaucratic collectivist" society. In 1947 the Tendency left the Workers Party and rejoined the Socialist Workers Party, which it exited again in 1951, breaking with Trotskyism and forming Correspondence Committees.

15   Later she articulated the multiplicity of forces of revolution this way: "[T]he Dialectics of Revolution is characteristic of all the four forces we singled out in the United States—labor, Blacks, youth, as well as women. All are *moments of revolution,* and nobody can know before the event itself who will be the one in the concrete, particular revolution.... In a word, no matter who the specific revolutionary force turns out to be ... the whole truth is in the dual rhythm of any revolution: the overthrow of the old society and the creation of new human relations. It requires the spelling out of the dialectic in its totality with *every individual* subject." ("Introduction to Morningside Edition," *Marxism and Freedom,* p. 12.).

Economic-Philosophic Manuscripts of 1844 or, as she often called them, his Humanist Essays, which quickly became central to her work.[16]

In the face of what she came to see as a total contradiction—counterrevolution coming from within the revolution—she turned to Marx's Humanism, and with it what she would later articulate as the question of what happens after the revolutionary conquest of power, the question of the needed depth of revolution, and the reach to philosophy for a total answer to the totality of crises of our age. Dunayevskaya's championing of the Manuscripts' importance resulted in her being the first to translate and publish selections in English in the 1958 first edition of *Marxism and Freedom, from 1776 until Today*. Her translations of two key 1844 essays, "Private Property and Communism" and "Critique of the Hegelian Dialectic," are included in the Appendix to this volume.

3.1   *The Philosophic Moment of Marxist-Humanism*

Her rediscovery of Marx's Humanism drew her to his transformation of the Hegelian dialectic into the Marxian dialectic, which made possible the creation of Marxist-Humanism. The direct encounter with Hegel's dialectic became increasingly central to these explorations.

The study of Hegel and of Marx's roots in Hegel became a shared project of the Johnson-Forest Tendency, which Dunayevskaya jointly led with C.L.R. James and Grace Lee (Boggs). In early 1949 she translated V.I. Lenin's Abstract of Hegel's *Science of Logic,* and her accompanying letters to her co-leaders initiated a three-way correspondence on the relationship of the dialectic to Lenin, to Marx, and to the present age.

That same year the general strike of coal miners broke out in West Virginia. Confronted by automation in the mines, the strikers raised the questions of what kind of labor a human being should do—a question at the heart of her economic theory ever since "Labor and Society," as she worked out a deeper opposition to state-capitalism calling itself Communism—and why there should be a division between thinking and doing. She would later see the miners' questioning as a manifestation of the movement from practice that is itself a form of theory, a key aspect of the new post-World War II stage of cognition. Dunayevskaya's involvement in this strike, immediately after having translated Lenin's notebooks, had a great impact on her:

---

16   Both of these articles are reproduced in Chapter 9 of *Russia: From Proletarian Revolution to State-Capitalist Counter-Revolution: Selected Writings by Raya Dunayevskaya*.

...the Miners' General Strike seemed to touch, at one and the same time, a concept Marx had designated as alienated labor *and* the absolute opposite to it, which Marx had spelled out as the end of the division between mental and manual labor.... It led me to conclude that two new vantage points were needed for the book I had been working on, titled *State-Capitalism and Marxism*. One was that the American worker should become a point of departure not only as "root" of Marxism but as a presence today.... The second vantage point was to be the dialectic as Lenin interpreted it in his Abstract of Hegel's *Science of Logic*.[17]

As part of this, she plunged into a study of the dialectical development of the structure of Marx's *Capital*. That had become a pressing issue for Dunayevskaya by 1944, when she found that Stalin's theoreticians had revised the Marxian theory of the law of value. Where Marx and Marxists had always held that law to be a mark of capitalist and not socialist society, the Stalinists in 1943 suddenly reversed their position to declare that it operated under socialism, meaning in the USSR. The same Stalinist article proposed that future teaching of *Capital* should omit its first chapter, which Dunayevskaya saw as a violation of the dialectical structure of *Capital*. In showing that the law of value is specific to capitalism, her "A New Revision of Marxian Economics"[18] exposed how fundamentally Stalin's regime was revising Marxian theory. As she put it in "Revision or Reaffirmation of Marxism?" answering Marxist defenders of the revision, including Paul Baran and Oscar Lange, "It is a question of severing the indissoluble connection between the dialectical method of Marx and his political economy."[19]

In 1949 she deepened this concept by delving into how Marx restructured *Capital* on the basis of what emerged from struggles from below, from the Civil War in the U.S. and the struggle for the eight-hour day to the formation of the First International and the 1871 Paris Commune. This became the basis of a unique analysis of the logic and structure of Marx's greatest theoretical work—an analysis that became entwined with the need for a new relationship between theory and practice and remains unrivaled today. She would return to this question with deeper insights with each new moment of development

---

17   Quoted from Chapter 21 of this volume. See the three-way correspondence in *The Raya Dunayevskaya Collection* (RDC), pp. 1595–734, 9209–327.

18   This is included in Chapter 9 of *Russia: From Proletarian Revolution to State-Capitalist Counter-Revolution*.

19   Originally published in the *American Economic Review*, September 1945, this piece is included in RDC, pp. 214–17.

achieved in the writing of what she called her "trilogy of revolution": *Marxism and Freedom, from 1776 until Today; Philosophy and Revolution: From Hegel to Sartre and from Marx to Mao;* and *Rosa Luxemburg, Women's Liberation, and Marx's Philosophy of Revolution.*

By 1953 attitudes to the dialectic became a point of divergence between the Johnson-Forest Tendency's leaders, as Dunayevskaya followed out the task they had set themselves of delving into Hegel's *Philosophy of Spirit (Philosophy of Mind)*, the last book of his *Encyclopedia of the Philosophical Sciences.* Though James had written that he had found nothing in *Philosophy of Spirit* "for us,"[20] she came to consider what she found by grappling with Hegel's Absolutes to be nothing less than a philosophical breakthrough for our epoch. This was expressed in her May 1953 letters on Hegel's Absolute Idea, Absolute Knowledge, and Absolute Mind.[21] In retrospect she would term it "the philosophic moment," or the philosophic point that governed all the concretizations that followed.[22] To her, the Absolute was no endpoint but a point of departure.

Crucial to this was Hegel's discussion of absolute negativity—to her, not only the first negation as overthrow of the existing state of affairs but the negation of the negation, the establishment of the new—as the "turning point" and "the innermost and most objective moment of Life and Spirit, by virtue of which a subject is personal and free."[23] Differentiating herself from James's earlier notes on the "positive in the negative" as *"only the general* development of socialism through overcoming Stalinism," she held that it was now possible to be more concrete. In addressing the problem of what happens after revolution, she stressed absolute negativity as subjectivity, self-movement, self-liberation, and the need for "a totally new revolt in which everyone *experiences* 'absolute liberation.' " She would later elaborate how this is integral to Marx's opposition to "vulgar communism" and his vision of transcending communism to establish "positive Humanism, beginning from itself," expressed in his 1844 *Manuscripts.*

In Hegel's Absolute Mind, Dunayevskaya's May 1953 letters found the new society, and a new relationship of theory and practice. The latter was not a goal left for the far future, but what is needed and possible for today's movements to achieve liberation and not fall prey to another bureaucracy arising after the

---

20   See the letter of C.L.R. James to Grace Lee Boggs of May 20, 1949, RDC, p. 1612.

21   Written soon after Stalin died, these letters can be found in *The Philosophic Moment of Marxist-Humanism* and Chapter 2 of *The Power of Negativity.* See Chapters 21 and 22 in this volume on what led to these letters, including Dunayevskaya's discussions with Charles Denby, who would later become the worker-editor of *News & Letters,* "about both Stalin's death and the affinity the American workers felt with the Russian workers."

22   See *The Philosophic Moment of Marxist-Humanism,* p. 7; *The Power of Negativity,* p. 5.

23   See *The Philosophic Moment of Marxist-Humanism,* p. 33; *The Power of Negativity,* p. 20.

conquest of power in revolution. This involved comprehending the practice of masses in motion for freedom as a movement from practice that is itself a form of theory, and the need to meet that with a movement from theory that is itself a form of philosophy and revolution. Pivotal to that was the vision of a new society that would abolish the opposition between mental and manual labor.

In embryo the May 1953 philosophic moment contained Dunayevskaya's unique characterization of the nature of our epoch, discussed earlier here. Part 4, Section A of this collection—titled "Marxist-Humanism"—describes how it involved a new stage of cognition, a new automated stage of capitalist production, and the revolt specifically against that new stage of production.

The next month, on June 17, East German workers erupted in the first revolt from under totalitarian Communism, followed quickly by a revolt in the Vorkuta slave labor camp within Russia itself. In 1956 the Hungarian Revolution challenging Russian Communist domination brought Marx's Humanist Essays onto the historic stage, as Dunayevskaya put it. In the other hemisphere, the Montgomery, Alabama, Bus Boycott marked the opening of the Black revolution in the U.S.

3.2   Marxism and Freedom: *The Movement from Practice and a New Concept of Theory*

After C.L.R. James broke with Dunayevskaya, she founded a new organization in 1955, News and Letters Committees, which continues to project her ideas in responding to social, political, and economic events. She wrote a regular column for its newspaper, *News & Letters,* first titled "Two Worlds"[24] and later "Theory/Practice." She led the Marxist-Humanist organization for three decades, until her death, and that direct engagement in the revolutionary movement remained inseparable from her theoretical work. She transformed the book she had been working on from *State-Capitalism and Marxism* to *Marxism and Freedom, from 1776 until Today.* It aimed to re-establish Marxism in its original Humanist form, now relating the question the miners had asked—"what kind of labor should a human being do?"—to Hegel's and Marx's dialectic of negativity with self-movement at its core.

The book was structured on the movement from practice, from the Great French Revolution through the revolutions of Marx's day and the Russian Revolutions to Hungary, Montgomery, and the workers' battles against automation. Looking back, it is difficult to fathom today the uniqueness of putting what was "only" a bus boycott in a Southern city together with a revolution

---

24   In the first few issues, the column was titled "Notes from a Diary: Two Worlds," after her unsigned "Two Worlds: Notes from a Diary" column for the *Correspondence* newspaper.

that shook Eastern Europe, long before the phrase "Black revolution" became a journalistic cliché.

Declaring, "There is nothing in thought—not even in the thought of a genius—that has not previously been in the activity of the common man" (p. 28), the book advanced a new concept of theory. Arguing that Marx, in writing *Capital* and in restructuring it in response to movements from below, had broken with the old concept of theory, she wrote in *Marxism and Freedom:*

> He who glorifies theory and genius but fails to recognize the *limits* of a theoretical work, fails likewise to recognize the *indispensability of the theoretician.* All of history is the history of the struggle for freedom. If, as a theoretician, one's ears are attuned to new impulses from the workers, new "categories" will be created, a new way of thinking, a step forward in philosophic cognition. (p. 89)

This flowed out of her analysis of the dialectical structure and process of formation of Marx's *Capital.* The question of structure was never separated from the philosophical content of the economic categories, from the split in the category of labor to the fetishism of commodities.

A concept of the "American roots of Marxism" is integral to *Marxism and Freedom* and was expanded in *American Civilization on Trial,*[25] which presented a comprehensive view of U.S. history through the lens of "Black masses as vanguard." A driving force of that history is not only slavery and the slave trade but slave revolts, the economic remains of slavery after its abolition, and the never-ending quest for freedom of African-American masses. Dunayevskaya had been active with Black liberation struggles since she worked with and wrote for *The Negro Champion* newspaper of the American Negro Labor Congress as a teenager in the 1920s. In the mid-1930s she was was a member of the Washington Committee to Aid Agricultural Workers, active in support of sharecroppers' struggles in the South. By the 1940s, in contrast to the typical U.S. Marxist position, she was writing theoretical analyses putting forward the importance of independent Black struggles, which must not be subsumed under the general class struggle. The Johnson-Forest Tendency chose Dunayevskaya to represent the tendency in its debate on the "Negro Question" with the Workers Party majority, which was represented by David Coolidge (Ernest Rice McKinney). *American Civilization on Trial,* published in 1963, incisively developed this theoretical direction, elaborating how Black masses have

---

25   *American Civilization on Trial: Black Masses as Vanguard* (Chicago: News and Letters, 2003) was first published in 1963.

been the vanguard in U.S. history, whose turning points arose when white labor coalesced with Black masses in motion.

3.3   Philosophy and Revolution: *"Absolute Idea as New Beginning" and Marx's Transformation of Hegelian Dialectic*

As the 1960s proceeded, mass movements exploded, including the African-American Freedom Now Movement, the movement against the Vietnam War, and the Women's Liberation Movement. Dunayevskaya welcomed them, listening carefully and at the same time warning of the contradictions within them, above all the shying away from philosophy and preferring to "pick up theory *en route.*" The failure of the revolutionary movements of the 1960s could not be ascribed only to the very real repression and counterrevolution they faced. Internal contradictions must be confronted. At the same time, these failures engendered what she called a "passion for philosophy."[26]

To Dunayevskaya these considerations spelled out the need for a new dive into Hegel's dialectic, particularly his Absolutes, from the vantage point of our time. That became the concept of the book *Philosophy and Revolution: From Hegel to Sartre and from Marx to Mao.* With "Why Hegel? Why Now?" as its point of departure, it examines philosophy and revolution in Hegel, Marx, and Lenin, then proceeds to test alternatives against Marx, and to analyze world economy and revolts in Africa, East Europe, China, the U.S., France, and Latin America. The fact that Marx's "social individual" could be found in Hegel's Absolute, and that freedom was Hegel's point of departure and point of return, linked his thought both to Marx and to today's freedom struggles. Thus, comprehension of Marx depends on grasping the relationship between his dialectic and Hegel's:

> From the very beginning Marx, in his critique of the Hegelian dialectic, dug so deeply into its roots in thought and in reality that it signaled a revolution in philosophy and at the same time a philosophy of revolution....
>
> To Marx, what was crucial was that man was not merely object, but subject, not only determined by history, but its creator. The *act* of world history is the self-development of labor, its class struggles. (pp. 48–49)

---

26   In the original introduction to *Philosophy and Revolution,* she linked the hunger for philosophy to the Black revolt as follows: "Not many professors of philosophy may have related to the Soledad Brother who was shot down in 1971. But so deeply grounded is the black dimension in 'absolute negativity,' in the desire for new beginnings through the 'syllogistic' resolution of alienation, that George Jackson's discovery of the dialectic of liberation in that hellhole, San Quentin Prison, can by no means be brushed aside as 'accidental'..." (pp. xxiii–xxiv).

Philosophy and Revolution aimed to articulate "the integrality of philosophy and revolution as the characteristic of the age, and [trace] it through historically," basing itself on "the Humanism of Marx, that philosophy of liberation which merges the dialectics of elemental revolt and its Reason."[27] This included a new view of Marx as creating a "new continent of thought and revolution" through his transcendence of and yet repeated return to Hegel's dialectic. With this new stage of Dunayevskaya's thought, an explicit critique of Lenin's "philosophic ambivalence" also became part of *Philosophy and Revolution*.

3.4   *Impact of Marx's* Ethnological Notebooks *and Women's Liberation: Marx as Philosopher of Revolution in Permanence vs. Post-Marx Marxism*

While the Women's Liberation Movement that arose in the 1960s was treated by most of the revolutionary Left as a diversion, Dunayevskaya welcomed it and hailed its challenge to the Left from the Left. The category she made of women as reason as well as force of revolution became central to her next two books, *Rosa Luxemburg, Women's Liberation, and Marx's Philosophy of Revolution* and *Women's Liberation and the Dialectics of Revolution: Reaching for the Future.*

The 1970s saw the publication of Marx's *Ethnological Notebooks* for the first time, 90 years after he had written them. These notebooks took up works of anthropology and history of Asian, Native American, and ancient European societies. To Dunayevskaya they "created a new vantage point from which to view Marx's *oeuvres* as a totality,"[28] illuminating much about Marx's method:

> Marx's historic originality in internalizing new data, whether in anthropology or in "pure" science, was a never-ending confrontation with what Marx called "history and its process." That was concrete. That was everchanging. And that ever-changing concrete was inexorably bound to the universal, because, precisely because, the determining concrete was the ever-developing Subject—self-developing men and women.[29]

To Dunayevskaya, the *Ethnological Notebooks* disclosed "new moments" discovered by Marx in the last decade of his life, on topics ranging from the Man/Woman relationship to non-capitalist societies, and from ancient communal

---

27   Preamble to the Constitution of News and Letters Committees, which can be found in RDC, pp. 7993–8003.

28   *Rosa Luxemburg, Women's Liberation, and Marx's Philosophy of Revolution*, p. xxi.

29   *Rosa Luxemburg, Women's Liberation, and Marx's Philosophy of Revolution*, p. 180.

social forms to revolutionary organization. The new moments were seen not as a break but as a development in continuity with his 1844 Humanism and *Capital.* She saw them as a new concretization of Marx's concept of revolution in permanence, which in turn was a re-creation of Hegel's negation of the negation, or absolute negativity. Not to be confused with Trotsky's theory of permanent revolution or Mao's "uninterrupted revolution," Marx's concept meant revolution could not stop with the overthrow of the old but must continue after the conquest of power to a transformation of human relations profound enough to abolish the division between mental and manual labor. The discoveries of his last decade, she wrote, extended his concept of permanent revolution because they

> made clear, at one and the same time, how very deep must be the uprooting of class society and how broad the view of the forces of revolution. It led Marx to projecting nothing short of the possibility of a revolution occurring in a backward land like Russia ahead of one in the technologically advanced West.[30]

The notebooks and Marx's last decade became a major focus of Dunayevskaya's third book, *Rosa Luxemburg, Women's Liberation, and Marx's Philosophy of Revolution.* The book was also responding to the international growth of the Women's Liberation Movement, the global economic crisis that began in the mid-1970s, the rise of the Third World, and the vitality of and yet grave contradictions within revolutions from Portugal to Iran. At the same time, the book viewed the great Marxist Rosa Luxemburg as a contemporary, both because of her previously disregarded feminist dimension, because she was a revolutionary and a serious theoretician, and because her writings impinged on the relationship of spontaneous mass actions to consciousness and organization, which remains as much a burning question today as it was for Dunayevskaya.

From this work arose her views of Marx as philosopher of revolution in permanence and, in contrast, of what she called post-Marx Marxism as a pejorative. The term "post-Marx" was not meant to be chronological but to refer to a truncated Marxism that failed to draw on the totality of Marx's philosophy. It was borne out by a neglectful attitude to Marx's archives. It was not limited to "neo-Marxism" but included the "orthodox," with the book critically exploring Luxemburg, Lenin, Trotsky and even Frederick Engels. She saw different

---

30   *Rosa Luxemburg, Women's Liberation, and Marx's Philosophy of Revolution,* p. xxi. For more on permanent revolution, see Chapter 31 of this collection, "Philosopher of Permanent Revolution and Organization Man."

approaches to the dialectic of transitions from one social order to another as
a vital distinction:

> What Marx, in the *Grundrisse*, had defined as "the absolute movement of
> becoming" had matured in the last decade of his life as new moments—
> a multilinear view of human development as well as a *dialectic duality
> within each* formation. From within each formation evolved *both* the end
> of the old *and* the beginning of the new. Whether Marx was studying the
> communal or the despotic form of property, it was the human resistance
> of the Subject that revealed the direction of resolving the contradictions.
> Marx transformed what, to Hegel, was the synthesis of the "Self-Thinking
> Idea" and the "Self-Bringing-Forth of Liberty" as the emergence of a new
> society. The many paths to get there were left open. As against Marx's mul-
> tilinear view, which kept Marx from attempting any blueprint for future
> generations, Engels' unilinear view led him to mechanical positivism.[31]

3.5   *Dialectics of Organization and Philosophy*

The 1980s were a time of retrogression with U.S. President Ronald Reagan in
the saddle, allied with British Prime Minister Margaret Thatcher. Reagan pre-
sided over the gutting of workers' hard-won gains, a resurgence of homelessness, poverty, and racist violence, a rollback of women's rights and civil rights,
military intervention, reactionary politicized religion, and the Third World
debt crisis. To Dunayevskaya their unprecedented "ideological pollution" was
just as crucial, and had contaminated the Left as well. Revolutions continued
to reveal their internal contradictions, as in the counterrevolution that came
from within Grenada's leadership. To her this meant a "two-fold problematic of
our age ... 1) What happens *after* the conquest of power? 2) Are there ways for
new beginnings when there is so much reaction, so many aborted revolutions,
such turning of the clock backward in the most technologically advanced
lands?" Dunayevskaya began working on a book—not yet finished when she
died—on "Dialectics of Organization and Philosophy: The 'Party' and Forms
of Organization Born out of Spontaneity." She had long before, while still in
the Johnson-Forest Tendency, broken with the concept of vanguard party associated with Lassalle, Lenin, and Marxist parties in general. The key now, she
wrote in one of her last writings,

---

31   *Rosa Luxemburg, Women's Liberation, and Marx's Philosophy of Revolution*, p. xxxvi.

is not the Party or the leader or leadership, but *philosophy,* the body of ideas, the dialectic of ideas and organization, as against the party as well as distinct from forms of organization born out of spontaneity. While these, of course, are correct, as against the elitism and ossification of the Party, the truth is that these forms also search for an organization different from their own in the sense that they want to be sure that there is a totality of theory and practice against the establishment of a power that has stopped dead with its conquest of state power—in short, altogether new beginnings.

The burning question of the day remains: What happens the day after? How can we continue Marx's unchaining of the dialectic organizationally, with the principles he outlined in his *Critique of the Gotha Program?*

... as opposed to the Party, we put forth a body of ideas that spells out the second negativity which continues the revolution in permanence after victory. The principle of revolution in permanence doesn't stop with a victory over capitalism; indeed, it doesn't stop until the full abolition of any division between mental and manual labor. Full self-development of Man/Woman that leads to truly new human relationships remains the goal.[32]

A major element of Dunayevskaya's work on dialectics of organization and philosophy was a new look at Marx's 1844 *Manuscripts.* They had always been crucial to her, with their explicit naming of his philosophy as a new Humanism, rooting it in Hegel's dialectic of negativity, and criticizing vulgar communism as well as alienated labor. She now designated the Manuscripts as his "philosophic moment" and examined their new Humanism as the ground of organization for him throughout his life, from the Communist League of the 1840s through his 1875 *Critique of the Gotha Program.* The organizational character of the *Critique,* in her view, led Marx

to develop a general view of where we're headed for the day *after* the conquest of power, the day *after* we have rid ourselves of the birthmarks of capitalism *when* a new generation can finally see all its potentiality put an end once and for all to the division between mental and manual labor.[33]

---

32   *The Year of Only Eight Months,* RDC, pp. 10690–726.

33   Quoted from "Presentation on Dialectics of Organization and Philosophy of June 1, 1987," in *The Philosophic Moment of Marxist-Humanism,* p. 7, and in *The Power of Negativity,* p. 5.

Thus, at the end of her life, her work was opening a tantalizing new vista on Marx's philosophy of revolution in permanence.[34]

4   The Form and Content of This Collection

Rather than a chronological sequence, this collection is organized around some of the central categories created by Dunayevskaya in her comprehension of Marx's body of ideas. Each Part thus reflects the totality of Marxist-Humanism's development while illuminating its distinctive re-creation of Marx for today.

Part 1, "The Philosophic Moment of Marx: Marx's Transformation of the Hegelian Dialectic," focuses on that 1844 philosophical creation of Marx's new Humanism. It begins with Dunayevskaya's "Preface to the Iranian Edition of Marx's 1844 Essays," which returned to Marx's philosophic moment with the new view brought about by her study of the new moments of Marx's last decade. At the same time it reflects the fact that she was asked to write the

---

34   Since Dunayevskaya's death in 1987, several books have been published collecting writings by her. These include *The Philosophic Moment of Marxist-Humanism: Two Historic-Philosophic Writings by Raya Dunayevskaya* (1989); *The Marxist-Humanist Theory of State-Capitalism* (1992); *The Power of Negativity: Selected Writings on the Dialectic in Hegel and Marx* (2002); *The Dunayevskaya-Marcuse-Fromm Correspondence, 1954–1978: Dialogues on Hegel, Marx, and Critical Theory* (2012); *Crossroads of History: Marxist-Humanist Writings on the Middle East* (2013); and *Russia: From Proletarian Revolution to State-Capitalist Counter-Revolution* (2017). By now her *Marxism and Freedom,* first published in New York in 1957 with a 1958 publication date, has appeared in many editions and translations: Italian (1962); Japanese (1964); French (1971 and 2016); British (1971 and 1975); Spanish (1976, 1990, and 2007); Chinese (1998); Farsi (2008); Russian (2011); Arabic (2011); and Indian (2013). The new chapter that was added to the 1964 edition, "The Challenge of Mao Tse-tung," was translated by a Chinese refugee at the start of the "Cultural Revolution." Other entire chapters were circulated in samizdat in the underground in East Europe and resulted in a dialogue with East European Marxist-Humanists. Some of them collaborated later in the writing of the chapter on state-capitalism in East Europe in *Philosophy and Revolution*. Other chapters were translated into Farsi in Iran, where revolutionaries included one of them in a pamphlet to celebrate May Day 1979. *Philosophy and Revolution: from Hegel to Sartre and from Marx to Mao,* first published in 1973, appeared in Spanish (1977, 1989, and 2004), Italian (1977), German (1981), Russian (1993), Chinese (2000), Farsi (2004), and a portion in Polish (1990). *American Civilization on Trial: Black Masses as Vanguard* was published in Spanish (2014). *Rosa Luxemburg, Women's Liberation, and Marx's Philosophy of Revolution* (1982) came out in a second edition introduced by Adrienne Rich in 1991, and in Spanish (1985, 1999, 2009, 2013, and 2017) and German (1998). *Women's Liberation and the Dialectics of Revolution: Reaching for the Future* was published in Spanish in 1993.

preface by young Iranian participants in the Revolution of 1978–79 who saw this writing as not merely scholarship but a way of intervening in the ongoing revolution under the whip of Ayatollah Khomeini's counterrevolution.[35]

Another piece, "A 1981 View of Marx's 1841 Dialectic," extends her new view of Marx after publication of his *Ethnological Notebooks* to the years before his break with bourgeois society. The indispensability of Hegelian dialectic, as transformed by Marx into a philosophy of revolution, is further elaborated in "The Theory of Alienation: Marx's Debt to Hegel" and "The Todayness of Marx's Humanism," both of which take up Marx's *Economic-Philosophic Manuscripts of 1844*.

The relationship between Marx's early analyses and his masterwork, *Capital*, goes far beyond the fact that he never let go of such essential categories as alienated labor. Marx's Humanism and dialectic permeate both the form and content and the method of *Capital*. That is seen in how *Marxism and Freedom* advanced a new concept of theory grounded in that very method. Her analysis of the dialectical structure and process of formation of Marx's *Capital* is elaborated with verve in "Capitalist Development and Marx's *Capital*, 1863–1883," which opens Part 2, "The Inseparability of Marx's Economics, Humanism, and Dialectic." It was continued in a new way for a different context as one of the elements of Chapter 3, "The Todayness of Marx's Humanism." This interpretation became central to every polemic with post-Marx Marxist interpretations of Marx's great work.

Dunayevskaya's concreteness was such that all her writings after the coal miners' general strike of 1949–50 were rooted in recognition of a new stage of production introduced by automation, together with a new stage of cognition represented by the miners' asking "what kind of labor" human beings should do. The question of what constitutes a dialectical Marxist response to automation as a new stage of production is addressed in her letter to Herbert Marcuse presented in Part 2, including both the attitude of the theoretician toward the workers and the attitude of the workers to automation.

That concreteness was manifested after the global recession of the mid-1970s in the way Dunayevskaya's writings from then on related to the structural crisis of capitalism and the responses to it by rulers, masses, and theoreticians. The crisis immediately engendered new debates about the relevance of Marx's theory. "Today's Epigones Who Try to Truncate Marx's *Capital*" combines the analysis of the crisis as no mere cyclical event with a critique of Trotskyist

---

35   *Crossroads of History: Marxist-Humanist Writings on the Middle East* by Raya Dunayevs-
     kaya (Chicago: News and Letters, 2013) includes a selection of her analyses of revolution
     and counterrevolution in Iran.

economist Ernest Mandel and clarification of Marx's theory as both economic and philosophical, in a way that speaks strongly to our contemporary situation.

As a deep restructuring of the economy continued in the 1980s, with the U.S. having become a debtor nation, Chapter 9, "Capitalist Production/Alienated Labor," investigated the economic situation and the illusions of the capitalist ideologues. The ideologues had forgotten not only the lessons of the Great Depression but that the foundation of capitalist economy is alienated labor—alienated "from the activity of self-development into an appendage to a machine," as she put it in "The Theory of Alienation: Marx's Debt to Hegel" (Chapter 2). The subjective dimension is brought to view in Chapter 9 both as struggles from below and as the positive in the negative that Marx outlined in his *Critique of the Gotha Program.*

Part 2 presents two letters that expand on the discussion in *Philosophy and Revolution* of Marx's *Grundrisse,* the first rough draft of *Capital.* They develop the question of Marx's restructuring of the book and his break with the concept of theory by viewing *"the self-development of the Idea,* in Marx's hands," and they take up the indispensability of Hegel and a critique of Martin Nicolaus, the English translator of the *Grundrisse* and author of a foreword to it.

After the discovery of the new moments of Marx's last decade, "Marx's Critique of Culture" expands the view of "economics" in a critique of the philosopher Louis Dupré, who corresponded with Dunayevskaya and has written much on both Hegel and Marx. Here she revisits Marx's concept of praxis in relationship to "culture" and "the wide gulf between Marx's multilinear view of human relations and Engels' unilinear view."

That new view of the differences between Marx and Engels, as well as critique of many varieties of Marxists, grew out of the concept of Marx's Marxism as a totality developed while Dunayevskaya was writing *Rosa Luxemburg, Women's Liberation, and Marx's Philosophy of Revolution.* It coalesced into her concept of post-Marx Marxism as a pejorative, beginning with Engels. Part 3, "Post-Marx Marxism and the Battle of Ideas," begins with an essay never published before that is directly on the concept of post-Marx Marxism. That is followed by two columns from *News & Letters* explicitly concretizing the concept in critiques of specific Marxists and Marxologists. Part 3 continues with a series of incisive critical discussions of Marxist interpretations and misinterpretations of Marx.

The four sections of Part 4, "Marx as Philosopher of Revolution in Permanence—Reading Marx for Today," show the ramifications of this return to Marx's thought as interventions into the contemporary terrain of revolution and counterrevolution. The first section, "Marxist-Humanism," retraces the road that led from the coal miners' general strike through the ramifications of Stalin's death to Dunayevskaya's letters on Hegel's Absolutes. In doing so, the return to Marx's Marxism reveals itself to be a re-creation, illuminating the philosophic moment of Marxist-Humanism and the original contribution that flowed from it as "Absolute Idea as New Beginning."

Marx's last works also provided Dunayevskaya with a new vantage point on his relationship to what she called the Black dimension, as seen in the second section of Part 4, "Black Liberation and Internationalism." It is summed up in "The Two-Way Road between the U.S. and Africa," together with the "multi-dimensionality" of Black masses in motion, from African-American women as reason to the African revolutions and the rise of the Third World. The section begins with an excerpt from *American Civilization on Trial: Black Masses as Vanguard*, presenting Marx's relationship to the Abolitionists and the Civil War as part of a comprehensive view of U.S. history with Black freedom movements at the center. How important African-American revolt was to her conception of U.S. Marxism from the very beginning is shown not only in her 1920s activities but in theory in her 1944 "Black Intellectuals in Dilemma" (Chapter 26).

"Marx's 'New Humanism' and the Dialectics of Women's Liberation in 'Primitive' and Modern Societies" opens the third section of Part 4, "Women's Liberation and the Dialectics of Revolution," by tracing Marx's treatment of the Man/Woman relationship in his works. At every period from his youth in the 1840s through to the end of his life, she shows how Marx took up that relationship in ways that illuminate how total the uprooting of society needs to be. "Marx and Engels' Studies Contrasted: Relationship of Philosophy and Revolution to Women's Liberation" contains an extended commentary on Marx's *Ethnological Notebooks*, relating them to the difference between Marx and Engels and to the contemporary Women's Liberation Movement, which Dunayevskaya contends was given little direction by Engelsian Marxism.

How this vantage point relates to questions of sexuality and women's liberation is taken up in Dunayevskaya's "Letter to Adrienne Rich." Responding to Rich's very serious review of Dunayevskaya's four books,[36] the letter expands on the reason for being of *Philosophy and Revolution,* and on her concepts of "woman as revolutionary reason as well as force" and "new forces and new passions" of revolution, especially in relation to her fourth book, *Women's Liberation and the Dialectics of Revolution: Reaching for the Future,* and her work-in-progress, *Dialectics of Organization and Philosophy.* In doing so, the letter illuminates her view of multilinearity in Marx's late writings as a dimension of his concept of revolution in permanence concerning not only class but all social relations.

---

36   Adrienne Rich, "Living the Revolution," *The Women's Review of Books* Vol. 3, No. 12, September 1986.

"Dialectics of Organization and Philosophy," the final section of Part 4, begins with "Spontaneity, Organization, Philosophy (Dialectics)" and "Philosopher of Permanent Revolution and Organization Man," both written in the process of composing *Rosa Luxemburg, Women's Liberation, and Marx's Philosophy of Revolution*. These writings hold thoughts on the relationship of dialectics and organization that were not included in the finished book. These are the first pieces Dunayevskaya wrote that draw out the connection of the theory of revolutionary organization to Marx's last decade and his concept of revolution in permanence, and contain one of her most comprehensive discussions of Marx's *Critique of the Gotha Program*.

Dialectics of organization and philosophy is also central to one of the very last writings by Dunayevskaya, "A Post-World War II View of Marx's Humanism, 1843–1883; Marxist Humanism, 1950s-1980s." The retrogression of the 1980s was the context for a new interpretation of the origin of Marxist humanism worldwide in the 1950s and of Marx's last decade. That includes new articulations on the relationship between organization, spontaneity, and philosophy.

We hope this collection will make a contribution to the living development of Marx's philosophy of liberation and of Marxist-Humanism, and therefore to the achievement of revolution in permanence. The reason for returning to Marx today remains what Dunayevskaya indicated in *Rosa Luxemburg, Women's Liberation, and Marx's Philosophy of Revolution:*

> What is needed is a new unifying principle, on Marx's ground of humanism, that truly alters both human thought and human experience. Marx's *Ethnological Notebooks* are a historic happening that proves, one hundred years after he wrote them, that Marx's legacy is no mere heirloom, but a live body of ideas and perspectives that is in need of concretization. Every moment of Marx's development, as well as the totality of his works, spells out the need for "revolution in permanence." This is the absolute challenge to our age. (p. 195)

PART 1

The Philosophic Moment of Marx: Marx's Transformation of the Hegelian Dialectic

∵

CHAPTER 1

Preface to the Iranian Edition of Marx's Humanist Essays

In 1980, young Iranian revolutionaries were preparing a Farsi edition of Marx's Economic-Philosophic Manuscripts of 1844 *and asked Dunayevskaya to write the preface. They saw this publication as not scholarship alone but a way of intervening "in the battle against a counterrevolution that not only threatens from outside Iran, but that arose so quickly from within the revolution itself," as Charles Denby, editor of* News & Letters, *put it. In writing the preface, Dunayevskaya returned to Marx's philosophic moment with the new view brought about by her study of Marx's last decade, as well as her analyses of the revolution and counterrevolution in Iran.*

Because there is nothing more exciting than addressing revolutionaries in an ongoing revolution, I feel very honored to have this opportunity, in 1980, to introduce Marx's 1844 *Economic-Philosophic Manuscripts,* which opened an entirely new continent of thought and revolution that Marx named "a new Humanism." The year that I was first able to publish these Humanist Essays as an Appendix to my work, *Marxism and Freedom, from 1776 until Today,* a quarter of a century ago, coincided with the Hungarian Revolution against Russian totalitarianism calling itself Communism. Thus, both from below, from an actual proletarian revolution, and from theory, a todayness was shed upon these Essays that had lain on the dusty shelves of archives and had never been practiced.

Because what the contemporary world needs most today is a unity of Marx's philosophy of liberation with an outright revolution, we must re-examine what it is that Marx had meant when, in his greatest theoretical work, *Capital,* he had declared "human power is its own end" [MCIIIK, p. 954; MCIIIP, p. 959]; and what, in his very first historical materialist analyses in 1844, he had meant by saying "communism, as such, is not the goal of human development, the form of human society"[1]—what the goal is, is the creation of totally new, classless, human relations.

When you turn to the Essays on "Private Property and Communism" and the "Critique of the Hegelian Dialectic," you will note three things at once. First and foremost is that the analysis of labor—and that is what distinguishes Marx

---

1 Quoted from the Appendix to this book, p. 340. Following text references are to this Appendix.

from all other Socialists and Communists of his day *and* ours—goes much further than the economic structure of society. His analysis goes to the actual *human* relations. Secondly, it was not only Hegel who Marx stood on his feet by uniting, instead of separating, thinking from being. It was also the "quite vulgar and unthinking communism [that] completely negates the *personality* of man" [Appendix, p. 331]. Thirdly, and above all, is Marx's *concept* of labor—that it is the creativity of the labor*er* as the gravedigger of capitalism which uproots all of the old. Whether capitalism achieves the domination of labor through ownership of or through control over the means of production, what Marx focuses on is this: *any* "domination over the labor of others" proves not only capitalism's exploitative but perverse nature. To further stress the perverse nature, Marx says that the whole of capitalism could be summed up in a single sentence: "Dead labor dominates living labor." This *class* relationship transforms the living laborer into "an appendage to the machine." Here is how Marx expresses it in the Humanist Essays:

> Private property has made us so stupid and one-sided that ... in place of all the physical and spiritual senses, there is the sense of possession which is the simple alienation of all these senses.... The transcendence of private property is, therefore, the total *freeing* of all the human senses and attributes.
>
> Appendix, p. 335

It is here, to make sure that one thereby does not jump to the conclusion that the abolition of private property creates a new society, that Marx rejected the substitution of one form of property—state—for private as any solution to the problems of exploitation. It is why he rejected "vulgar and unthinking communism," focusing instead on two other problems: (1) truly new human relations, the "new Humanism" in place of communism; and (2) *the totality of the uprooting of all old relations* so that the *dual* rhythm of social revolution—the abolition of the old and the creation of the new—would run their full course.

In order to fully grasp Marx's Historical Materialism, the foundation for which was laid by these Humanist Essays, let us turn to the history of Marx's day as well as of today. What we see, first and foremost, is that Marx, in laying the foundation of Historical Materialism, was also creating the theory of proletarian revolution, the dialectic of liberation. Marx's greatest discovery—his concept of labor which revealed the laborer to be not just a force of revolution, but its Reason—meant that the proletariat was the "Subject," the *Universal* Subject that was not just a product of history, but its shaper, negating, i.e., abolishing, the exploitative reality. The exploited proletariat is *the transformer of reality*. It is here that Marx saw the core of the Hegelian dialectic, naming "the dialectic of negativity as the moving and creating principle" [Appendix, p. 344].

In actuality, continued Marx, there lies hidden in Hegel's *Phenomenology of Mind* "the movement of history" [Appendix, p. 341]. The mystical veil Hegel threw over it must be removed, but far from turning his back on philosophy, Marx transformed Hegel's revolution *in* philosophy into a philosophy *of* revolution. Which is why Marx held that "Humanism distinguishes itself both from Idealism and Materialism, and is, at the same time, the truth uniting both ... [and] capable of grasping the act of world history" [Appendix, p. 347].

"Grasping the act of world history" meant that he had to proclaim "revolution in permanence" when he saw that no sooner had the masses helped the bourgeoisie gain victory over feudalism in the 1848 revolutions than the bourgeoisie turned against them. And when he witnessed the greatest revolution in his time, the 1871 Paris Commune, and saw the masses take destiny into their own hands, Marx declared that non-state to be *the* "political form at last discovered to work out the economic emancipation of the proletariat" [MECW 22, p. 334]. As Marx expressed it:

> We should especially avoid re-establishing society as an abstraction, opposed to the individual. The individual *is the social entity*.
>
> Appendix, p. 334

Marx raised the question of "revolution in permanence" not only for his day but as the way out for all unfinished revolutions. No age can understand that better than our own, plagued *both* by transformations into opposite after each revolution—such as that which saw the first workers' state that arose from the Russian Revolution turn into the state-capitalist monstrosity that Russia is now; *and* by the aborting of today's revolutions before ever they come to completion.

The question is: *What happens after* the first act of revolution? Does conquest of power assure a classless society or only a new class bureaucracy? Our age, which has witnessed a whole new Third World emerge from the struggle against Western imperialism (U.S. imperialism most of all) in Latin America as in Africa, in the Middle East as in Asia, needs to demand that "grasping the act of world history" means spelling out total freedom.

Here again, Marx can illuminate our task in the manner in which he spelled out how total must be the uprooting of the old and the creation of the new. He turned to the most fundamental of all human relations—that of man to woman. In it we see why Marx opposed both private property and "vulgar communism":

> The infinite degradation in which man exists for himself is expressed in this relation to the *woman* as the spoils and handmaid of communal lust. For the secret of the relationship of man to man finds its *unambiguous*, definitive, *open*, obvious expression in the relationship of *man* to *woman*, and, in this way, the *direct, natural* relationship between the sexes. The direct, natural, necessary relationship of man to man is the *relationship of man to woman*.
>
> Appendix, p. 332

Clearly, "each of the human relations to the world—seeing, hearing, smell, taste, feeling, thought, perception, experience, wishing, activity, loving" [Appendix, p. 335] must transcend mere equality, a needed first achievement but not yet the needed total reorganization of human relations. Abolition of the old is only the first mediation. "Only by the transcendence of this mediation ... does there arise *positive* Humanism, beginning from itself" [Appendix, p. 352].

As one follows Marx's view of total freedom, one can see how far beyond technology Marx's philosophy of revolution extended. Long before the atom was split and out of it came, not the greatest productive force, but the most destructive A-bomb, H-bomb and N-bomb, Marx wrote in these Essays: "To have one basis for life and another for science is *a priori* a lie" [Appendix, p. 338]. With Hiroshima, we saw what a holocaust the lie of separating the reason for being from the reason for scientific development can become. Now, with the eruption of the worldwide anti-nuclear movement, we can see all over again how urgent it is to study and practice Marx's new continent of thought. As the great English poet William Blake expressed it, nothing is more binding than "mind-forged manacles."[2] Let us finish with those manacles once and for all.

It is with the striving for such a manifesto of total freedom that I, as Marxist-Humanist, express my solidarity with the Iranian revolutionaries as we all aspire to a new internationalism. The struggle continues.

November 1, 1980
Detroit, Michigan

---

2 Blake, "London," *Songs of Experience.* —Editor.

CHAPTER 2

The Theory of Alienation: Marx's Debt to Hegel

First published in The Free Speech Movement and the Negro Revolution *(Detroit: News & Letters, 1965), this article was described in the Foreword to that pamphlet as "the lecture by Raya Dunayevskaya most frequently requested both by college students and civil rights activists because it deals with the problem with which they are themselves grappling—'Alienation and Freedom.'"*

The topic "Marx's Debt to Hegel," is neither merely academic, nor does it pertain only to the historical period of Marx's lifetime. From the Hungarian revolt to the African revolutions, from the student demonstrators in Japan to the Negro revolution in the U.S., the struggle for freedom has transformed reality and pulled Hegelian dialectics out of the academic halls and philosophy books onto the living stage of history.

It is true that this transformation of Hegel into a contemporary has been via Marx. It is no accident, however, that Russian Communism's attack on Marx has been via Hegel. Because they recognize in the so-called mystical Absolute "the negation of the negation," the revolution against themselves, Hegel remains so alive and worrisome to the Russian rulers today. Ever since Andrei Zhdanov in 1947 demanded that the Russian philosophers find nothing short of "a new dialectical law," or, rather, declared "criticism and self-criticism" to be that alleged new dialectical law to replace the Hegelian and objective law of development through contradiction,[1] up to the 21st Congress of the Russian Communist Party where the special philosophic sessions declared Nikita Khrushchev to be "the true humanist," the attack on both the young Marx and the mystic Hegel has been continuous. It reached a climax in the 1955 attacks on Marx's Early Essays[2] in theory. In actuality it came to life as the Sino-Soviet Pact[3] to put down the Hungarian Revolution.

One thing these intellectual bureaucrats sense correctly: Hegel's Concept of the Absolute and the international struggle for freedom are not as far apart as would appear on the surface.

---

1   For Dunayevskaya's analysis of this see *Marxism and Freedom*, p. 40. —Editor.
2   Marx's *Economic-Philosophic Manuscripts of 1844*. —Editor.
3   Once the Sino-Soviet conflict came into the open, Chinese Communism actually dared boast of the fact that it urged Khrushchev to undertake the counterrevolutionary intervention. For the latest Chinese attacks on Marxist-Humanism which it calls the "revisionist" concept of Man, see text of this pamphlet [Mario Savio, Eugene, Walker, and Raya Dunayevskaya, *The Free Speech Movement and the Negro Revolution* (Detroit: News & Letters, 1965)], p. 39.

I   The Ideal and the Real are Never Far Apart

It is this which Marx gained from Hegel. It is this which enabled the young Marx, once he broke from bourgeois society, to break also with the vulgar communists of his day who thought that one negation—the abolition of private property—would end all the ills of the old society and be the new communal society.

Marx insisted on what is central to Hegelian philosophy, the theory of alienation, from which he concluded that the alienation of man does not end with the abolition of private property—*unless* what is most alien of all in bourgeois society, the alienation of man's labor from the activity of self-development into an appendage to a machine, is abrogated. In the place of the alienation of labor, Marx placed, *not* a new property form, but "the full and free development of the individual."

The pluri-dimensional in Hegel, his presupposition of the infinite capacities of man to grasp through to the "Absolute," *not* as something isolated in heaven, but as a *dimension* of the human being, reveals what a great distance humanity had traveled from Aristotle's Absolutes.

Because Aristotle lived in a society based on slavery, his Absolutes ended in "Pure Form"—mind of man would meet mind of God and contemplate how wondrous things are.

Because Hegel's Absolutes emerged out of the French Revolution which put an end to serfdom, Hegel's Absolutes breathed the air, the earthly air of freedom. Even when one reads Absolute Mind as God, one cannot escape the earthly quality of the unity of theory and practice and grasp through to the Absolute Reality as man's attainment of total freedom, inner and outer and *temporal*. The bondsman, having through his labor gained, as Hegel put it, "a mind of his own,"[4] becomes part of the struggle between "consciousness-in-itself" and "consciousness-for-itself." Or, more popularly stated, the struggle against alienation becomes the attainment of freedom.

In Hegel's Absolutes there is imbedded, though in abstract form, the full development of what Marx would have called the *social* individual, and what Hegel called individuality "purified of all that interfered with its universalism,"[5] i.e., freedom itself.

---

4   G.W.F. Hegel, *The Phenomenology of Mind,* translated by J.B. Baillie (New York: The MacMillan Co., 1931), p. 239.

5   Hegel, *Philosophy of Mind,* translated by William Wallace (Oxford: Oxford University Press, 1892), ¶481.

Freedom, to Hegel, was not only his point of departure. It was his point of return. This is what makes him so contemporary. This was the bridge not only to Marx but to our day, and it was built by Hegel himself.

As Lenin was to discover when he returned to the Marxian philosophic foundations in Hegel during World War I, the revolutionary spirit of the dialectic was not superimposed upon Hegel by Marx; it is in Hegel.[6]

II   Marx's Critique of, and Indebtedness to, the Hegelian Dialectic

The Communists are not the only ones who try to spirit away the integrality of Marxian and Hegelian philosophy. Academicians also think that Marx is so strange a progeny that he has transformed Hegelian dialectics to the point of non-recognition, if not outright perversion. Whether what Herbert Melville called "the shock of recognition" will come upon us at the end of this discussion remains to be seen, but it is clearly discernible in Marx.

Marx's intellectual development reveals two basic stages of internalizing and transcending Hegel. The first took place during the period of his break with the Young Hegelians, and thrusts at them the accusation that they were *dehumanizing* the Idea. It was the period when he wrote both his *Criticism of the Hegelian Philosophy of Right*, and the *Critique of the Hegelian Dialectic* [see Appendix].

There was nothing mechanical about Marx's new materialist outlook. Social existence determines consciousness, but it is not a confining wall that prevents one's sensing and even seeing the elements of the new society.

In Hegel, too, not only continuity as relation between past and present, but as attraction exerted by the future on the present, and by the whole, even when it does not yet exist, on its parts, is the mainspring of the dialectic.

It helped the young Marx to found a new stage of world consciousness of the proletariat, in seeing that the material base was not what Marx called "vulgar" [Appendix, pp. 331–32], but, on the contrary, *released* the subject striving to remake the world.

Marx was not one to forget his intellectual indebtedness either to classical political economy or philosophy. Although he had transformed both into a new world outlook, rooted solidly in the actual struggles of the day, the sources remained the law of value of Adam Smith and David Ricardo, and Hegelian dialectics. Of course Marx criticized Hegel sharply for treating objective

---

6   For Dunayevskaya's analysis of Lenin's study of Hegel see *Marxism and Freedom*, Chapter 10, and *Philosophy and Revolution*, Chapter 3. —Editor.

history as if that were the development of some world-spirit, and analyzing self-development of mind as if ideas floated somewhere between heaven and earth, as if the brain was not in the head of the body of man living in a certain environment and at a specific historic period. Indeed Hegel himself would be incomprehensible if we did not keep in front of our minds the historic period in which he lived—that of the French Revolution and Napoleon. And, no matter how abstract the language, Hegel indeed had his finger on the pulse of human history.

Marx's *Critique of the Hegelian Dialectic* is *at the same time* a critique of the materialist critics of Hegel, including Ludwig Feuerbach, who had treated "the negation of the negation only as the contradiction of philosophy with itself." [Appendix, p. 341].

Marx reveals, contrariwise, that principle to be the expression of the *movement of history* itself, albeit in abstract form.

Marx had finished, or rather, broken off his *Critique of the Hegelian Dialectic*, just as he reached Absolute Mind. Marx's rediscovery of the Absolute came out of the concrete development of the class struggles under capitalism, which split the Absolute into two:

(1)   The unemployed army which Marx called "the general absolute law" of capitalist development, the reserve army of unemployed [MCIK, p. 707; MCIP, p. 798]. That was the negative element that would cause its collapse.

(2)   "The new forces and passions" [MCIK, p. 835; MCIP, p. 928], the positive element in that negative, which made the workers the "gravediggers" [MCIK, p. 837, note 1; MCIP, p. 930, note 2] of the old society, and the creators of the new.

It is here—in the second stage of Marx's relation to the Hegelian dialectic— that Marx fully transcended Hegel. The split in the philosophic category of the Absolute into two, like the split of the economic category of labor into labor as activity and labor-power as commodity, forged new weapons of comprehension. It enabled Marx to make a leap in thought to correspond to the new, the creative activity of the workers in establishing a society on totally new foundations which would, once and for all, abolish the division between mental and manual labor and unfold the full potentialities of man—a truly new human dimension.

III   The Human Dimension

Of course it is true that Hegel worked out all the contradictions in thought alone while in life all contradictions remained, multiplied, intensified. Of course where the class struggle did not abolish contradictions, those contradictions plagued not only the economy, *but its thinkers*. Of course Marx wrote that beginning with the first capitalist crisis, the ideologists turned into "prize-fighters" for capitalism [MCIK, p. 19; MCIP, p. 97].

But, first and foremost, Marx did *not* separate ideology and economics as if the latter were the only fundamental, and the former nothing but "show." Marx maintains that they are both as real as life. Throughout his greatest theoretic work, *Capital*, Marx castigates "the fetishism of commodities" *not only* because relations of men at production appear as "things," *but especially because* human relations under capitalism are so perverse that that is not appearance; that is indeed what they really are: Machine is master of man; not man of machine.

Marx's main point was that the driving force of the dialectic was man himself, not just his thought, but the *whole of man*, beginning with the alienated man at the point of production; and that, whereas bourgeois ideologists, because of their place in production, have a false consciousness because they must defend the *status quo* and are "prisoners of the fetishism of commodities," the proletarian, because of his place in production, is *the* "negative principle" driving to a resolution of contradictions.

In the *Philosophy of History* Hegel had written, "It is not so much *from* as *through* slavery that man acquired freedom."[7] Again we see that "Praxis" was not Marx's discovery, but Hegel's. What Marx did was to designate practice as the class struggle activity of the proletariat. In Hegel's theory, too, praxis stands higher than the "Idea of Cognition" because it has "not only the dignity of the universal but is the simply actual."[8]

It is true that Hegel himself threw a mystical veil over his philosophy by treating it as a closed ontological system. But it would be a complete misreading of Hegel's philosophy were we to think that his Absolute is either a mere reflection of the separation between philosopher and the world of material production, or that his Absolute is the empty absolute of pure or intellectual intuition of the subjective idealists from J.G. Fichte through F.H. Jacobi to F.W.J. Schelling, whose type of bare unity of subject and object—as Prof. J.B. Baillie has so brilliantly phrased it—"possessed objectivity at the price of being inarticulate."[9]

Whether, as with Hegel, Christianity is taken as the point of departure, or whether—as with Marx—the point of departure is the *material* condition for

---

7 Hegel, *The Philosophy of History* (New York: Dover, 1956), p. 407. —Editor.
8 Hegel, *Science of Logic*, Vol. II, translated by W.H. Johnston and L.G. Struthers (New York: The MacMillan Co., 1951), p. 460. —Editor.
9 Hegel, *The Phenomenology of Mind*, p. 38. —Editor.

freedom created by the Industrial Revolution, the essential element is self-evident: man has to *fight* to gain freedom; thereby is revealed "the negative character" of modern society.

Now the principle of negativity was not Marx's discovery; he simply named it "the living worker"; the discovery of the principle was Hegel's. In the end, Spirit itself finds that it no longer is antagonistic to the world, but is indeed the indwelling spirit of the community. As Hegel put it in his early writings, "The absolute moral totality is nothing else than a people ... [and] the people who receive such an element as a natural principle have the mission of applying it."[10]

The humanism of Hegel may not be the most obvious characteristic of that most complex philosophy, and, in part, it was hidden even from Marx, although Lenin in his day caught it even in the simple description of the Doctrine of the Notion as "the realm of Subjectivity or of Freedom."[11] Or man achieving freedom not as a "possession," but a dimension of his being.

It is this dimension of the human personality which Marx saw in the historical struggles of the proletariat that would once and for all put an end to all class divisions and open up the vast potentialities of the human being so alienated in class societies, so degraded by the division of mental and manual labor that not only is the worker made into an appendage of a machine, *but the scientist* builds on a principle which would lead society to the edge of an abyss.

One hundred years before Hiroshima, Marx wrote, "To have one basis for science and another for life is *a priori*, a lie" [Appendix, p. 338]. We have lived this lie for so long that the fate of civilization, not merely rhetorically, but *literally*, is within orbit of a nuclear ICBM. Since the very survival of mankind hangs in the balance between the East's and the West's nuclear terror, we must, this time, under the penalty of death, unite theory and practice in the struggle for freedom, *thereby abolishing the division between philosophy and reality and giving ear to the urgency of "realizing" philosophy*, i.e., of making freedom a reality.

---

10   Hegel, *Natural Law,* translated by T.M. Knox with an introduction by H.B. Acton (Philadelphia: University of Pennsylvania Press, 1975), pp. 128–29. —Editor.

11   Lenin, Abstract of Hegel's *Science of Logic.* Citations to Lenin's Abstract will be to Dunayevskaya's translation, which is included in *Russia: From Proletarian Revolution to State-Capitalist Counter-Revolution: Selected Writings by Raya Dunayevskaya* (Leiden: Brill, 2017). The above quotation is on p. 89.

CHAPTER 3

The Todayness of Marx's Humanism

This chapter was written in response to a request by Erich Fromm for an essay for a book he was editing, which was published in 1965 as Socialist Humanism: an International Symposium, *in which it was titled "Marx's Humanism Today." Dunayevskaya was one of only three people in the U.S. to be included in the symposium, which was later published in many editions in various languages. This chapter, which she had originally titled "The Todayness of Marx's Humanism," was published separately as pamphlets in Japanese (1967) and in Spanish (1974), the latter under the title* El humanismo de Marx en la actualidad.

It was during the decade of the First International (1864–74)—a decade that saw both the Civil War in America and the Paris Commune—that Marx restructured[1] the many drafts of *Capital* and published the first two editions of Volume I.

Capital sets forth a new concept of theory, a new dialectical relationship between theory and practice, and a shift of emphasis from the idea of history as the history of theory to the idea of history as the history of production. It signifies Marx's "return" to his own philosophic humanism after more than a decade of concentration on economics and empiric studies of the class struggles of his day. Not surprisingly, this return is on a more concrete level, which, rather than diminishing Marx's original humanist concepts, deepens them. This is obvious in the chapter "The Working Day," which Marx first decided to write in 1866 under the impact of the mass movement for the shortening of the working day following the conclusion of the Civil War in the United States. It is obvious in "The Fetishism of Commodities," which Marx informs us he changed "in a significant manner"[2] after the Paris Commune. It is obvious in the original categories he created for his economic analysis and the creative practice of the Hegelian dialectic. Humanism gives Marx's magnum opus its force and direction. Yet most Western scholars of Marxism are content either to leave the relationship between the now famous *Economic-Philosophic*

---

1   In his Preface to Volume II of Marx's *Capital* (Kerr edition), Friedrich Engels lists the original manuscripts in such a way that the pagination tells the story of the restructuring. For my analysis of this, see pages 87–91 of *Marxism and Freedom* (New York: Twayne Publishers, 1958, 1964).

2   See Marx's Afterword to the French edition of *Capital*, in *Capital*, Vol. I [MCIP, p. 105]. —Editor.

Manuscripts of 1844[3] and *Capital* implicit, or to make the continuity explicit only insofar as the ethical foundations of Marxism are concerned.[4] This leaves the door wide open for those who wish to transform Marx's humanism, both as philosophy and as historic fact, into an abstract which would cover up concrete economic exploitation, actual lack of political freedom, and the need to abolish the conditions preventing "realization" of Marx's philosophy, i.e., the reunification of mental and manual abilities in the individual himself, the "all-rounded" individual who is the body and soul of Marx's humanism.

The 1844 *Manuscripts* didn't just "pave the way" for "scientific socialism." Humanism wasn't just a stage Marx "passed through" on his voyage of discovery to "scientific economics" or "real revolutionary politics." Humanist philosophy is the very foundation of the integral unity of Marxian theory, which cannot be fragmented into "economics," "politics," "sociology," much less identified with the Stalinist monolithic creation, held onto so firmly by Khrushchev and Mao Zedong.

Of all the editions of *Capital*, from its first publication in 1867 until the last before Marx died in 1883, the French edition (1872–75) alone contained the changes that had, as Marx put it in the Afterword, "scientific value independent of the original." The revolutionary action of the Parisian masses in "storming the heavens"[5] and taking destiny into their own hands clarified for Marx the two most fundamental theoretical problems: the accumulation of capital, and the fetishism of commodities. Just as his analysis of the struggles to shorten the working day became pivotal to the structure of *Capital*, so these additions became crucial for its spirit, i.e., for the future inherent in the present. The changes were of two kinds. One was tantamount to a prediction of what we today call state capitalism—the ultimate development of the law of concentration and centralization of capital "in the hands of one single capitalist, or those of one single corporation" [MCIK, p. 688, MCIP, p. 779]. The second was the illumination of the fetishism of commodities inherent in the value-form as emanating from "the form itself" [MCIK, p. 82, MCIP, p. 164].

---

3   Marx's 1844 *Manuscripts* are now available in several English translations, including one issued in Moscow, but the one more readily available here is by T.B. Bottomore, and is included in *Marx's Concept of Man* by Erich Fromm (New York: Frederick Ungar Publishing Co., 1961). Outside of the essay on "Alienated Labor," I am, however, using my own translation and therefore not paginating the references.

4   See especially *The Ethical Foundations of Marxism* by Eugene Kamenka (New York: Frederick A. Praeger, 1962).

5   *The Civil War in France*, by Karl Marx, is widely available in many languages both as a separate pamphlet and in Marx's *Selected Works* and *Collected Works*. ["Storming the heavens" is quoted from a letter from Marx to Ludwig Kugelmann, April 12, 1871 [MECW 44, p. 132]. —Editor.].

Marx concluded that only *freely* associated labor can abrogate the law of value; *only* "freely associated men" [MCIK, p. 92, MCIP, p. 173] can strip the fetishism from commodities.

At this moment in history, when established state powers claim "to practice" or to base themselves on Marxism, it is essential to re-establish what Marx himself meant by practice. It was freedom. The notion of freedom, always Marx's point of departure and of return, is concretized through a most painstaking and original analysis of the "inexorable laws" of capitalist development. This discloses *how* the proletariat, as "substance" (or mere object of an exploitative society) becomes "subject," i.e., revolts against the conditions of alienated labor, *thereby* achieving "the negation of the negation," or self-emancipation. In a word, *Capital* is the culmination of the 25 years of labor that began when Marx, in 1843, first broke with bourgeois society and melded what he considered its highest achievements in thought—English political economy, French revolutionary doctrine, Hegelian philosophy—into a theory of liberation, a new philosophy of human activity which he called "a thoroughgoing Naturalism or Humanism."

The Hungarian Revolution of 1956[6] transformed Marx's humanism from an academic debate to a question of life and death. Interest in it intensified the following year when the "100 Flowers" blossomed briefly in China before the totalitarian state caused them to wither abruptly.[7] From 1958 to 1961 the

---

6   For Dunayevskaya's writings on the Hungarian Revolution of 1956, see "Spontaneity of Action and Organization of Thought: In Memoriam to the Hungarian Revolution," Political Letter of September 17, 1961, included in Chapter 11 of Dunayevskaya, *Russia: From Proletarian Revolution to State-Capitalist Counter-Revolution*. See also Chapter 18 of *Marxism and Freedom*, "Two Kinds of Subjectivity." —Editor.

7   The indispensable book for the English reader is *The Hundred Flowers Campaign and the Chinese Intellectuals* by Roderick MacFarquhar (New York: Frederick A. Praeger, 1960). The voices of revolt in China should then be compared with those in Eastern Europe. By now the books, not to mention pamphlets and articles, on the Hungarian Revolution are legion. A few which I consider important for tracing the role that Marx's humanism played are the following: *Imre Nagy on Communism* (New York: Frederick A. Praeger, 1957); François Fejtö, *Behind the Rape of Hungary* (New York: David McKay Company, 1957); *The Hungarian Revolution, A White Book* edited by Melvin J. Lasky (New York: Frederick A. Praeger, 1957); *Bitter Harvest*, edited by Edmund O. Stillman with Introduction by François Bondy (New York: Frederick A. Praeger, 1959). For eyewitness reports, and especially those relating to the Workers' Councils, the issues of *The Review* (periodical published by the Imre Nagy Institute, Brussels) are quintessential. Some reports also appeared in the magazine *East Europe*, which did a competent job on Poland, especially in the publication of the debate on Marx's humanism between the leading philosophers in Poland, Adam Schaff and Leszek Kolakowski. Both of these philosophers are also translated in the collection entitled *Revisionism*, edited by Leopold Labedz (New York: Frederick A. Praeger, 1962).

African revolutions gave proof of a new, third world whose underlying philosophy, again, was humanism.[8]

The Cold War and McCarthyism helped keep the United States isolated from the West European rediscovery of Marx's 1844 Humanist Essays in the mid-1940s and early 1950s. Now, however, Americans have an opportunity to make up in comprehensiveness of discussion what was lost in the belated start.[9] The Freedom Now movement of the Negroes, on the one hand, and, on the other hand, the 1962 missile crisis over Cuba, which made real the nuclear threat, have helped rekindle the debate. In his own way, the scholar too must grapple with the inner identity of the Marxian economic, political, sociological, scientific, and philosophic categories. It was the late, non-Marxist, anti-Hegelian economist, Joseph Schumpeter, who pinpointed Marx's genius as "the *idea* of theory," the transformation of "historic narrative into historic raisonné."[10]

Elsewhere[11] I have made a detailed analysis of all four volumes of *Capital* and their relationship to the 1844 *Manuscripts*. Here space considerations limit

---

8   *African Socialism* by Léopold Sédar Senghor (New York: American Society of African Culture, 1959); Sekou Toure's "Africa's Path in History" was excerpted for the English reader in *Africa South*, April-June 1960, Capetown; now available only abroad. See also my *Nationalism, Communism, Marxist-Humanism and the Afro-Asian Revolutions* (American, 1958, and English, 1961), editions available at *News & Letters*, Detroit, Michigan [Chicago, Illinois, 1984].

9   I do not mean to say that I accept the West European intellectual's attitude on either the question of the degree of belatedness, or the low level of discussion in the United States. Four or five years before Europe's first rediscovery of Marx's early essays, when Europe was under the heel of fascism, Herbert Marcuse dealt with them in his *Reason and Revolution*. It is true that this was based on the German text of the essays, that no English translation was available, and that the discussion of Professor Marcuse's seminal work was limited to small groups. It is also true that I had great difficulty in convincing either commercial publishers or university presses that they ought to publish Marx's Humanist Essays or Lenin's *Philosophic Notebooks*. I succeeded in getting both these writings published only by including them as appendices to my *Marxism and Freedom* (1958). Even then they did not become available to a mass audience. It was not until 1961, when Erich Fromm included a translation of the 1844 *Manuscripts* in *Marx's Concept of Man*, that Marx's humanism reached a mass audience in the United States, and received widespread attention in American journals. Nevertheless, I see no substantive reason for the intellectual arrogance of the European Marxologists since, in Europe as in the United States, it was only after the Hungarian Revolution that the discussion of humanism reached the level of either concreteness or urgency. When I refer to the belatedness of the discussion, I have in mind the long period between the time the 1844 *Manuscripts* were first published by the Marx-Engels Institute in Russia, in 1927, under the editorship of Ryazanov, and the time they received general attention.

10   *A History of Economic Analysis* by Joseph Schumpeter (Oxford: Oxford University Press, 1954).

11   *Marxism and Freedom*. See especially Chapters V through VIII.

me to the two basic theories—the Marxian analysis of value and the fetishism of commodities—which are, in reality, the single, decisive, unified theory of alienation, or historical materialism, dialectically understood.

Marx's discovery that "It is not the consciousness of men that determines their existence, but, on the contrary, their social existence that determines their consciousness"[12] was no departure from either his own theory of alienated labor or the theory of alienation as the central core of the Hegelian dialectic. But Marx's precise analysis of the actual labor process under capitalism is more concrete, alive, shattering—and, of course, revolutionary—than any stage of alienation in Hegel's *Phenomenology of Mind*. In true Hegelian fashion Marx focuses on creativity, but, unlike Hegel, he bases it on the actual process of production. There, facing not just an idea but a *human being* who has ideas, Marx develops his earlier concept of the worker's "quest for universality."[13] The "new passions and new forces" [MCIK, p. 835; MCIP, p. 928] he now sees are born not only to overthrow the old order, but to construct a new one, "a society in which the full and free development of every individual is the ruling principle" [MCIK, p. 649; MCIP, p. 739].

So organically related are the economic, political, and philosophic concepts in *Capital* that when, in 1943,[14] the Russian theoreticians first openly broke with the Marxian analysis of value, they had to deny the dialectic structure of *Capital* and ask that, in "teaching" it, Chapter I be omitted. It does not speak highly of "Western" philosophy that it never saw the philosophic implications in this economic debate, and therefore also failed to discern the reason why the theoretical magazine of Soviet Marxism (*Under the Banner of Marxism*), which had carried on the tradition of Marx's dialectic philosophy, ceased its publication. Thereafter, without further ado or any reference to any previous interpretation of Marxian economics, the revision of the Marxian analysis of value became the standard Communist analysis. The wholeness of Marxian theory has always been the *bête noire* of established Marxism. It took the

---

12   *A Contribution to the Critique of Political Economy* (Chicago: Charles H. Kerr, 1904), p. 11 [MECW 29, p. 263].

13   *Poverty of Philosophy* (Chicago: Charles H. Kerr, 1910), p. 157 [MECW 6, p. 190].

14   *Pod Znamenem Marxizma* (*Under the Banner of Marxism*), Nos. 7–8/1943. The crucial article on the law of value from this issue was translated by me under the title, "Teaching of Economics in the Soviet Union." Along with my commentary, "A New Revision of Marxian Economics" [included in Chapter 9 of Dunayevskaya, *Russia: From Proletarian Revolution to State-Capitalist Counter-Revolution*], the article was published in The *American Economic Review* (September 1944). The controversy around it, in which Professors Oscar Lange, Leo Rogin, and Paul A. Baran participated in the pages of the journal, lasted for a year, at the end of which (September 1945) my rejoinder, "Revision or Reaffirmation of Marxism?" was published [RDC, pp. 214–17].

collapse of the Second International and a break with his own philosophic past to make Lenin, at the end of 1914, fully grasp the organic connection of Marxian economics with Hegelian philosophy. And from then on he became uncompromising in his criticism of all Marxists, himself included. In one of his "aphorisms" he wrote, "It is impossible fully to grasp Marx's *Capital,* and especially the first chapter, if you have not studied and understood the *whole* of Hegel's *Logic.* Consequently, none of the Marxists for the past half century has understood Marx!"

There is no more remarkable piece of analysis in the annals of political economy—and no more Hegelian kind of writing in Marx's "early Hegelian period"—than the final section of Chapter I of *Capital,* entitled "The Fetishism of Commodities." There philosophy and economics are connected with history as integrally as content and form are welded together in a great work of literature. By the time Marx introduced further changes into the French edition, after the Paris Commune, those fifteen pages were as tightly drawn as the strings of a violin. We must remember that Marx considered the greatest achievement of the Commune to be "its own working existence" [MECW 22, p. 339]. The *totality* of the reorganization of society by the Communards gave Marx a new insight into the whole question of the *form* of value, not only as it was historically determined, but also as it conditioned bourgeois thought in turn. Under capitalistic conditions of production, philosophy had been reduced to an ideology, i.e., false consciousness. The categories of thought proper to capitalistic production were uncritically accepted by all, including even Adam Smith and David Ricardo, the authors of the epoch-making discovery that labor was the source of all value. This is why, despite their discovery, they could not dissolve the fetishism of commodities. Classical political economy, concludes Marx, met its historic barrier here.

The commodity form of the products of labor became a fetish because of the perverse relationship of subject to object—of living labor to dead capital. Relations between men appear as the relation between things because in our alienated society that is all "they really are" [MCIK, p. 84; MCIP, p. 166]. Dead capital is the master of living labor. The fetishism of commodities is the opiate that, to use a Hegelian expression, passes itself off as "the very *nature* of the mind"[15] to all *except* the proletariat who daily suffer from the domination of dead labor, the stranglehold of the machine. Therefore, concludes Marx, no one can strip the fetishism from the commodities *except freely associated labor.*

---

15   See Hegel on "The Third Attitude to Objectivity": "What I discover in my consciousness is thus exaggerated into a fact of the consciousness of all and even passed off for the very nature of the mind" (Hegel's *Logic,* first Wallace translation, Oxford University Press, 1892).

Obviously the Russian theoreticians, in 1943, were determined that no one should.

The necessary ideology to cover up the exploitation of the laborer did not change its essence when it changed its form from the private to the state capitalism that calls itself Communism. Nor has the ideological rift between China and Russia undermined the exploitative relationship in either land. Were Marx to return to earth, he would have no difficulty whatever in recognizing in its new form—the State Plan and its fetishism—the state capitalist development he predicted as the ultimate effect of the inexorable laws of capitalist development. Our generation should understand better than any previous generation that it is not a question of nationalized vs. private property. It is a question of freedom. Wherever and whenever freedom was limited, Marx struck out against the barrier, in practice and in theory. Thus, when classical political economists spoke of "free labor," by which they meant wage labor, Marx wrote caustically: "For them there was history, but history is no more" [MCIK, p. 93, note 2; MCIP, p. 175, note 35].

It should be obvious that Marx's primary theory of value, or "abstract," "value-producing" labor, is a theory of alienated labor. In the Humanist Essays Marx explained why he analyzed economic facts "in conceptual terms as *alienated labor*.... How does it happen, we may ask, that man *alienates his labor?* How is this alienation founded in the nature of human development? We have already done much to solve the problem insofar as we have *transformed* the question concerning the *origin of private property* into a question about the relation between *alienated labor* and the process of development of mankind. For in speaking of private property one believes oneself to be dealing with something external to mankind. But in speaking of labor one deals directly with mankind itself. This new formulation of the problem already contains its solution."[16]

By the time he completed *Capital,* however, Marx felt the need to create economic categories to analyze the alien character of labor under capitalism both as an activity in the factory and as a commodity in the market where "alone rule Freedom, Equality, Property and Bentham" [MCIK, p. 195; MCIP, p. 280].

Marx created special economic categories not only to expound his theory of value and surplus-value, but also to show how degraded human relations were at the point of production itself. By splitting the category of labor into labor as activity and labor-power as a commodity—as if the laborer could indeed disjoint his hands from his body and have them retain their function—Marx was able to show that, since labor-power cannot be so disembodied, it is the laborer himself who enters the factory. And in the factory, continues Marx, the

---

16   See "Alienated Labor" in *Marx's Concept of Man* by Erich Fromm, pp. 103, 108.

laborer's ability becomes a mere appendage to a machine and his concrete labor is reduced to a mass of congealed, abstract labor.

Now there is, of course, no such creature as an "abstract laborer"; one is a miner or a tailor or a steelworker or a baker. Nevertheless, the *perverse* nature of capitalist production is such that man is not master of the machine; the machine is master of the man. By the instrumentality of the machine, which "expresses" itself in the ticking of a factory clock, a man's skill becomes unimportant so long as he produces a given quantity of products in a given time. Labor time is the handmaiden of the machine which accomplishes the fantastic transformation of all concrete labors into one abstract mass.

Marx considered his analysis of concrete and abstract labor his original contribution to political economy, "the pivot on which a clear comprehension of political economy turns" [MCIK, p. 48; MCIP, p. 132]. In the process of his analysis of the capitalist's "werewolf hunger for surplus labor" as "a live monster that is fruitful and multiplies" [MCIK, pp. 268, 217; MCIP, pp. 353, 302], Marx creates two other new categories: constant *capital* (machines) and variable *capital* (wage labor). All labor, paid or unpaid, he insists, is *forced* labor. And this labor is so alien an activity that it has itself become a *form of capital.*

The precision, as well as originality, of this description of alienated labor is not, of course, merely a category of the "deductive Hegelian dialectic." It is a category of the dialectic *empiricism* of Marx re-creating an altogether new level of truth. Only politically motivated, self-induced blindness can, when reading Marx's pages upon pages on the labor process under capitalism, conclude either that the mature Marx departed from his theory of alienated labor, or that alienated labor is a "leftover" from Marx's "left Hegelian days" before he worked his way out of "Hegelian gibberish" into "scientific materialism." At the same time, because Marx's economic categories have so incontrovertible a class character, it is impossible to denude them of their class content. Although some of today's near-Marxists loudly proclaim the "neutralization" of these categories, they apply them *to capitalism and to capitalism only.* Because the Marxian law of value is the supreme manifestation of capitalism, not even Joseph Stalin—at least not for very nearly two decades after he already had total power, the State Plan, and the monolithic party—dared admit its operation in Russia since he claimed the land was "socialist." It was only in the midst of a world war that the Russian theoreticians openly broke with the Marxian concept; in practice, of course, the ruling bureaucracy had long since followed an exploitative course.

In 1947 Andrei Zhdanov dramatically (or at least loudly) demanded that "the philosophical workers" replace the Hegelian dialectic with "a new dialectical law": criticism and self-criticism. By 1955 the critique of Marxian concepts concerned his humanism. V.A. Karpushin wrote in "Marx's Working Out of the Materialist Dialectics in the Economic-Philosophic Manuscripts in the Year 1844": "Marx was the first philosopher who went beyond the confines of philosophy and from the point of view of practical life and practical needs of the proletariat analyzed the basic question of philosophy as a truly scientific method of revolutionary change and knowledge of the actual world."[17]

The Russian Communists were not, however, about to favor "revolutionary change" where "revolutionary change" meant *their* downfall. Therefore, when the Hungarian Revolution tried the following year to transform reality by *realizing* philosophy, that is to say, by making freedom from Russian Communism a reality, the debate ended in machine-gun fire. Thus the violation of the *logos* of Marxian theory was followed by the destruction of liberty itself.

Soon after, the Russian theoreticians unloosed an unbridled, vitriolic attack on all opponents of *established* Communism, whom they gratuitously labeled "revisionists." Unfortunately, too many Western scholars accepted the term and referred to the ruling Communists as the "dogmatists," despite such wild gyrations and "flexibility" as, on the eve of World War II, the Hitler-Stalin Pact and the united front between Mao Zedong and Chiang Kai-shek; and, more recently, the rift between Russia and China. At the same time, the single grain of truth in the duality of Lenin's philosophic legacy—between the vulgarly materialistic *Materialism and Empirio-Criticism* and the creative dialectics of his *Philosophic Notebooks*—has provided a field day for the innate anti-Leninism of "the West." Elsewhere[18] I have analyzed "Mao's Thought," which is supposed to have made "original contributions to Marxism," especially his *On Practice* and *On Contradiction,* as they relate to his rise in power. Here I must limit myself to the fact that the humanist debate was in danger both of becoming a purely academic question, and of being separated from the "political" debates on "revisionism." Fortunately Marxism does not exist only in books, nor is it the possession only of state powers. It is in the daily lives of working people trying to reconstruct society on new beginnings.

The liberation from Western imperialism, not only in Africa but in Latin America (Fidel Castro too first called his revolution "humanist"), unfurled a humanist banner. Thereupon the Russian Communist line changed. Where, at first, it was claimed that Leninism needed no sort of humanization, nor any

---

17   *Voprosy Filosofii (Questions of Philosophy)*, No. 3/1955.

18   See the new chapter, "The Challenge of Mao Tse-tung" in the paperback edition of *Marxism and Freedom* (New York: Twayne, 1964). For an analysis of a similar perversion of Lenin's partisanship in philosophy into Stalin's monolithic "party-ness in philosophy," see the well-documented and perceptive analysis *Soviet Marxism and Natural Science, 1917–1932* by David Joravsky (New York: Columbia University Press, 1961).

of the reforms proposed by the proponents of "humanist socialism," the claim now became that the Soviets were the rightful inheritors of "militant humanism." Thus M.B. Mitin, who has the august title of Chairman of the Board of the All-Union Society for the Dissemination of Political and Scientific Knowledge, stated that Khrushchev's Report to the Twenty-first Congress of the Russian Communist Party was "the magnificent and noble conception of Marxist-Leninist socialist humanism."[19] And in 1963, at the thirteenth International Congress of Philosophy, held in Mexico, it was the Soviet delegation that entitled one of its reports "humanism in the Contemporary World."[20] Thus, curiously, Western intellectuals can thank the Russian Communists for throwing the ball back to them; once again, we are on the track of discussing humanism.

Let us not debase freedom of thought to the point where it is no more than the other side of the coin of thought control. One look at our institutionalized studies on "Marxism-Leninism" as the "know your enemy" type of course will show that, in methodology, these are no different from what is being taught under established Communism, although they are supposed to teach "opposite principles." The point is this: unless freedom of thought means an underlying philosophy for the realization of the forward movement of humanity, thought, at least in the Hegelian sense, cannot be called "an Idea." Precisely because, to Hegel, "only that which is an object of freedom can be called an Idea," even his Absolutes breathed the earthy air of freedom. Our age can do no less. It is true that the Marxian dialectic is not only political or historical, but also cognitive. However, to claim that Marx's concept of the class struggle is a "myth" and his "glorification" of the proletariat only "the end product of his philosophy of alienation"[21] flies in the face of theory and of fact. In this respect, George Lichtheim's criticism that such an American analysis is "a sort of intellectual counterpart to the late Mr. Dulles's weekly sermon on the evils of communism"[22] has validity.

Marx's humanism was neither a rejection of idealism nor an acceptance of materialism, but the truth of both, and therefore a new unity. Marx's "collectivism" has, as its very soul, the individualistic element. That is why the young Marx felt compelled to separate himself from the "quite vulgar and unthinking

---

19   *Pravda*, February 6, 1959. The English translation used here appears in *The Current Digest of the Soviet Press*, June 3, 1959.

20   The report of this conference by M.B. Mitin appears in *Voprosy Filosofii*, No. 11/1963. For a different report of the same conference see *Studies in Soviet Thought*, No. 4/1963 (Fribourg, Switzerland).

21   *Philosophy and Myth in Karl Marx* by Robert Tucker (Cambridge: Cambridge University Press, 1961).

22   George Lichtheim's "Western Marxist Literature 1953–1963" appears in *Survey*, No. 50, January 1964.

communism [that] completely negates the *personality* of man" [Appendix, p. 331]. Because alienated labor was the essence of *all* that was perverse in capitalism, private or state, "organized" or "anarchic," Marx concluded his 1844 attack on capitalism with the statement that "communism, as such, is not the goal of human development, the form of human society" [Appendix, p. 340]. Freedom meant more, a great deal more, than the abolition of private property. Marx considered the abolition of private property to be only "the first transcendence." Full freedom demanded a second transcendence. Four years after these Humanist Essays were written Marx published the historic *Communist Manifesto. His* basic philosophy was not changed by the new terminology. On the contrary. On the eve of the 1848 revolutions, the Manifesto proclaimed: "The freedom of the individual is the basis of the freedom of all."[23] At the end of his life the concept remained unchanged. His magnum opus, like his life's activity, never deviated from the concept that only "the development of human power, which is its own end" is the true "realm of freedom" [MCIIIK, pp. 954–55; MCIP, p. 959]. Again, our age should understand better than any other the reasons for the young Marx's insistence that the abolition of private property is only the first transcendence. "Not until the transcendence of this mediation, which is nevertheless a necessary presupposition, does there arise positive Humanism, beginning from itself" [Appendix, p. 352].

"Positive Humanism" begins "from itself" when mental and manual labor are reunited in what Marx calls the "all-rounded" individual. Surely our nuclear age should be oppressively aware that the division between mental and manual labor, which has been the underlying principle of all class societies, has reached such monstrous proportions under capitalism that live antagonisms characterize not only production, but science itself. Marx anticipated the impasse of modern science when he wrote in 1844: "To have one basis for life and another for science is *a priori* a lie" [Appendix, p. 338]. We have been living this lie for one hundred and twenty years. The result is that the very survival of civilization as we have known it is at stake.

The task that confronts our age, it appears to this writer, is, first, to recognize that there is a movement from practice—from the actual struggles of the day—to theory; and, second, to work out the method whereby the movement *from theory* can meet it. A new relationship of theory to practice, a new appreciation of "Subject," of live human beings struggling to reconstruct society, is essential. The challenge of our times is not to science or machines, but to men. The totality of the world crisis demands a new unity of theory and practice, a new relationship of workers and intellectuals. The search for a total

---

23   MECW 6, p. 506: "[W]e shall have an association, in which the free development of each
      is the condition for the free development of all." —Editor.

philosophy has been disclosed dramatically by the new, third world of under-developed countries. But there are also evidences of this search in the struggles for freedom from totalitarian regimes, and in the West. To discern this mass search for a total philosophy it is necessary only to shed the stubbornest of all philosophies—the concept of "the backwardness of the masses"—and *listen* to *their* thoughts, as they battle automation, fight for the end of discrimination, or demand freedom *now*. Far from being intellectual abdication, this is the beginning of a new stage of cognition. This new stage in the self-liberation of the intellectual from dogmatism can begin only when, as Hegel put it, the intellectual feels the "compulsion of thought to proceed to ... concrete truths."[24]

The espousal of *partiynost* (party principle) as a philosophic principle is another manifestation of the dogma of "the backwardness of the masses," by which intellectuals in state-capitalist societies rationalize their contention that the masses must be ordered about, managed, "led." Like the ideologists in the West, they forget all too easily that revolutions do not arise in the fullness of time to establish a party machine, but to reconstruct society on a human foundation. Just as *partiynost*, or monolithism, in politics throttles revolution instead of releasing the creative energy of new millions, so *partiynost* in philosophy stifles thought instead of giving it a new dimension. This is not an academic question for either the East or the West. Marxism is either a theory of liberation or it is nothing. In thought, as in life, it lays the basis for achieving a new *human* dimension, without which no society is truly viable. As a Marxist humanist, this appears to me the whole truth of Marx's humanism, both as philosophy and as reality.

---

24   Hegel, *Logic,* translated by William Wallace (Oxford: Oxford University Press, 1892), ¶12.

CHAPTER 4

A 1981 View of Marx's 1841 Dialectic

Dunayevskaya's study of Marx's Ethnological Notebooks, *after they were finally published in 1972, led to her perceiving "new moments" of his "revolutionary philosophic-historic concepts." She extended this to an evaluation of his life's work as a totality, and in turn a fresh look at the years before his break with bourgeois society, leading up to his 1844 "philosophic moment." In this chapter, a letter to Charles Denby that was then printed in the June 1981 issue of* News & Letters, *she looks back to Marx's 1839–41 work. There she sees Marx making his first challenge to Hegel and the Left Hegelians, "in order to discover the inadequacy of the principle which* compelled *[Hegel's] accommodation" to existing reality, in search of new beginnings. That work, Dunayevskaya believed, illuminated the birth and nature of his philosophy of revolution in permanence.*

May 5, 1981

Dear CD [Charles Denby]:

I'd like to discuss with you the reason for my beginning the part of the book on Marx[1] in 1841 rather than 1843. The latter is the usual starting point for analyzing Marxism since that is the year Marx broke from bourgeois society. I find the year 1841 especially exciting because there we see Marx as a revolutionary before ever he developed a totally new body of ideas—a whole new continent of thought and of revolution we know as Marx's Marxism. We become witness to him speaking to himself, so to speak. In preparing his doctoral thesis on ancient Greek philosophy, specifically Epicurus and Democritus, we become witness to the fact that, despite his erudition and concentration on Greek philosophy, what preoccupies him is the reality of Germany, 1840, the great irresolvable contradiction between Hegel's Absolute Idea and Prussian reality.

To the extent to which 1841 was mentioned at all by Marxists, it was simply to show that, even in the realm of thought, and even when Marx himself was still a Hegelian, he "deviated" from Hegel's analysis of those Greek philosophers. What, however, is of the essence, as his Notebooks rather than just the thesis show, is truly phenomenal: Marx is actually probing heretofore unprobed depths of consciousness as well as of reality:

---

1 *Rosa Luxemburg, Women's Liberation and Marx's Philosophy of Revolution* is still in manuscript form, but should be off the press next year.

> While philosophy has sealed itself off to form a consummate, total world.... The world confronting a philosophy total in itself is therefore a world torn apart.... He who does not acknowledge this historical necessity must be consistent and deny that men can live at all after a total philosophy. (p. 491)[2]

Naturally, it isn't Epicurus and Democritus that interest us, but how Marx, in writing on that, was having his eyes fixed on and opposing the German reality of his day. As a young Hegelian he is asking himself: where is humanity heading? And it is this which leads him to the conclusion to break with the bourgeoisie as he begins his struggle against Prussian censorship, and feels the urgency to oppose the status quo. He starts to engage in *"ruthless criticism of all that exists,* ruthless in the sense that the criticism is neither afraid of its own results nor of confronting the powers that be" (Letter to Arnold Ruge, September 1843 [MECW 3, p. 142]).

Clearly, what is tugging at the young Marx in reality and in thought is something in the air—revolution. The key word for the young Marx is history. The contemporary history which was pulling at the student Marx was in his thesis stated as if it were only the history of thought, but the non-muted form in which it was expressed in his so-called Notebooks makes it clear that it was actual history—the crisis in contemporary Germany in reality as well as in thought. And because that was so, it was both Hegel and the Left Hegelians (of whom he was one) that Marx was breaking from. His point was that it is insufficient simply to show that the master (Hegel) had accommodated himself to reactionary reality. One must analyze the accommodation not merely to expose it, but in order thereby to discover the inadequacy of the philosophical principle which *compelled* that accommodation. Only in that way could the critique produce an advance in knowledge which would create the possibility of a new beginning.

Marx held that because Hegel's philosophy *wasn't* the unity of reason and reality which it claimed to be—the present period of crisis revealed the total diremption of the two separate totalities. Reality and Reason confronted each other hostilely: "This duality of philosophical self-consciousness appears finally as a double trend, each side utterly opposed to the other" (p. 86).

---

2 Both the Notebooks and the doctoral thesis on Epicurus and Democritus are quoted from *Karl Marx, Frederick Engels: Collected Works*, Volume 1, International Publishers, 1975. The disparity in the pages referred to above in these two works is due to the fact that, whereas the thesis, pp. 25–108, appears in Sec. 1, the Preparatory Materials, i.e., Notebooks, (pp. 403–509) do not appear till the end of the volume.

Discerning the inadequacy in both Hegel and the Young Hegelians, Marx was heading, his Notebooks reveal, toward both attacking philosophy and opposing reality. He turned first to a search for what he called a new "energizing principle" (p. 73 [alternate translation]) as he wrote:

> It is a psychological law that the theoretical mind, once liberated in itself, turns into practical energy.... But the *practice* of philosophy is itself *theoretical*. It is the *critique* that measures the individual existence by the essence, the particular reality by the idea. (p. 85)

The question that Marx kept asking himself is: where and how to begin anew both in philosophy and in trying to transform reality. The new beginning that Marx had worked out over the next two to three years was nothing short of a whole new continent of thought and of revolution. For, as he left the academic world and became a journalist, a revolutionary journalist, he was at once engaged both in battles with Prussian censorship and the legal system, specifically the laws on wood theft, taking, instead, the part of the rebellious peasants. Just as revolutionary journalism led to a break with the bourgeoisie and its state, so the Philosophic-Economic Essays led in 1844 to a new world view—"a new Humanism"—and a new concept of revolution—proletarian revolution.

What I found most exciting about that year, 1841, is to see the idea while it is germinating rather than when it is already a conclusion. The process of breaking, moreover, is what shows, at one and the same time, what is old and what is newborn, not as just "influences," but discontinuous with old: the great divide in historic age. And what sets off one age from another both as birthtime of history and of philosophy are those breaking-points of departure from old which point to the direction forward.

It is true that Marx would not work out that new beginning until he had broken with bourgeois society as he had already in 1841 broken with religion and Prussian censorship, and until he discerned the working class as Subject. But, philosophically, there is no doubt where he was headed, as he contrasted practice to theory and developed his most original interpretation of *praxis*. That was to remain his unique category for breaking both with "idealism" *and* "materialism."

Finally, can I confide in you something that may sound fantastic: may I ask you whether you see any relationship between the questions that preoccupied Marx in 1841 to what has been happening in our age in the early years of the 1950s? You remember, I am sure, two very different events in the early 1950s that would disclose, at one and the same time, the new stage of production—Automation—and a new stage of cognition, whether that be the break I saw in the Absolute Idea as reflecting not just a movement from theory, but a movement *from practice* that was itself a form of theory, or something as seemingly simple as your own life's story which you called *Indignant Heart*[3] and which actually was pointing to a new stage of Black consciousness that was soon to be revealed in the Montgomery Bus Boycott. Well, it happened that in this year's lecture tour, when I spoke on the book and on the year, 1841, I was asked by Iranian and Latin American revolutionaries about those early 1950s when, on the one hand, U.S. imperialism was acting in a most brutal imperialist way by bringing back the Shah in Iran, and causing a counterrevolution in Guatemala; and, on the other hand, there was a second, revolutionary USA, which today's revolutionaries wished to get a feeling about.

Let's discuss that when we begin the pre-plenary discussions[4] next month, O.K.?

Yours,

Raya

---

3   Charles Denby, *Indignant Heart: A Black Worker's Journal* (Boston: South End Press, 1978). —Editor.

4   This refers to discussions in preparation for the annual national gathering of News and Letters Committees. —Editor.

PART 2

The Inseparability of Marx's Economics, Humanism, and Dialectic

∵

CHAPTER 5

Capitalist Development and Marx's *Capital,* 1863–1883

The dialectical development of the structure of Marx's Capital *was central to Dunayevskaya's understanding of Marx ever since the Stalinists tried to bury its first chapter. Under the impact of her work translating Lenin's Abstract of Hegel's* Science of Logic *and her involvement with the 1949–50 coal miners' general strike, she dug into how Marx restructured* Capital *on the basis of the dialectic that emerged from below. This became the basis of a unique analysis of the logic and structure of Marx's greatest theoretical work—an analysis that became entwined with the need for a new relationship between theory and practice. She would return to this in* Marxism and Freedom; Philosophy and Revolution; *and* Rosa Luxemburg, Women's Liberation, and Marx's Philosophy of Revolution*. Her analysis of the dialectical structure and process of formation of Marx's* Capital *is elaborated with verve in this chapter, taken from the 1952 second draft of what became* Marxism and Freedom.

1   The Civil War in the United States and the International Workingmen's Association

There were a few stupid Marxists in the United States who, when the Civil War broke out, contented themselves with signing a statement that they were opposed to "all" forms of slavery, wage slavery as well as chattel slavery. Marx would have nothing to do with those who were quick to make a "general" attack on slavery but remained nothing but disinterested bystanders in the actual civil war that broke out. As he was to write in *Capital*: "Labor in the white skin cannot be free so long as labor in the black skin is enslaved" [MCIK, p. 329; MCIP, p. 414]. This was not an agitational statement but the simple truth. The trade union movement in America developed first on a *national* scale *after* the Civil War and the giant steps labor will take then will bring it up to the level of the activity of the First International.

There were thousands of workers in England, non-Marxists, who held a monster demonstration against their Government's attempt to intervene in the Civil War in the United States on the side of the pro-slavery South. This movement Marx was interested in and followed very closely.

In 1863 there was an insurrection in Poland against the tsarist Russian imperialist domination over them. "This much is certain," wrote Marx to Engels, "The era of revolution at length has been reopened in Europe."[1]

The turbulent 1860s also engulfed France. Napoleon III's regime was shaken by the many strikes and "combinations" (unions) which kept springing up despite the strictest anti-Combination laws and harshest prison terms for the strikers. Louis Bonaparte conceived the idea of gaining the support of the workers by giving amnesty to a *few* of the thousands of those imprisoned for participation in strikes. At the same time he announced that the workers could elect their own delegates to attend the World Exhibition to be held in London in 1862, where the capitalists would display not only their machines, raw materials, and finished products, but also their technicians, statisticians, *and* manual operatives in order "to inspire" them to ever greater production. Two hundred thousand workers voted in the French election and sent delegates to the English capital. Once there, the delegation split and contacted the British trade unions. Those workers had other ideas than to continue to work as the capitalists ordered. Out of the contact with the British trade unions, there grew, first, joint action in favor of the Polish insurrectionists who had been bloodily put down, and then the decision to establish an "international workingmen's association." To that meeting in 1864 Marx was invited.

Many write as if the historic significance of the International Workingmen's Association or, as it is now known, the First International is that Marx "organized" it. Nothing could be further from the truth. It was Marx who *recognized* at once the historic significance of this crystallization of the empiric acts of labor into a *new formation*. At every critical stage in the *objective* development of capital, the *subjective* development of the opposing element in capitalism—labor—tells the *specific* stage the proletariat has reached in its attempt to *reorganize society*. Thus the *organizations* formed at every stage tell the *concrete* stage of development of labor. It was one thing when it created utopian societies, quite something else when it built Chartism and unions, and something alee again when it reached the stage of an *international* organization. Marx was always looking at the revolts of the workers and the organizations they formed. He said the one merit of utopianism was that it reflected the first instinctive desire to reorganize society. It became a reactionary sect precisely when this universal aim to establish a new social order gained new impulses from the concretely developing capitalism and its revolt now took the form of the fight for the normal working day while the Utopians insisted on preserving the old type of organization. Marx, on the other hand, prided himself because

---

1   Letter of Marx to Engels, February 13, 1863 [MECW 41, p. 453]. —Editor.

what he had written out for the first congress was precisely what the workers in Baltimore had already concluded by "correct instinct":

> The first and great necessity of the present, to free the labor of this country from capitalistic slavery, is the passage of a law by which eight hours shall be the normal working day in all States of the American Union.

The Congress at Geneva[2] had made this an *international* goal.

Neither was it the fact that Marx wrote the Inaugural Address and Statutes of the International that made it a historic occasion. It was that the Inaugural Address and Statutes disclosed *what* the concrete development of labor, in relation to the concrete development of capital, 1848–1864, had achieved and what it had not achieved. With the defeats of the 1848 revolutions and break-up of party organizations of the proletariat, wrote Marx, the "dreams of emancipation vanished before an epoch of industrial fever, moral marasme, and political reaction."[3] Under those conditions the development of capitalism meant the growing accumulation of capital at one end, and the growing misery at the other pole. Although capitalism had succeeded in bribing some workers and turning them into "political blacks," the revolts of the workers were continuous and they did achieve:

(1) Establishment of the Ten Hours Bill, thus placing its political economy in the place of the political economy of the capitalist ideologues whose prostitute cry was that "all" profit came only in the last, the eleventh hour.

(2) Workers established some cooperative factories, thus proving that *capitalist management was useless*. But that was its *only* value.

(3) Since cooperative factories cannot arrest the growth of monopolies, therefore the working class must aim for political power, with this one reservation, that the great *end* is economic emancipation, to which every political movement is subordinate as a *means*.

The greatness of the Address is that, starting from the given concrete, and disciplined by the *variety* of forces coalescing to establish the First International, from trade unionists to Proudhonists to anarchists, it nevertheless contained *all* the implications of communism when it declared in its statutes:

> That the emancipation of the working classes must be conquered by the working classes themselves; that the struggle for the emancipation of the

---

2 The International held its first General Congress at Geneva, Switzerland, in September 1866. —Editor.

3 "Inaugural Address of the Working Men's International Association," MECW 20, p. 10.

working classes means not a struggle for class privileges and monopolies, but for equal rights and duties, and the abolition of all class rule;

That the economical subjection of the man of labor to the monopolizer of the means of labor, that is, the sources of life, lies at the bottom of servitude in all its forms, of all social misery, mental degradation, and political dependence;

That the economical emancipation of the working classes is therefore the great end to which every political movement ought to be subordinate as a means.[4]

2   *The Working Day and Marx's* Capital

Marx had been laboring on the theory of surplus value. To scientifically extricate it from being a mere *implication* in Ricardo's theory of value, Marx found he had to study the working day: how was it *divided* between that part which was *necessary* to produce the value of labor-power to pay the laborer his wages and that which produced the *surplus* value which the capitalist appropriated. But there was nothing static about this working day. The struggle to establish a normal working day was a veritable civil war between capital and labor. Thus to the revolutionary theoretician wrestling with the theory of surplus value the "mere historic connection" disclosed:

(1)   that capitalism's "single life impulse" [MCIK, p. 257; MCIP, p. 342] to create surplus value had led to such unlimited expansion of the working day at the long birth of capitalism, from the 14th to the 17th centuries, that it produced the premature exhaustion and death of labor-power itself. It was only labor's struggle against this self-destructive nature of capitalist production that saved society.

(2)   But the industrial revolution in the last third of the 18th century broke all bounds—moral and natural, age, sex, day, night—twenty-four hours was the day of the machine and was to be the day of labor. Again it took the *revolt* of the working class, this time united and organized by the mechanism of production itself, to infuse capitalist society with a *social* consciousness which made it a life-and-death question for bourgeois society as a whole compulsorily to shorten the working day.

(3)   However, once the limits of the working day were set, the capitalist's "were-wolf hunger for surplus value" [MCIK, p. 268; MCIP, p. 353] which is in the very *nature* of production sought a way to extract *within* the same

---

4   "Provisional Rules of the Association," MECW 20, p. 14.

working day ever greater amounts of surplus value. Through constant revolutions in the method of production *and* through the intensity of labor, the capitalist was able to *force* more surplus out of labor within the limited working day.

Thus what Marx called "the mere historical connections" revealed the general groundwork of capitalism to be the prolongation of the working day beyond the time necessary to produce the value of the labor-power.

That is not a peaceful process in the factory, where the surplus is forced out of the worker through the domination of the machine and the factory clock. And it most certainly is not a peaceful dispute in the open class struggle, where it takes the proportions of a veritable civil war. That Ricardo's "bourgeois skin" didn't let him see this struggle in understandable. But *Marx* himself didn't have a section on the Working Day in the first draft of *Capital*. When he began to study the science of the machine and the degradation of the laborer, it is then that he also saw how inelastic were the limits of the working day. The working out of the theory of surplus value led him to the struggle of the *division* of the working day and that division into the *division* of labor into concrete and abstract. When he wrote about abstract labor in the *Critique*, it looked as if it were an intellectual deduction. Now the dominance of the machine over man showed what a *reduction* of all human faculties this was. For there is no such animal as an abstract laborer. One is either a tailor, a miner, an assembly line worker. It is the dominance of the machine that forces all concrete labor to produce so much in such a such a time, no matter what the individual skill or ability is, into one abstract mass. The struggle then at the point of production between concrete and abstract labor is what is reflected in the struggle of labor against capital for the normal working day:

> In place of the pompous catalogue of the "inalienable rights of man" [Marx wrote in *Capital*] comes the modest Magna Charta of a legally limited working-day, which shall make clear "when the time which the worker sells is ended, and when his own begins." *Quantum mutatus ab illo.*[5]
>
> MCIK, p. 330; MCIP, p. 416

Marx's full transcendence of Ricardo proved that it wasn't a question of not "understanding." There are no "misunderstandings" in history. The historic differences are *class* differences. Production for production's sake without regard to the birth throes of wealth produces one theory, and blinds one as to its implications. Production which includes the self-development of men produces

---

5   The Latin phrase means "What a great change!" —Editor.

the opposite theory and reveals the other's "blind spots." There is no mediating ground where "good men" can clear up "misunderstandings." *The revolt clears them all up by overthrowing the conditions which create the birth throes and the ideology.*

The turbulence of the 1860s, Marx's close observation of the revolts and the organizational form illuminated his theoretic work with a light no intellectual deductions can substitute for. He was now ready for his great work. *Capital,* as it was published in 1867, is *substantially* the structure we now have. But there are two deficiencies:

(1)   the law of concentration and centralization is not developed to its ultimate form, and, above that,

(2)   the fetishism of the commodity, although it has taken some giant advances over the *Critique* where it appeared a simple matter, has still failed to explain the *why* of this fantastic form of appearance of a production relationship. He said that "only freely associated labor" can tear the veil off. But there he stopped, for freely associated labor had not yet torn off the veil.

3   The Paris Commune Destroys the Fetishism of Commodities

Social revolution broke out in Paris on March 19, 1871, when the Republic of France showed itself as ready as Napoleon III to capitulate to Bismarck. The spontaneous mass outburst took the form of the Commune of Paris and was the first historic attempt of the workers to establish a workers' state. It lasted only two months before the Parisian workers were massacred by the bloodiest terror in history. But in those two short months the workers accomplished more miracles than capitalism in as many centuries in (1) realizing full democracy, and (2) releasing all the potentialities of the proletariat so that the world could see how fully-sized human beings manage their lives. Within two days after its fall, Marx delivered an Address to the First International on the historic significance of the Commune. It is this description of the struggle of the proletariat for a new social order which reveals also the essence of *Capital* in its final classic form. I add emphasis when the specific point is one that shows its dialectic relationship to *Capital* and thereby finally tears off the veil of bourgeois fetishisms.

First and foremost the Paris Commune did not take over but *smashed* the centralized state power with its ubiquitous organs of standing army, police, officialdom, "*organs wrought after the plan of a systematic and hierarchic division of labor."* In doing so it got rid not only of the absolutist Empire but *"the Parliamentary Republic* ... the proper form of their joint-stock Government."[6]

In its place it established the armed people, officials at workingmen's wages and subject to immediate recall, and a *working*, not a parliamentary body of bureaucrats. The Commune thus superseded not only monarchical rule but class rule itself. It was the *"self-government of the producers"* [MECW 22, p. 332].

In contrast to all previous forms of political rule, which were always repressive, it was a thoroughly *expansive* political form, "the political form at last discovered under which to work out the economical emancipation of labor. *Except on this last condition,* the Communal Constitution would have been an impossibility and a delusion. The political rule of the producer cannot coexist with the perpetuation of his social slavery" [MECW 22, p. 334].

The Commune thus established the *inseparability* of politics and economics and hence the first step to abolishing the most monstrous division of all, which comprises the whole history of capitalism—the division between mental and manual labor. Capitalist *parliamentarism* kept this division alive and could do so because while the bourgeois governed the workers kept on working. But a workers' state aiming at the abolition of class property and transforming the means of production into mere instruments of *"free and associated labor"* [MECW 22, p. 335] could not. Everyone becomes a worker and the *"plain worker"* [MECW 22, p. 336] becomes the ruler. Thus while work loses its class stigma and becomes a way of life and self-development, *no form* of production, not even cooperative production, is left out from under *"workers' control"* [MECW 22, p. 335]. With no officialdom, no standing army, no police, the workers themselves would work it out. *Nobody else can.*

Marx then adds that it did not offer and could not have offered a blueprint of the future. It merely *"set free the elements of the new society"* [MECW 22, p. 335]. Here then is what the Commune was:

(1) direct and active participation of the masses in controlling production and public affairs;

(2) suppression of a *social hierarchy* by making all work at workmen's wages; *that is suppression of all bureaucracy;*

(3) unification of legislative and executive power in one *working* body meant also control not only of the administrative apparatus but of the production apparatus;

(4) maximum activity of mass and the minimum for its elected representatives, who were at all times subject to recall.

---

6 Quoted from *The Civil War in France,* MECW 22, pp. 328–29. —Editor.

It was the totality of the reorganization of society that threw new insight into the totality of bourgeois society of commodity production. Being the self-government of producers and smashing both empire and the parliamentary republic, the commune disclosed to Marx that value production is a form of organization.[7]

Marx then returned to *Capital* and to the question, whence then the mystery of the product of labor so soon as it assumes the form of a commodity, he answered simply: "Clearly from the form itself" [MCIK, p. 82; MCIP, p. 164].

Had value been only congealed labor, it need not have had a form other than its bodily form—a product of labor would be simply a product of labor. But the fact that a product of labor is not just a thing, but a "commodity," that it makes a social relationship appear in the disguise of an exchange of things, *that* has a reason. Marx now for the first time adds the *why* of the fantastic form. It is because under capitalism relations between people *"really are* material relations between persons and social relations between things" [MCIK, p. 84; MCIP, p. 166]. In a society where man is not master of the machine, but the machine is master of him, the *"perverse* relations" find a form suitable to it. *It can have no other form.*

Value production is that form of organization which dominates over everything. Though the cooperation between laborers is part of capitalist production itself, it cannot be an end in itself, but must be a mere means to the end of value production. So every single thing that issues from the process of production has the *value-form.* The commodity itself is not a product of the market. *It arises at the point of production itself and reflects the dual character of labor.*

The value form of organization in the factory means despotic plan *plus* perversity of relation of man to machine.

In the market it means free competition *plus* monopoly.

In the state it means parliamentary democracy *plus* empire, because, once the struggle is not among *individuals* but among *classes* and when it is a question of class, the vaunted democracy is nothing but a public force for social enslavement. Even the middle classes in Paris that followed the proletariat recognized empire to be the *"natural* offspring" of the party of class order [MECW 22, p. 330], and concluded it must be *"either* the Empire *or* the Commune" [MECW 22, p. 336]. There is no middle road.

---

7   In *Marxism and Freedom,* p. 101, Dunayevskaya added: "What was *new* was that the Commune, by releasing labor from the confines of value production, showed *how* people associated freely without the despotism of capital or the mediation of things.... The Commune transformed the *whole question of form* from a debate among intellectuals to the serious *activity* of workers—'facing with sober senses the conditions of their being and their relations with their kind.' "

You do not wish to face this *duality* in the commodity and that is why the fetishism of commodities has you by the throat, Marx is saying to classical political economy. You cannot move from it at all. Now that Marx fully transcended Ricardo, he saw that Ricardo not only "deviated" on the question of money, *but this greatest production economist of the bourgeoisie had never got away from the market at all.* They not only never entered the factory to see *how* labor was producing its products in the form of commodities, they knew the *law* of value only by the way it expressed itself in the market when it came crashing over their heads. Marx adds a subtle but hilarious footnote [MCIK, p. 93, note 1; MCIP, p. 174, note 34]. You never paid any attention to the *form* of value not only because you were concerned only with its magnitude. But it is the concrete universal of the whole being and soul of capitalism. You therefore cannot transcend your *historic* limitations. Were not the value-form but the reorganization of society the "concrete universal" of society, the debate moves from a debate among intellectuals, to a question of the establishment of a new social order. That is the *theoretic* achievement of the Paris Commune.

CHAPTER 6

Today's Epigones Who Try to Truncate Marx's *Capital*

In response to two events—the continuing global economic crisis that had be-
gun in 1974, and the publication of a new English-language translation of Marx's
Capital—News and Letters Committees published the pamphlet Marx's "Capital"
and Today's Global Crisis in January 1978. Written as the introduction to the pam-
phlet, this essay was a revision and expansion of a "Political-Philosophic Letter"
written December 15–30, 1976, and titled "Today's Global Crisis, Marx's Capital,
and the Marxist Epigones Who Try to Truncate It and the Understanding of
Today's Crises." The December 1976 document is included in The Raya Dunayevs-
kaya Collection, pp. 5282–99. Marx's "Capital" and Today's Global Crisis also
contained four chapters on Capital from Dunayevskaya's Marxism and Freedom,
her "Tony Cliff Reduces Lenin's Theory to 'Uncanny Intuition' " (which is repro-
duced in Chapter 17 of Russia: From Proletarian Revolution to State-Capitalist
Counter-Revolution), and a preface by the great Scottish revolutionary Harry
McShane. The pamphlet is included in The Raya Dunayevskaya Collection,
pp. 5824–59.

> Accumulate, accumulate! That is the Moses and the prophets! ... Accu-
> mulation for the sake of accumulation, production for the sake of pro-
> duction: this was the formula in which classical economics expressed
> the historical mission of the bourgeoisie in the period of its domina-
> tion. Not for one instant did it deceive itself over the nature of wealth's
> birth-pangs.
>
> MARX, CAPITAL

> If Marx did not leave behind him a *"Logic"* (with a capital letter), he did
> leave the *logic* of *Capital* ... the history of capitalism and the analysis of
> the *concepts* summing it up.
>
> LENIN

> It has often been claimed—and not without a certain justification—
> that the famous chapter in Hegel's *Logic* treating of Being, Non-Being,
> and Becoming contains the whole of his philosophy. It might be claimed
> with perhaps equal justification that the chapter dealing with the fetish

character of the commodity contains within itself the whole of historical materialism....[1]

LUKÁCS

Marx's greatest theoretical work, *Capital*,[2] has once again marched onto the present historic stage even among bourgeois ideologues, since there is no other way to understand today's global economic crisis. Thus, *Businessweek* (June 23, 1975)[3] suddenly started quoting what Marx was saying on the decline in the rate of profit as endemic to capitalism. It even produced official graphs from the Federal Reserve Board, the Department of Commerce, Data Resources, Inc., as well as its own data, all of which goes to show that the post-World War II boom has ended in a slump in the rate of profit. They have stopped laughing long enough at Marx's alleged "false economic theories" to show that, not just in theory but in fact, Marx's analysis of the "law of motion" of capitalism [MCIK, p. 14; MCIP, p. 92] to its collapse, "insofar as a decline in the rate of profit" is concerned, is reality.

While, with the "economic upturn" in 1975, the authors hoped it was only a "passing phenomenon," by the end of 1976 (December 27, 1976), *Businessweek* didn't sound quite so optimistic. Thus, while it still gloated over the 30 percent increase in net profits, it could not skip over the following determinates:

(1) the low *rate* of growth; (2) the hardly moveable high rate of unemployment of 7 percent officially, which does not change the truth that this is "average," but among Black youth it is at the fantastic rate of 34.1 percent; (3) the volatile undercurrent of dissatisfaction in the relationship between the

---

1 Georg Lukács, *History and Class Consciousness* (Cambridge, Mass.: MIT Press, 1971), p. 170. See my article "Lukács' Philosophic Dimension" in *News & Letters*, February and March, 1973 [reproduced in *Russia: From Proletarian Revolution to State-Capitalist Counter-Revolution*]. See also Lucien Goldmann's speech, "The Dialectic Today," given at the 1970 Korcula, Yugoslavia, Summer School (published posthumously in the collection of essays *Cultural Creation in Modern Society*, Telos Press, 1976). The speech acknowledges the correct chronological as well as philosophic "recovery" of Hegelian categories in Marxism and their actualization in the period 1917–23, by correctly stating that first came Lenin's *Philosophic Notebooks*, second came Lukács' *History and Class Consciousness*, third was Antonio Gramsci. All others—from Georgi Plekhanov to Karl Kautsky, from Franz Mehring to even Lenin *prior* to 1914—were simply acting as positivists whose "academic science" was materialism. Goldmann adds that it was not accidental, because 1917 actualized the dialectic, and 1923, with the defeat of the German revolution, signaled the end of the dialectical renaissance.

2 The Pelican Marx Library edition of Vol. I of Marx's *Capital* (London: Penguin Books, 1976) includes as "Appendix" the first English translation of the famous "Sixth Chapter" of *Capital* from the Marx-Engels Archives, Vol. II (VII) [in Russian].

3 "What the Marxists See in the Recession" (*Businessweek*, June 23, 1975).

underdeveloped countries and the industrialized lands to whom they are indebted at an impossible-to-meet $60 billion; (4) hard-core inflation of 6 percent as against the 1–2 percent inflation characteristic of most of the 1960s. Moreover, this "hard-core inflation" is actually *not* what it is, but what it is hoped it will be brought down to; and (5) the unevenness of growth within the country, which shows that so basic an industry as steel has undergone a 17 percent drop in growth. At the same time, so bleak is the international outlook that *Businessweek*, in summing up the outlook, cannot exclude even depression: "If Washington fails, fears of new world depression will intensify."

The capitalists may not be ready to "agree" with Marx that *the* supreme commodity, labor-power, is the only source of all value and surplus value, but they do see that there is such a decline in the *rate* of profit, compared to what *they* consider necessary to keep investing for expanded production, that they are holding off—so much so that now their ideologists are saying low investment is by no means a temporary factor that the capitalists would "overcome" with the next boom. *There is to be no next boom.* It is this which makes them look both at the actual structural changes—overwhelming preponderance of constant capital (machinery) over variable capital (living labor employed)—as well as the *world* production and its interrelations.

Thus, the "miracle" of post-World War II West Germany has stopped, as has the "miracle" of Japan. The *Financial Post*[4] ran a special piece on "West Germany: The Troubled Giant" pointing to the fact that there is a visible crack in the "social peace" (though the government got organized labor not to demand "extraordinary" wage increases). Not only that, but the nuclear issue, besides encountering U.S. opposition to West Germany's nuclear reactor sales to Brazil, produced at home such massive anti-nuclear demonstrations that even the German courts had to ban further nuclear power stations "until the issue of waste disposal had been resolved." Meanwhile, actual capital investment in real, rather than inflated, prices has fallen for three years in a row—and unemployment keeps increasing.

As for Great Britain and Italy, no significant recovery has yet begun. With oil revenue expectations, prospects may not be as grim for Britain as for Italy, but unemployment there has now officially reached 1.4 million—highest since the Depression. Prime Minister Callaghan immediately admitted that he could see only more unemployment in the immediate future, as public spending cuts

---

4 *Financial Post*, Special Report: "West Germany: The Troubled Giant," by Peter Foster (Toronto, September 17, 1977).

demanded by the International Monetary Fund take effect. In Italy, inflation is currently running at 20 percent, and oil price increases have so devastated the economy that no growth at all is forecast for 1977. Other forecasts—in Europe, and in the underdeveloped world—are either only marginally better, or worse.

By 1977, it was not only an academic—the serious bourgeois economist, Simon Kuznets—who, ever since the end of World War II, maintained that the "emergence of the violent Nazi regime in one of the most economically developed countries of the world raises grave questions about the institutional basis of modern economic growth—if it is susceptible to such a barbaric deformation as a result of transient difficulties."[5] It was a high Western government leader, none less than the President of France, Giscard d'Estaing, in 1977 who questioned the survival of the capitalistic system. Solzhenitsyn-inspired, retrogressionist intellectuals complain that capitalism has seen the emergence of a "strange siren whose body is capital and whose head is Marxist."[6]

But U.S. governmental statistics show good cause for those capitalistic headaches: the biggest increase in poverty since 1959 occurred in 1975 and has persisted. No less than a rise of 10 percent in the number of poor, totaling now 25.9 millions, are below poverty level. That means that no less than 12 percent of all Americans had an income of less than $5,500 annually for a family of four.

That this—the fifth post-World War II recession—is so hard to come out of, has brought the capitalists themselves face-to-face with the reality that the overriding fact of present-day capitalist economy is the decline in the rate of profit as well as poverty, unemployment *and* stagnation.

It is the age of state-capitalism as a *world phenomenon*. This development has no more solved its deep economic crisis than when full state-capitalism came to a single nation, Russia, China, etc.[7] As for inflation, it is true that the deep recession, which was triggered by the quadrupled oil prices after the 1973

---

5   Simon Kuznets, *Postwar Economic Growth* (Cambridge, Mass.: Harvard University Press, 1964), p. 121. See also his *Capital in the American Economy*.

6   *Barbarism with a Human Face*, translated by George Holoch (New York: Harper & Row, 1979), calling itself "The New Philosophy" by its guru, Bernard-Henri Levy, hails from the same famous university that produced Louis Althusser in the early 1960s, and in the mid-1970s had produced this Solzhenitsyn-inspired elitism with the ex-Althusserite, André Glucksmann, who now calls Alexander Solzhenitsyn "the Shakespeare of our time." Their works have not yet appeared in English, but a preview of them can be read in *The Manchester Guardian* (June 26, 1977), "Despairing Voice of France's Lost Generation," by Walter Schwarz. As against this critique, the "Le Monde" section of *The Manchester Guardian* (July 10, 1977) published a panegyric by Philippe Sollers.

7   For an analysis of Russian and Chinese state-capitalism see *Marxism and Freedom*, Chapters 13 and 17. —Editor.

Arab-Israeli war, was by no means the only reason for the double-digit inflation, any more than that "sickness in the economy" could be ascribed, as Big
Capital wishes to ascribe it, to workers' wages. The overwhelming reality is this:
Just as monopoly growth inhibited national economic growth, so the oil cartel
has actually lowered world economic growth.

As opposed to the 1950s and early 1960s, when Western Europe held attrac-
tions for capitalism with its cheaper labor and latest technology, in the 1970s
U.S. capital has added a new incentive for world capital: a safe haven for its investments, now that European capital has decided the U.S. proletariat is not as
revolutionary as the European workers. As against the oil monopolists who are
spending their billions on buying Western technology and military hardware,
and whose actual investments in the U.S. are not directed to the capital goods
market, West German, French and British capital *is*. However, so deep is the
economic crisis in the U.S. and in the world that such European investment
in the U.S. is likewise only a palliative, even as the massive super-profitable
investments upholding apartheid South Africa[8] cannot substitute for the insufficient investment capital and plant expansion in the U.S.

Thus, Lawrence A. Veit, International Economist and Deputy Manager at
Brown Brothers, Harriman & Co. (not to mention his previous position as
economist at the State and Treasury Departments), openly speaks of a "premature cyclical downturn"[9] rather than what Ernest Mandel calls "the generalized
economic recession coming to an end in 1975."[10] Further, Veit points not only
to the economic problems, but "the changing attitudes to work itself among
the younger generation." Here it can already be seen that *serious* bourgeois
analysts do see that the question of Alienated Labor is not "just theory." It is
concrete. It is urgent. It affects the "premature cyclical downturn."

---

8   A single glance at U.S. investments in South Africa shows them to be both massive and
     growing. Where, a decade ago, U.S. companies had $600 million invested in that apartheid
     land, it has skyrocketed to no less than $1.46 billion in 1974 (the last year for which data
     is available). Further projects are being built by Kennecott Copper and Caltex Petroleum
     (owned jointly by Standard Oil of California and Texaco, Inc.). Moreover, some Canadian-
     sounding names are mainly American-owned, as witness Quebec Iron & Titanium, two-
     thirds owned by Kennecott and one-third by Gulf and Western Industries, which has a 39
     percent interest in a proposed $290 million mining and smelting complex. As one State
     Department official explained, "the large and growing role" (no less than 15 percent of
     total foreign investment in South Africa is U.S.!) of U.S. investments is because "business-
     men don't have to fear their operations in South Africa are going to be nationalized...."
9   *Foreign Affairs*, January, 1977, "A Troubled World Economy."
10   Ernest Mandel, "A Hesitant, Uneven and Inflationary Upturn," *Intercontinental Press*,
     November 29, 1976.

The deep recession, in the U.S. and globally, is by no means over, though some who consider themselves Marxists like Mandel think that it has come "to an end in 1975." The false consciousness that has permeated even economists who are revolutionaries emanates from the fact that capitalism has, in the post-World War II period, come up with ways of keeping the economy going, stopping short of the type of Great Depression, 1929–32 (actually until 1939), that led to World War II. Since this time it would lead to World War III, it is "unthinkable," because it would, of necessity, be a nuclear war that would end civilization as we have known it.[11]

Under these circumstances, consider the irony of a famous Trotskyist economist, Ernest Mandel, who holds that the present deep recession "has come to an end."[12] Under the guise of praising "the validity of parts of Marx's *Capital* [which extend] also into the future," Mandel hangs upon Marx's shoulders his (*Mandel's*) analysis of state-capitalist monstrosities as "not yet fully-fledged classless, that is socialist, societies: the USSR and the People's Republics of Eastern Europe, China, North Vietnam, North Korea and Cuba."[13]

That this can pass muster with Penguin Books "in association with *New Left Review*," which is the editor of their Pelican Marx Library, speaks volumes for the sad state of today's scholarship. Whether, in this case, the choice of Mandel has come about by virtue of his name as author of *Marxist Economic Theory*, or otherwise, is their problem, not ours. Elsewhere I had already criticized that work. There[14] I have shown that, while bourgeois ideologues were enamored with Mandel's statement that he had "strictly abstained from quoting the sacred texts," it was not true, as *The Economist* claimed, that it was because Mandel replaced "Marx's Victorian facts and statistics by contemporary empirical

---

11   Even that "unthinkable" war is now flirted with by the U.S. rulers with the latest horrifying approval by the Carter administration of the neutron bomb. As I wrote in the 1977–78 Perspectives Thesis: Nothing in Hitler's Germany, from the "secret weapon" with which Hitler threatened world destruction, to the actual genocide he practiced within his domain, is any match for the *actual* military technology now in the hands of the superpowers, U.S. especially. What dehumanized creature could compete with the super-scientist-military-industrial complex of State Planners which dares describe a bomb as "clean" because, though this neutron bomb can mass-kill by radiation, it leaves property intact! (See "Time Is Running Out." *News & Letters*, August-September, 1977.).

12   *Intercontinental Press*, November 29, 1976.

13   Ernest Mandel's Introduction to the Pelican Marx Library edition of Vol. 1 of Marx's *Capital*, p. 16. All other references to the Introduction and to Vol. 1 will include the pagination directly in my text. [The Pelican edition is the same as the Penguin edition and corresponds to the Vintage edition, published in the U.S. —Editor.].

14   See " 'True Rebirth' or Wholesale Revision of Marxism?" *News & Letters*, May and June-July, 1970.

material." Rather, it was because Mandel tailended the Keynesian *theory* of "effective demand." Here what concerns us is not so much Mandel's "Marxist analysis of contemporary material" as Mandel's utter perversion of nothing short of Marx's monumental work, *Capital.*

Capitalism's ways of containing its economic crises within recession level, rather than uncontrollable Depression, are judged by Mandel to be a "stabilizer," even though it is precisely that type of concept that led to the collapse of the established Marxist (Second) International with the outbreak of the First World War.[15] Where that shocking event had Lenin return to Marx's origins in Hegel, and the dialectic of transformation into opposite, today's Marxists plunge not only into the latest series of economic "facts" sans any dialectical rudder, but also to a violation of the dialectical structure of Marx's *Capital* itself. That, too, is not "just theory," but that which gives, *or could give when not violated*, action its direction.

It becomes necessary, therefore, not to limit oneself to the economic-political data of the year, but have that data be a new beginning for the battle of ideas which refuses to be shifted back and forth empirically between the theoretical and the practical and vice versa, *both* reduced to the immediate level. Bereft of Hegelian-Marxist[16] dialectics, not to mention the *strict relationship* of workers' revolt against the "Accumulate, accumulate!" exploitative relationship, one can hardly escape trying to hem in the analysis of today's crises within the bounds of bourgeois—private and state—ideology, and thus inflict structuralism and the latest twist in pragmatism on Marx's greatest *original* work, *Capital.*

In our day, we have the situation where a new French translation of *Capital* is introduced by that official Communist-structuralist, Louis Althusser, who stooped to pseudo-psychoanalysis to express his venom against Marx's *Critique of the Hegelian Dialectic* as "the prodigious 'abreaction' indispensable to the liquidation of his [Marx's] 'disordered' consciousness."[17] And, for the

---

15   For Dunayevskaya's analysis of the failure of the Second International see Chapter 9 of *Marxism and Freedom*, "The Second International, 1889 to 1914." —Editor.

16   I hyphenate Hegelian-Marxian, not to state my own view and thus taunt the vulgar materialist-scientists like Althusser and Mandel, but because in the very section of Marx's own Postface to the second edition of *Capital*, to which Mandel refers to "prove" that Marx was a materialist, not "idealist," dialectician, Marx writes: "The mystification which the dialectic suffers in Hegel's hands by no means prevents him from being the first to present its general forms of motion in a comprehensive and conscious manner" [MCIK, p. 25; MCIP, p. 103]. And within the text itself, as we know, Marx further stresses that Hegelian dialectics is the "source of *all* dialectics" [MCIK, p. 654; MCIP, p. 744; emphasis added].

17   Louis Althusser, *For Marx* (London: Penguin Press, 1969), p. 35. Althusser's new Preface to the French edition of *Capital*, Vol. I, is reproduced in the British edition of *Lenin and Philosophy and Other Essays*, translated by Ben Brewster (London: New Left Books,

English world, the beautiful new translation of *Capital* is, as we saw, burdened with an introduction by the Trotskyist epigone, Ernest Mandel, who spreads himself over some 75 pages of "Introduction."

From the very beginning—in the first section Mandel dares entitle "The Purpose of *Capital*"—he does not merely peddle his view of Russia as "socialist," and does not only seek to disjoint the "scientific" from its revolutionary content, but unashamedly hooks these views to "the distinction" Marx drew between "utopian and scientific socialism" [MCIP, p. 16], as if Marx would not have stopped short of tolerating forced labor camps!

That the two—the new edition of Marx's *Capital*, and analyses of today's global crises—do not hang apart, but are integrally related, is clear enough. What is clearer still is that Mandel is presenting, not Marx's views, but his own. No wonder he also sees "stabilizers" in private capitalism's development, though, as revolutionary, he wishes that overthrown. Vulgarization of Marxism has its own dialectic. It is necessary, therefore, to disentangle Marx from Mandel, to remain rooted in Marx's philosophy of liberation *as a totality*, and to face with sober senses the alienated world reality that must be uprooted if we are to release the revolutions-to-be from the crisis-ridden state-capitalist age.

It is not a question of needing "to know" Marx's *Capital* "in order correctly" to be able to analyze today's global crises. Rather, it is that today's economic crises *compel* one not to separate economics from politics, and not only as the capitalists naturally do from their class point of view, but objectively as the antagonistic relationships *at the point of production* are seen to produce market crises created in production.

Thus, it is not just that the "investment drought" is a great deal more than just "hesitant." What is interesting in the *Foreign Affairs* analysis of "The Troubled World Economy" is that it recognizes that inseparable from that pivotal "investment drought," even when there is some growth, is the rise in energy cost, which means that, along with the rising cost of automated equipment, too much value is invested compared to labor productivity, when so little living labor is being used in production. Therefore it is telling "the West" not to be overly happy with their "petro-recyclers," that is to say, Big Capital's way of getting those oil billions from the fourfold increase of prices back from the Middle East potentates, and into its own hands by selling machinery and military hardware.

The point is that the recession is so deep, so internal, as well as so linked with the *world* market, that the highly industrialized countries are not programming great expenditures for new plants and equipment. This is at a time

1971), pp. 69–101. See also my "Critique of Althusser's Anti-Hegelianism," *News & Letters*, October, 1969.

when profits are high, and so shaky are European economies and so great the fear of revolutions (or at least "Communists in government"), that the U.S. has become a magnet for foreign capital investment even as Europe was that magnet for U.S. Big Capital's investment going abroad in the 1950s.

Finally, even bourgeois economists understand that the centerpiece, the nerve, the muscle as well as the soul of all capitalist production is labor—the extraction from living labor of all the unpaid hours of labor that is the surplus value, the profits—and that, therefore, neither the market, nor political manipulation by the state, nor control of that crucial commodity *at this moment*—oil—can go on endlessly without its relationship to the life-and-death commodity: labor-power. *Foreign Affairs* concludes: "Cartels do not have infinite lives and ... [thus] will one day narrow the difference between the price of energy and the cost of production."

One would think that so erudite an economist as Mandel knows the relationship of value to price, and I do not doubt that *abstractly* he does. But watch what he does as he hits out at Marxists who have criticized him for attaching too much importance to the market. He lectures them thusly:

> ... capitalist production is production of *commodities* ... this *production* in no way implies the automatic *sale* of the commodities produced ... the sale of commodities at prices yielding the average rate of profit ... in the final analysis.[18]

As if this vulgarization of Marx's analysis of the dialectical relationship between production and its reflection in the market crisis were not far enough a distance from Marxian "economics," Mandel reaches for Marx's most crucial analysis of the unemployed army as "*the absolute general law*" of capitalist production. Here is how he strips the "absolute general law" to fit, in answer to the monetarist Prof. Karl Brunner's bourgeois defense of the need to lower inflation, even though its "price is unemployment":

> There can be no better confirmation of the analysis of Karl Marx made in *Capital*, more than a century ago: in the long run capitalism cannot survive without an industrial reserve army....[19]

Though one acquainted with Mandel's economist specialization should be accustomed to the many ways he has of turning Marx upside down, this is enough to make one's hair stand on end. Far from saying that capitalism

---

18   *Intercontinental Press*, November 29, 1976.
19   Ibid.

"cannot survive without an industrial reserve army," Marx says *the absolute general law of capitalist accumulation*"—the unemployed army "and the dead weight of pauperism"—would bring capitalism down. The antagonistic character of capitalist accumulation sounds "the knell of capitalist private property. The expropriators are expropriated" [MCIK, p. 837; MCIP, p. 929].

Now it isn't that Mandel doesn't "know" such ABC's of Marxism. It is that a pragmatist's ideology is as blinding as the "science" of today's myriad market transactions, and one extra moment's look at the market, away from irreconcilable class contradiction at the point of production, and the inescapable turns out to be the violation of the Marxism of Marx! It is high time to turn to Marx's methodology in his greatest theoretical work, *Capital*. It was no accident, whatever, why, *precisely why*, Marx refused to deal with the market until after—some 850 pages after—he dealt dialectically and from every possible angle with the process of production. It is time we took a deeper look at Mandel, away from the market, as "pure" theoretician and revolutionary.

As we showed before, Mandel, from the very first section of his Introduction to *Capital*—"The Purpose of *Capital*"—tries to hang on Marx a 20th-century epigone's contention that Russia is "socialist." By the end of that section, Mandel has separated Marx's "scientific ... cornerstone" by still another restatement about capitalism creating "the economic, material and social preconditions for a society of associated producers" (p. 17). Such "rock-like foundation of scientific truth" left out but a single word—*"freely"* (my emphasis). Freely is the *specific* word, concept, living reality that was *the* determinate of Marx's "objective and strictly scientific way" not only of distinguishing his analyses from all others, but characterizing his *whole life*. Marx's own words read:

> Let us finally imagine, for a change, an association of free men, working with the means of production held in common.... The veil is not removed from the countenance of the social life-process, i.e., the process of material production, until it becomes production by freely associated men, and stands under their conscious and planned control.
>
> MCIK, pp. 90, 92; MCIP, pp. 171, 173

Marx's sentence is from that greatest and most concise of all sections in *Capital*, on the dialectical method. Though dialectics is not only method, but the dialectics of liberation, the last section of Chapter 1 of *Capital*—"The Fetishism of Commodities"—makes no entrance in Mandel's section entitled "The Method of *Capital*." In my text that follows from *Marxism and Freedom*,[20] I have gone

---

20   This refers to Chapters 5 through 8 of *Marxism and Freedom*, as reproduced in the pamphlet *Marx's "Capital" and Today's Global Crisis*.

into great detail on the relationship of the historic experience of the Paris Commune to Marx's dialectical concept of the "fetishism" of the commodity-form. Here it is sufficient to point to the fact that neither friends nor enemies, no matter how "new" and "independent" they thought their own philosophy to be (as, for instance, Sartre's Existentialism[21]), has denied the pivotal role of that section to any comprehension of Marx's *Capital*, especially its dialectics.

Fetishism contained Marx's very original dialectic, which, though rooted, as is all dialectics, in the Hegelian, has a live, concrete, revolutionary subject—the proletariat. This is not "a political conclusion" tacked onto economics. Rather, it is the "variable capital" in its live form of the wage worker who, *at the point of production*, is so infuriated at the attempt to transform him into "an appendage" to a machine, that he rises up—from strikes to outright revolutions—to uproot the old society and create totally new, truly human relations as *freely* associated men. Mandel, however, as we saw, not only makes no mention of the section on Fetishism,[22] but perverts the whole concept of freedom by reducing "*freely* associated men" to just "a society of associated producers." And so proud is he of his interpretation that that phrase becomes, literally, the final word of the whole Introduction (p. 86).

Marx, on the other hand, after devoting a lifetime to completing Vol. I of *Capital* in 1867, did not feel satisfied with his concretization of "the fetishism" of the commodity-*form*. It was only after the Paris Commune, as he worked out the French edition of *Capital*, 1872–75, that he reworked the section yet once again, *and* called attention to it and other changes by asking all to read that edition as "it possesses a scientific value independent of the original and should be consulted even by readers familiar with the German" [MCIP, p. 105].

As for Lenin, it took nothing short of the outbreak of the First World War and the collapse of the Second International, *and* his own restudy of Hegel's *Science of Logic* in that cataclysmic period, to write:

> It is impossible completely to understand Marx's *Capital*, and especially its first chapter, without having thoroughly studied and understood the *whole* of Hegel's *Logic*. Consequently, half a century later none of the Marxists understood Marx!![23]

---

21   See Jean-Paul Sartre's *Search for a Method* (New York: Alfred A. Knopf, 1965), and *Critique de la Raison Dialectique* (Paris: Librairie Gallimard, 1960). See also my critique "Jean-Paul Sartre: Outsider Looking In," Chapter 6, *Philosophy and Revolution* (New York: Delacorte Press, 1973), pp. 188–210.

22   By no accident whatever, Mandel's half-sentence reference (p. 74) to the existence of the section on "Fetishism of Commodities" is in what could be called the sales section of his Introduction, "Marx's Theory of Money."

23   Lenin, *Collected Works*, 38:180.

Evidently, Mandel thinks he has done Lenin one better when, in explaining dialectical method, he points to the fact that Marx's dialectical method helps "pierce through new layers of mystery" not alone by contrasting appearance to essence, but in showing "why a given 'essence' appears in given concrete forms and not in others" (p. 20). Too bad it made Mandel think that he has pierced through that mystery, not by sticking with the *specificity of the commodity-form*, but by plunging into "sales," to which he adds "real history." What he fails to cite is that the *real history* of that first chapter, as well as its dialectics, is exactly what, in 1943, Stalin ordered excised in the "teaching" of *Capital*.[24]

On the contrary. Mandel skips over both the fact *and the why* of Stalin's "academic" order in the midst of the holocaust and, instead, hails as a "rebirth of true Marxism" the 1954 codification of that very revision of the law of value in the *Textbook of Political Economy*. The Russians labored ten years before they could write as if that had always been the interpretation of Marxian economics. Mandel begins there straightaway.

This is not because Mandel is the brilliant one. The Russians have a twenty-year priority in that field. But the Communist state-capitalists *had to*, first—upon the direct orders of Stalin—make the admission that they were changing "the teaching" of Marxian political economy. They then *had to* make sure that the texts prior to 1943 did a "disappearing act" in order, from then on, to begin writing without further ado about the "orthodox" interpretation of the law of value. Above all, they had to work out the consequences of the break with the structure of *Capital* which reveals not only the exploitative nature but also the perversity of capitalism: The machine is master of man, which gives rise to

---

24   This was first revealed in the article in *Pod Znamenem Marxizma* (*Under the Banner of Marxism*), No. 7–8, 1943. However, the magazine did not reach this country until 1944, at which time I translated it into English and it was published in the *American Economic Review*, Vol. 34, No. 3, 1944, under the title, "Teaching of Economics in the Soviet Union." See also Will Lissner ["Soviet Economics Stirs Debate Here"] in the *New York Times*, Oct. 1, 1944. [Lissner also took it up in "No Change Is Seen in Soviet Economy," *New York Times*, July 29, 1945. —Editor.] The controversy in this country, on the startling reversal in Marxian teachings, continued in the pages of the *American Economic Review* for an entire year. See especially Paul Baran's "New Trends in Russian Economic Thinking," December, 1944. My rebuttal, "Revision or Reaffirmation of Marxism," *American Economic Review*, Vol. 35, No. 4, appeared in September, 1945. [All of the documents from this controversy are included in *The Raya Dunayevskaya Collection*. For the articles as they appeared in *American Economic Review*, see pp. 193–217. For Dunayevskaya's correspondence surrounding the publication of the articles, see pp. 8962–81. Dunayevskaya's article in the September 1944 *American Economic Review* accompanying her translation, "A New Revision of Marxian Economics," sparked the debate. It is included in Chapter 9 of *Russia: From Proletarian Revolution to State-Capitalist Counter-Revolution.* —Editor.].

the fetishistic appearance of commodities and presents the relations between men as if they were mere exchange of things.

Then, and only then, could the Russian theoreticians, Stalinized and "de-Stalinized," write as if the startling 1943 revision was "Marxism." It isn't that the erudite Mandel hadn't "read" the controversies. Rather, the loss of memory was planned for purposes of presenting a "true rebirth": "After Stalin's death, and especially after the effects of Khrushchev's reforms had been exhausted, Soviet economic thought underwent a true rebirth."[25]

Mandel's "real history" turns out to be a complete jumble—"presuppositions," plus mixing up dead and living labor: "Commodity production as a basic and dominant feature of economic life *presupposes* capitalism, that is a society in which labor-power and instruments of labor have themselves become commodities" (p. 21, my emphasis). Turning Marx so far upside down that "instruments of labor" are on the same level as the *differentia specifica* of capitalism—labor-power as a commodity—cannot but lead to his climactic separation of logic and history: "In that sense it is true that the analysis of Vol. I of *Capital* is logical (based upon dialectical logic) and not historical" (p. 21).

Now Marx *methodologically* left the genuine historic origins of capitalism to the end of the volume, so that its *tendency—law* of motion, not, as Mandel would have it, laws of motion—should not become a matter of diverting us from what is the result of strict, commodity-production capitalism, no matter how that "first dollar," so to speak, was obtained. Just as trying to take Chapter 1 out of its structural order (as Stalin felt compelled to do in 1943 *as he prepared to make sure that the workers in post-World War II Russia would work hard and harder*) was a total violation of the dialectical structure of Marx's *Capital*, so, too, is Mandel's mixing up the "real history" of the rise of capitalism instead of presenting it dialectically. Marx moved it to the end, *not* because there is a division between history and dialectics, but because dialectics contains both, and, *therefore*, the discernment of the law of motion of capitalist production, strict commodity production, could be grasped best when one limited oneself to capitalist production and capitalist production alone.

Marx never tired of repeating that his original contribution was the split in the category of labor—abstract and concrete labor; labor as activity and labor-power as commodity; labor as not only the source of all value which includes surplus value, but the subject who would uproot it. So "single purpose" a revolutionary theoretician was Marx in all his multitudinous and basic discoveries that, though he devoted some 850 pages (it is over 1,000 pages in the Pelican edition, which includes the famous heretofore unpublished "Chapter 6" of the

---

25   Ernest Mandel, *Marxist Economic Theory* (New York: Monthly Review Press, 1970), p. 726.

Archives) in Vol. I to that question, he no sooner started Vol. II than he repeated: "The peculiar characteristic is not that the commodity labor-power is saleable, but that labor-power appears in the shape of a commodity" [MCIIK, p. 37; MCIIP, p. 114].

Mandel, however, is convinced that—once he has "explained" what he calls "historical dimension"[26] (p. 16) as being the opposite of the eternal; and contrasted appearance to essence where nevertheless appearance is significant; and then separated logical from historical where nevertheless "the logical analysis does reflect some basic trends of historical development after all" (p. 22)—he has thereby been faithful to Marx, as against those "from Bernstein to Popper" who called for the "removal of the dialectical scaffolding" as "mystical." Mandel thereupon plunges into "The Plan of *Capital*," as if that were only a matter of dates and pages, instead of the actual restructuring of *Capital* on the basis of what did come not only historically, but *from below*.

What Marx did, in restructuring *Capital*, was based on these struggles from below—the workers' struggle for the eight-hour day and the Civil War in France where the Paris Communards had "stormed the heavens."[27] There was no State Plan, no State Property, no Party. The Commune's greatest achievement, he concluded, was *"its own working existence"* (my emphasis) [MECW 22, p. 339].

But what does Mandel choose to illustrate what a commodity is? Here is his definition: "If a pound of opium, a box of dum-dum bullets or a portrait of Hitler find customers on the market, the labor which has been spent on their output is socially necessary labor" (pp. 43–44). Nothing could possibly be a more total absolute opposite of what Marx analyzed in socially necessary labor *time* which, in the case of capitalism, is "dead labor dominating living labor" and, in the case of socialism, is the "place for human self-development."[28]

---

26   "The historical principle" is exactly what the Russians used as the reason for cutting out
      Chapter 1 of *Capital*. As I wrote in my commentary then (1944): "The ideas and meth-
      odology of the article are not accidental. They are the ... methodology of an 'intelligen-
      tsia' concerned with the acquisition of 'surplus products.' What is important is that this
      departure from 'past teaching of political economy' actually mirrors economic reality.
      The Soviet Union has entered the period of 'applied economics.' Instead of theory, the
      article presents an administrative formula for minimum costs and maximum produc-
      tion. It is the constitution of Russia's post-war economy." [From "A New Revision of Marx-
      ian Economics." See Chapter 9 of *Russia: From Proletarian Revolution to State-Capitalist
      Counter-Revolution*.].

27   Quoted from a letter from Marx to Ludwig Kugelmann, April 12, 1871 [MECW 44, p. 132]. —
      Editor.

28   See MECW 33, p. 493; see also MECW 20, p. 142; MECW 32, p. 390; *Grundrisse*, p. 708. —
      Editor.

Mandel is oblivious to all this. Instead, he writes of "Marx's key discovery: his theory of surplus value" (p. 46), as if that too involved mostly market, sales, money—the whole distributive sphere which Marx held would blind us not only to the primacy of relations of production, but make us, indeed, fall victim to the fetishism of commodities, which freely—*and only freely*—associated men can possibly strip off.

Marx, however, was so determined to stress the freedom that he warned the Paris Communards that unless control is totally in their own hands, even cooperative labor can become a "sham and a snare" [MECW 22, p. 335]. He returned to the subject in Vol. II of *Capital*:

> ... we must not follow the manner copied by Proudhon from bourgeois economics, which looks upon this matter as though a society with a capitalist mode of production would lose its specific historical and economic characteristics by being taken as a unit. Not at all. We have in that case to deal with the aggregate capitalist.
>
> MCIIK, p. 503; MCIIP, p. 509

Today's global crises elicited from Mandel what is not obvious in his introduction to Marx's *Capital*, but in fact underlies his total *misconception*, and that is the concept of an existing equilibrium—and in our crisis-ridden age, at that. Thus, as he got to the "Deeper Causes" in his analysis of "A Hesitant, Uneven, Inflationary Upturn," he cited what in fact characterizes all his books and articles, and that is Kondratiev's "long wave theory."

The fact that the editor—*New Left Review*—of this new edition of Marx's *Capital* can, in two succeeding issues of *New Left Review*, both praise Mandel's *Late Capitalism* and also catch the revisionism[29] both of Marxism *and* Trotskyism inherent in Mandel's adherence to Kondratiev's "long wave theory," shows the confusion prevalent in all modern-day Marxist theoreticians who try to keep away from the theory of state-capitalism, leaving all their "newness" contained in the time-abstraction of "Late Capitalism"—not to mention academicians à la Daniel Bell who call it "post-industrial." As if the transformation into opposite of Lenin's into Stalin's Russia were a mere *passing* "historical detour," from which "dark interlude" it "slowly began to emerge in the 1950s" (p. 85), Mandel shows further how very "*au courant*" he really is by referring not only to James Burnham's *Managerial Revolution* of the early 1940s but also

---

29   *New Left Review*, No. 99, September-October, 1976, "The Theory of Long Waves: Kondratiev, Trotsky, Mandel," by Richard B. Day: "No amount of subtlety can overcome the basic fact that, in Trotsky's view, long-waves—or long cycles—were incompatible with a Marxist periodization of the history of capitalism."

John Kenneth Galbraith's "technostructure" *New Industrial State* of the 1960s (p. 81), not to mention Paul Samuelson's concept of "mixed economy"—every thesis except the real issue which tore Trotskyism apart before World War II, and wreaked havoc within Stalinism in the post-World War II period and is continuing to this day in Eastern Europe.

What did split Trotskyism and what is at issue at this very moment, whether we look at the global crisis of "the West" or the whole world and its "restructuring," especially the North-South dialogue, is the question of the class nature of Russia.[30] To treat the question seriously, we must neither stop at journalistic phrases, nor at Mao Zedong's late discovery *after* he broke with "deStalinized" Russia and first then began to designate Russia as "state-capitalist." No, we must begin at the beginning, when Marx first projected, in the crucial, famous, irreversible French edition, 1872–75, the idea that the law of concentration and centralization of capital would reach its ultimate when "the entire social capital was united in the hands of either a single capitalist or a single capitalist company" [MCIK, p. 688; MCIP, p. 779].

Now, though Mandel does even less about this addition to *Capital* than he did with fetishism, which he mentioned in a single phrase, the fact is that this is not all Marx said of the ultimate development of concentration and centralization of capital. Nor is it only that his closest collaborator, Frederick Engels, who edited Vols. II and III of *Capital*, added some statements about Marx's prediction of monopoly. The additions to the 1872–75 French publication were, in turn, followed by *Anti-Dühring*, upon which Marx collaborated with Engels. It reads:

> The more productive forces it (the state) takes over, the more it becomes the collective body of capitalists, the more citizens it exploits.... State ownership of the productive forces is not the solution of the conflict....
> MECW 25, p. 266

---

30   It isn't that Mandel doesn't know of the class nature of Russia that was designated as state-capitalism. Ernest Mandel happened to have been the person who debated me in 1947 when I presented the theory of state-capitalism, which I was the first to work out from original Russian sources on the basis of the first three Five-Year Plans, when the Russians were still denying the operation of the law of value in their "socialist land." (See "Analysis of the Russian Economy," *New International*, December, 1942, January, 1943, February, 1943; and again in December, 1946, and January, 1947. After World War II, I analyzed the fourth Five-Year Plan, "New Developments in Stalin's Russia," in *Labor Action*, October, 1946.) Following that conference of the Fourth International, the French Trotskyist theoretical journal, of which Mandel was an editor, published my article on the Eugene Varga controversy (see *Quatrieme Internationale*, January-February, 1948). [Dunayevskaya's series of articles, "New Developments in Stalin's Russia," is included in RDC, pp. 448–53. For Dunayevskaya's writings on the Varga controversy, see "The Case of Eugene Varga," RDC, pp. 12456–62. —Editor.].

Far from "ownership" alone determining the class relationship, Marx, from his first break with bourgeois society in 1843, through his leadership in the Workingmen's (First) International Association in 1864, to his death in 1883, never varied from "dead labor dominating living labor" as *the* determinant of capitalism.

As always, however, it is only when a concrete objective crisis makes philosophy a matter of concrete urgency for revolutionaries, that theory becomes "practical." It was not only when the Second International collapsed along with private, competitive capitalism, that Lenin saw the dialectical transformation into opposite, the counterrevolution *within* revolution. He saw it in the workers' state itself. He worried about its *revolutionary* leadership—its main "theoretician," Nikolai Bukharin, and *his* mechanical materialism. Lenin suddenly feared that his co-leader was not "fully a Marxist" since he "did not fully understand the dialectic."[31]

It wasn't a question of the word, "state-capitalism." Bukharin had used the expression "state-capitalism." So did Leon Trotsky, who, in 1919, in the *First Manifesto of the Third International*, wrote:

> The state control of social life for which capitalism so strived, is become reality. There is no turning back either to free competition or to the domination of trusts.... The question consists solely in this: who shall control state production in the future—the imperialist state, or the state of the victorious proletariat?

Now it is true that Trotsky recognized this only theoretically, and, in fact, did not accept state-capitalism as the designation for Stalinist Russia, though he fought Stalinism and held that "The Revolution [Was] Betrayed."[32] It is not true that Lenin didn't see both state-capitalism and its absolute opposite—the revolutionary, self-determining subject, the proletariat that was the whole, without which there was no new society. Which is why his *Will* was almost as adamant against the "administrative mentality" (Trotsky and Bukharin) as against the one whose removal he demanded—Stalin.

In any case, once World War II ended, and capitalism had also learned "to plan" and "to nationalize," Varga saw no signs of a general economic crisis coming any earlier than a decade hence, whereupon Stalin had the whole Institute

---

31   See Dunayevskaya's discussion of Lenin's Will in *Marxism and Freedom,* Chapter 12, "What Happens After." —Editor.

32   This refers to Leon Trotsky's book *The Revolution Betrayed*, trans. Max Eastman (New York, Pathfinder, 1937). —Editor.

of World Economics turn against him. Varga was made to repudiate his written view of the post-war economy as any new stage of world economy. Maria Natanovna Smit was left standing alone, defending the position that the stage of world economy was "state-capitalism" and quoting Lenin, who had seen its element in World War I:

> During the war, world capitalism took a step forward not only toward concentration in general, but also toward state-capitalism in even a greater degree than formerly.[33]

Just as Stalin buried Lenin's first grappling with elements of state-capitalism, so the Trotskyist epigones evaded the whole theoretical question of state-capitalism in Russia, which had led to such deep splits in the Fourth International that Mandel now (and not only in his journalistic writings but in his new book *Late Capitalism*) has "rehabilitated" Kondratiev and his long-term equilibrium analysis!

In Stalinist Russia, with its Draconian laws against labor, and dehumanized forced-labor camps, the 1943 revision in the law of value was followed by Andrei Zhdanov's 1947 revision in philosophy, which invented nothing short of "a new dialectical law"—"Criticism and Self-Criticism"—in place of the objectivity of the contradiction of class struggle and "negation of negation," that is to say, proletarian revolution. DeStalinized Russia did nothing to change this wholesale revision of Marx's Historical-Dialectical Materialism.

Mandel's bringing in "history" now is indistinguishable from Stalinism's claim that the commodity-form and law of value have existed before capitalism and after, and are not "only" capitalistic. It is sad, indeed, to have to record also that Trotskyism, despite the fact that Trotsky had always fought Stalinism, thus not besmirching any concept of socialism, nowadays keeps its political battles so far afield from its economics and philosophy that its major leader, Mandel, can actually hail Russian post-war revisions as a "true rebirth" of Marxism.

The result is a violation of both Marxian theory and practice, not only "in general," but as it affects the view of the present global crises, not just on the question of analysis of any set of crises. The question goes far beyond any "rejiggering of the world's economic balance sheet" by playing around with the latest bag of tricks on bourgeois *and* developing countries, such as "indexing" the prices of raw materials.

---

33   Lenin, *Collected Works*, 38:300 (Russian edition). The Stenographic Report of that debate was published in English by Public Affairs Press, Washington, D.C., 1948.

The point is that, even if one didn't wish to accept our analysis of state-capitalism as *the* total contradiction, absolute antagonism in which is concentrated nothing short of revolution, *and counterrevolution*, one would have to admit that the totality of the contradictions compels a total philosophic outlook. Today's dialectics is not just philosophy, but dialectics of liberation, of self-emancipation by all forces of revolution—proletariat, Black, women, youth. The beginning and end of all revolves around labor. Therein is the genius of Marx, who, though he wrote during a "free enterprise, private property, competitive capitalistic era," saw that, instead of plan vs. market chaos being the absolute opposites, the chaos in the market was, in fact, the expression of the hierarchic, despotic plan of capital *at the point of production*. "Materialism" without dialectics is "idealism," *bourgeois* idealism of the state-capitalist age. As I pointed out in my critique of Mandel's *Marxist Economic Theory*:

> No wonder that the bourgeois reviewers were so pleased with Mandel's view of the market mechanisms acting as "stabilizers." Mandel wanted to synthesize the overproduction, underconsumption disproportionality theories of crises with Marx's, which is related strictly to the law of value and surplus value. But as Marx said of Proudhon, "He wishes to be a synthesis, he is a composite error."[34]

---

34   Karl Marx, *Poverty of Philosophy* (Chicago: Charles H. Kerr, 1906), p. 228 [MECW 6, p. 178].

CHAPTER 7

Letter to Herbert Marcuse on Automation

On August 8, 1960, Herbert Marcuse wrote Dunayevskaya, requesting help for his work on a book that was published as One-Dimensional Man: Studies in the Ideology of Advanced Industrial Society (*Boston: Beacon Press, 1964*). *She related automation, state-capitalism, workers' subjectivity, and the dialectic in response to this query from Marcuse:*

> *One of my problems will be the transformation of the laboring class under the impact of rationalization, automation and particularly, the higher standard of living. I am sure you will know what I mean if I refer to the discussion among the French sociologists in* Arguments *and especially Serge Mallet's articles. It is a question of a changing—that is to say—a more affirmative attitude of the laborer not only towards the system as a whole but even to the organization of work in the more highly modernized plants. Mallet's field study of French workers in the Caltex establishment in France points up sharply the rise of a highly co-operative attitude and of a vested interest in the establishment.*
>
> *Now, what I should like to ask you is first, your own considered evaluation as far as the situation in this country is concerned, and secondly, if it isn't asking too much—reference to American literature on this problem pro and contra. I know that your own evaluation runs counter to the thesis of reconciliatory integration of the worker with the factory but I would also like to know whether there is any sensible argument for the other side.*

August 16, 1960

Dear HM:

...Your letter of the 8th came at an auspicious time since the special issue of *News & Letters,* which will be issued as a special pamphlet, *Workers Battle Automation,*[1] has just come off the press and should be of value to you because you will see the workers speaking for themselves on the conditions of labor and the alleged high standard of living. I know, from the time I last spoke to you, that you consider these views as being the result of my influence. While

---

[1] *Workers Battle Automation* by Charles Denby et al. (Detroit: News and Letters, 1960) is included in RDC, pp. 2843–905. —Editor.

it is true that Charles Denby and some (by no means all) of the writers of this pamphlet are Marxist Humanists, you would make a serious mistake if you considered their views so exceptional that they did not represent the American proletariat. They represent a very important segment of the American workers and in all basic industries—auto, steel, coal—and the conditions they describe are what they experience on the line, not what some sociologists see in a "field study." I would like to call your attention also or especially to p. 6, "Which Way Out," because, contrary to the monolith not only of Communists but radicals who think they must have a "united voice" when they face the public, workers here disagree openly. Angela Terrano, whom you may recall I quote in *Marxism and Freedom* because she has raised the question of what kind of labor in the true Marxist sense, and who then used the expression that work would have to be totally different, "something completely new, not just work to get money to buy food and things. It will have to be completely tied up with life" (p. 275) here rejects Automation altogether, whereas the editor insists that if the workers managed the factory it would not be a House of Terror and works along the more traditional channels of workers' control of production, shorter workday, etc.

Secondly, I happen to know a Caltex engineer who says some very different things than Serge Mallet. I had him add a special paragraph on the question you raised, but his study of "Oil and Labor" published in the *Fourth International* in 1948[2] was quite a comprehensive one and as I doubt you have it I enclose that too. (But when you have finished please return at your convenience.) At the same time I am not sure that you have my article in *Arguments* on "State Capitalism and Bureaucracy,"[3] which deals with some of the sociologists you no doubt have in mind, as C. Wright Mills, who speak on somewhat a higher level than the epiphenomenal "Organization Man," and contrasts that to a state capitalist analysis of the times we live in. Since it was simultaneously published also in English I am enclosing the *Socialist Leader* of January 2, 1960,[4] which does so. I will also try to locate the "Two Worlds" article at the beginning of the year which dealt with the American economy in the postwar years as it goes from recession to recession.[5]

---

2   "Oil and Labor," by John Fredericks (John Dwyer), *Fourth International,* May 1958, August 1948, and September 1948, is included in RDC, pp. 1297–310. —Editor.

3   "Bureaucratie et capitalisme d'état," by Raya Dunayevskaya, Arguments #17, Paris 1960 is included in RDC, pp. 2746–49. —Editor.

4   "State Capitalism and the Bureaucrats," by Raya Dunayevskaya, *Socialist Leader,* January 2, 1960, is included in RDC, pp. 9488–93. —Editor.

5   "Stagnation of U.S. Economy," by Raya Dunayevskaya, *News & Letters,* January 1960.

Now then, the American literature on the subject: I have long since stopped paying attention to sociologists who have rather degenerated into the school of "social psychology" which the workers in the factory rightly call "head shrinking" so my list cannot be exhaustive, but I can give you the major references. Since the class struggle was never accepted in American sociology as the framework of analysis, your reference to those who speak of alleged cooperative attitude of worker to management and even "organization of work"(!), must have in mind ex-radicals and near radicals whose recent toutings of the virtues of capitalism are sort of summed up in the person of Daniel Bell and his strung-out articles called a book, *The End of Ideology*, by which they mean, of course, the end of the class struggle. Certainly *they* are struggling no longer now that their philistinism cannot even assume the veneer of the West European enders of the class struggle (not only the French but even the British "New Left") but the crassest apologia for State Department "culture." (Now, isn't that a better euphemism than "the line"?)

Perhaps the most solid of these is Seymour Martin Lipset. His *Political Man: The Social Bases of Politics* is dominated by his attempt to "document" the attenuation of the class struggle: The modification of late capitalism by welfare legislation, redistribution by taxation, powerful unions and "Full Employment" legislation. Lipset's thesis is that

> the fundamental political problems of the industrial revolution have been solved; the workers have achieved industrial and political citizenship; the conservatives have accepted the welfare state; and the democratic left has recognized that an increase in over-all state power carries with it more dangers to freedom than solutions to economic problems.

(Even here the American is very different from the French, who, when they espouse the attenuation of the class struggle, go for the Plan with a capital P while the American remains "the free enterpriser," although the State Department itself, when it is a question of *export* of ideology, goes for "people's capitalism.")

A book that has recently gotten a lot of attention both because it is new and sort of summarizes in bright journalistic language some half century of sociology is *The Eclipse of Community* by the Princeton University sociologist, Maurice R. Stein. There are all sorts of shouting on "the End of Industrial Man" (Peter Drucker),[6] the end of political man, *The Politics of Mass Society* by

---

6   An apparent reference to Peter Drucker's *The Landmarks of Tomorrow* (New York: Harper and Brothers, 1959).

William Kornhauser. Now none claim that the end of this economic, industrial, political man, even as his thinking too has been taken over by the electronic brain, is happy or content with his work. In that respect the ambivalence is seen clearest in Daniel Bell's *Work and Its Discontents*, whose claim is that the attenuation of the class struggle has nevertheless occurred, if not in the factory, then by "the new hunger, the candied carrot."[7] How much have we heard of those TV sets and "occupational mobility" and David Riesman's flip side record from the Lonely Man to *Individualism Reconsidered*[8] of the need "to increase automatization in work—but for the sake of pleasure and consumption and not for the sake of work itself." At least Bell has one good catch phrase that the descriptions that issue from the so-called "human relations" projects are "not of human, but of cow, sociology."

If you take the economists, you also have a choice of the flip side, so that Louis M. Hacker now touts "The Triumph of Capitalism"[9] and while everyone is ashamed of such past as *The Decline of American Capitalism*,[10] which—like all so-called Marxist books from Lewis Corey to that Stalinist apologist who passes for "the" Marxist authority (even Joseph Schumpeter's monumental but quite lopsided, or, as we say more appropriately in Jewish, "*tsidreit*," work, *History of Economic Analysis* refers to him as such) Paul Sweezy—are one and all underconsumptionist, so that, whether you take the period of the 1930s when "all" were Marxists to one degree or another and some serious works were done, or you take now when nearly the only works against capitalism are issued by the Stalinists, there really is no genuine Marxist analysis of the American economy either historically, sociologically or as economic works. But, at least, from the economists one does get figures and they do show that in *The Affluent Society*[11] some are very much more affluent than others. Otherwise, the sociological works, even before McCarthyism for whom they lay prostrate, were specialized studies of one or another aspect, like occupational mobility by sociologists Reinhard Bendix and S.M. Lipset, or the Lynds' *Middletown* or Lloyd Warner's *Yankee City* or Louis Wirth's *The Ghetto* or Florian Znaniecki on the Polish peasant in America.[12] Even the more broad dislocations as *Class and*

---

7   *The End of Ideology,* p. 254. —Editor.

8   David Riesman wrote *The Lonely Crowd* (New Haven: Yale University Press, 1950) and *Individualism Reconsidered* (Glencoe, Ill.: The Free Press, 1954). —Editor.

9   Louis M. Hacker, *The Triumph of American Capitalism: The Development of Forces in American History to the End of the Nineteenth Century* (New York: Simon and Schuster, 1940).

10   Lewis Corey, *The Decline of American Capitalism* (New York: Covici, Friede, 1934).

11   John Kenneth Galbraith, *The Affluent Society* (Boston: Houghton Mifflin, 1958).

12   Reinhard Bendix and Seymour Martin Lipset (eds.) *Class, Status and Power: A Reader in Social Stratification* (Glencoe, Ill.: The Free Press, 1953); Robert S. Lynd and Helen Merrell

Caste in Southern Town by Dollard[13] had no comprehensive view of American society as a whole. When both the muckrakers before World War I (Lincoln Steffens' *Autobiography*[14] if you happen not to have read it will do for that) and the specialized studies of the 1930s and some in World War II stopped flowing, we then went into the most famous Elton Mayo's Hawthorne studies on *The Human Problems of an Industrial Civilization* (New York: MacMillan, 1933), which were to replace, I suppose, the statistical studies of sharecroppers, breadlines, etc.

Now everything has moved to Automation. In addition to those I list in *Marxism and Freedom*, there is now *Automation and Technological Change,* Hearings before Joint Commttee on the Economic Report, 84th Congress, Washington, D.C. [1955]; Howard B. Jacobson and Joseph S. Roucek, eds., *Automation and Society* (New York: Philosophical Library, 1959), Charles R. Walker, *Toward the Automatic Factory: A Case Study of Men and Machines* (New Haven: Yale University Press, 1957) and Floyd C. Mann and L. Richard Hoffman, *Automation and the Worker: A Study of Social Change in Power Plants* (New York: Holt, 1960), which, despite its title, is not what the worker feels but a specialized study in power plants by the University of Michigan. There is a good bibliography, issued in 1959, called *Economic and Social Implications of Automation: Abstracts of Recent Literature,* Michigan State University, East Lansing, Mich. [1958]. I doubt any of these are really what you wish to waste your time on, but it is a fact that the new (since 1958) "The Society for the History of Technology" with its journal *Technology and Culture* (Vol. I, #1, Winter 1959) at least doesn't write with the guilt complex that the sociologists do and therefore can both be somewhat more objective as well as free from the attempt to identify the end of *its* ideology with that of the "masses." Not being concerned much with the masses (their outpost away from the publishing center here at Wayne State University and its editor Melvin Kranzberg of Case Institute of Technology, Cleveland, is really Chicago and the "Christian Humanism" of the sociologist-technologist John U. Nef) it can pay attention to the technological base as it impinges on other fields. For example, it would definitely be worthwhile if your book is not going to press right this minute to gets its next issue, which it

---

Lynd, *Middletown: A Study in Contemporary American Culture* (New York: Harcourt, Brace and Company, 1929); Lloyd W. Warner and Paul S. Lunt, *Yankee City,* Vols. I–v (New Haven: Yale University Press, 1941–1959); Louis Wirth, *The Ghetto* (Chicago: University of Chicago Press, 1928); W.I. Thomas and Florian Znaniecki, *The Polish Peasant in Europe and America: Monograph of an Immigrant Group,* Vols. I–v (Boston: Badger, 1918–1920).

13   John Dollard, *Caste and Class in a Southern Town* (New York: Harper, 1937).

14   Lincoln Steffens, *The Autobiography of Lincoln Steffens* (New York: The Literary Guild, 1931).

promises to devote entirely to that monumental five-volume study *A History of Technology*,[15] which is edited by Charles Singer and which series of articles on it, critical and otherwise, will be prefaced by him.

Now then, as you see, I could not give you the listing of the American literature on the subject without giving you my views as well. I wish now to summarize my considered evaluation not merely of books of the American society as I see, which differs very radically from your views. If I may, I would like to say that I hope at least that you have not, in your preoccupation with "the transformation of the laboring class" fallen into the trap of viewing Marxian socialism as if it were a distributive philosophy. I do not mean to insult you and put in the underconsumptionist category but such great revolutionaries as Rosa Luxemburg were in it, despite the fact that her *Social Reform or Revolution* was based precisely on removing the question of the class struggle from its reduction to a question of "personal fortunes" to one of production relations. Engels certainly wrote many works on production relations and never was even conscious of any deviations, and yet by not being the dialectician and humanist Marx was, wrote tracts that were far afield. Rudolf Hilferding had undertaken his *Finance Capital* as a bringing up to date of *Capital* yet the "organized capitalism" with its "stability" inclinations reduced socialism to a matter of "taking over" not reorganized from the ground up, least of all by the spontaneous actions of the workers. Of course, you may say that is exactly where Marx was "wrong" and you of course are not only entitled to your view but writing probingly for many years, and I may be doing you great injustice since I do not have your manuscript at hand (I do hope you will send it to me so that view can be concrete instead of based on assumptions) but I just have a feeling that this preoccupation with the alleged high standard of living shifts the weight from what you yourself state in the Preface to my book as "the integral unity of Marxian theory at its very foundation: in the humanistic philosophy."

Therefore, allow me to recapitulate some fundamentals although all are familiar to you. First you no doubt recall that on p. 125 of *Marxism and Freedom* where I quote from *Capital* Vol. I, pp. 708–09, on law of accumulation, I argue against the popular concept that now that the worker is "better off," etc., pointing to Marx's statement that "in proportion as capital is accumulated, the lot of the laborer, *be his payment high or low,* must grow worse" (emphasis added). That his lot has grown worse is evidenced in the conditions of labor under Automation and in the unemployment it has produced. The "pockets of depression" may sound very incidental to those who do not have to live in them but when, in 1960, even a Jack Kennedy (now that electioneering is in the air) must

---

15   Charles Joseph Singer, ed., *A History of Technology* (Oxford: Clarendon Press, 1954).

stand appalled at conditions in West Virginia where actual cases of mothers selling themselves into prostitution to try to keep from starvation, isn't it time for the exponents of higher standard of living to take a breather and look into the lot of the 5 million unemployed who with their families make up 13 million. And it isn't only the unemployed, nor even the snail's pace of the rate of growth of the American postwar economy which has produced three recessions, but the so-called normal conditions under Automation. I have seen miners' shacks who had an outhouse instead of a toilet but had a TV on the installment plan, but that did not signify either contentment or that they "chose" thus the "candied carrot," but only that TV could be installed whereas before plumbing could be it would need a great deal more that a $5 down payment—you'd have to root out altogether those hovels, including the miserable excuses for roads leading to them in this most road-conscious industrially advanced free land.

The answer of those who seem to take the opposite view is that, 1, they have never even bothered to build a labor party, 2, the labor leadership they have they "deserve" since they wanted for the Reuthers, Meanys, Hoffas, and 3, that they are not "active" i.e., rechanging society this very moment. Striking, wildcats, *and* organization of their own thinking seem not to count for very much. For the moment I'll accept this non-acceptable view and ask whether that is any more than the "bourgeoisification of the British proletariat" Marx and Engels so bemoan or "the aristocracy of labor" that Lenin saw as the root cause of the collapse of the Second International.

This brings me to the second basic Marxian view, on the question of going to *ever deeper and lower* strata of the proletariat for its revolutionary essence. You may recall that on p. 187 of *Marxism and Freedom* I bring in Marx's speech of September 20, 1871 [MECW 22, pp. 614–15], after the collapse of the Paris Commune and the cowardly running even before then of the British trades union leaders. (I have seen that speech only in Russian, but it may be available in German; I don't know.) I there also show that Lenin hadn't "discovered" this, which he now called "*the quintessence* of Marxism," until he himself was confronted not only with the betrayal of the Second International *but with the ultra leftism of Bukharin* who was thereupon ready to castigate not only the Second International's leadership but the proletariat itself. It is the last paragraph on that p. 187 where I deal with Lenin's approach on two levels, the real and the ideal, that I would now like to call to your attention, if I may.

It is true that Automation and state capitalism are not only "quantitative" but qualitative changes in our contemporary society and that that predominant fact would also affect a *part* of the proletariat. But a part is not the whole. Indeed, the fact that gives the appearance of an affluent society not only in the bourgeois sector but in the masses—the millions of employed so that the

5 millions unemployed look "little"—does not show that those unemployed are *predominantly in the production workers.* No suburbia here. It is all concentrated in the industrial centers, among an organized but wildcatting proletariat and aggravated by the Negro Question, which is by no means quiescent, and among a youth that has shown that they are not rebels without a cause but with one. I know you do not accept my view that they are in search of a total philosophy and are not getting themselves ready for the dustbin of history. But it is a fact that not only among the proletariat and the million that were striking just when Khrushchev was visiting and Eisenhower wanted to show him American superiority in industry, not industry at a standstill,[16] it is a fact that, in just the few months that Negro college youth began sitting in, the whole question of freedom and youth "coming up to the level of the West European" has been moved from the stage of the future to that of the present.

That will do until I actually see your book in manuscript and get the development of your thought. I should be very happy to write again then. Meanwhile, my work—and I still labor with the Absolute Idea despite the activist pressures you are free from—moves slowly, but I do hope after Labor Day to get more time to concentrate on the book....

YOURS,

RAYA

---

16   A strike from July to November 1959 shut down the steel industry in the U.S.

CHAPTER 8

Marx's *Grundrisse* and the Dialectic in Life and in Thought

The 1973 publication of the first English translation of Marx's Grundrisse, *also called the "Rough Draft" of Capital, was hailed by Dunayevskaya for how it showed the self-determination of the Idea. The two letters presented here take up the illumination shed by the* Grundrisse *on the break in Marx's concept of theory, his restructuring of Capital, and the relationship between the dialectic in life and in theory. The second letter addresses these themes and Marx's method rooted in the Hegelian dialectic through a detailed critique of the Foreword by the translator, Martin Nicolaus. The letters are included in* The Supplement to the Raya Dunayevskaya Collection, *pp. 15099–100 and 12435–39.*

September 24, 1978

To all teachers, students, readers and re-readers of *Marxism and Freedom*
Dear Colleagues:
I should like to call your attention to p. 89, ¶2, of *Marxism and Freedom*:

> He who glorifies theory and genius but fails to recognize the *limits* of a theoretical work, fails likewise to recognize *the indispensability of the theoretician.*

Although the last five words of the sentence are underlined, it has heretofore had little attention since the other underlined word, "*limits*," had to be stressed in this section on "The Working Day and the Break with the Concept of Theory."

However, it has to be stressed now that, first, I then had only a bowdlerized[1] version of the *Grundrisse*. Indeed, I began stressing that as soon as I was able to get *Grundrisse* translated for me at the end of the 1960s, at which point I was so

---

1 I found the *Grundrisse* about the same time Roman Rosdolsky did in the immediate post-World War II period; we probably both used that same copy. In any case, I asked Grace [Lee Boggs] to translate it and she presented twelve pages of quotations which were so busy proving that Marx, 1857, was not Marx, 1867, on twofold labor and the decline in the rate of profit that she left out entirely the crucial section on Pre-Capitalist Economic Formations—in fact she seems to have skipped all the way from somewhere in the 300s (pages) to the 600s. That was way back in the mid-1940s, and I rediscovered that section in the early 1960s as I was working on the Third World, especially China.

anxious that all others read it that I made it a condition for preparing *Philosophy and Revolution* to be published, at which point it was to be an Appendix. That became unnecessary to insist upon, as by then, 1973, a full translation appeared in England. Needless to say, far from agreeing with Nicolaus's Foreword to it, I wrote a special section on it for *Philosophy and Revolution*: "The 1850s: The *Grundrisse*, Then and Now." *I now propose that those pages (61–75) of* Philosophy and Revolution *be made part of the study of* Marxism and Freedom, *as without it the 1850s are incomplete* in *Marxism and Freedom,* which concentrates on what followed the *Grundrisse*, i.e., *Critique of Political Economy.*

From those pages in *Philosophy and Revolution* you will see that—while everything said in *Marxism and Freedom* is correct on the question of the relationship of history and theory, on the discarding by Marx of these first forms of *Capital,* to which the actual movement from practice of the 1860s was indispensable—yet, the fact that "*the indispensability of the theoretician*" could have been slighted over shows that, until the actual *Grundrisse* was known, it remained an abstraction. As we know, not only from *Philosophy and Revolution,* but from the objective world situations of the *1950s*—the Chinese Revolution, which forced Russia and European Communism to turn back to just how Oriental society had brought a new stage of revolution to the European stage 100 years ago, the Taiping Revolution—*the self-development of the Idea,* in Marx's hands, went a great deal further than Marx gave himself credit.

Put another way, Marx was absolutely right to be dissatisfied with the *form* of the *Grundrisse*, to feel he was only "applying" the Hegelian dialectic, not recreating it on the basis of his own new continent of thought and the dialectic that came out of the Civil War in the U.S. and the Paris Commune. *But once he had worked out that* magnificent form of *Capital,* he had to discard much of the historical material of the *Grundrisse.* That not only did *not* mean that what he discarded was "wrong," but in fact could, and indeed would, have been rewritten for Volumes II and III, which remained incomplete. Those who taught us that, in their own truncated form, were the Chinese revolutionaries; at least for them what Marx said on Oriental society was both concrete and crucial. For our age—and here I am referring to the post-1968 period—it became as crucial as V.I. Lenin's *Philosophic Notebooks*, which is why both subjects became crucial for *Philosophy and Revolution.*

There is another reason for *my* proposing that the *Grundrisse* section in *Philosophy and Revolution* be taken up in the study of *Marxism and Freedom.* (Incidentally, I don't know whether you received from Eugene [Gogol] his outline of the classes in *Marxism and Freedom* that Los Angeles will conduct at Compton College; it is good, except that I suggested it have an extra lecture on the 1850s. In fact, it was not seeing it that led to my present proposal for all.) That reason concerns Herbert Marcuse. In his Preface to *Marxism and Freedom*, though he praises me highly for taking Marx's Humanism further than ever before, he excuses previous failure on the ground that "a most decisive link was still missing, the *Grundrisse*" from 1939–41 when it was first published (p. xxi), without explaining why then till 1957 when *Marxism and Freedom* was going to press? I thought we were nevertheless talking the same language when he said that Marx departed from Hegelianism, not only the old, but the "Young Hegelians," of which Marx had been a member, and I gave Marcuse credit for doing a pioneering work (p. 349, ftn. 30). It turned out, however, that whereas I had taken for granted that it meant what we called a new continent of thought, Marcuse had reduced it to Frankfurt School type of sociology. Which proves all over again "don't take matters for granted" when it comes to serious theory.

YOURS,
RAYA

P.S. I would also recommend that everyone reread my July 1, 1973, letter on the English translation of the *Grundrisse*. It was reproduced in part as a "Two Worlds" column in the November 1973 *News & Letters*.

•••

July 1, 1973

Dear Friends,

Grundrisse has finally been translated into English and published in full....

Unfortunately, this edition is burdened by so fantastic a Foreword by its translator, Martin Nicolaus, that we must all over again divert from Marx to his interpreters. You, of course, have the chapter on the *Grundrisse* in *Philosophy and Revolution,* and since you will soon have the whole of Marx's work, you could skip over the 60-page Foreword. However, the Foreword has a signifi-cance because it is by the youth who, in giving us a rigorous translation and having the advantage of being or knowing Greek, translated also all those pas-sages that are always left to tantalize, and who, being New Left, gives us an indication of all that will befall us in the battle of ideas.

By stating that his Foreword is "fantastic," *I do not* mean it departs *in any* fundamental way from established Marxism, which, with reformism, be-gan demanding the removal of the "Hegelian dialectic scaffolding" of Marx's works. And I certainly do not mean that "orthodoxy" resting with Joseph Stalin, who threw out "the negation of the negation" from the "dialectic laws," much less with Mao Zedong, who perverted contradiction from the elemental class struggle to "principal" and "subordinate" forever changing places in "bloc of four classes." (The latter two, especially Mao, get praised to the skies, so that we read that *On Contradiction* and *On Practice* "are at one and the same time strictly orthodox in the Marxist sense and highly original" (p. 43, ftn. 39)). I mean that the pull of pragmatism, state-capitalism, and the administrative mentality that characterizes our age are so overwhelming that all the years put into the translation, the recognition that "The *Grundrisse* challenges and puts to the test every serious interpretation of Marx yet conceived" (p. 7), and the subjective wish to be revolutionary, are still no shield from the *objective* pull of the state-capitalist age once your ears are not close to the ground so that you see all the elemental forces *from practice uniting* with the self-determination of the philosophy of liberation.

From the very first page, first paragraph, Nicolaus announces that the 1857–58 Notebooks (that did not see publication in Marx's time; were kept from public eye till World War II when they were first published in the original German only in Moscow; didn't really reach front center stage *until after* Chinese Revolution and Korean War in 1953; and were disregarded for two further decades before they reached Anglo-Saxon world) "display the key elements in Marx's development and *overthrow* of the Hegelian philosophy" (p. 7, my emphasis). With this as his ground, how could the translator possibly learn anything from the 893 pages?

(Add to this false beginning also the first footnote on that same page, which shows the heavy dependence on Rosdolsky's work, which Nicolaus himself later (p. 23, ftn. 16) admits is exclusively economic and results in "the virtual exclusion of the question of method (and of Hegel) from the debates of this epoch" and, of course, in Rosdolsky himself. In footnote 1 (p. 7), Nicolaus also quotes Rosdolsky as stating "that only three or four copies of the 1939–41 edition ever reached 'the western world.' " I myself, however, knew of more than that many copies in New York alone. While it certainly was no "mass" circulation, the truth was that so great was the hunger for philosophy, for *Marx's* original philosophy, so great the disgust with what the Communists made of it *plus* Trotskyists' disregard of it, that passages would be translated and passed around in small circles of revolutionary Marxists long before the current dissenters in Russia made *Samizdat*, the popular self-publication, a universal.)

The next fifteen pages of his Foreword Nicolaus devotes to background plus a few pages in trying to summarize the first chapter of Marx's "On Money" and into the first section "On Capital." All is devoted to the translator's view of "the structure of the argument" (p. 23), only to conclude: "All that follows in the remaining four hundred pages of the *Grundrisse* is built on the basic elements here outlined."

Having thus cavalierly virtually dismissed one-half of the book (he will later return in bits and pieces), he is off on his own. It is here, then, that we have to search for his method and aim and originality of contribution. Quoting Marx on the difference between a method of presentation and a method of inquiry, which Nicolaus translates as *"method of working"* (p. 26), Nicolaus concludes that this is *the* unique feature of the *Grundrisse*. Directly after this he once again quotes Marx, this time Marx's letter to Engels (January 16, 1858) on the fact that Marx did indeed find Hegel's <u>Logic</u> of great service "in the method of working." Unfortunately, Nicolaus has no comprehension whatever, either of this sentence or of the one he quotes from Lenin that it was "impossible completely to understand Marx's *Capital,* especially Chapter 1, without having thoroughly studied the <u>whole</u> of Hegel's *Logic."*

Far from basing himself on either, Nicolaus *is* on his way to construct something altogether different. First, he brings in a character from Bertholt Brecht's dramas who states that, though Hegel could have been "one of the greatest humorists among philosophers, like Socrates ... he sold himself to the state." Nicolaus concludes: "That is to say, Hegel's philosophy was at once dialectical, subversive, as was Socrates', and idealist, mystical like a priest's" (p. 27). So satisfied is he with that red herring of old, that he reiterates, "it left Hegel towards the end a philosopher-pope bestowing benediction, as popes must, on the temporal emperor." As for the dialectic, he returns us to the origin of the word: in "Greek, *'dia,'* meaning split in two, opposed, clashing; and *'logos,'* reason; hence, 'to reason by splitting in two' " (pp. 27–28).

But just as we are about to think he is finally, more or less, on the right track (that is, though it is in Greece and times of Socrates rather than in Germany in the times of the French Revolution and Napoleon), he develops neither contradiction nor self-motion, but jumps at once to *Begriff* (concept). As if Hegel *didn't* grasp that any more than he grasped that very unique Hegelianism, "moment" (p. 29, ftn. 23), because, allegedly, it was from Isaac Newton, from mechanics, and not from history's self-movement, that Hegel took the word "moment." While this flies in the face of Marx's critique of the dialectic as rooted in history, self-development, the self-making of labor, Nicolaus stresses how "profoundly contrary to Hegel's method" is Marx's. (Nicolaus here limits himself to the concreteness of Marx's concept of time especially on the question of production, which is, of course, crucial, but we will see later that what he leaves out, in turn, is *the whole* of Marxism: SUBJECT, self-development, *masses as reason and not just as labor time.*)

At the moment Nicolaus was altogether too busy denying Hegel: "The idealist side of his philosophy was that he denied the *reality* of what the senses perceive" (p. 27). Not a word about the fact that so great was Hegel's discovery, according to Marx—the second negativity, the creativity, and so rooted in the revolutionary period—that Hegel *had* to "throw a mystical veil" over that *reality*. It is of course at reality where Marx did transcend Hegel—and so did the historic period of 1848 as against 1789—but, again, it was the Subject, the proletariat, that made the Great Divide between Hegel, the bourgeois philosopher, and Marx, who had discovered a new continent of thought that was not merely materialism vs. idealism but the *unity* of the two in "the new Humanism," and that carried through into Vol. III of *Capital* as "human power is its own end" [MCIIIK, p. 954; MCIIIP, p. 959].

So preoccupied is Nicolaus with contrasting materialism to idealism (though he himself will later (p. 34) need to admit that if it were only a question of "standing Hegel right side up" then that "was accomplished in the early 1840s by *both* Feuerbach and Marx..." [my emphasis]) that he forgets the true uniqueness of Marx and repeats outworn revisionisms about "Hegelian language" to tell us that "before *Capital* found its way into print Marx discarded most of this lexicon as baggage which had served for its journey but outlasted its day" (pp. 32–33). Then what did that "service" that Hegel rendered Marx achieve? Nicolaus's answer is indeed the most petty-bourgeois intellectualistic idealism yet heard: "The usefulness of Hegel lay in providing guide-lines for what to do in order to grasp a moving, developing totality with the mind" (p. 33).

Now if it is nothing less than "guide-lines" that Hegel provided and if he also provided "a grip on the entire realm of the 'independent objective Mind' which Hegel had sent floating into the heavens..." what exactly was *new* in Marx's discovery? Where was that proletariat Marx held onto as *the* Subject for transformation of society, the shaper of history, the mass that is a product of history but also "makes" it? Nicolaus can't seem to get further than "standing right side up" and "removing mystical shell from rational core."

He does get to two other philosophic concepts: where to begin? and Mediation. And, at one point I even thought he would get to a genuine divide, when he pointed to the difference between starting with the abstract Being and Nothing in Hegel, and the concrete Commodity—which Marx didn't reach till the very last page of the *Grundrisse* (p. 881) but which then became the beginning both of *Critique of Political Economy* built on *Grundrisse*, and of *Capital*. But he was altogether too eager to stick at the "overthrow of the Hegelian system":

> This is the critique of Hegel's *dialectic method,* therefore a critique of his theory of contradiction, hence a critique of the fundamental processes of the Hegelian *concept*, of Hegel's basic grasp of movement. (p. 34)

The result was self-paralysis, blindness to that crucial Chapter 1 of *Capital,* which (1) Lenin called attention to as requiring the *whole* of *Logic* but which

Nicolaus reduces to zero, stating, "it would be a misreading of Lenin's intent to argue that.... This is a project for a long term in prison" (pp. 60–61). (2) He never once questions himself as to that constant reappearance of Chapter 1 at each revolutionary period and *counter*-revolutionaries demanding it be thrown out of the teaching of *Capital,* as Stalin did in 1943. Moreover, and above all, (3) *what* exactly is Chapter 1, and its 1872–75 rewriting by Marx himself of its final section "Fetishism of Commodities" and *why* did Marx ask readers of the German edition which did not have that essential part to please read the French edition *following the Paris Commune?*

Nothing, *nothing whatever,* is greater proof of the recreation of the dialectic on the basis of this elemental outpouring *and* the self-development of Marx's *Begriff* of Commodity. In *"nothing whatever"* I include all the great dialectical developments in *Grundrisse,* even its Hegelian-Marxian "absolute movement of becoming" [*Grundrisse,* p. 488]. For the most mature, most creative genius *learned* from the Parisian masses that that perverse form, a commodity, the value-form of a product of labor, can never he stripped of its fetishism except by *"freely associated* labor." So his beginning, as against Hegel's in *Science of Logic,* was not only concrete, tangible as against abstract universal of Being, but it was also the not-concrete, not-tangible bourgeois fetish which reduced labor itself to the commodity, labor-power. *And this was not only production exploitation vs. market equality, but that Absolute, the specifically capitalistic stage of production, whose Notion had to be split into two:* bourgeois reification vs. freely associated labor showing it is all relations of production that must be uprooted *and* recreated on altogether other foundations.

Having "overthrown Hegelian philosophy," he goes into Mediation, a central category surely but not an Absolute, and furthermore long since cleansed by Marx of its "idealism" once he stated "immediate identities leave immediate dualities intact." Nicolaus quotes that statement on p. 39[2] only as preliminary to first going in on his own. By no accident, therefore, on the very next page (p. 40, ftn. 36), though he wishes to criticize Louis Althusser's "overdetermination" concept, he ends by saying that Althusser is "ambiguous." If anything can be said about Althusser, despite his deliberately obfuscating "complex" style, it is that he is "brave," not at all ambiguous, in his attack not only on Hegel but on Marx, whose affinity to Hegel he calls nothing short of "abreaction."

No, dear Nicolaus, all your praise of Lenin's *Philosophic Notebooks* means nothing, nothing at all, once you consign anyone who wishes to study *Logic* to fully comprehend *Capital* to "a long term in prison" and think, now that you

---

2   The quotation is actually Nicolaus's paraphrase of Marx's statement: "The immediate unity in which production coincides with consumption and consumption with production leaves their immediate duality intact" (p. 91). —Editor.

have presented (and how presented!) *Grundrisse,* which Lenin hadn't known about, no further need is there for Hegel. Is there any for *Capital* or *Grundrisse* when you assure us that, in place of awaiting a long term in prison, "meanwhile, much can be gained from *Wages, Price, and Profit* and *On Contradiction"* (p. 61), having already (p. 43, ftn. 39) assured us that Mao's essays are "at one and the same time strictly orthodox in the Marxist sense and highly original." In their *perversity,* they surely are "highly original" for a Marxist, but shouldn't you ask yourself: how did it happen you went back to *1937* when, in fact, the Chinese Revolution is what brought onto the historic stage "Pre-Capitalist Economic Formations" (you more precisely do translate it as "Forms which precede capitalist production. (Concerning the process which precedes the formation of the capital relation or of original accumulation.)")?

Let me expand on this. Nicolaus stopped before he reached that crucial section (pp. 471–514) of the *Grundrisse,* which he barely mentions anywhere as if what he called "the structure of the argument" could possibly have been made on what preceded it. Clearly, the section was neither merely economy nor even "merely" historic, that is to say, history as past instead of as present *and future.* The dialectic in that historic period had all the elements of a new role for peasantry, a new role for so-called "Oriental despotism," a more comprehensive view of becoming. For all those reasons, it is only *when* an actual revolution occurred in China *and* that country actually was the first to translate the section on pre-capitalist formations, that all established Communist regimes were *compelled* to grapple with what Marx had written in 1857–58. Insofar as the question of "backwardness" is concerned, Marx reiterated that in altogether new form in the very last year of his life, 1882–83. Put in a different way, he now said that "backward" Russia might, *ahead* of the "advanced" countries, have a social revolution. He showed the same type of attitude in his relationship to the "Automaton." Nicolaus does mention that section more often than the one on Oriental society. But again, his hostility to Hegel—and being stuck *in* the mud of our age's administrative mentality—limited his perception of that section as if it were only against the "New Left's" view that engineers will, with automation, invent machines that will replace the proletariat, etc., etc. In actuality it is the multidimensionality that Marx was analyzing. He saw the *limitations* of both the Hegelian dialectic sans Subject and his own economics, great as it was, sans the masses in motion. In the 1850s this is what made him discard all, start anew, and include both the Civil War and the Paris Commune. Both the struggle for shortening the working day and the new Black Dimension releasing labor led to the restructuring of *Grundrisse* as *Capital.*

The *new* in the *Grundrisse* even now is not merely "method of working," great as that is. It is the *continuity* of the affinity of the Marxian and Hegelian dialectic. From the *moment of break* with bourgeois society, 1843, all the way through *Grundrisse* and total break with vulgar materialists (not merely as utopians or Proudhonists but as Lassalleans), to *Capital* and the First International, Marx's self-development is in no sense a break from the young Marx that discovered a new continent of thought.

Any who question, as Nicolaus does, whether "it is any longer necessary to read Hegel's *Logic* in order to completely understand *Capital*" (p. 60) when *Grundrisse* is finally available; *and then claim that Grundrisse is just to see a mind at work,* are indeed the worst kind of petty-bourgeois "idealists." They are completely dead to the whole of the past two decades when *from below,* from the East German Revolt in 1953 on to Paris *and* Peking, 1968, as well as from "above" (self-determination of Idea finally catching up with self-determination of nations), "new passions and new forces" have arisen. This movement surely has passed by progeny of the Stalins, Maos, not to mention the Trotskyists and all who thought they can catch theory "*en route.*" The task for us, however, has just begun.

YOURS,
RAYA

CHAPTER 9

Capitalist Production/Alienated Labor

As a deep restructuring of the economy continued in the 1980s, Dunayevskaya investigated the economic situation and the illusions of the capitalist ideologues. The ideologues had forgotten not only the lessons of the Great Depression but that the foundation of capitalist economy is alienated labor. The subjective dimension is brought to view here both as struggles from below and as the positive in the negative that Marx outlined. This chapter is excerpted from "Capitalist Production/Alienated Labor: This Nuclear World and its Political Crises," Part II of the Marxist-Humanist Draft Perspectives, 1986–87, *published in* News & Letters, *July 1986. The text of the full* Draft Perspectives, *completed by Dunayevskaya on June 17, 1986, is included in the* Supplement to the Raya Dunayevskaya Collection, *pp. 11026–34.*

The basis of the economy of the most powerful imperialist land, the U.S., is that it is now a debtor nation. The global ramifications of that fact, as well as its implications at home, have not been seriously dealt with. Paul Volcker, head of the Federal Reserve Board, and considered by economists to be the "second most powerful man" in the land, did not bother to attend the [G7] Economic Summit. He refused to be deluded by all the hoopla about the great state of the world economy, especially that of the U.S. Volcker claimed the U.S. "put all the necessary solutions off on other countries.... The action taken so far is not enough to put the deficit on a declining trend." The strength of the economy, Volcker concluded, "is not an unalloyed joy."

The Grand Illusion, however, that all capitalist ideologues, including Volcker, have created about this nuclear world with its robotized production, was achieved by them through forgetting that Alienated Labor is *the* irreplaceable foundation, essence and universal form—*the* creator of all values and surplus-values. That is exactly what produces both capitalist profits and what Marx called the "general absolute law of capitalist accumulation"—its unemployed army.

What the industrial giants cannot hear is the death-knell that labor, employed and unemployed, as well as the homeless, are ringing out. The industrialists are under the illusion—never more so than in this robotized stage of production—that the unemployed army can be made to rampage against the employed.

Their ideologues are busy "proving" that Marx was wrong. They have never understood that other fundamental Marx prediction, that the failure to reproduce labor means the death of their whole system. Political crises reflect the general absolute law of capitalist production differently in different historic periods. Thus, the Great Depression produced a John Maynard Keynes, with his *General Theory of Employment, Interest and Money*, which proved to the capitalists that they cannot get out of economic crisis *unless* they couple production with employment. All kinds of "New Deals" were thereby contrived to save capitalism from revolution.

Today, modern profit-hungry capitalists, both state and private, think they can do the exact opposite—that is, "uncouple" employment from production. They think they can still go merrily on with their computerized stock market, false super-profiteering through mergers, playing the margins, and alternating ownerships from corporations to "private entrepreneurs." They now talk of factory "incubators," where former large plants are leased out to small producers who employ far fewer workers at far lower wages. They act as if higher labor productivity can come from somewhere other than sweated, living labor; as if it can come out of computers.

The favorite word of today's economists is "uncoupling." Peter F. Drucker has written for *Foreign Affairs* (Spring, 1986) on "The Changed World Economy."[1] There, he arrogantly, and yet in an offhand manner (as if the changes he is talking about are the true status of the world economy), insists that it is necessary to recognize the three truths of the uncoupling that he elaborates:

(1) "uncoupling" employment from production.

(2) "uncoupling" capital from capital investment, reducing capital to money by calling it "capital movement": "Capital movements rather than trade (in both goods and services) have become the driving force of the world economy. The two have not quite come uncoupled, but the link has become loose and, worse, unpredictable."

(3) "uncoupling" industrial production from the whole economy, by which he tries to explain that he means uncoupling it from the "weak" sectors like the farm economy and raw materials. It is as if digging out the raw materials is done without labor. Or, for that matter, as if our so-called post-industrial world is so "advanced" with its computers, its plastics, its synthetics, its "high technology," that labor which is not on a production line is not labor.

What they choose to disregard is that even those robotized, unimated[2] production processes are built on sweated labor. A recent NBC television special[3] on

---

1   See also the Special Report by Norman Jonas on "The Hollow Corporation" in *Businessweek*, March 3, 1986.

2   "Unimation" (for "universal automation") refers to use of industrial robots in manufacturing.—Editor.

3   "The Japan They Don't Talk About," April 22, 1986, NBC *White Paper*.

that most high-tech land, Japan, which has completely shaken up the global market, revealed how fully its production is rooted in the most wretched, low-paying, non-union, piecework labor, done by subcontractors for its high-tech corporations.[4]

Indeed, all of the ideologues are rightly screaming against the astronomical indebtedness of the capitalist economy since President Ronald Reagan has been in power. There is no way that even Reagan can deny that we have become a debtor nation. What the ideologues (who supposedly differ from the supply-siders and monetarists) have to recognize is this: once they have "uncoupled" industrial production from their whole economy, and capital from investment in production, reducing capital investment to money alone, they are left with what they supposedly rejected—monetarism.

These are not mere stock market fantasies; the monstrous reality they have created is a land in which at one pole we see a thousand new millionaires, while at the other we see the pauperization of millions of the unemployed, of the homeless, of the masses of Blacks and women living so far below the poverty line that hunger stalks the richest land in the world.

Once capital is not tied to investments in production, once even trade has been "uncoupled" from trade of products and reduced to mere exchange of services, there is nothing left but an exchange of monies and investment for more monies. The reason that the U.S., though itself a debtor nation, is nevertheless still at the top of the heap is because the international capitalists feel safe in only one country—the counterrevolutionary Reagan's USA. It is not only "flight capital" leaving "unstable" lands that gets to the U.S.; Japan and West Germany have "invested" heavily here as well.

Let's take another look, then, at the "safe" U.S. and all of Reagan's victories in his ongoing counterrevolution at home against unions, against Blacks, against women, against the youth.

– It is true that the union bureaucracy has given too many concessions. But one look at Hormel's ongoing strike[5] shows that militants know how to fight their own leaders, as well as the capitalists.

---

4   Back in the early 1940s, when Plan, with a capital "P," was the rage among the Left, the first study of the Five-Year Plans of Russia by those working out a State-Capitalist Theory debunked the Plan as any kind of socialism, showing that "feudal" Japan, in the very same 1932–37 period, was outproducing "socialist" Russia. [See Raya Dunayevskaya's original 1942 study of the Russian economy, included in *Marxism and Freedom*, p. 233 and p. 358, ftn. 220. — Editor.].

5   Approximately 1,500 meatpacking workers in Local P-9 of the United Food and Commercial Workers carried on a strike against Hormel in Austin, Minn., from August 1985 to June

- It is true there is no ongoing General Strike. But if we count up all the "little" strikes from Minnesota to Chicago, from New York's sweatshops to California farmworkers, and every place in between, we will see that U.S. labor is in daily, unrecorded revolt.
- It is true that the Women's Liberation Movement has seen a retrogression of all its hard-won gains of the 1960s and 1970s. But anyone who thinks that the sudden mass demonstration of 100,000 in Washington, D.C., on March 9 was "just" against Reagan's stand on abortion has not heard the voices of the Black and white women who have made their rejection of Reaganism known on every front from housing to childcare and from affirmative action to freedom of choice—and that is not the question of abortion alone, but the passion for human relations.
- It is true that the youth today are not the youth of the 1960s. But, as we have seen, the internationalism that was present in the anti-Vietnam War movement has reached a new dimension. Nor can one rewrite the history which has proved that the two-way road of the Black dimension between Africa and America has never separated its struggles from its ideas of freedom, its search for a philosophy of revolution.

The Black masses see right through Reagan-Weinberger's "conceptual arsenal,"[6] as the ceaseless nuclear arming and genocidal imperialism that it is. The utter barbarism of the Holocaust is what shows us where this post-World War II world of capitalism-imperialism is heading.

The significance of the *new*, the concrete, is not only the general fact that these struggles and crises point to the need to uproot the system. The significance is that this new *form* of production, which Drucker and others tout, is hiding the essence, by creating the illusion that this Particular, this specific appearance, is the new Universal. It is necessary to work out the new and concrete forms as they appear. That does not mean merely saying that it is only form rather than essence. Rather, it is to see that only revolution can abolish these forms; that only revolution can abolish the illusion some Marxists have that these forms are the new Universal. This kind of transformation can be achieved only by the dialectic of Absolute Method.

As Hegel articulated it:

1986 with national grassroots support, though undermined by the national union leaders. —Editor.

6 Secretary of Defense Caspar Weinberger touted a "conceptual arsenal" for "a new defense strategy for the 1990s" (Bill Keller, "Weinberger Describes U.S. Strategy for 90's," *New York Times*, Oct. 10, 1985). —Editor.

To hold fast the positive in *its* negative, and the content of the presupposition in the result, is the most important part of rational cognition;
also only the simplest reflection is needed to furnish conviction of the
absolute truth and necessity of this requirement, while with regard to the
examples of proofs, the whole of the *Logic* consists of these.[7]

Karl Marx projected his concept of the positive that would follow only after the
old capitalist society was thoroughly uprooted:

In a higher phase of communist society, after the enslaving subordination of individuals under the division of labor, and therewith also the
antithesis between mental and physical labor, has vanished; after labor,
from a mere means of life, has itself become the prime necessity of life;
after the productive forces have also increased with the all-round development of the individual, and all the springs of co-operative wealth flow
more abundantly—only then can the narrow horizon of bourgeois right
be fully left behind and society inscribe on its banners: from each according to his ability, to each according to his needs!

   Critique of the Gotha program, MECW 24, p. 871

The positive in the negative was not—*was not*—that Alienated Labor under
capitalism is the human activity, much less that science is the human activity.
Rather, it was the *struggles* of the Alienated Laborers against capitalism, and
the laborers' passion for an actual unity of mental and manual labor, that spells
out the urgency of revolution.

 What the revolutionary theoreticians need to do is *listen* to the voices from
below, and *concretize* that new unity by *practicing* it in their own publications,
activities, relations, as they prepare for revolution, anticipate it, labor for it.
The absolute opposite of that is what oozes out from the ideologues under
capitalism—which is why Marx called them the "prizefighters" for capitalism
[MCIK, p. 19; MCIP, p. 97].

---

7 *Science of Logic*, Vol. II, translated by Johnston & Struthers (New York: MacMillan, 1929),
 p. 476; trans. Miller (London: Allen & Unwin, 1969), p. 834.

CHAPTER 10

Marx's Critique of Culture

After the discovery of the new moments of Marx's last decade, this essay, which originally ran as the "Theory/Practice" column in the October 1984 issue of News & Letters, *expands the view of "economics" in a critique of the philosopher Louis Dupré, who corresponded with Dunayevskaya and has written much on both Hegel and Marx. In reviewing his book* Marx's Social Critique of Culture, *she revisits Marx's concept of praxis in relationship to "culture" and "the wide gulf between Marx's multilinear view of human relations and Engels' unilinear view."*

Professor Louis Dupré's *Marx's Social Critique of Culture*[1] is a most original critique of all of Marx's works by an independent scholar who has previously made a serious contribution to the study of the young Marx with his *Philosophical Foundations of Marxism*. He achieves this, not by extending his study, nor merely by now focusing on what Marx is best known for—his "Economics." Rather, he has embarked on a totally new venture, which is at once disclosed in the Foreword, where he states:

> What started as an attempt to correct and further explore certain theses I proposed in an earlier publication eventually led to a wholly new assessment of Marx's significance in the history of Western consciousness. (p. vii)

The uniqueness of a study of Marx as "the first major critic of a process of cultural disintegration that began with the modern age and has continued unabated to our time" challenges both Marxists and bourgeois interpreters of Marx.

1   Culture and Ideology

Dupré grasps most presciently the impact of Marx's concept of ideology as a false consciousness when he writes, toward the end, that "the term *ideology* receded almost as suddenly as it had risen to prominence. But the *concept* re-emerges ..." (p. 217). To stress that it was not limited to Marxists, Dupré prefaced that statement with: "No aspect of Marxist work has more profoundly affected the modern mind than his critique of ideology" (p. 216).

---

1   *Marx's Social Critique of Culture,* by Louis Dupré (New Haven: Yale University Press, 1983) $25.

Nevertheless, none before—and this includes Marx himself—had ever viewed Marx's works from the vantage point of culture. Furthermore, far from that vantage point having been embarked upon by Prof. Dupré as some sort of specialized study, it indeed excludes no major work, be it philosophic, economic or political, from his purview. Let me begin with the most specialized field—that of the "law of motion" of capitalism [MCIK, p. 14; MCIP, p. 92] to its collapse, and not restrict that to Chapter 4, "Economics as Sociocultural Activity," which is entirely devoted to "Economics," since it pervades the whole work.

Thus, in the second chapter, "Culture as Historical Process," Dupré not only deals with "Base and Superstructure" but touches on something as pivotal for that final decade of Marx as his critique of Mikhailovsky, who tried to make a universal of Marx's law of accumulation of capital. Marx insisted that he had been analyzing West Europe only and that precapitalist societies could find another path to revolution. Thus, in Chapter 3, "Structural Dialectic," Dupré tackles the whole question of "The Dialectic of Economic Concepts" as well as "The Historical Principle Radicalized: *Capital*"; and in Chapter 5, "The Uses of Ideology," to which we have already referred, what stands out is the relationship of ideology to superstructure.

There is no escaping from Dupré's preoccupation with "Economics" as both what he considers his most pivotal analysis of Marx's concepts and his concern with righting the record on the manner in which critics of Marx have not given sufficient attention to Marx as a serious, indeed "the first major critic of a process of cultural disintegration" in Western consciousness (p. vii). To further emphasize that, he keeps returning to the point that it simply isn't true that Marx meant to completely subordinate culture to economics. Furthermore, he seldom says anything on economics without stressing it as a social phenomenon. Therein precisely lies also the weakness because it leads to very nearly so subordinating human activity to "social" as to make the two appear synonymous. I therefore will start with the very first chapter, where Dupré is strongest and most convincing, as he tackles the question of fetishism of commodities.

2   Alienation or Class Struggles?

His subtitle for the section on *Capital* is "Alienation as Economic Contradiction." Dupré holds (correctly in this writer's view) that alienation and fetishism are not at all synonymous, that fetishism of commodities is directly related to the process of production where the "reification of all aspects of man's productive activity" occurs. He also denies a direct relationship of fetishism as

Marx develops it in *Capital* to his concept of the fetish as he presented it in his 1842 Notebooks, when he was summarizing Charles De Brosses's famous 1785 work, *Ueber den Dienst der Fetischgötter*. Dupré approvingly quotes Theodore Adorno's letter to Walter Benjamin: "The fetish character of commodities is not a fact of consciousness, but dialectic in the eminent state that it produces consciousness" (p. 50).

At the same time, however, Dupré shows an affinity to what the Frankfurt School later did by extending the question of fetishism to the whole cultural field. His ambiguity continues though he is well aware of the fact, as he himself put it, that thereby "we have left the area of Marxist hermeneutics for what is in fact a critique of Marx" (p. 50). Nowhere is this more jarring than on the question of praxis. No wonder that in a "Provisional Conclusion" to that chapter, Dupré suddenly questions why Marx concentrates "primarily on the capitalist mode of production and its exclusive orientation toward the production of exchange value" (p. 55). He points to the determining factor of "the negativity of praxis, in alienation, in the total dialectic of society, and indeed of all history" (p. 57), which is exactly where Dupré's ambiguity stands out most sharply. It is only now that we can turn to that Chapter 4 on "Economics" and, with it, the greatest weakness of the whole work.

Dupré fails to see that it is because of the priority of the mode of production and the relations between capital and labor at the point of production that Marx is not dealing only with "economic laws." It is there that Marx hears the "stifled voice" of the worker, follows his actions of resistance in the factory and extols the workers' struggle for the shortening of the working day. Dupré pays no attention whatever to the 80 pages Marx devotes to the chapter in *Capital* on "The Working Day." While Western ideologists have dismissed that as a sob story, it is precisely there that Marx credited the workers with creating the ground for a philosophy greater than what the Declaration of Independence expounded:

> In place of the pompous catalogue of the "inalienable rights of man" comes the modest Magna Charta of a legally limited working-day, which shall make clear "when the time which the worker sells is ended, and when his own begins." [MCIK, p. 330; MCIP, p. 416].

All this is missing from Dupré, as if it had nothing to do with "culture." Marx, on the other hand, as early as the *Communist Manifesto,* referred to it as "class culture" [MECW 6, p. 501]. But to see that, one has to not separate culture any more than philosophy from revolution. So all-present was that concept of revolution to Marx that he called the whole struggle nothing short of a civil war:

The creation of a normal working day is, therefore, the product of a pro-tracted civil war, more or less dissembled, between the capitalist class and the working class. [MCIK, p. 327; MCIP, pp. 412–13]

3   Marx's Labor Theory of Value

Dupré prefers, when he comes to that "Economics" chapter, to make the usual beginning—critique of Marx's law of labor value, and to stress the fact that "... outside the strictly Marxist ambit no living economist accepts Marx's value theory" (p. 178). The expression "living economist" is supposed to hide the fact that Dupré is both relying on bourgeois economists, and, at the same time, excluding Third World economists. It is true that he quotes two great econo-mists who are sympathetic to Marx—Joan Robinson and Joseph Schumpeter, but both are pragmatists, hostile to Hegelian dialectics, which Dupré certainly is not. Somewhere (I believe in the very essay Dupré quotes) Joan Robinson expresses her great indignation at Marx for constantly allowing Hegel to "stick his nose" into the field of economics:

> The concept of *value* seems to me to be a remarkable example of how a metaphysical notion can inspire original thought, though in itself it is quite devoid of operational meaning.[2]

Schumpeter, who is just as hostile to Hegelian dialectics in the economic field, nevertheless, was most profound in understanding why it was impossible to argue with Marx on strictly economic grounds, asking how you can argue with an "economist" like Marx when he is forever "transforming historic narrative into historic reason."[3]

The very first sentence of the "Economics" chapter states: "While the tenden-cy in the modern age has been to emancipate itself from any other functions of the cultural process, Marx's theory aims at reintegrating economic activity with the overall process of socialization" (p. 165). Despite that declaration, and despite the fact that Prof. Dupré over and over again disclaims any attempt on his part to consider Marx an economic determinist, we will see him here falling into what I consider the Engelsian trap, that is to say, quoting Engels as if that were a statement of Marx.

---

2   Joan Robinson, *Essay on Marxian Economics* (London: Macmillan, 1967), p. xi.
3   Joseph A. Schumpeter, *Capitalism, Socialism and Democracy* (London and New York: Rout-ledge, 1994), p. 44.

4   Marx and Engels Aren't One

On the second page of that "Economics" chapter he suddenly declares: "... Ever since he (Marx) had read Engels's 'Outline of Political Economy' (1844), he had known that an economic system, once established, cannot be simply dislodged by a better one" (p. 166). It is true that the young Marx as a philosopher was overly impressed with Engels' early essay on political economy. It is not true that he first got from Engels the concept of the solidity of the capitalist system.

Marx's *Economic-Philosophic Manuscripts*—which he described only orally to Engels that same year—had already singled out a great deal more than the need to break with capitalist society. Marx's Promethean view of new human relations had projected not only the need to overthrow capitalism but to establish such totally new human relations that communism was also rejected as "the goal of human society" [Appendix, p. 340]. On the contrary. Marx insisted: "Only by the transcendence of this mediation, which is nevertheless a necessary presupposition, does there arise positive Humanism, beginning from itself" [Appendix, p. 352].

Prof. Dupré has such a profound grasp of those 1844 *Manuscripts* and so much stresses the fact that Marx totally opposes a purely economic view, that it is hard to know how Dupré could have fallen into the trap. I believe it results from not grappling with the last decade of Marx's life. Despite Dupré's appreciation of Marx, not Engels, as the founder of a whole new continent of thought and revolution, he still treats Marx and Engels very nearly as one. Thus he writes as though Engels was right to claim that his *Origin of the Family, Private Property and the State* was a bequest of Marx:

> It is, of course, impossible to verify this claim, yet Marx's recently published ethnological notebooks appear to support it. Hence there is every reason to take Engels's work as, at least in substance, concordant with Marx's latest development. (p. 99)

Nothing could be further from the truth, as can be seen from the actual transcription of Karl Marx's *Ethnological Notebooks*, which discloses the wide gulf between Marx's multilinear view of human relations and Engels' unilinear view.

Engels' near identification of Lewis Henry Morgan as a "materialist" differs sharply from Marx's critical attitude to Morgan; Engels' view of women as suffering from some sort of "world historic defeat of the female sex" ever since the victory of patrilineal over matrilineal society sharply contrasts to Marx's multidimensional view of all human development.

Dupré couldn't have fallen into this trap if what he calls Marx's "application" of the dialectic to economic categories were actually Marx's transformation of that dialectic of thought to the dialectic that emerges out of the actual praxis of the masses, of the historic events that shaped and reshaped history, and developed into the dialectic of revolution itself—not only as an opposition, as a first negation, but as a continuity, as what Marx called "revolution in permanence."

5   What is Economics to Culture? And What is it to Revolution?

Dupré himself—despite his deep comprehension "in general" that Marx had the category of praxis as the divisive line between all different varieties of socialism and his own philosophy and practice of revolution—nevertheless makes this fantastic conclusion:

> Since the production of surplus value by means of surplus labor practically vanishes, revolutionary action loses its purpose. Marx did not pursue this line of thought. If he had, it might have changed his entire political program. (p. 192)

It is true he, himself, rejects that as Marx's view, but he nevertheless continues to manifest this ambiguity when he writes:

> Our present criticism bears only on the fact that Marx *singled out economic relations of production ... from the social complex as a whole as being more fundamental,* and that his work displays a *tendency* to regard these relations as being primarily determined by the *means* of production.... Yet the ambiguity remains.... (p. 215)

The "ambiguity" is Dupré's, not Marx's.

From Dupré's Introduction, "The Reintegration of Culture," to his Conclusion, "Culture Reintegrated through Praxis," he develops the unique view of Marx as a social critic of culture without in any way trying to hide Marx's disdain of bourgeois culture as he shows that Marx "the great critic exposed the spurious claims of a culture which had erected itself into an independent, quasi-religious reality, a dehumanized, denaturalized fetish" (p. 3).

And though he sees that praxis is a dividing line also within the Marxist movement, Dupré himself does not fully comprehend what Marx meant to express in the category of praxis. It was certainly a great deal more than practice, especially as intellectuals consider practice to be merely the practice of theory, rather than grasping that theory itself emerges out of praxis—and that praxis is an activity both manual and mental. Put differently, and as we have tried to show throughout this review, Marx saw workers' activity not only as action, not only as practice, but as Reason. Dupré grapples with it, and does tend to conclude that:

> Marx rescued productive labor from its cultural isolation. In his concept of praxis he attempted to reintegrate all facets of culture, the theoretical and aesthetic as well as the practical. (p. 280)

But since revolution is not exactly a preoccupation of Prof. Dupré, his view of Marx's Economics is presented quite ambiguously—for, without revolution, "Marxism" is not Marx's Marxism. Nevertheless, Marxists as well as non-Marxists will find it a serious study to grapple with as a challenging interpretation by an independent scholar.

PART 3

Post-Marx Marxism and the Battle of Ideas

∵

CHAPTER 11

Post-Marx Marxism as a Category

Dunayevskaya's full view of the differences between Marx and Engels, as well as her critique of many varieties of Marxists, grew out of the concept of Marx's Marxism as a totality that she developed while writing Rosa Luxemburg, Women's Liberation, and Marx's Philosophy of Revolution. *It coalesced into her concept of post-Marx Marxism as a pejorative, beginning with Engels, as a critical rather than chronological concept. This piece is included in* The Supplement to the Raya Dunayevskaya Collection, *pp. 15318–25.*

Three elements in relationship to a 1980s view in *Rosa Luxemburg, Women's Liberation, and Marx's Philosophy of Revolution* revolve around the making of post-Marx Marxists into a category that is derogatory and yet, in making up the index, I was opposed to listing every post-Marx Marxist, thus both giving too much "publicity" to characters who are very secondary, whether Maximilien Rubel or Jean-Paul Sartre or David Ryazanov. It is natural, of course, to oppose mixing up counterrevolutionaries with revolutionaries, but that is not what is stressed. A good part of our being "smarter" is not us but the maturity of the age, while the other equally important part was the movement from practice, along with our having all of Marx's documents. I stressed the fact that I was concerned only with revolutionaries.

Thus it happened that in the post-revolutionary citings in the index, we actually were concerned with revolutionaries, and, therefore, with the designation of post-Marx Marxism merely as a chronological idea.

In a word, for the post-Marx Marxists *as a category*, a derogatory category, I made it a phenomenon that begins with Engels, *not just* at the point when Marx died, but when Engels was collaborator with a live Marx. My main point was to show how we could be totally diverted from dialectics as a most original re-creation by Marx, by the very good intentions of Ryazanov, when he discovered that the first draft of the *Communist Manifesto* was written by Engels, publishing that and then having all the other post-Marx Marxists publishing *Marx's Communist Manifesto*, with a double signature of Karl Marx and Frederick Engels. And as if that were not bad enough, therefore to give the impression that the footnote [Engels added] after Marx's death, where Engels brought in his interpretation of Lewis Henry Morgan's *Ancient Society* as a *"correction,"* needed by the new developments in anthropology. Now let's go into this in great detail by repeating these facts but tying them strictly to methodology:

(1)   1847. Engels writes draft. It is in the form of a catechism, asking questions, answering questions, all of which are "correct," or at least not wrong, but it moves absolutely nowhere.

(2)   1847. Marx sees the draft and decides not to use that as ground. Instead, we have the work of a revolutionary genius, which challenges the whole bourgeois world and, with that specter haunting Europe, assuring the bourgeoisie that its days are numbered, while the proletariat is conquering power. It becomes the manifesto not only of the little Communist League that commissioned it, not only of the actual 1848 revolutions that follow, but the mark of all revolutions, climaxed in November 1917 in Russia.

(3)   1882. In the numberless texts published between 1847 and 1882, in having become a *world*-historic manifesto, no change is ever introduced into it, though errors have been acknowledged. Quite the contrary, the errors too are stressed as historic and not to be touched. What is touched is that 1882 Russian edition to which a P.S.[1] is added that outlines so new a perspective that it will actually not become reality until the death of both Marx and Lenin.

(4)   1883–1888. Engels issues a new edition in which, supposedly because Marx had not lived to see the great new developments, Engels puts a star into the very first sentence of that great historic challenge of [Chapter 1 of] the *Communist Manifesto:* "All history is the history of class struggles" [MECW 6, p. 482]. Engels claimed that that meant all *"written"* history and what had become available since that day *in writing* are the new findings by the new science of anthropology and for the analysis of those findings by Morgan, people should read Engels' *Origin of the Family, Private Property, and the State,* which was supposedly a bequest of Marx.

Now, first, Engels stopped both the poetic flow and the dialectic flow of that world-historic pronouncement. Secondly, he reduced the historic significance by making it a question of factual data. Thirdly, it isn't true that the facts he was talking about that the new science of anthropology discovered were found after Marx's death. The truth, rather, is that Marx not only knew them and made no less than a 98-page summary and commentary, but that he was trying very hard to convince Engels to please read Morgan's work. And Engels acknowledges as much when August Bebel and Karl Kautsky keep asking how it happens that Engels didn't know that Marx had left many, many, many unpublished manuscripts that Engels didn't know about. Engels then uses a twofold answer:

---

1   An apparent reference to the new preface signed by Marx and Engels for the 1882 Russian edition of the *Communist Manifesto.* —Editor.

(1) that, had he known, he would have bothered Marx to finish them; (2) Marx felt absolutely confident that Engels would be scrupulous and precise as to how he presented Marx.

Whatever it is that Engels thought he did, the point is: Why did the post-Engels Marxists, who were by now acquainted in part and knew material unknown to Engels, not only continued Engels' off-handed way, but what is worse and what really disoriented the next generation, raised up Engels to Marx's level? Isn't it *because* the *real* ground was Engelsian, and that includes Rosa Luxemburg? It is this—*just this*—which transformed post-Marx Marxists from a question of chronology to a derogatory category. They, at one and the same time, took liberties with what Marx had written and published *and* did not delve into all the new that they learned from these unpublished documents to create a true Marx-ground for both comprehending Marx and, in a Marx way—Marx, not Engels—to interpret their own period. Thus:

(1)   When the *Nachlass*[2] was first published, it was the person who published, edited, and introduced it, who became the big shot, and that was by no means restricted to Engels. It continued with Franz Mehring on the early material, with Kautsky on the *Theories of Surplus Value*, with Ryazanov on the 1844 *Manuscripts*. A truly serious confrontation with what was new in Marx and therefore in their comprehension of what they thought was Marxism occurred only after revolution. That is to say, the 1917 revolution brought the manuscripts to light, but it was only after still other total crises, like the 1930s and further revolutions which compelled original contributions for one's own age.

Therefore, when we confront our own age and do have the overwhelming part of his heritage available, we must in turn not limit ourselves to what is new but reconsider Marx from the very beginning as Marx and Marx alone.

---

2 *Nachlass,* meaning "legacy," refers to Marx's papers, including works unpublished during his lifetime. The word is used in the title of *Aus dem literarischen Nachlass von Karl Marx, Friedrich Engels und Ferdinand Lassalle* ("From the literary legacy of Karl Marx, Friedrich Engels and Ferdinand Lassalle"), several volumes of works by Marx, Engels, and Lassalle, edited by Franz Mehring and published beginning in 1902. It included some important early writings by Marx. Dunayevskaya criticized Mehring's editorializing and Luxemburg's commentary on it in *Rosa Luxemburg, Women's Liberation, and Marx's Philosophy of Revolution,* pp. 116–18. — Editor.

CHAPTER 12

Hobsbawm and Rubel on the Marx Centenary, but Where is Marx?

This essay originally appeared as the "Theory/Practice" column in the August-September 1982 issue of News & Letters.

With the approach of the centenary of Marx's death (March 1883), "specialists" are publishing their summations of the 64 years of Marx's life as well as the world impact Marxism still maintains 100 years after his death. Two such works in English are already off the press:

(1) *Rubel on Karl Marx*,[1] edited by Joseph O'Malley, consists of five essays by Maximilien Rubel, editor of the volumes of Marx issued by the prestigious French Bibliothèque de la Pléiade. Rubel's edition of Marx's works (to which we'll return) attempts to rival the "official" Russian-East German projected 100-volume collected works. Most of Rubel's essays appeared originally as introductions to the three volumes that have thus far appeared.

(2) *Marxism in Marx's Day*[2] is Volume I of *The History of Marxism,* edited by the English historian Eric J. Hobsbawm. It consists of eight essays by international scholars plus three essays and a Preface by Hobsbawm, whose contributions range from "Marx, Engels and Pre-Marxian Socialism" (Chapter 1), through "Marx, Engels and Politics" (Chapter 8), to a final Chapter 11 on "The Fortunes of Marx's and Engels' Writings."

Marx and Engels are here presented, if not as identical twins, surely as equal co-founders of Marxism—an attitude characteristic of *established* Marxism, whether of the period of the Second or of the Third International. Hobsbawm is in the tradition of that same superficial attitude, although on this centenary of Marx's death, when we finally do have substantially all of Marx's works, it is surely time to put an end to this "tradition." Isn't it time to focus on the fact that Marx's heirs kept the voluminous writings that had not been published in Marx's lifetime in that same unpublished state until the Russian Revolution unearthed them? And that soon thereafter—i.e., in Stalin's time—their publication was once again "arrested"? Isn't it time to end the myth that Marx

---

1 *Rubel on Karl Marx,* edited and translated by Joseph O'Malley and Keith Algozin, Cambridge University Press, 1981.

2 *The History of Marxism,* Volume I, edited by Eric J. Hobsbawm, Indiana University Press and Harvester Press (London), 1982.

and Engels are very nearly "one" and, instead, let us hear Marx, himself, as he continuously developed his ideas for 40 long creative years?

1   The Strange Affinity between Rubel and Hobsbawm

What is needed here is to see how such opposites as Hobsbawm and Rubel, who hold to politically opposite conclusions, nevertheless display an equally superficial attitude *to Marx's own discoveries*. How does it happen that neither Hobsbawm (who treats Marx and Engels as equal co-founders) nor Rubel (who maintains that not only are they not "one" but that Engels alone is the "founder of Marxism" and that, had Engels not invented "the legend of Marxism," there would be no Marxism) allow Marx to speak for himself?

Ignoring that Marx's life, activities and writings add up to a dialectical yet rigorous body of thought that constitute "Marxism," Rubel proceeds on his merry way to attribute his own view on Ethics to Marx, while Hobsbawm, who holds to the "scientific attitude" of Marx (i.e., "Economics" and some history), concludes that Marxism adds up to method alone, not deeply rooted in Hegelian dialectics. Therein, indeed, lies their strange affinity: both are anti-Hegelians.

Hobsbawm does include one essay on philosophy—"Marx 'Philosopher,'" by István Mészáros. Rubel's essays don't have that single redeeming feature. The question is why Rubel's editor, Professor O'Malley,[3] who knows both Hegel and Marx's "addiction" to Hegel, glosses over all the contradictory statements in Rubel? In his present Introduction, he declares: "Rubel is one of the world's foremost authorities on Marx" (p. vii).

It is true that Rubel, as editor of the independent French collection of Marx's writings, has brought out some heretofore unpublished works which included needed corrections to those Engels published.[4] It was especially great to see the re-establishment *in toto* of the genuine French edition of Marx's Volume I of

---

3   Joseph O'Malley has given us a profound, scholarly, superb translation and editing of Marx's *Critique of Hegel's "Philosophy of Right."* Perhaps I should have caught a whiff of his dependence on Rubel's "scholarship" when I read that work and called to Prof. O'Malley's attention the fact that he wrongly attributed the end of Marx's creative years to 1878, whereas new moments had been discovered anew by Marx in his *Ethnological Notebooks,* 1880–1882. (See my letter of August 30, 1979, included in the *Raya Dunayevskaya Collection: Marxist-Humanism 1941 to Today, Its Origin and Development in the U.S.* available on microfilm from the Wayne State University Labor History Archives Library.) In my forthcoming work *Rosa Luxemburg, Women's Liberation, and Marx's Philosophy of Revolution* (Humanities Press and Harvester Press, 1982), I have detailed Marx's New Moments in the 1880s as a Trail to the 1980s.

4   See Kevin A. Barry's comparison between Engels' editing of Marx's French edition of *Capital,* Vol. I, and Marx's own 1875 edition (*News & Letters,* October 1981).

Capital—that is, the one Marx himself checked, edited, and expanded. Unfortunately, though not one-sided in the manner of the Stalinist version, Rubel's is just as one-sided in its vision of Marx, and a great deal more arbitrary in the selections he has made than the liberties Engels allowed himself. Thus, Rubel's Volume II of *Capital,* while it does include some sections and paragraphs Engels left out, takes impermissible liberties with what Rubel chooses to single out. And he leaves out a great deal more than Engels did.[5]

Evidently, the fact that Maximilien Rubel is "an independent Marxist" (independent, that is, *of Marx*) carries enough attraction for Prof. O'Malley that not only does he not criticize Rubel's substitution of a self-created ethical Humanism for Marx's Humanism as the dialectics of revolution, but he goes to some length to praise Rubel's "Ethics" as if that were *Marx's* Marxism. The unfortunate result is seen in the very sequence of the five essays, which are not presented in the order in which they were written, but begin (and in a fundamental sense end with the same view) with "The 'Marx Legend,' or Engels, Founder of Marxism."

2   The Single Article on Philosophy

Does the single article on philosophy in Hobsbawm's collection of 11 essays plus preface save his book from the myths about Marx? Hardly. First, Mészáros does not deal with that subject at all. It is true that—in a non-polemical way, concentrating on Marx alone and refusing to limit himself to the young Marx as "philosopher"—Mészáros makes clear that

> Marx never stopped stressing the gigantic character of Hegel's achievements, brought to realization at an immensely important juncture of historical development in the aftermath of the French revolution in response to the most complex and dynamic interplay of social forces—including the emergence of labor as a hegemonic movement—in world history.

Furthermore, in showing that the mature Marx, like the young Marx, rooted his dialectic in the Hegelian dialectic, Mészáros opposes the one-sidedness of

---

5   Nothing is quite so unwarranted as the so-called volume on Philosophy, Vol. III of Rubel's editions, which has just come off the press in France. But that is not what we are concerned with in these essays, which were written long before.

interpretations which claim that Marx moved away from Hegelian idealism as if that meant a shift from philosophy to "science."

In sharp contrast to the pragmatism and the general scientistic orientation that pervades the rest of the Hobsbawm collection, Mészáros writes:

> ... the speculative verbal supersession of philosophy by "Theory," "Theoretical Practice," by the so-called "rigorous scientific concept of experimental reasoning," and the like, can only lead to a conservative rejection of the unity of theory and practice and to the sceptical dismissal of Marx's values as unrealizable dreams. (p. 109)

In documenting his insistence that the young Marx's attitude to philosophy (that one "cannot supersede philosophy without realizing it") characterized the mature Marx as well, Mészáros makes a powerful critique of Georg Lukács' view that there is an "identical Subject-Object" not only in Hegel, but in Marx. Mészáros writes that it was precisely Marx's critique of that "identical Subject-Object" which "helped Marx to reconstitute the dialectic on a radically different footing." "In Marx," he stresses, "the movement is *open-ended* and its fundamental intent is subversive, not reconciliatory." "Quite unlike Hegel," Mészáros concludes, Marx concentrates on "the unity of *the ideal and the material,* mediated through the dialectic of *theory and praxis.*"

The one weakness of the Mészáros contribution, to this writer, is that it centers around philosophy only "in general," rather than delving into the dialectics of revolution. The "historians" and theorists of political economy proceeded to fill the loophole thus created, which allows them to act as if they are the revolutionary realists and true heirs of Marx. In truth, they are the ones—as their editor, Eric J. Hobsbawm, proves all over again by not taking issue with post-Marx Marxists—who practice the most vulgar reductionism not alone of dialectics to "flexibility" but of revolution to statist class-collaborationism.

3   Ahistorical History

Because he is the editor as well as the author of three essays plus the Preface, it is Hobsbawm who gives his stamp to the entire work, and it is in the final chapter that he attempts to summarize the whole Marx legacy and its relevance for our age. The very title of that summation, "The Fortunes of Marx's and Engels' Writings," tells the ahistoric, empty rhetoric of this noted English historian. Thus, the revolution of 1917, in which Prof. Hobsbawm certainly believes, is mentioned somewhere, but is not seen as the ground for the total change in attitude toward Marx's works, which had remained until then entombed in the Second International's vaults. Instead, he begins with David Ryazanov, the scholar entrusted to head the Marx-Engels Institute.[6]

Along with this disregard of the historic, revolutionary motivation for creating the Institute, is the disregard of the philosophic transformation of no less a person than the leader of 1917, V.I. Lenin, who was the only one to break with his philosophic past and turn directly to Hegel, not for any scholastic reason, but because of the compulsion that arose from the outbreak of World War I and the Second International's betrayal.

It was this actual historic compulsion to grapple with Marx's origins in the Hegelian dialectic which continued *after* the revolutionary conquest of power. In the early 1920s Lenin urged the editors of *Under the Banner of Marxism* to call themselves a "Society of the Materialist Friends of Hegelian Dialectics," and to make sure "to print excerpts from Hegel's principal works."[7] And, of course, it was Lenin who inspired the establishment of a Marx-Engels Institute.

While it was the famous scholar-editor Ryazanov who became the first head of that Institute, it was Lenin, not Ryazanov, who had laid the ground for a serious study of Marx, for the publication of all his works, and for never forgetting that the Marxian dialectic is rooted in the Hegelian dialectic. There is no doubt that, both in erudition and in seriousness of excavating many unknown works of Marx, Ryazanov had a name none could equal. But there is also no doubt that Ryazanov displayed the usual intellectual arrogance not only to Lenin but to Marx, as can be seen in his attitude to Marx's work during the last decade of Marx's life—and to the *Ethnological Notebooks* in particular, which he dared to characterize as "sheer pedantry" without ever having read them.[8] It was this attitude that contributed to their remaining unpublished until our own age.

There can be little doubt today about Stalin's outright revisionism of Marxism, and the total transformation into opposite of the first workers' state into a state-capitalist society. That, however, is not the reason behind Ryazanov's

---

6   A longtime revolutionary, Ryazanov became the Marx-Engels Institute's first director and was instrumental in acquiring tens of thousands of manuscripts by Marx and Engels and other documents, publishing some previously unknown ones as important as Marx's 1844 *Economic-Philosophic Manuscripts*. Ryazanov was executed in Stalin's purges of the 1930s. —Editor.

7   V.I. Lenin, "On the Significance of Militant Materialism," *Collected Works*, Vol. 33 (Moscow: Progress Publishers, 1973), p. 234.

8   I deal with Ryazanov's 1923 Report on all the new writings he had discovered, in my forthcoming book [*Rosa Luxemburg, Women's Liberation, and Marx's Philosophy of Revolution*]. The report is available only in Russian and German. However, part of his report, but not including the reference to "sheer pedantry," is quoted in *The Ethnological Notebooks of Karl Marx* by its editor, Lawrence Krader. See especially pp. 355, 357, 374.

presumptuous attitude to the last writings of Marx. The removal of Ryazanov from his post in 1931 was part of the Stalin retrogressionism. But it was Ryazanov who, when he unearthed Marx's last writings in 1923, set the attitude to that legacy.

4   The Myth of Marx and Engels as One, and "Anti-Dühring"

It is not just Ryazanov whom Hobsbawm treats so uncritically. What is far more serious is that he has not a single word of criticism of any "official" post-Marx Marxist, and that Engels is treated very nearly as indistinguishable from Marx himself. It is true, of course, that without Engels we would not have had Volumes II and III of *Capital*; and it is true Engels was Marx's lifelong collaborator. It is *not* true that their close collaboration differed only to the extent that there was an agreed-upon "division of labor" between them *or* that the difference was only a question that Marx was a genius and the others were, at best, only talented. Engels himself admitted that. Now that we do have the over 500 pages of Marx's *Ethnological Notebooks* as against the few paragraphs Engels cites in his *Origin of the Family, Private Property, and the State,* in which he claims he is presenting their joint views, the myth must surely be ended, and the truth disclosed. This is *not* for academic reasons, but because of the urgency and relevance for our age, when a whole new Third World has emerged and a new Women's Liberation has moved from an Idea whose time has come to a *movement*, and because Marx laid the ground for penetration and action on both of these problematics.

It is a question not only of the *Origin*, published after Marx's death, which Engels claimed was a "bequest" of Marx, but of Engels' famous *Anti-Dühring*, which was published during Marx's lifetime when no claim was made that it represented both Marx and Engels; It was only in the editions published *after* Marx's death that Engels suddenly claimed the work represented both of them. This, unfortunately, became the ground of *Engels'* "Marxism" which was accepted by all post-Marx Marxists as such. Here is what Hobsbawm claims:

> There is no evidence whatever that Karl Marx expressed or felt any reservations about such works as Engels' *Anti-Dühring*, which is today often considered to embody specifically Engelsian positions.

The actual facts about *Anti-Dühring* begin in 1868 when Marx, after reading Eugen Dühring's review of *Capital*, called Engels' attention to that professor most critically (Letter of January 8, 1868), but got no response from Engels.

It was not until 1875–76, when Dühring's works got a following in the socialist movement and Wilhelm Liebknecht appealed to Engels to answer Dühring, that Engels turned to a review of all of Dühring's writings. But, far from submitting a plan for his work to Marx, he simply asked Marx to write a piece, not on Dühring's philosophy, but on his political economy. This Marx did; Engels cut it; and, without acknowledging Marx's contribution, it was made into Chapter 10 [of Part II], "Out of the *Critical History*."

Serious study and documentation about Marx's limited knowledge of Engels' *Anti-Dühring* has been done by Terrell Carver in his essay, "Marx, Engels and Dialectics," which was published in the September 1980 issue of *Political Studies*. Why does Eric Hobsbawm persist in the "official" myth? Hand in hand with philosophic indifference to the distinctions between Marx and Engels goes Hobsbawm's ahistorical attitude to questions of polemics.

Whenever this historian reaches a fundamental "polemical" divide, he searches not for its meaning, but for how to escape taking a position. The isolation of "scholarship" on Marx from the Russian Revolution was not the only instance. By skipping from the 1920s all the way to 1956, be avoided a single word about the very first opposition to Stalin by no less a person than Lenin's co-leader of the Russian Revolution, Leon Trotsky. Hobsbawm's attempt to disregard all differences within Marxism by claiming that his work is not "polemical" doesn't stand up when another state arises—Mao's China—and Hobsbawm finally uses the term "polycentric Marxism," which he has assigned to a future volume.

Thus far, the English reader has only the first volume of *The History of Marxism*—which was supposed to center on "Marxism in Marx's Day." The question is: Where, then, is Marx? We don't see him. What we are given are today's interpretations by a select few who deal with some aspects of Marx's multidimensional new continent of thought and of revolution. Far from expanding the expression, "polycentric Marxism," Hobsbawm has used it as a way to take back his one admission—that he hasn't paid attention to Marxists who have "attracted insignificant numerical support"—by also claiming: "but this statement implies no judgment about the relative contributions of the various organizations, large or tiny, to the Marxist analysis."

Hobsbawm's way of omitting history that he calls "polemical" is hardly distinguishable from expunging history as it is being made. Historians have ever been more adept at rewriting than at writing history. For that we must return to Marx and let him speak for himself.

DETROIT, MICH., JULY 30, 1982

CHAPTER 13

Marx's Philosophy of Revolution vs. Non-Marxist Scholar-Careerists in "Marxism"

This essay was originally published as the "Theory/Practice" column in the April 1984 issue of News & Letters.

The writings of non-Marxist scholars who are careerists in Marxism have become an industry unto itself. One such scholar, Terrell Carver, who has spent more than a decade in the field, published his first, quite promising study, *Karl Marx: Texts on Method*,[1] in 1975. His latest work, *Marx and Engels: The Intellectual Relationship*,[2] will be followed (in a soon-to-be-published 1984 symposium, *After Marx*[3]) with an article entitled "Marxism as Method," a title very similar to the first book he published. But the recent works appear to be totally the opposite of what Carver first seemed to be saying.

The reader had every right to read into that 1975 work, which focused on Marx's methodology, that the author meant dialectic methodology as Marx had transformed the Hegelian dialectic, which had created a revolution *in philosophy*, into a dialectics *of revolution*. That principle had permeated Marx's entire adult life, so that it mattered not at all whether the subject under discussion was philosophy or political economy; whether it was a matter of working out in theory a dialectics of revolution and writing a Manifesto for an organization that called for revolution, or actual participation in an ongoing revolution and even after its defeat declaring for "revolution in permanence."[4] Therefore, it did not seem to matter at all whether a study of Marx was undertaken by a Marxist or a non-Marxist who had delved into the field merely as a scholarship pursuit.

The two texts Carver had chosen to concentrate on seemed most impressive and objective in that regard. One was the Introduction to the *Grundrisse*, which

---

1 *Karl Marx: Texts on Method*, translated and edited by Terrell Carver (Oxford: Basil Blackwell, 1975).
2 Terrell Carver, *Marx and Engels: The Intellectual Relationship* (Bloomington: Indiana Univ. Press, 1983).
3 *After Marx*, edited by T. Ball and J. Farr, is soon to be published by Cambridge University Press.
4 See [March 1850] *Address to the Communist League*, available in many sources, including *Karl Marx and Frederick Engels, Collected Works*, Vol. 10. (New York: International Publishers, 1978) [MECW 10, pp. 277–87].

had first come to light in our age and proved—even to opponents of the Hegelian dialectic and proponents of "scientific economics," like the Althussers—that the "mature Marx" had most definitely not discarded "philosophy" as he made his profound analysis of "the economic law of motion of modern society" [MCIK, p. 14; MCIP, p. 92]. It is true that Carver was presenting a new translation and commentary on only the Introduction of the *Grundrisse*, but there was no way of missing Marx's multidimensionality, his sweep of human development as the absolute opposite to capitalist wealth and alienated labor as well as to pre-capitalist society. Marx had, after all, held out a Promethean vision of a new society "where man does not reproduce himself in any determined form, but produces his totality. Where he does not seek to remain something formed by the past, but is in the absolute movement of becoming" [*Grundrisse*, p. 488].[5]

Carver furthermore made some quite original contributions as he called attention to the fact that, profound and comprehensive as was Marx's Introduction, the post-Marx Marxists had narrowed their vision to make the only reigning principle of Marxian methodology to be a "development from the abstract to the concrete." Carver correctly stressed that that was *not* the method that characterized the Preface to Marx's *Critique of Political Economy*. As Marx explained:

> I omit a general introduction which I had prepared as on second thought any anticipation of results that are still to be proven, seemed to me objectionable, and the reader who wishes to follow me at all must make up his mind to pass from the particular to the general....[6]

The second "Marx text" Carver chose to translate anew and comment on—"Notes (1879–80) on Adolph Wagner"—further reinforced the view that Carver was entering the contemporary field of challenging reigning Marx-interpretations by self-appointed Marx "specialists" who imprison everything in so-called "orthodoxy" when what is needed is a serious grappling with Marx's Marxism instead of inventing unbridgeable gulfs between the "young" and the "mature" Marx. Here was a document from Marx's last years in which he was reaffirming that his dialectic methodology and the historically concrete commodity were inseparables. Moreover, commodity related not to a mere thing; the twofold

---

5 See Karl Marx, *Pre-Capitalist Economic Formations* (New York: International Publishers, 1965), p. 85.

6 Karl Marx, *A Contribution to the Critique of Political Economy* (Chicago: Charles H. Kerr, 1904), p. 9 [MECW 29, p. 261].

nature of the commodity reflected the twofold character of labor—abstract and concrete—Marx's original contribution without which, he claimed, no scientific understanding of political economy is possible.

Nothing in all this could possibly have prepared the reader for the shock of reading Carver's latest article on "Marxism as Method," as he rushes to conclude:

> Marx's actual method in dealing with political economy was *eclectic* and very complex. He used classical and Hegelian logic, and the *techniques* of mathematical, sociological, economic, historical and political analysis.... This *eclectic* method included a notion of dialectic as the *specification* of conflictual, developmental factors in analyzing social phenomena, and we know that Marx found this helpful in dealing, for example, with the concepts of money and profit. (My emphasis)

So opposite a picture of Carver emerges from his first book and his most recent writings that one is tempted to ask: Who is the "real" Terrell Carver? The answer, I believe, is revealed in an article—"Marx's Commodity Fetishism"[7]— written the same year as *Karl Marx: Texts on Method* was published. It is there we read: "In 1842 he (Marx) had read a 1785 German translation of Charles de Brosses's *Cult of the Fetish-Gods,* published anonymously in Paris in 1760." Supposedly, "Marx used the word 'fetish' in this eighteenth- and nineteenth-century sense" (p. 50). This is further substantiated by him with a definition straight from the Oxford English Dictionary: "An inanimate object worshipped by savages on account of its supposed inherent magical powers, or as being animated by a spirit."

It is absurd to consider that Marx would have followed an Oxford English Dictionary definition after a full quarter of a century of labor studying the commodity—at the end of which he was still so dissatisfied that, following the Paris Commune, he returned to his masterpiece, *Capital,* to introduce fundamental changes both in Chapter 1 and in the section on "Accumulation of Capital," asking even the reader familiar with the original edition to nevertheless read that 1872–75 French edition.[8]

---

7 Terrell Carver, "Marx's Commodity Fetishism," *Inquiry,* 18, pp. 39–63.
8 Over the years, I have traced not only Marx's concept of the fetishism as he described it in 1867 and in the 1872–75 French edition, but how Chapter 1, especially its concluding section on fetishism, has become central to all the debates over Marx the dialectician and Marx the "economist" at every single critical turning point in the objective situation. These debates begin with the call by the first revisionist, Eduard Bernstein, for the removal of the "dialectical scaffolding"; achieve a Great Divide in Marxism with Lenin's Abstract of Hegel's *Science*

It is in the section on fetishism—in which Marx had seen that the mystical character which has human relations reduced to "material relations between persons and social relations between things"—that he now, after the Paris Commune, declared that only "freely associated" men and women can strip away that fetish. Carver makes short shrift of all of this by paying no attention whatever to such *historical* truths and dialectical relations.

The truth is that Carver totally rejects Marx's dialectic, including the whole labor theory of value and surplus value. He is so eaten up with hostility to Marx that in this article he strikes out also against the great economist Joan Robinson,[9] who, though she rejects Marx's dialectics, recognizes his great contributions to economics. Here is the arrogance with which Carver wipes his hands of all that:

> If the arguments for his critical re-presentation of the labor theory of value are unconvincing, then there is no reason to accept his views precisely as he expressed them, and that is that. (p. 59)

The one-paragraph Preface to *Marx and Engels: The Intellectual Relationship,* in which Carver calls attention to his Marx-Engels Chronology, may shed some illumination—but for very different reasons than he had in mind when he wrote that he hoped "the reader will find the Marx-Engels Chronology at the end of the book useful in following my account of two complicated careers ..." The Chronology illuminates not so much the Marx-Engels relationship as the pragmatic, non-revolutionary presuppositions that are weighing heavily on the author.

Thus: 1) Missing entirely are the 1848 Revolutions or any writings during that period. No wonder there is not a word of the famous March 1850 *Address to the Communist League,* written after the defeat of those Revolutions, in which Marx and Engels declared for the "revolution in permanence." In place of revolution—either the particular ones in France and Germany, or "in

---

of Logic; and reach the post-WWII period with Sartre on one side and Althusser on the other. See *Marxism and Freedom,* especially Chapter x ("The Collapse of the Second International and the Break in Lenin's Thought"); *Philosophy and Revolution,* Chapter 2, Section C ("The Adventures of the Commodity as Fetish"), as well as Chapter 6, on Jean-Paul Sartre, especially Section B ("The Dialectic and the Fetish"); and *Rosa Luxemburg, Women's Liberation, and Marx's Philosophy of Revolution,* Part Three ("Karl Marx—From Critic of Hegel to Author of *Capital* and Theorist of 'Revolution in Permanence' ").

9   One way Joan Robinson rejected dialectics was expressed when she told me that she wished Marx had told Engels all his economic theories, so Engels could have presented them in clear English.

permanence"—what determines this so-called independent study of Marx is the concept of "career," "vocation." Carver goes so far as to picture, in this latest book, Engels losing out to Marx because he "lacked Marx's single-minded political thrust and unifying sense of vocation" (p. xiii).

2) The 1860s fare as badly in the Chronology as the revolutions that covered Europe in the 1840s. We are told nothing of the Polish Revolt, or the Civil War in the U.S., or the General Strikes in France—all of which resulted in the establishment of the International Workingmen's Association (First International), headed by Marx. Not only that. Along with Marx's activities came also the many restructurings of *Capital,* which led, at one and the same time, to relegating the history *of theory* to Volume IV. *Instead, "history and its process" became the center, the determinant for Marx. This means little to Carver, as is obvious from the fact that he also leaves out of his Chronology what was the greatest revolution in Marx's time—the Paris Commune*—which led to the definitive French edition of Marx's greatest Work, *Capital,*[10] and which, in illuminating that intellectual relationship between Marx and Engels, would have thereby revealed what Marx's Marxism is.

3) Instead, Carver presents the last years of Marx's life so loosely that outright factual errors have crept in. The reader doesn't know whether Carver really does know the *Ethnological Notebooks* or was led to believe by Engels that they were concerned only with Morgan's *Ancient Society,* and to believe, further, that Engels had included all of Marx's study in his own very first work after Marx's death—*The Origin of the Family, Private Property, and the State*—as a "bequest" of Marx. No wonder that Carver does not subject Engels' very first "substantial" work after Marx's death to any critical examination. [*This author considers that work to be the most serious deviation from Marx's Marxism, whether that be the concept of Man/Woman in the 1844 Essays or as it was developed in the full* Ethnological Notebooks.[11]] A reading of those Notebooks would have proved to Carver that his conclusions that Marx and Engels are not "one" is by no means limited to the difference in Engels' presentation of

---

10   See Chapter X of *Rosa Luxemburg, Women's Liberation, and Marx's Philosophy of Revolution,* especially Section 2 ("*Capital:* Significance of the 1875 French Edition of Vol. I"). See also "The French Edition of *Capital,* 100 Years After," a paper presented by Kevin Anderson to the Conference of the Eastern Sociological Society, Philadelphia, March 19, 1982.

11   In 1972, Marx's Notebooks, titled *The Ethnological Notebooks of Karl Marx* (Assen: Van Gorcum, 1972), were finally transcribed by Lawrence Krader. For my analysis see especially Chapter XII, Section 2 ("The Unknown *Ethnological Notebooks,* the Unread Drafts of the Letter to Zasulich, as well as the Undigested 1882 Preface to Russian Edition of the *Communist Manifesto*") in *Rosa Luxemburg, Women's Liberation, and Marx's Philosophy of Revolution.*

Anti-Dühring before and after Marx's death. It is no wonder that the way Carver presents the situation ends with his total rejection of Marx and praise of Engels, though it began the other way around.

In his latest work, *Marx and Engels: The Intellectual Relationship,* Carver devotes no less than two of the five chapters of the book to Engels, *before* the lifelong association was established in the autumn of 1844. This presentation, indeed, overshadows Marx's development in the crucial 1842–44 period. The first encounter between Marx and Engels in 1842, presented by Carver in Chapter 1 ("The False Start"), led nowhere, but Carver shows in great detail what Engels wrote in that period. The same holds true for 1843, which was a great turning point in Marx's life—not only personally, as his break with bourgeois society shows, but objectively, as his writing shows. But, again, the focus is on Engels, not on Marx, specifically on the article, "Outlines of a Critique of Political Economy," which Engels had submitted to Marx's journal in Paris, and which greatly impressed Marx.

What is important is not that it greatly impressed Marx *then,* but that Carver is so overwhelmed by it *now,* 140 years later, that he elevates it to a status above Marx's famous 1844 Essays, which initiated the discovery of a whole new continent of thought and revolution. Completed the month before the meeting with Engels in mid-August, Marx's views had so great an impact on Engels himself (even though he heard the concepts only in an abbreviated oral form) that a lifelong collaboration of the two revolutionaries resulted.

Terrell Carver, the hidebound eclectic, turns all this upside down. Thus: 1) Carver claims (p. 41) that since Marx's "excerpt-notes" contain a resume of Engels' "Outlines," it is, in fact, Engels who inspired Marx's now famous 1844 *Economic-Philosophic Manuscripts.*

2) Not only that. Carver further considers those 1844 *Manuscripts* "an *intermediate* stage of conceptual elaboration between Engels' critique of the economists' basic categories, and the much crisper 'premises' of *The German Ideology*" (p. 41, my emphasis), a collaborative effort of the two in 1845, which they later consigned to the "gnawing criticism of the mice."

3) Still not satisfied with his reduction of Marx's 1844 *Manuscripts* as something reflecting Engels' "methodology," Carver concludes: "The methodology, however, was *adopted from Engels' 'Outlines,'* where there was a focus on 'contradictions' in social life" (p. 54, my emphasis).

4) Finally, Carver concludes that "The theoretical, empirical and even in some respects political and historical virtues of Engels' work were substantially degraded when he settled into his role as Marx's 'second fiddle' " (p. 155).

Of course, when one has praised Marx's "eclecticism," spelled out his scientific, rigorous and voluminous concrete economic studies, stressing the meticulousness of his studies, how can one conclude that Marx's methodology, which led to his conclusion about the law of motion of capitalism, is mechanically "derived" from Hegel's categories in the Logic? Fiction in place of fact oozing out of Carver's eclecticism should not surprise us any more than his crediting Marx's methodology in the 1844 Manuscripts to Engels.

What all this proves, to this author, is that the totality of the crises of our age, in thought as well as in material conditions, is so unrelenting in its stranglehold over pragmatism that it becomes impossible for the non-Marxist scholars to cut themselves free and make any real contribution to the knowledge of *Marx's* Marxism as a totality.

CHAPTER 14

Paul Mattick: Economism vs. Marx's Humanism

Today's revival of interest in Marx's crisis theory, especially since the onset of the 2008 economic meltdown, includes a significant strain of economism and has revived controversies and issues addressed by Dunayevskaya. This review-essay of Paul Mattick's book Marx and Keynes *first appeared in the "Two Worlds" column of the January 1970* News & Letters.

Marx and Keynes: The Limits of the Mixed Economy, by Paul Mattick (Boston: Extending Horizons Books, 1969), is a most disappointing book. Or perhaps the more correct description would be: a most revealing book. In part, this is due to its sheer length (364 pages), which allows the author to make explicit what, heretofore, as essayist, he left only implicit. But the more fundamental reason for the revelatory character of the book is the *timing*. Ever since the Hungarian Revolution moved the Humanism of Marxism front-center of the historic stage, it has become impossible for *economism* to hide its underlying anti-Marxism.

Thus, though there was no backtracking on the part of Mattick from his wide knowledge of Marxian as well as Keynesian economics, and though the lucidity of his style in book form is as illuminating as it has been these many years in essay form, *the full book-length form, and the timing, revealed a shocking truth: his anti-Leninist obsession is, in reality, anti-Marxism.*

Should this description of a Marxian *economist* sound defamatory, the reader must listen to Mattick himself. The revelation of his rejection of Marx's Humanism is his, not mine. It is he, not I, who is appalled at

> the recent vogue of the socialist humanism of the young Marx, who considers the alienation of labor in capitalism a result of the "alienation of man from his true nature." This *unMarxian Marx* well fits the welfare state and can even be used in the ideological war against the ideological Marxism of the state-capitalist adversary. (p. 282, emphasis added)

1   The Rewriting of History

How like the state-capitalist ideologists calling themselves Communists—as well as today's Trotskyists—Paul Mattick sounds! *His* rewriting of history, no doubt, has different motivations than either those holding state-capitalist power, or hungering to do so. But this does not turn untruths into truths.

It was not the "welfare state," but the Hungarian Freedom Fighters, the *proletarian* revolutionaries, who brought Marx's Humanism from the musty bookshelves onto the world historic stage. It is not "the recent" welfare state ideologist's "use" of the "unMarxian Marx" that has produced the "vogue," but the ceaseless East European revolts, from East Berlin, 1953, to Czechoslovakia, 1968, that keeps Marx's Humanism alive. The "young Marx's" philosophy of liberation became, also, the underlying philosophy of the African Revolutions against Western Imperialism. Nor did Marx's Humanism, in circling the globe, come to a standstill as it reached the so-called welfare states. On the contrary. In reaching the world citadel of the "welfare states," the U.S., the theory of alienation of the "unMarxian Marx," far from "fitting" the welfare state, gave birth to a new generation of revolutionaries, Black and white, who sought and are seeking to uproot it.

Indeed, to come from the sublime to the petty, even the aloof and mature Paul Mattick has been compelled to acknowledge the history-making long life of the now famous 1844 Economic-Philosophic Manuscripts, *albeit in a slanderous form.*

No doubt the "mature" Marxist *economist* had known of these long before now (1969, the year of publication of his *Marx and Keynes*). No doubt he knew about them long before the very first East European uprising of the East German workers who dared challenge both Russian Imperialism and their own state-capitalist overlords of the productive process. Simultaneously with that movement *from below* in the birthplace of Marx, a few brave intellectuals also confronted the Communist ideologists with Marx's Humanism. This *dual* movement, from practice and from theory, however, had no more effect on Mattick's *economist* interpretation of Marx than the very first discovery of Marx's Humanist Essays in the late 1920s by the great Marxist scholar David Ryazanov. It needed a social revolution as great as October 1917 before it became possible to pry this unpublished heritage of Marx from the vaults of the Second International, where they had lain buried since the death of Engels.

In a word, at no time from their first discovery, through the period they made history anew in live class battles, until today, did the authentic voice of Marx— of Marx, not Lenin, of Marx's philosophy of liberation, not of Lenin's theory of the "vanguard party"—cause Mattick to question his economist interpretation of Marx.

On the contrary, instead of facing the reality of his failure to fully comprehend the philosophy of Marx, he stoops to Stalinist-type amalgam-building. The "vogue" of Marx's Humanism, he now dares claim, "fits" the welfare state!

2   What is Economism?

Paul Mattick's presumptuousness in declaring the authentic voice of "the young Marx" to be that of some "unMarxian Marx" has one salutary effect upon the reader who has had to struggle through 282 pages before being thrown this curve. Till then, he had been wondering why the lucid author had thrown 42 chapters at him without doing so simple a thing as dividing the many chapters into a few leading parts to give the reader some indication of where the author was headed. Now the reader, having been made wiser by this unexpected curve, feels compelled to return to the beginning of the formless book to see what is Mattick's comprehension of Marxism.

The first chapter where Paul Mattick deals directly with Marx on Marx's own, not John Maynard Keynes', foundations is Chapter 3, "Marx's Labor Theory of Value." This, and the chapters on "Accumulation and the Falling Rate of Profit" as well as the two chapters on "The Realization of Surplus Value," and "Capitalism in Crises" are the best in the book. Mattick has always written seriously when criticizing Marxists who departed from the "materialism" of Marx. On that point he is even capable of escaping his own narrow economism.

Thus, in taking other Marxian *economists* to task, he writes:

> When Marx speaks of the "law of value" as *relating* to a deeper reality which underlies the capitalist economy, he refers to the "life process of society based on the material process of production." (p. 29)

Thus, also, he criticizes George Lichtheim for identifying the Ricardian and Marxian law of value while heaping empty praise upon Marx as "the last, as well as the greatest of the classical economists." Mattick comments: "Even though Marx accepted and developed Ricardo's value theory, he was not the 'greatest' of the classical economists, but their adversary" (p. 28).

Here he himself draws a sharp distinction between narrow economism and Marx's concept of the "life process of society based on the material process of production." Nor does Mattick limit his criticism to reformists, but extends it to revolutionary Marxists. Thus, he hits out against Rudolf Hilferding for reducing Marx's materialist conception of history to the value theory:

> ... the materialist conception of history is not identical with the labor theory of value. It discusses social development in general, of which capitalism is only a special case. (p. 34)

Nor, Mattick continues, is it "merely a question of conscious as against uncon-
scious regulation" (p. 35). *The law of value, and, inseparably from it, the law of
surplus value, applies to capitalist societies and only to them.*

It is true Mattick conveniently skips over my exposé of Stalin's open break
with Marx's theory of value in 1943 at the time it happened, but, at least in 1969,
he does write of it. It helps him also to expose Paul Sweezy's apologia of Russian state-capitalism as if statification of industry plus "the principle of planning" is all that is needed to establish "socialism." But, while Mattick hits away
at reformist and Communist economists, he himself does not break out of
economism's confines in the full tradition of the revolutionary Marx, who did
not separate philosophy from economics *because his* Promethean vision of a
classless society united, instead of divided, materialism and idealism into that
new human dimension he called "a thoroughgoing Naturalism or Humanism."

3   What is Philosophy?

So foreign, to Mattick, is the integrality of Marx's philosophy of history with
his economic categories that he makes a total hash out of Marx's *original* economic categories. Mattick forces into identity Marx's split of classical political
economy's category of labor into *abstract* and *concrete* labor, and the further
singling out from labor, as activity, its commodity-form of appearance, *labor-
power.* Where Marx speaks of the twofold character of labor, Mattick "restates"
it as "the twofold character of labor-power" (p. 57).

The obtuseness of Mattick to *Marx's* philosophic analysis of the all-pervading
fetishism of commodity-*form*, literally calls for him to make such false identification as if it were, indeed, the commodity rather than the activity which
"produces" value and surplus value. The twofold character of the commodity—
use-value and exchange-value—is of course only the phenomenal expression,
the cover-up of the exploitative relationship at the point of production, all of
which Mattick "knows" very well. Then why attempt, with a single stroke of
the pen, to do away with the fetishism of commodities by identifying Marx's
analysis of labor, as activity, with labor-power as commodity?

Had the mature Mattick followed Marx into the labor process itself, he
could not have mixed up "economic categories" and could not have escaped
seeing the labor-capital relationship as not only an exploitative one, but also a
perverted one. Throughout the four volumes of *Capital*, the most mature Marx
pounds away at this capitalistic perversion—the reification of labor, the transformation of man into a thing *and* the revolt of the workers against this.

Evidently, for the knowledgeable Paul Mattick, the commodity-form holds no secrets; labor and labor-power may appear synonymous to one who doesn't feel the full weight of the capitalistic *perversion* of subject to object, of man into mere appendage to machine, of the transformation of concrete labor into the abstraction, value. But Marx, after laboring more than a decade with the exposition of the fetishism of the commodity-*form* which, on the surface, appeared so simple that all "took it for granted," was still dissatisfied even after the first edition of *Capital* was published in 1867.

It was *only after* the workers had shown themselves anew as creative "Subject," and not merely as exploited "substance," by "storming the heavens"[1] and creating a totally *new form* of workers rule—the Paris Commune; and *only after* Marx himself analyzed this greatest revolution of his lifetime—*The Civil War in France*—that he again reworked that most famous section of Chapter 1, "The Fetishism of Commodities" in the French edition of *Capital*, 1872–75. Only then was he finally satisfied with the simplicity of his answer to the question: Whence the fetishism of commodities? "From the form itself" [MCIK, p. 82; MCIP, p. 164].

The whole point was that not only is the form "fantastic" that makes "social relations appear as material relations between things," but that, under capitalism, that is what "they really are" [MCIK, p. 84; MCIP, p. 166].

Without full comprehension of *this* philosophy, Mattick ends, not only by separating what Marx had united—philosophy and economics—but, inescapably, isolates himself from the voices from below in his era and thus falls prey to Keynes. This is so, not because he *doesn't*, as a Marxist economist, criticize Keynes as bourgeois. It is so because, in his preoccupation with Keynes, he proceeds undisturbed by proletarian attitudes to the decades from the 1930s to the end of the 1960s; that is to say, from the Depression to the technological revolutions culminating in Automation.

The result is that his only "original" category for world economic development of our era is "mixed economy." Even the concept of state-capitalism becomes subordinated to the "theory" of the mixed economy. No wonder he falls such easy prey to the Keynesian "revolution" in economics that he reverses history itself to make it fit the economic theories of Keynes. "Though carried out in the name of Marx," writes Mattick (in referring both to the 1917 Revolution and to the imperialist adventures of present-day Russian Communism, *as well as the African*

---

1   Quoted from a letter from Marx to Ludwig Kugelmann, April 12, 1871 [MECW 44, p. 132], referring to the Paris Commune. —Editor.

Revolutions[2] *which broke out spontaneously,* totally unconnected with Communism), "the state capitalist or state socialist revolutions would be better described as 'Keynesian revolutions' " (p. 279).

4   Mattick's Hostility to the Proletariat

We have no time to waste on exposing such a fantastic turning upside down of actual social revolutions which produced phenomenal changes in bourgeois economics, not to mention Mattick's *retiming* of history so that Keynesian economics, which was not born until the 1930s, nevertheless "fits" 1917. What is of importance is that this has led him to bring into the open his anti-proletarian "philosophy," which, both objectively and subjectively, does indeed fit in with state-capitalism *and* "welfare state" ideologists as well as with all who have departed from Marxism.

Like all of them, Mattick abuses Marx's vision of the revolutionary nature of the proletariat—"The proletariat is revolutionary or it is nothing"—in order to shout loud his hostility to the proletariat: "At present it (the proletariat) is nothing ..." (p. 337).

It is this anti-proletarian attitude that is his one true underlying "philosophy," be it in his analysis of Marx, whom he is supposed to be following, or of Keynes, whom he is supposed to be opposing; be it in his professional anti-Leninism or in his deliberately ambiguous degrading of the African Revolutions. It is this hostility to the proletariat that has caused his self-paralysis every time he faces the integrality of philosophy and revolution.

---

2   For a discussion of the African Revolutions, see my *Nationalism, Communism, Marxist Humanism and the Afro-Asian Revolutions*. For an on-the-spot report directly from Africa, see my *Political Letters*, Nos. 34 thru 39. Both are available through News and Letters Committees.

CHAPTER 15

Bertell Ollman: Pitting "Human Nature" against Marx's Humanism

This essay first appeared as the "Two Worlds" column in the November 1972 issue of News & Letters.

The intellectual's alienated life in a world in crisis and disarray, his organic empiricism and isolation from the worker, bid fair to inundate us with still more books on the "backwardness" of the proletariat. As if the 308 pages of *Alienation* by Bertell Ollman (New York: Cambridge University Press, 1971) weren't proof enough of that being its underlying concept, its author informs us: "I intend to explore the workers' difficulty in attaining class consciousness in greater detail in a forthcoming work" (p. 307).

This promise is no individualistic exception. Hard as it is to believe that academia will once again attempt to return us to the McCarthyite 1950s when bourgeois intellectuals were busy proclaiming an "end to ideology," the Nixon age unnerves even some intellectuals sympathetic to Marx. This has been a fact of life ever since the near-revolutions in 1968 proved to be stillbirths. Not only does the mass passion for a philosophy of liberation, when so many aborted revolutions are all about us, appear incomprehensible to the intellectual separated from the workers by a wall of books, but Marx's works themselves, if not totally incomprehensible, get so fragmented as to become abstract, losing their proletarian pivot as well as their dialectic totality.

Thus, where the left intellectual, in the activist mid-1960s, would not have thought of trying to bring about a division between Marx's theory of alienated labor and its inseparable absolute opposite, "the quest for universality" [MECW 6, p. 190] the same intellectual, in the early 1970s, strives so intensely to be original as to attribute to Marx a theory of human nature he never enunciated, while denying Marx *his* new continent of thought—historical materialism as a "new Humanism." Professor Ollman acts as if the "attempt to make Marxism 'respectable' to a hostile American public" compelled Erich Fromm "to abstract his (Marx's) remarks on human nature from the rest of his theories in order to present him as a humanist" (p. 75).

1   The Unity of Idealism and Materialism

It wasn't Fromm, but Marx, who spelled out his new Humanism as a thoroughgoing Naturalism, or Humanism, [which] distinguishes itself both from Idealism and Materialism, and is, at the same time, the truth uniting both ... [and alone] capable of grasping the act of world history.[1]

Moreover, this historic unity of idealism and materialism was expressed by Marx over and over again throughout the now famous 1844 *Economic-Philosophic Manuscripts* that dealt so profoundly with the concept of alienation which is the centerpiece of Ollman's book.

So determined was Marx, in his critique of capitalistic alienated labor, to present the absolute opposite of this—labor as creative activity—that he separated himself also from "vulgar communism" which thinks that alienated labor can be abolished through the abolition of private property. Marx held that, crucial as it is to abolish private property, a new form of property (though it be collective) would not abolish what is most dehumanizing in all class societies: the division between mental and manual labor.

Therefore, though he credits communism with being "transcendence of private property," he concludes: "Only by the transcendence of this mediation, which is nevertheless a necessary presupposition, does there arise *positive* Humanism, beginning from itself" [Appendix, p. 352]. That, and that alone, would denote the end of the *pre*-history of mankind imposed by class society, and begin the true self-development of men and women and children by creating the new human dimensions which can come only with total freedom. Then, and only then, would we know "human nature." Then, and only then, would a new society initiate "the development of human power which is its own end."[2]

Ollman would not deny this. Why then could this scholarly left intellectual not grasp the dialectics of Marx's analysis of alienation *and* humanism, of the capital/labor relationship not merely as an "internal" versus an "external" relationship, but as so antagonistic a class relationship that he couldn't possibly have written so narrowly, so one-sidedly and in so non-revolutionary a manner as Ollman about alienated labor, i.e., the very subject who is destined to achieve self-emancipation?

---

1 There are many translations finally available of the Humanist Essays of Marx, but I was the first to translate them for the American public, and I am quoting that translation which appeared as an Appendix to the first (1958) edition of *Marxism and Freedom* [Appendix, p. 347].

2 It is important to hold in mind that this is not from the early Humanist Essays, but from Marx's greatest mature theoretical work, *Capital* (Vol. III, p. 954 [MCIIIK, p. 954; MCIIIP, p. 959]). This does not mean, as Bertell Ollman implies, that Marx's thirty years of mature work was a matter of gathering "supporting material" for his early works. That unhistorical view tells the whole story about Ollman's disregard of Marx's self-development as well as of the historical development itself in those critical three decades when Marx was writing *Capital*.

2   Dialectics vs. Empiricism

Far from having to go in for abstractions as to "human nature" to get a view of "future" "communistic" society, as the professor has him do, Marx was most specifically, rigorously and solely concerned with the concrete capitalistic society under which he lived, *its* "law of motion" [MCIK, p. 14; MCIP, p. 92], *its* antagonistic class duality, *its* reified labor (its reified labor, not reified products) out of which, nevertheless, dialectically emerge the "new passions and new forces" for uprooting the old and reconstructing society on totally new, humanist foundations.

Just as Marx couldn't have written of capital without writing of its opposite, its gravedigger, so he couldn't have written about the *theory* of alienation without its opposite, the philosophy of liberation Marx called "the new Humanism."

3   Dialectics vs. Linguistics

The trouble with Professor Ollman, as with all empiricists, is that he has reduced dialectics to a question of linguistics. The very first chapter of his book on Marx—"With Words like Bats"—holds that Vilfredo Pareto has thereby made the most "profound observations ... on our subject" for "one can see in them [bats] both birds and mice" (p. 3). That attitude carries through the last chapter, in which he writes: "If Marx is given highest marks for creating Marxism, he can only be given a mediocre rating for his skills as a communicator" (p. 236). This is hardly an original critique on the part of academia. The great English economist Joan Robinson told me in all seriousness that she wished Marx had told all his views to Engels and had him present Marx's discoveries since Engels wouldn't have had Hegel "stick his nose between Ricardo and me."

Ollman does her one better. He *invents* words for Marx! Marx's whole philosophy of liberation, his analysis of the law of motion of capitalist production, along with the antagonistic capital/labor production relationship, get subsumed under Ollman's description of Marxism as a "philosophy of internal relations." In pursuance of his original "discovery," especially the capitalization of Relation, miracles are indeed wrought in "Marx's vocabulary" as Ollman not only treats Marx and Engels as one on the very subject—dialectics—on which they most certainly were not identical (as none, indeed, knew better than Engels), but elevates Joseph Dietzgen's primitive dialectics as the equivalent of Marx *and Hegel!*[3]

---

3   Marx did all he could to spread Dietzgen's writings because he was a worker and did try to grapple with dialectics, but in the serious correspondence about him, Marx bemoaned the fact that Dietzgen hadn't studied Hegel. As he put it in his letter to Engels on Oct. 4, 1868

I doubt that a single worker will understand Professor Ollman's "vocabulary," but to the extent that it has helped some intellectuals understand Marx's historic analysis of reality (judging by the rave reviews *Alienation* has received), to that extent it has made a contribution which will, of necessity, send them to the study of Marx's work themselves. Or so we hope.

[MECW 43, p. 121]: "My opinion is that J. Dietzgen would do best to condense all his ideas into two printer's sheets.... If he publishes them in the size he is proposing, he will discredit himself by the lack of dialectical development...."

The Dialectic of Labor in Marx and "Critical Thought"

The journal Paunch *published a special issue (#44–45) in May 1976 featuring Bill J. Harrell's "Marx and Critical Thought."¹ The editor, Arthur Efron, published with it seven commentaries on Harrell's study, including Raya Dunayevskaya's.*

> Time is the place of human development.
>
> MARX

Marx's Humanism—and that is what Marx named his discovery of a new continent of thought: "a new Humanism"²—is either a revolutionary philosophy of liberation or it is nothing at all. Just as a *revolutionary* philosophy of liberation is not just a "philosophy" (much less Harrell's concept of "sociology"), but a struggle for actuality, the actuality of freedom, so the uprooting of the exploitative system, existing reality, is a great deal more than freedom from economic exploitation, rooted though it is in that necessity. Rather, the process of liberation—"the negation of the negation"—creates what Marx called "new forces, new passions."³ Having uprooted the exploitative class structure of society, the Subject (the proletariat) has achieved a whole new human dimension. Because "the individual *is* the social entity"⁴ [Appendix, p. 334], the contradiction between the individual and society is transcended. Even when this was still expressed in the abstract philosophic language of Hegel, instead of Marx's

---

1 B.J. Harrell's article may be found on https://web.archive.org/web/20120114174004/http://people.sunyit.edu:80/~harrell/billyjack/marx_crt_theory01.htm. The article appears in numbered paragraphs. Dunayevskaya's references to the article will appear in the text by paragraph number. —Editor.

2 Lest this be identified only with the young Marx of the famous *Economic-Philosophic Manuscripts of 1844*, consider also Volume III of *Capital* where he defines freedom as "development of human power, which is its own end, the true realm of freedom" [MCIIIK, pp. 954–55; MCIIIP, p. 959].

3 *Capital*, Vol. I, contains a paragraph on "new forces and new passions" [MCIK, p. 835; MCIP, vp. 928], and "negation of the negation" [MCIK, p. 837; MCIP, p. 929]. (Charles H. Kerr edition is used throughout.)

4 Again, lest only the 1844 *Manuscripts* be thought of when identifying individual and social, consider the expression in the *Communist Manifesto*: "the free development of each is the condition for the free development of all" [MECW 6, p. 506].

analysis of concrete class struggles and historic revolutions, the dialectics of liberation were unambiguous: "Individuality purified of all that interferes with its Universalism, i.e., freedom."[5]

Harrell is right when he says labor is "central to Marxian critical *analysis*" [¶52] (my emphasis)—and totally wrong when he speaks of it as "ultimate end" [¶52], as if it were not Marx's specific description of capitalism and capitalism only, but of any society. All that did was permit Harrell to impose on Marx's "ambiguous" conception [¶67] some sort of kinship with today's state-capitalist societies that call themselves Communist. Though Harrell feels compelled to qualify that allegedly theoretical affinity, holding that the "totalitarian result" "clearly violates its [Marx's] spirit" [¶75], he never lets go of his perverse definition:

> Perhaps the most succinct way in which one could summarize Marxian political-economy is: *a theory of the development of workers' control as the prerequisite for a society based upon work.* [¶57]

Far from looking toward "*a society based upon work*" as an "ultimate end," Marx was so appalled by labor that he, at first, called for "the abolition of labor."[6] What convinced him otherwise, that is to say, had him concretize the concept, and call, instead, for "the emancipation of labor"[7] was the labor*er*, *his* class struggles, his *daily* resistance at the point of production, where the instrumentality, machinery, dead labor dominated living labor. The revolt of the laborer against his exploiter, the capitalist, was also directed against the ideology, the false consciousness, which represented him as what he is *not*.

Marx's critique of classical political economy's great discovery that labor was the source of all value was that labor was treated only as "source," not as Subject, the "gravedigger" [MECW 6, p. 496] of the system resting on alienated labor. Naturally, workers' control of production would change that mode of labor, but for that to be the *absolute* opposite of capitalistic reification of labor, transformation of man into thing, labor has to become self-activity, development not only of production, but the self-development of man/woman,[8] the

---

5 Hegel, *Philosophy of Mind*, ¶481.

6 *The German Ideology*, p. 69 [MECW 5, p. 52].

7 For example, in the "Inaugural Address" to the First International [MECW 20, p. 12] and *The Civil War in France* [MECW 22, p. 334]. —Editor.

8 In the same *Economic-Philosophic Manuscripts* where Marx wrote, "The secret of the relationship of man to man finds its *unambiguous*, definitive, *open*, obvious expression in the relationship of *man* to *woman*" [Appendix, p. 332] he attacked not only capitalist private property but also "quite vulgar and unthinking communism" [Appendix, p. 331] which

human dimension. Over 100 years before Hannah Arendt discovered the difference between labor and work,[9] and profoundly *misread* Marx, and Harrell read Arendt as an improvement on Marx's concept [¶52], Marx had spent a lifetime developing the concept of the *duality* of labor. It is "about"[10] the only category Marx takes credit for creating.

This is no empty concern with who was the "first." Rather, my point is the dialectics, which so escape Harrell, who is busy piling up "failures" of Marx as if he were the first in this century plus 33 years to be burying Marx, and this, though he himself admits that Marx keeps living, living globally, agreeing with Georges Sorel's accounting for Marxism's "historic tenacity" [¶59]. Instead of rushing to declare labor and freedom "ambiguous in conception and unclear in its implications" [¶67], ought Harrell not at least have asked himself: "though I deny Marx is any such genius as his adherents claim him to be, how does it happen that a genius credited with discovering a whole new continent of thought, lays claim to originality in but a single category, the *duality* in labor? What is so crucial in Marx's concept of alienated labor (whether or not 'lifted' from Hegel's theory of alienation), that has, in Marx's hands, led (1) to break with other socialists, revolutionaries, so that on the one hand stands Marx and his evaluation of the class struggles, and, on the other hand, all others, from the anarchist Pierre-Joseph Proudhon to Marx's adherent, Ferdinand Lassalle

---

thought all evils would be done away with once private property was abolished instead of going on to "second negation" and going on to self-development of mankind, putting all his stress on the fact that it must not be only a "to have," but a "to be": "Private property has made us so stupid and one-sided that ... in place of all the physical and spiritual senses, there is the sense of possession, which is the simple alienation of all these senses.... Each of his human relations to the world—seeing, hearing, smell, taste, feeling, thought, perception, experience, wishing, activity, loving.... To such absolute poverty has human essence had to be reduced in order to give birth to its inner wealth" [Appendix, p. 335]. (I am using my own translation as I was first to translate these now famous essays, but they can be found in many editions.)

9   Harrell refers to Hannah Arendt, *The Human Condition* (Chicago: University of Chicago Press, 1958). —Editor.

10   The only other category Marx claimed credit for is the split in the category of capital into constant capital and variable capital, but since capital was treated not as a thing but a relationship of production of capitalist to laborer, and since constant capital was but another name for dead labor and variable capital for living labor, the latter is the only element that underwent a variation in magnitude *because* of all the millions of commodities exchanged daily; this alone was living and could be and was exploited to produce all surplus values as well as its own exchange-value, wages. They all ended with the split in the category labor, thus: concrete and abstract; labor/labor-power; living labor/dead labor; constant/variable capital; fetishism of commodities.

(whom Marx called 'first workers' dictator').[11] (2) A century before 'Third World' as concept was developed, why did Marx himself move from the concept of China as 'vegetating in the teeth of barbarism'[12] to such 'embrace'[13] of the T'aiping Revolution as to necessitate a second deeper look at labor as work of artisans? Moreover, (3) the concepts of labor and of freedom and of 'becoming'[14] were so deepened that, if anything moved Marx from being an 'economist' to being a 'sociologist' that surely is clearest seen in the *Grundrisse* which I, Harrell, have dismissed as if it simply proved there was no difference between the young and the mature Marx? Finally, (4) in *Capital*, Marx claims originality for the concept of duality of labor, a split sharpened as 'concrete and abstract labor.' Marx feels an urgency to work out a totally new section, 'The Fetishism of Commodities,' which, to this day, has served schools of thought as different as Existentialism in France and the Frankfurt School in Germany (not to mention political economists and sociologists and other specialized 'sciences' Marx as revolutionary has rejected), but I, Harrell, concerned with the 'inadequacy of Marxian thought as a critical sociology' fail to examine."

Now then, since I had to ask the questions "for" Harrell, but Harrell himself spent not a single word on them, limiting himself to some isolated quotations from Marx, let us take a look at Marx's thought, as a totality, no matter in what abbreviated form allotted space demands. Great as the Marx quotations were that Harrell chose, they are no substitute for the singularity of that split in the category, labor. Because it is original with Marx, and "is the pivot on which a clear comprehension of political economy turns,"[15] Marx raises it in the very first chapter of Volume I of *Capital*, no matter how many new discoveries of

---

11   Letter of Marx to Engels, April 9, 1863, MECW 41, p. 467. —Editor.

12   Marx's expression was "vegetating in the teeth of time" [MECW 16, p. 16]. —Editor.

13   Read especially the articles he wrote for *The New York Daily Tribune*, reproduced now in *The American Journalism of Marx and Engels* (N.Y., The American Library) [MECW volumes 11–17 and 19]. And if you cannot read the massive *Grundrisse* at least read those parts reproduced in abbreviated form, *Pre-Capitalist Economic Formation* (N.Y.: International Publishers, 1965) [Grundrisse, pp. 471–514]. Marx also brought the question of T'aiping into a footnote in *Capital* itself, which the American edition omitted. [The footnote was since published in MCIP, p. 164. —Editor.]

14   *Grundrisse*: "When the narrow bourgeois form has been peeled away, what is wealth, if not the universality of needs, capacities, enjoyments, productive powers, etc. of individuals, produced in universal exchange? ... What is this, if not a situation where man does not reproduce himself in any determined form, but produces his totality? Where he does not seek to remain something formed by the past, but is in the absolute movement of becoming?" [*Grundrisse*, pp. 487–488].

15   *Capital*, Vol. I, p. 48. [MCIK, p. 48; MCIP, p. 132].

economic laws (none of which are "iron"),[16] leading to the discernment of "the economic law of motion" of capitalism [MCIK, p. 14; MCIP, p. 92], to its collapse; and no matter how broad the historical developments, philosophic insights and literary allusions Marx traces through in the four volumes[17]—he does not stray far from the duality of labor as pivot since, indeed, it is not only pivot for comprehension of political economy, but is ground for revolution— the dialectical development from the revolution *in* philosophy to philosophy *of* revolution *to* actuality.

None before Marx had split the category, labor, but it is this, just this, which discloses the perversity of capitalism, whose mode of production, with its factory clock, pounds all the many varieties of concrete labor into one abstract mass of "socially-necessary labor-time" [MCIK, p. 46; MCIP, p. 129].[18] Marx, having followed the worker from the marketplace, where the worker, though "free," had sold himself, or rather his ability to labor, *labor-power, as a commodity*, proceeded to the workshop. The centerpoint of Marx's *Capital* is the analysis of "The Labor Process and the Process of Producing Surplus-Value" [Chapter 7]. There he traces the laborer as he is turned into an appendage of a machine. This dead labor (labor congealed into the form of machine) dominates living labor, after which "it," as commodity, be he employed or unemployed, is traced back into the market. There—and *this* there is not only in the marketplace but includes the whole of bourgeois culture—"The Fetishism of Commodities" reigns supreme not only over capital/labor, but also over independent intellectuals, including the discoverers of labor as the source of all value [MCIK, pp. 92–93;

---

16   Harrell encloses "iron laws" in quotation marks as if they summed up Marx's own attitude. In fact, he directed one of his latest works against such expressions used by Lassalle, whose famous expression was "iron law of wages"; "If I abolish wage labor, then naturally I abolish its laws also, whether they are 'iron' or sponge" (*Critique of the Gotha Program*) [MECW 24, p. 91].

17   *Capital* is, generally, referred to as a three-volume study because that is all that bear that name. But, in fact, *The Theories of Surplus Value*, edited and misedited by Karl Kautsky, was, by Marx, considered Volume 4 of *Capital*, and I always include those volumes as integral to *Capital*.

18   Contrast this view of time by factory clock and world market to Marx's concept, quoted at the top of my commentary, which maintains that time is the "place of human development" [MECW 33, p. 493; see also MECW 20, p. 142; MECW 32, p. 390; *Grundrisse*, p. 708]. The same totally different world relates to all the criticisms piled on "immiseration" as against Marx's insistence that, be the worker's payment *"high or low"* [MCIK, pp. 708–709; MCIP, p. 799], capital ("value big with value") "vampire-like" sucks him dry of "free individuality" [MCIK, pp. 217, 257, 835; MCIP, pp. 302, 342, 927]. (See the whole of Part VII, "Accumulation of Capital," and the penultimate chapter, "The Historical Tendency of Capitalist Accumulation." *Capital*, I.)

MCIP, pp. 173–75].[19] This is no accident, says Marx, as only *"freely* associated men" can strip the fetishism from commodities [MCIK, p. 92; MCIP, p. 173].

Obviously, Harrell thinks he is the exception and can give a more "substantive" view of freedom whose thought, as it moved to materialist "political economy," was "so wrong as to be irrelevant" [paraphrasing ¶58, 85] and became "progressively narrower" [¶77]. To correct that, Harrell empties the specificity of Marxian categories, introducing such total confusion into that most precise expression, "capital accumulation," as to make it both equivalent to bourgeois culture and acceptable to Marx since "bourgeois culture provides the necessary capital accumulation as well as the abstract insight as to the ultimate end of universal freedom" [¶26]. On the way to *his* conclusion of the know-it-all, be-it-all "sensual needs," Harrell arms himself with what he conceives as support from "Critical Thought." (Incidentally, while that is what the Frankfurt School called itself and also what it directed toward Marx, it is not what Marx named his new continent of thought. So opposed was he to labels that, outside of "the new Humanism" as the *dialectic unity* of the material and the ideal, he never tried pasting labels upon his total outlook. Historical Materialism was Engels' expression; Dialectical Materialism was Plekhanov's. And, while the Frankfurt School tried to leave their designation "open" enough to "include" Marxism, it is *they*, not revolutionary Marxism, that narrowed itself to "Critical.")

Unfortunately, though his sympathy lies in their direction, Harrell hardly presents a total picture of the Frankfurt School, whether in relation to Marx or "as such." First, he fails to show the division *within*: what they were in the 1930s and early 1940s, and what they became in the postwar years hardly makes them a unified outlook—not totalitarian, need it be added—but nevertheless motivated by Marxism, independent, and separate from both the German Social Democracy and the Russian *"state* socialism." Secondly, he acts as if the present "school"—the Habermas "school" is altogether removed from both Marxism and the original Critical school—speaks with a like voice.

The most telling mix-up relates to the one—Herbert Marcuse—Harrell so admires as to credit one of his works, *Eros and Civilization,*[20] as being nothing

---

19   In *The Eighteenth Brumaire of Louis Bonaparte*, Marx explained why it was he considered intellectuals "petty bourgeois" like "shopkeepers," though in "their education and individual position they may be separated from them as widely as heaven from earth. What makes them representatives of the petty bourgeoisie is the fact that in their minds they do not get beyond the limits which the latter do not go beyond in life, that they are consequently driven theoretically to the same problems and solutions to which material interests and social position drive the latter in practice" [MECW 11, pp. 130–131].

20   Herbert Marcuse, *Eros and Civilization: A Philosophical Inquiry into Freud* (New York: Vintage, 1962).

short of "one of the most important works in social philosophy since Marx" [¶121]. We do not see the Herbert Marcuse of *Reason and Revolution*,[21] from which work Harrell could have learned a great deal about both Marx and Hegel. He makes no note of the open departures from Marxism since then.[22] And, though he analyzes more of Marcuse's works as against none of Adorno's and little of Horkheimer, the founders of the Frankfurt School, the truth is that his preoccupation is just *Eros and Civilization*. Or, more precisely put, sensuality sans history, applicable to "all" cultures, as *substitute* for, not just Marx's "economics" or "sociology"—*but passions*, striving to reconstruct exploitative capitalism on humanist beginnings. Instead, Harrell redefines needs as "timeless erotic needs" [¶140]. That, of course, is Harrell's privilege, but it certainly wasn't Marx's perspective, and I doubt it is Marcuse's.

Harrell may argue that that was precisely his point, a critique of Marx which showed that "in the effort to avoid considering" just such sensual human needs and restricting "his analysis to the negative or to given historical trends, the critical perspective is crippled" [¶105]. The trouble is that thereby Harrell rejects more than Marx and/or "critical thought" as he rushes, helter-skelter, to conclude: *"There must not only be the negation of the negation but negation through the identification of positive possibilities"* [¶105].

Language is no stranger to reductionism, but this violates simple common sense, which I am sure Harrell has plenty of. But so anxious was he to drive the nail into his accusation of just how far "Marxian theory fell short of its liberating purpose" [¶105] that he violated even the simple linguistic meaning of two negatives equaling a positive.

Before Harrell, to friend and foe alike, negation of negation meant a positive, not just a positive "possibility," but a positive, a *new* positive. Marx took seriously the Hegelian dialectic which, at the very apex of second negativity, affirmed "the most important part of rational cognition" to be "to hold fast to the positive in the negative...."[23] As Marx opposed blueprinting the future, he allowed but one intimation of "the future" and that because it was so rooted

21   Herbert Marcuse, *Reason and Revolution: Hegel and the Rise of Social Theory* (Amherst, New York: Humanity, 1999).

22   Marcuse surely makes no secret of this, with the sole exception that the 1960 new preface to *Reason and Revolution*, originally published in 1941, is presented as if the author had not undergone some very fundamental changes that were quite discontinuous. We have been friendly enemies for many years, and I believe the first serious change is seen in his reexamination of Marxism that he wrote as Preface, in 1957, to my *Marxism and Freedom*. (It has been recently reproduced in the 4th English edition of my work.)

23   Hegel, *Science of Logic*, Vol. II, p. 476. In the new one-volume translation by A.V. Miller, the quotation appears on p. 834. (N.Y., Humanities Press).

in the concrete, in the present. He spelled it out as "permanent revolution."[24] That "negation of negation" would assure not stopping at first negation—the overthrow of the exploitative system—but would recognize and develop *the wealth of human needs*" so that "there arises *positive* Humanism, beginning from itself" [Appendix, pp. 339, 352].[25]

As for Harrell's dramatic climax, that the inclusion of "sensual needs" into "socio-historical categories" would assure the conquest of "unhappy consciousness"—"'unhappy consciousness' resolves itself through the discovery of the sensual in the form of its particularity" [¶148]—I wish him happiness. But let him not forget that the "unhappy consciousness" is only a quite early stage in Hegel's *Phenomenology*, and in Marx's new continent of thought and in critical thought to the present; there is a long, long road still ahead.

---

24 The idea of permanent revolution was first developed by Marx after the defeat of the 1848 revolutions, in his March 1850 *Address to the Communist League* [MECW 10, pp. 277–87]. It has been developed, first, by Trotsky, who, however, while holding to the concept of world revolution, nevertheless introduced a duality into it by glossing over the revolutionary role of the peasantry. Then, in the hands of Mao as "uninterrupted revolution," it not only violated the Hegelian concept of negation of negation by "declaring" it "non-existent," but Marx's concept of proletarian revolution, which got lowered to "cultural revolution." There are all kinds of ways of decapitating the dialectic since the first revisionist, Eduard Bernstein, found its revolutionary nature burdensome up until the present Russian chief philosopher, Kedrov, who tried to force a separation between Lenin's *Philosophic Notebooks* and the Hegelian concept of negativity. See "Why Hegel? Why Now?" in my current work, *Philosophy and Revolution* (New York: Dell, 1973).

25 The East European revolts, beginning with the East German uprising on June 17, 1953, and the 1956 Hungarian Revolution, through the 1968 Czechoslovak call for "socialism with a human face" which the Russian tanks rolled over, have been quite a philosophic development of thought of the 1844 Humanist Essays on the historic stage of today. A collection, an international symposium, *Socialist Humanism*, edited by Erich Fromm, includes quite a few of these philosophers speaking for themselves. (New York: Doubleday, 1965) .

CHAPTER 17

Gramsci's "Philosophy of Praxis"

This essay appeared as the "Two Worlds" column in the November 1977 issue of
News & Letters.

> The philosophy of *praxis* is consciousness full of contradictions in which
> the philosopher himself, understood both individually and as an entire
> social group, not merely grasps the contradictions, but posits himself as
> an element of the contradictions and elevates this element to a principle
> of knowledge and therefore of action.
>
> A. GRAMSCI, "Problems of Marxism" in *Prison Notebooks*

Fifty-one years ago this month, on November 8, 1926, Antonio Gramsci, revolutionary leader of the Turin Factory Councils, a founder of the Communist Party of Italy, a Marxist theoretician-activist, was arrested by Benito Mussolini's police. When, after nearly a year of incarceration, Gramsci was brought to face fascist courts, the Prosecutor, demanding condemnation of Gramsci, mouthed Mussolini's injunction: "We must prevent this brain from functioning for twenty years!"

It meant a life sentence for the frail revolutionary. Indeed, he died before the twenty-year sentence had expired. But fascism could not stop the brain from functioning. The eleven years of brutal fascist imprisonment produced profound philosophic-political writings that retain relevance for our day. Naturally, that was not the lived revolutionary life any Marxist would have wished, much less one who had experienced the *Biennio Rosso* (the Two Red Years, 1918–1920) of the General Strike, the Factory Councils, the near-revolution that turned into the failed revolution. But it was the period that laid the ground for working out anew the integrality of philosophy and revolution as Gramsci thought through the experiences of the *Biennio Rosso* as well as its philosophy, history as well as triangular relationship of class, factory councils, party. That is to say, spontaneity and organization, to Gramsci, could no more be narrowed to an elitist party ordering the masses around than spontaneous actions could be squeezed dry of the creative thought that produced the action of masses in motion.

1   Factory Councils in Italy

Rather than either only a vanguard party to lead, or philosophy sans revolution, what had to be worked out was the inseparability of philosophy and revolution. So solidly grounded in philosophy was Gramsci's concept of the Russian Revolution and the soviets which brought the Bolsheviks to power that he hailed them as opening a "new stage of humanity." And when he wrote of the Factory Councils in Italy as "the model of the proletarian state," he knew that, far from arising from his head, it was the Fiat factory workers who had spontaneously formed them during the summer of 1919; that universalism and the anti-state would concretize *State and Revolution:* "The Russian Revolution is the triumph of freedom; its organization is based on spontaneity, not on the dictates of a 'hero.' ..."[1]

Consider, then, the irony that among Gramsci's detractors are not only state-capitalists in power calling themselves Communists, as in Russia, or those who hunger for state power in the existing parliamentary, bourgeois states (with or without a King, be it Spain or Italy or France) who are busy attempting to make that great revolutionary Gramsci sound like a Eurocommunist class-collaborationist.[2] No, the detractors also include those who fight Eurocommunism and try to restore Gramsci as the revolutionary he was, like the Trotskyists (all varieties), as well as some from the New Left. The latter try to intellectualize Gramsci as if he, as philosopher who had a certain concept of the function of intellectuals, could possibly have assigned a revolutionary role to intellectuals who kept themselves apart from the proletariat, from masses in motion. It all adds up to fear, on the one hand of philosophy and on the other of proletarian revolution, thus reducing the proletariat to robot. It therefore is essential, though in very abbreviated form, to restore the wholeness of Gramsci's "philosophy of praxis." Indeed, the very phrase itself shows how inseparable are thought from action, theory from practice, philosophy from revolution.

By no stretch of the imagination can one excuse moving away from the central core of Gramsci-ism—"philosophy of praxis"—on the ground that since the fascist prison guards were looking over his shoulder, and since many a time when Gramsci would have used the word, revolution, he had to use the phrase

---

1   Antonio Gramsci, *Selections from Political Writings, 1910–1920,* edited by Quintin Hoare, translated by John Mathews (London: International Publishers, 1977), p. 54.

2   This is especially ludicrous in view of Gramsci's singling out for criticism class collaborationism as well as the then existing Socialist Party. See *Selections from the Political Writings, 1910–1920,* p. 43: "The political decadence which class collaboration brings is due to the spasmodic expansion of a bourgeois party which is not satisfied with merely clinging to the state, but also makes use of the party which is antagonistic to the state...."

"philosophy of praxis," both for Marx and for revolution, as if that were not his own worldview.[3]

Quite the contrary. First and foremost, the substance of his *Prison Notebooks* is directly on philosophy. Far from adhering to a "Crocean idealist" analysis of Hegel, Gramsci's most profound and violent attack is precisely on that type of "historicism": "This [Benedetto Croce's—RD] historiography is a degenerated and mutilated Hegelianism because his fundamental concern is the panicky fear of Jacobin movements of every active intervention of the great popular masses as historically progressive factors."[4]

2   Spontaneity

To Gramsci, "history" was always masses in motion shaping history. So much so that it is not only the bourgeois and petty-bourgeois interpretations he attacked, but also Marxists', from Georgi Plekhanov to Nikolai Bukharin, because their mechanical and scientific views had no conception of what V.I. Lenin called "the dialectic proper," whose central Marxian core was the proletariat as Subject transforming history. So solidly grounded in Hegelian-Marxian philosophy was Gramsci all his adult life, that his "purely" journalistic writings before he became a leader of the Communist Party of Italy—the early Gramsci of the *Biennio Rosso* period—were permeated with the dialectic of thought as well as of liberation. That is first and foremost and is not at all something forced upon him by prison life, which kept him from activism. In truth, the few times Gramsci created ways to send out uncensored messages, or was able to talk in person to visitors, there never was any separation between philosophy and revolution.

Indeed, this is what gave birth to such designations as "insurrectionist" and "spontaneist" in addition to attempting a forced identity between Gramsci's concept of "Council Communism" and the anarcho-syndicalist concept. It is this which led the Stalinist-Communist leader, Palmiro Togliatti, not to publish Gramsci's *Prison Notebooks* for ten long years, and then to truncate them in the post-war years as the Communists became part of the bourgeois government

---

3   The French edition of the truncated version of Gramsci's writings is profoundly criticized by Attilio Baldan in "Gramsci as an Historian of the 1930s." He gives both a more comprehensive view, though abbreviated, of the whole literature, as well as a critique of the French structuralist misinterpretation. It appears in *Telos,* Spring 1977, which includes other articles as well as reviews of the available translations in English.

4   *Selections from the Prison Notebooks* (London, New York: International Publishers, 1971), pp. 404–05.

and capitulated to the Catholic Church monopoly of education. Now that the writings are being published as written, it has no more stopped the present-day Communists from perverting this revolutionary's "philosophy of praxis" than did the truncated version, which had likewise fooled no one. Eurocommunist reformism just reflects the hunger Communists have for state power, displayed abroad as in Russia when *it* was transformed from the early workers' state into its present opposite, a state-capitalist society.

What is of the essence for our age, which has witnessed more aborted revolutions than any, is Gramsci's *revolutionary* legacy, which so integrated philosophy as to create ground for working out a new, urgent need for integrality of philosophy and revolution for our age. For this it is necessary to turn to the most fundamental of all of Gramsci's views—what he called "absolute 'historicism,' " "absolute humanism."

3   Absolute "Historicism," Absolute Humanism

Nothing so scares economists, even when they are Marxists, as the word "absolute," as if it really could mean only God or something equally mystical *they* attribute to Hegel. Because of this, even when they wish to restore to Gramsci his revolutionary stature, the greatest part of the time is spent endlessly revealing the Stalinist distortions, while they themselves so drain philosophy out of Marxian economic categories as to turn Marx himself into an "economist." In a word, what bothers them most in Gramsci is "lack" of economics.[5] It must have been just such vulgar materialism that Gramsci had in mind when he wrote:

> It has been forgotten that in the case of a very common expression (historical materialism) one should put the accent on the first term—"historical"—and not on the second, which is of metaphysical origin. The

---

5   See Chris Harman's two-part spread in *International Socialism* (#98 and #99), which, though it tells much that is available against Eurocommunist distortions, ends with an economist summation which totally disregards Gramsci's philosophic totality: "Although he provides a correct *abstract* account of the relation between economics and politics, Gramsci is alone among the great Marxists in not integrating a concrete economic dimension into his political writings. This is an arbitrariness...." To be that distant from Gramsci's working out the concept of totality is to be deserving of all Gramsci wrote against Bukharin's economist disregard of "the dialectic proper." See my analysis of other *International Socialism* disdain for philosophy: "Tony Cliff Reduces Lenin as Theoretician to an 'Uncanny Intuition,'" in the forthcoming News and Letters Committees joint British-U.S. publication, *Marx's Capital, Today's Epigones, and the Global Crisis,* off the press January 1978. [The critique of Cliff is included in *Russia: From Proletarian Revolution to State-Capitalist Counter-Revolution,* Chapter 17. —Editor.]

philosophy of praxis is absolute "historicism," ... an absolute humanism of history. It is along this line that one must trace the thread of the new conception of the world.[6]

Gramsci hit out not only against Croce but also against Bukharin, who kept stressing "objectivity," "science":

> Objective always means humanly objective, what may correspond exactly to "historically subjective," in other words, objective would mean "universally subjective" ... the Hegelian "Idea" is resolved into the structure as much as into the superstructure and the whole method of conceiving philosophy has been "historicized"....[7]

On this, the fifty-first year since the arrest of Gramsci, with which the fascists thought they would "prevent this brain from functioning," let us return to the study of Gramsci's own writings, not just as "legacy," and not uncritically but as ground to build anew, both as integrality of philosophy and revolution, and to work out so new a relationship of theory to practice that the triangular relationship of class, spontaneity, organization can first come alive in a successful revolution.

---

6   *Prison Notebooks,* p. 465.

7   Parts of the *Prison Notebooks* were incorporated in *The Modern Prince and Other Writings* (London, New York: International Publishers, 1957). It is from there that I quote here pp. 106–09. It is the central article for our purposes, which Gramsci called: "Critical Notes on an Attempt at a Popular Presentation of Marxism by Bukharin," pp. 90–117.

CHAPTER 18

Rosdolsky's Methodology and Lange's Revisionism

This essay originally appeared as the "Two Worlds" column in the January-February 1978 issue of News & Letters.

Among non-Stalinist but leadership-conscious Marxists, there is hardly a work that has gained the acclaim accorded to *The Making of Marx's "Capital"* by Roman Rosdolsky. Published in Germany in 1968, it has now been brought out by Pluto Press in an English translation for the fantastic sum of $35. It is as if the price itself testifies to its importance. If not a "classic," it is, after all, about the only available lengthy, serious commentary on Marx's *Grundrisse,* which has only recently been published in English for the first time.

Roman Rosdolsky, a well-known Marxist theoretician, tells us that ever since 1948, when he obtained one of the rare copies of the *Grundrisse* then available, he has been studying that "Rough Draft" of *Capital* and set himself a twofold task: (1) to write a commentary, or more precisely, an exposition of the new discovery "mainly in Marx's own words"; and (2) "to make a scientific evaluation of some of the new findings which it contained" (p. xi). The preoccupation with the latter comprises Roman Rosdolsky's original contribution. To it he devotes Parts One and Seven—"Introduction," i.e., mainly the origin and structure of the work; and "Critical Excursus." To these 225 pages should really be added some 35 pages (Part Six, "Conclusion") which summarize what he found in the exposition and commentary of the work.[1] Since, as he correctly notes, "Of all the problems in Marx's economic theory the most neglected has been that of his method both in general and, specifically, in relation to Hegel" (p. xi), methodology is the underlying motif not only of his "critical excursus," but the reason for writing the whole of the 581 pages.

I wish I could report that a genuine contribution to dialectical methodology had been made by Rosdolsky. Unfortunately, nothing could be further from the truth. If there is anything that is totally missing in his massive study, it is dialectics. To the extent to which he does make a contribution to the

---

1 Contrast this to Chapter 2, Section B, entitled "The 1850s: The *Grundrisse*, Then and Now," pp. 61–76, *Philosophy and Revolution, from Hegel to Sartre and from Marx to Mao*; also for changes in the structure of *Capital*, see *Marx's "Capital" and Today's Global Crisis*, especially sections entitled "The Relationship of History to Theory," pp. 29–36, and "Appearance and Reality," pp. 77–82. [These are sections from Chapters 5 and 8 from *Marxism and Freedom.* —Editor.]

comprehension of the *Grundrisse* (lots of quotations, especially on Money, but no self-movement of the whole), the reader gets neither a view of the historical sweep of Marx's concept of *what* the totality of his greatest work was to be, nor an understanding of *why* Marx nevertheless decided to start everything "*anew*."

1   The Missing Dialectic

This is said not to play down the significance of the *Grundrisse*, much less to say that "starting *anew*" meant Marx discarded the validity of the range of the "Rough Outline" just because, instead of the six books there listed, Marx readied for publication only three, and finished only one. Quite the contrary. While he definitely rejected its shapelessness, comparing it to the formlessness of "sauerkraut and carrots," Marx meant to develop further some of the most brilliant and profound of his writings that could not find their way into the new dialectic structure of *Capital*, Volume I—like "The Pre-Capitalist Economic Forms," and "the absolute movement of becoming" [*Grundrisse*, p. 488]. We get a whiff of this in a footnote in the totally new "Fetishism of Commodities" when Marx refers to the Taiping Revolution, as against the quiescent European workers following the 1848 revolutionary defeats, as if China embarked on their revolution "to encourage" the Europeans to revolt.

Rosdolsky, on the other hand, who writes 581 pages to expound the *Grundrisse*, has not a word to say about the originality, dialectic, and dimension of the new, *totally new*, concept of the Orient, China especially, contained in "Pre-Capitalist Economic Forms," though the period he was writing in *followed* the 1949 Chinese Revolution, which was the compulsion for the European Marxists to publish, first, that very section, and finally the whole of the *Grundrisse*. (The English translation, however, first came out in 1973.)

It was the specific section on the economic forms preceding capitalist production that became most relevant to the new birth of a "Third World." Nor was it only a question of relevance. It was the dialectics of liberation that gave the dialectic of thought a new dimension of revolution. It is the dialectic that is missing from Rosdolsky's methodology. By using it synonymously with methodology, he has managed to reduce both to mere presupposition.

2   The Presupposition

Let's take a second look at Rosdolsky's claimed preoccupation with methodology. It has led him, among other things, to create a special Appendix directly to Part One on Rosa Luxemburg's *Accumulation of Capital* rather than wait for the end of his work, where he deals with all debates on Volume II of *Capital*, including, of course, Luxemburg's critique of Marx's theory of accumulation (pp. 490–505). What, in the first part, he entitles "Methodological Comments on Rosa Luxemburg's Critique of Marx's Schemes of Reproduction" (pp. 63–72) turns out to be a question of Marx's presupposition of a "closed capitalist society."

Luxemburg uses neither the word "dialectic" nor "methodology," making it clear that she is arguing against Marx's "theoretical assumption of a society of capitalists and workers only," and not against the dialectical development flowing from this. It is the assumption that, she claims, is "a bloodless theoretical fiction" as against the reality of "third groups" and capitalism being surrounded by non-capitalist lands. Indeed, she stresses that it is "the spirit of Marxist theory" that demands we "abandon the premise of the first volume."

The issue has been debated for more than a half century. What is new in Rosdolsky is the claim that it was not done methodologically, that her error in grappling with the problems in Volume II of *Capital* was that she "underestimated the so-called 'Hegelian inheritance' in Marx's thought" (p. 492). The irony is that what Rosdolsky cites as proof was her criticism, not of Volume II, but of Volume I. So aroused was she over the attacks on her *Accumulation of Capital* that far from "underestimating Hegelian inheritance," she hit out against Marx's "famed Volume I of *Capital* with its Hegelian rococo ornamentation," which she now (March 8, 1917) wrote "is quite abhorrent to me." Rosdolsky, however, proceeds on his merry way, exposing "the dialectical content hiding behind Marx's 'Hegelian style' " (p. 493, ftn. 123)—as if style were the issue.

In truth, so total is his blindness to dialectic as content as well as form, as self-movement, self-development, self-activity—all internal, with external being the objectification, manifestation, the non-human—that, by the end of his 445 pages of exposition, Rosdolsky succeeds in reducing to absurdity the very meaning of the word, the very specific word that Marx, and Marx alone, used so incisively and originally: Reification.

Where Marx used the word to prove the horrors of capitalistic alienation of the laborer, reducing man to thing, Rosdolsky applies it to economic category, entitling the concluding chapter of his exposition, "The Reification of Economic Categories...." Where Marx demonstrates that the mystification of economic categories, the fetishism of commodities, all arise from the very "perversity" (Marx's expression) of relation of object to subject, relations between men assuming the "fantastic form of relations between things" [MCIK, p. 83; MCIP, p. 165], Rosdolsky puts mystification of things on a par with "reification of labor."

Marx does the exact opposite, demonstrating that the reason why the per-version of subject to object assumes *that* form is due to the fact that, *in the process of production,* that is what production relations *"really are"* [MCIK, p. 84; MCIP, p. 166]: laborers are mere appendages to machines. The reader can now see that my criticism of Rosdolsky sticking so narrowly to the *Grundrisse* meant, not a way of playing down the importance of *Grundrisse*, but stressing that, in form, and in content and articulation of economic categories, econom-ic laws of development through contradiction and crises—the "law of motion" [MCIK, p. 14; MCIP, p. 92] of capitalism to its collapse—*Marx's final statement is not in* Grundrisse, *but in* Capital.

Rosdolsky, however, is preoccupied with the changes "in general" rather than in the particular, with the number of books rather than the changes *within* the first volume of *Capital*, which is, after all, the only one Marx fully prepared for the printer, 1867. After that, he again introduced changes he considered so important that he asked even those who had read it in the original to read the new French edition (1872–75) since it "possesses a scientific value independent of the original."[2] Rosdolsky, on the other hand, is veritably obsessed with "the movement from the abstract to the concrete" as if the dialectic never gets to the concrete.

It is true Rosdolsky has made some valuable contributions, the most impor-tant being that he makes clear that the Humanism of the young Marx, 1844, the relationship of Marx to Hegel of the mature Marx, the Marx of the *Grundrisse*, 1857–58, and the "scientific" socialism of the Marx of *Capital*, 1867–83, are all one and the same. It is surely valuable when the one who says this is not a "Hegelian Marxist," but an "economist."

It is also valuable when Rosdolsky demonstrates that, although Marx fin-ished only three books after he outlined six, what *seemed* to have been left out, like the book on Landed Property, actually was incorporated in the part on Rent in Volume III. And Rosdolsky does indeed make mincemeat of Karl Kautsky's contentions: (1) that the historic sweep of Marx's famous chapter, "Historical Tendency of Capitalist Accumulation," is but a variation of "Change in the Appearance of the Law of Appropriation"; and (2) that the outline in 1862–63 was already the finished new outline of *Capital*, 1866, which Rosdolsky correctly shows would have meant "nothing short of disregarding the Working Day, Simple Cooperation, Division of Labor, etc." (p. 17). But Rosdolsky himself

---

2   Elsewhere I go into detail on these changes. See especially "The Paris Commune Illuminates and Deepens the Content of *Capital,*" and "The Breakdown of Capitalism: Crises, Human Freedom, and Volume III of *Capital*" in *Marx's "Capital" and Today's Global Crisis.* [These are Chapter 6 and Section 3 of Chapter 8 of *Marxism and Freedom.* —Editor.]

fails to see that the writing of some 75 pages on "The Working Day" directly into the "abstract" theoretic Volume I, while relegating to Volume IV the contending with all the other "Theories of Surplus Value," meant an actual break with the very concept of theory, both as dialectics of thought and dialectics of liberation.

Instead, Rosdolsky decided to conclude his "Critical Excursus" with a special chapter in praise of Oscar Lange's *Political Economy*, which, says Rosdolsky, "is to our knowledge the only work in more recent academic Marxist literature which consciously, and in detail, takes up the question of the methodology of Marx's *Capital*" (p. 552). This would, to say the least, sound peculiar to all except Rosdolsky, who is himself deaf to the dialectic. It was Lange who rushed to the defense of the Stalinist break with the dialectic structure of *Capital* and—integral to that break—the revision of the Marxist analysis of the law of value, when I translated that article from *Pod Znamenem Marxizma* (*Under the Banner of Marxism*) in the *American Economic Review* of September 1944. The authors had proposed that, in the future, Russian teaching should not follow the structure of *Capital*.

In my commentary, I stated that this was but the reflection of "economic reality," that is to say, the state-capitalist, not socialist reality.

With the excuse that, "tempting" as discussions of value would be, it is outside the confines of his study, Roman Rosdolsky has not a word to say of this debate.[3] I doubt that that is the reason for his silence, and not only because he chose, as the very climax of his work, to end with a discussion of Lange, full of praise of his *Political Economy* for devoting three chapters to "methodology." No, my doubt is due to the fact that this is not a question of debates, inside or outside of Russia. It is a question of the *actual* revision of Marx's view that the law of value is the motivating force of capitalism. It is a question of *timing*—the height of World War II—and the Russian workers could have told Rosdolsky that Stalin was announcing that there was to be no change in the exploitative reality even after the successful end of the war.

What is actually at stake, whether Roman Rosdolsky was or was not conscious of it, is that tailending Stalinist economism is unavoidable when the Subject—*freely* associated labor—is left as an abstraction. This leads inexorably to the failure to grapple with the dialectic. To understand how this is so, we must return to Marx.

---

3   Which is less, I might add, than even Lange did in his very last compilation of his writings before his death. It is true he does not mention me, but he does mention his own article in the *American Economic Review*, and there is no way to read that without knowing the new Stalinist thesis, and his defense of it.

Marx wrote 881 pages of the "Rough Draft" of what was to be *Capital,* i.e., the *Grundrisse,* and only in the very last paragraph he writes, "The first category in which bourgeois wealth presents itself is that of the *commodity,*" and then notes that "This section is to be brought forward." To Engels he writes that, now that he wishes to single out some of these chapters and rework them for publication, "before the deluge"—that is, before the economic crisis of 1857–58 runs its course, perhaps even to revolution—he finds that he must first construct a new first chapter, as he doesn't have one on Commodity. And this he did for the 1859 publication *Critique of Political Economy.* But this too is no sooner published than, once again, Marx is dissatisfied both with "the form of presentation," and structure of the whole six books he outlined.

By the time—eight years later—Marx had completed his analysis of the economic laws of capitalist production and, as an active revolutionary, was head of the first International Workingmen's Association, Marx had decided to start *ab ovo.* Nor was it only a matter of a new outline of three instead of six books. Everything was new, and nothing more so than the split in the category of labor into abstract and concrete labor.

Because Marx considered that split in the category of labor his most original contribution, crucial to "all understanding of political economy," he no sooner began Chapter 1, "Commodities," with their twofold nature—use-value and exchange-value—than he made it clear that that was not the essence, that he must at once go to the essence—the twofold character of labor itself. By the time he had finished that first chapter, there was also a totally new section, the last, entitled "The Fetishism of Commodities." It was clear by then that he had "thrown out" what had previously followed Commodity, and Money—history of the theory of each category, all of which had been relegated to Volume IV of *Capital.*

"The Fetishism of Commodities" has since become not only one of the most famous of Marx's writings, but so bothersome to all exploitative state powers, especially those calling themselves "socialist," that evidently they just cannot live with it. What Stalin declared necessary for "the teaching" has since been codified, without any acknowledgment such as they *had* to make in 1943 when it flew in the face of all previous "teaching" by friend and foe alike. Discarding, or making an abstraction, of the concrete imperative of *freely*-associated labor taking destiny into its own hands, stripping away the fetishism of commodities, of Plan, of anything and everything non-human, and declaring, with Marx, "Human power is its own end" [MCIIIK, p. 954; MCIIIP, p. 959], inexorably leads one to tailend Stalinism, that is to say, state-capitalist "methodology."

Just as Lange's "methodology" was pragmatic, Stalinist eclectic, so was Rosdolsky's. Despite all *talk* of dialectic, and relationship of Marx to Hegel,

Rosdolsky, by no accident whatever, concluded that one need "no longer bite into the sour apple, study the whole of Hegel's *Logic* in order to understand Marx's *Capital*—one can arrive at the same end, directly, by studying the *Rough Draft*" (p. 570). Too bad that all Rosdolsky arrived at by the end of his study of the "Rough Draft" was the quagmire of Polish neo-Stalinism which Rosdolsky calls "neo-Marxism."

Thus does the dialectic wreak its vengeance on non-Stalinist pragmatists who skip over Marx's admonition that the Hegelian dialectic "is the source of all dialectic" [MCIK, p. 654; MCIP, p. 744] as well as Lenin's conclusion that it is, indeed, impossible to understand Marx's *Capital*, "especially its first chapter, without studying the *whole* of Hegel's *Logic*."

CHAPTER 19

Adorno, Kosík, and the Movement from Practice

This essay originally appeared as the "Two Worlds" column in the March 1978 issue of News & Letters.

Negative Dialectics by Theodor Adorno (New York: Seabury Press, 1973)
Dialectics of the Concrete by Karel Kosík (Dordrecht, Holland and Boston: D. Reidel Publishing Company, 1976)

The above two works are not only the most serious contributions to the study of dialectics in the past half-century, but pathbreaking originals. Adorno's *Negative Dialectics* is the most comprehensive, and is not only one man's life's legacy, but a veritable philosophic testament of the celebrated Frankfurt School's total existence from its founding. That only a few have chosen to review it is only in part due to the difficulty of the text and originality of the concept of negative dialectics. That is so radical a departure from the dialectics of negativity that Adorno opens his work with an attack on "the negation of the negation," that is to say, the positive that flows from a double negation, and declares: "This book seeks to free dialectics from such affirmative traits without reducing its determinacy" (p. xix).

Rather, despite the comprehensiveness of the 416-page volume, the total view of philosophy is written in so aphoristic a style that it looks, if not chaotic, surely not the type of continuity that characterizes a serious work, but more like essay-type analyses of individual topics, with each just a very few pages. At the same time, the relationship of concrete to abstract always comes as a shocker rather than as something emerging out of what Hegel calls "the self-determination of the Idea," or as an illumination of an original and abstract idea that is specifically Adorno's.

When I first started grappling with the book, keeping in mind the period of its formation—the mid-1950s to the mid-1960s—I was forced to conclude that Adorno was deaf to the objective situation, the movement from practice, especially the revolts in Eastern Europe. The two magnificent decades since the very first revolt from under totalitarianism—East Germany, June 17, 1953—had, indeed, undermined regimes as well as opened vast new theoretical vistas. They were historic challenges to all that was both in practice and in theory. Yet, *Negative Dialectics* has little to do with *that* dialectic of negativity, least of all with the concept of Subject, with which Hegel distinguished his from all other philosophers who left the search for truth at Substance only. As "concretized" by Marx for the proletarian class, Subject is supposed to have been accepted also by Adorno, but, again, he keeps his distance and originality locked into his work.

Naturally, Adorno also keeps his distance from "positivists" and the vulgarisms of the knighted Karl Popper of the infamous "Hegel and fascism" school. Nevertheless, Adorno, very nearly out of nowhere, suddenly brings in Auschwitz, seeing some sort of kinship between it and absolute negativity:

> Genocide is the absolute integration.... Auschwitz confirmed the philosopheme of pure identity as death.... Absolute negativity is in plain sight and has ceased to surprise anyone. (p. 362)

By "nearly out of nowhere," I naturally do not mean Auschwitz wasn't the reality of fascism, nor do I mean only the suddenness and shock of introducing the subject-matter in the climax to the book, "Meditations on Metaphysics." Rather, I mean it is "wrong," that is to say, totally illogical, non-dialectical, from his own point of view of an adult lifetime devoted to fighting fascist "ideology" as the very opposite of Hegelian dialectics, its very death in Nazi Germany.

Perhaps a better word than "wrong" would be Adorno's own swearword: "naive." I mean that, as late as 1957, in *Aspects of the Hegelian Dialectic,* he was—almost—defending even subject-object identity:

> Subject-object cannot be dismissed as mere extravagance of logical absolutism.... In seeing through the latter as mere subjectivity, we have already passed beyond the Speculative idealism.... Cognition, if it is genuine, and more than simple duplication of the subjective, must be the subject's objectivity.[1]

And, indeed, in *Negative Dialectics* he reiterates the same truth when he writes that, despite the fact that Hegel "deifies" subjectivity, "he accomplishes the opposite as well, an insight into the subject as a self-manifesting objectivity" (p. 350).

Why, then, the vulgar reduction of absolute negativity? Therein is the real tragedy of Adorno (and the Frankfurt School): one-dimensionality of thought once you "give up" Subject, once you do not listen to the voices from below— and they certainly were loud and clear and demanding in that decade of mid-1950s to mid-1960s—once you yourself return to the ivory tower and reduce

---

1 Translated from the original German text (1957). A different translation can be found in Adorno, *Hegel: Three Studies* (Cambridge, Mass.: MIT Press, 1993), pp. 5–6. —Editor.

your purpose: "the purpose of discussing key concepts of philosophic disciplines and centrally intervening in those disciplines ..." (p. xx). Irresistibly came the next step, the substitution of a permanent critique not alone for absolute negativity, but also for "permanent revolution."

Now, whether the enduring relevance of Hegel has stood the test of time because of the devotion and rigor of analysis of Hegel scholars, or because *from below* there upsurged a movement for freedom that was *followed* by new cognition studies, there is no doubt that *because* Absolute Negativity signifies transformation of reality, the dialectic of contradiction and totality of crises, the dialectic of liberation, that Hegel comes to life at critical points of history which Hegel himself characterized as "birth-time of history." And there were Marxist scholars, revolutionary dissidents, who built on new ground.

It is this which not only distinguishes Karel Kosík's "optimism" from Adorno's pessimism, but accounts for the fact that his *Dialectics of the Concrete,* though written in as abstract a philosophic form as Adorno's book and thus as difficult for the "common reader," sees what *historic* concrete the dialectic concrete "has in mind." Karel Kosík's work, instead of being shunted aside, is intensely discussed, and not only in Czechoslovakia but internationally. It is the type of philosophic work, it is felt, which has something very important to say. In a very significant way, Karel Kosík's work both anticipated the Prague Spring, 1968, *and,* at the same time, was a theoretical departure which said, if defeated, this can become a new jumping off point for the next revolution.

Thus, though abstractly and indirectly articulated, no one doubted that it was an attack on the ruling bureaucracy, even if that were expressed, not in political terms, but a philosophic critique of fetishized existence. In his sharp first chapter's critique on the pseudo-concrete—an important new contribution of Karel Kosík's—he reminds the readers that "man's fetishized praxis ... is not identical with the revolutionary-critical praxis of mankind" (p. 2).

To try to draw from his use of the generic Man (with a capital "M"), instead of specific worker, the conclusion that Karel Kosík was shunting aside the revolutionary proletariat, in the manner of the so-called "New Left,"[2] is to fly in the face not only of Kosík's view of the role of the proletariat, but also his praise of philosophy as the "*indispensible activity of mankind*" (p. 4). Rather than playing up generic Man as opposed to the "classic" revolutionary proletariat, what Kosík is doing is rejecting the reductionist Communist concept of subjectivity, as if it meant nothing but petty bourgeois egoism, and re-establishing subjectivity as, *at one and the same time,* the ground of Hegelian dialectics and distinctively Marxian dialectics of Subject who shapes his own history.

---

2   See "Czech Marxism: Karel Kosík" by Paul Piccone, in *Critique,* #8, 1977.

Kosík is most explicit in his description of exploitation as resulting from

> dead labor ruling over live labor, object ruling over man, product over its producers, the mystified subject over the real subject, the object ruling over the subject. Capitalism is a dynamic system of total reification and alienation, cyclically expanding and reproducing itself through catastrophes in which "people" act behind masks of officers and agents of this mechanism, i.e., as its own components and elements. (p. 110)

Kosík's greatest contribution is the reintroduction of the dialectic as the revolutionary pivot of Marxism. We see this especially clearly in the crucial third chapter of the work, which deals with Marx's *Capital*. Here, too, though Kosík sticks strictly to *Capital* as the concrete greatest work of Marx, with rigorous analysis of both its construction and its development of categories, he manages, though indirectly, to make it an attack on mechanical materialism, i.e., the ruling bureaucratized teaching of *Capital,* as if, once you counterpose social to individual, you have come to Marx's concept of the class struggle, not to mention the philosophy. As Kosík puts it,

> Man is *walled in* in his socialness. Praxis, which in Marx's philosophy had made possible both objectivation and objective cognition, and man's openness toward being, turns into social subjectivity and closedness: man is a prisoner of socialness. (p. 106)

And a few pages later he contrasts to this "socialness" Marx's revolutionary way out:

> *Capital* turns out to be the "odyssey" of concrete historical praxis which proceeds from the elementary labor *product* through a series of real formations in which the practical-spiritual activity of people in production is objectified and fixed, to conclude its journey not in the cognition of what it is in itself, but rather in a *revolutionary* practical action based on this cognition. (p. 111)

No one need think that, because "Philosophy and Economy" is the most important chapter, Karel Kosík limits himself to either economics or philosophy. Rather, his work is a far-ranging and far-reaching critique on the glorification of science and culture, which he calls the metaphysics of science and culture. The East Europeans will feel a great affinity for Kosík's profound critique of Georgi Plekhanov, and they will easily guess that it's not only a critique of Plekhanov but of "socialist realism," *Lukács included*. He considers that Plekhanov's work on art "lacks the 'human sensory activity' which cannot be reduced to 'psyche' or to the 'spirit of the times' " (p. 77), and holds that Plekhanov's method is a "one-sided approach smacking of Enlightenment" (p. 61). In the land of Franz Kafka, the readers will know that reality is as irradiated by a great work of philosophy as by great works of literature and film.

The movement from practice over the past two decades that produced new theoretical departures was by no means limited to East Europe but covered the world. This was most brilliantly articulated by Frantz Fanon, when he wrote that the Africans' struggles for freedom were "not a treatise on the universal, but the untidy affirmation of an original idea propounded as an absolute."[3] There is no doubt, of course, that once action supersedes the subjectivity of purpose, the unity of theory and practice is the form of life out of which emerge totally new dimensions; in the 1960s, these heralded women's liberation as well as Black, youth as well as labor.

It is these live forces that made the near-revolutions of the late 1960s. What is needed now is the singling out of the dialectic of Reason in so inseparable a manner from the movement from practice that freedom can be made a reality. It's this type of role for new, revolutionary subjectivity that Marx disclosed:

> Not only do the objective conditions change in the act of reproduction, e.g., the village becomes a town, the wilderness a cleared field, etc., but the producers change, too, in that they bring out new qualities in themselves, develop themselves in production, transform themselves, develop new powers and ideas, new modes of intercourse, new needs and new language. (*Grundrisse*, p. 494)

---

3   Frantz Fanon, *The Wretched of the Earth* (New York: Grove Press, 1963), p. 41.

PART 4

Marx as Philosopher of Revolution in Permanence—Reading Marx for Today

∴

SECTION A

Marxist-Humanism

∵

CHAPTER 20

Introduction to *Philosophic Notes*

Philosophic Notes *was the title given to the first mimeographed pamphlet pub-*
lished by News and Letters Committees. Issued in November 1955, it included
the first English translation of Lenin's Abstract of Hegel's Science of Logic *and*
Raya Dunayevskaya's Letters of May 1953 on Hegel's Absolutes. In April 1956 a
second edition was issued, for which Dunayevskaya wrote two introductory notes:
one on Lenin's "Abstract," the other on her own 1953 Letters, the founding text of
Marxist-Humanism. The latter piece is presented here. The text of the first edition
is included in The Raya Dunayevskaya Collection, *pp. 2431–66. The original text*
of the Introduction presented here is included in the Supplement to the Raya
Dunayevskaya Collection, *pp. 12098–12101.*

When the great German philosopher, Hegel, reached the end of his *Science of
Logic,* and entitled the final chapter "The Absolute Idea," he suddenly began to
realize that under that tent all his philosophic enemies and all sorts of religion,
including the worship of the golden calf, would try to find a hiding place. He
therefore warned:

> It is certainly possible to indulge in a vast amount of senseless declama-
> tions about the idea absolute. But its true content is only the whole sys-
> tem, of which we have been hitherto examining the development. (*Logic,*
> ¶237)

Now the true content of what the writer of the present exchange of letters was
dealing with was a study of working-class struggles and working-class thought
as they appeared in history and were analyzed by Marx and as they appear
in the daily lives of workers nowadays. But the greatest illumination of these
struggles in the year 1953 was thrown by a reading of Hegel's Absolute Idea,
which the present writer identified with a concept of the new society and the
struggle for total freedom.

A new era of struggle for freedom had certainly opened in the year 1953.
That was the year of Stalin's death on the one hand, and the East German Revolt, on the other hand. This was followed within a few weeks by a revolt in the
slave labor camps of Vorkuta inside Russia itself. Clearly, Stalin's death symbol-
ized the beginning of the end of totalitarianism. We leaped generations ahead
when the workers in a satellite country and those in the slave labor camps took
matters into their own hands. The two new pages of history illuminated the

road to a new society by answering in the affirmative what had preoccupied both the average man on the street and the philosopher in his ivory tower: Can man be free in this age of totalitarianism?

In a sense the 1953 European struggles had been anticipated in America in 1950 with the great miners' strike. A new era in production had been opened with the first serious introduction of automation in the form of the continuous miner. Under its impact there was also born a new attitude to theory.

From the first industrial revolution, the newly born factory proletariat gained the impulse to struggle for the shortening of the working day, and thereby established a new philosophy. "In place of the pompous catalogue of the 'inalienable rights of man,'" Marx wrote in his greatest theoretical work, *Capital,* "comes the modest Magna Carta of a legally limited working day, which shall make clear 'when the time which the worker sells is ended, and when his own begins.' What a distance we have travelled!" [MCIK, p. 330; MCIP, p. 416]

The present industrial revolution of automation was being translated the world over into a new humanism. Never have they posed the question more clearly as not being one of material possessions nor annual wages, but of conditions of labor and a fundamentally new way of life. Without this universal philosophic form, state capitalism as a tendency[1] would remain economist and incomplete.

Although the leaders of the state capitalist tendency had been saying for years that we live in an age of absolutes, that the task for the theoreticians was the working out materialistically of Hegel's last chapter on the Absolute Idea, we were unable to relate the daily struggles of the workers to this total conception. The maturity of our age, on the other hand, disclosed itself in the fact that, with automation, the workers began to question the very mode of labor. Thus they began to make concrete, and thereby extended, Marx's profoundest conceptions. The innermost core of the Marxian dialectic, around which everything turns, is that the transformation of society must begin with the material life of the producer, that is, the worker.

In 1953, during the preparations to come out with a paper that would be a break from all previous radical papers, I turned to philosophy and saw, in the Absolute Idea, the breakdown of the division between theory and practice— the movement to total freedom.

What was new was that there was movement (a dialectic) not alone in the development from theory to practice, but from practice to theory. That, in essence, was the gist of the letters to Hauser (Grace Lee), the

---

1   This refers to the Johnson-Forest Tendency, which held that Russia had become a state-capitalist society. —Editor.

philosopher-designate, who, after demurring a day or so, came back with her usual hyperbole: "I think that these notes represent our Philosophic Note-books, comparable to those of Lenin in 1915."

Johnson (C.L.R. James), the titular founder of the state capitalist tendency, however, had other ideas. He never bothered to inform anyone what these were. However, he was very active in seeing that no one was moved by those ideas on practice contained in the letters on the Absolute Idea. When Hauser came to him with enthusiasm for all the "discoveries" I had made, he managed to shut her up. That was not too hard to do. What had previously been a liter-ary clique now became a philosophic clique. No one else had a chance to see these letters.

The titular head of the state capitalist tendency failed to grasp the new stage of production and the new stage of workers' revolt.[2] He could not do so because he was altogether preoccupied with probing the "social personality" of "origi-nal characters" and the "uniqueness" of the great literary writer and the greater literary critic.[3] The new humanism of the great East German Revolt played a secondary role to the humanism of "the great writer." That alone should have called for the abolition of the division between "theoretical leaders" and "the rank and file." It is high time to abolish that division as well as the division between "the inside" and "the outside." While the form in which the ideas first evolved in the mind of the author is rough and even abstruse, no stage in the evolution of the book[4] need be kept private. These notes and these letters are being published for all who are interested.

---

2 The new stage of production was automation, the focus of the 1949–50 miners' strike. See next chapter. —Editor.

3 A reference to C.L.R. James, *Mariners, Renegades and Castaways: The Story of Herman Melville and the World We Live In* (New York: privately printed, 1953). Reissued, London: Allison & Busby, 1984. —Editor.

4 The book is what became Dunayevskaya's *Marxism and Freedom.* —Editor.

CHAPTER 21

The Emergence of a New Movement from Practice that is Itself a Form of Theory

The 1949–50 coal miners' strike was one of the most important events in U.S. labor history and yet is little known. Dunayevskaya held that it signaled both a new automated stage of production and a new stage of cognition. It was pivotal to the creation in the ensuing years of Marxist-Humanism as philosophy and organization. This essay originally appeared as Part II of the pamphlet A 1980s View: The Coal Miners' General Strike of 1949–50 and the Birth of Marxist-Humanism in the U.S. *(Chicago: News and Letters, 1984) by Andy Phillips and Raya Dunayevskaya (*RDC, *pp. 8123–73).*

The dialectic of the 1949–50 Miners' General Strike, as it was transformed from a Lewis-authorized strike that already had lasted some six months into a challenge to John L. Lewis himself, laid the ground for new ways of thinking. The historic rejection by the miners of Lewis' order to return to work had imbued the old slogan, "No Contract, No Work," with new meaning because of the totally new question the miners raised: "What *kind* of labor should man do?" In a word, by being concerned not just with the unemployment that is always caused by new machinery, but with the unbridgeable gulf between manual and mental labor, which the continuous miner widened, they were pointing to new directions. I had for some years been developing the theory of state-capitalism, and to me the Miners' General Strike seemed to touch, at one and the same time, a concept Marx had designated as alienated labor *and* the absolute opposite to it, which Marx had spelled out as the end of the division between mental and manual labor.

Indeed, the todayness of Marxism shone through brilliantly in the miners' attitude to a passage I had read to them from Marx on the "automaton": "The lightening of the labor, even, becomes a sort of torture since the machine does not free the laborer from work, but deprives the work of all interest ..." [MCIK, p. 462; MCIP, p. 548]. Even the fact that the miners did not know that this passage was from Marx created a translucence when they insisted that the man who wrote that must have been in their mine, it was so perfect a description of Automation, specifically their continuous miner, which they called a "man-killer."

It led me to conclude that two new vantage points were needed for the book I had been working on, titled *State-Capitalism and Marxism*.[1] One was that the American worker should become a point of departure not only as "root" of Marxism but as a presence today. I therefore proposed to my co-leaders in the Johnson-Forest Tendency (JFT)—C.L.R. James and Grace Lee—that a worker be present at future discussions of the drafts of the book. The second vantage point was to be the dialectic as Lenin interpreted it in his Abstract of Hegel's *Science of Logic*. Four months before the strike erupted, I had finished the first-ever English translation of that historic 1914 encounter of Lenin with Hegel and, with brief comments, had transmitted it to James and Lee. A three-way correspondence resulted, centered on the relationship of the dialectic to Lenin as well as to our age.[2]

While we seemed to be as one on the need to work out the relationship between objective and subjective for the state-capitalist age that Lenin had worked out for the monopoly stage of capitalism, that relationship between objective and subjective was spoken of only "in general." Now, however, with an ongoing strike in progress, what had been a discussion of ideas assumed, to me, concreteness and urgency. Indeed, it gained a whole new dimension through what the miners were doing and thinking.

On February 14, something quite momentous happened. The workers who had voted down Lewis' order to return to work had been debating what to do next. They were already near starvation. The only relief they were getting came through "charity." Then, on February 14, miners in Scotts Run voted for the motion that "Red" and Andy brought to a meeting to establish a committee of miners to go to the rank and file of other unions to ask for help. Clearly, a great

---

1 This first version of what was to become *Marxism and Freedom* was submitted to Oxford University Press in 1947. I then sent it to prof. Joan Robinson. (The outline I sent her with her critique noted on it is included in the Wayne State University Archives of Labor and Urban Affairs, *Raya Dunayevskaya Collection*, pp. 472–503.) It was the year that I first visited West Virginia with the aim of establishing a new local [of the Socialist Workers Party] there of miners and students. The following year (on my return from France, where I presented my state-capitalism position in a debate with Ernest Mandel before a conference of the Fourth International), I moved to Pittsburgh so I could work with both steelworkers in Pittsburgh and miners in West Virginia.

2 See Appendix A to this pamphlet for a descriptive chronology of thirty-five letters written between February 18, 1949 and January 15, 1951. The full text of all these letters is included in the Archives collection, pp. 1595–1734. [The pamphlet's appendices are not included here, but the descriptive chronology Dunayevskaya mentions is on pp. 1595–96 of the RDC. The letters cited, and additional letters collected later, can be found at www.rayadunayevskaya. org, as can the Guide to The Raya Dunayevskaya Collection. The latter contains a descriptive chronology of twenty-seven additional letters from 1948 to 1951 plus associated manuscripts, covering RDC, pp. 9209–9327. —Editor.]

deal more than just getting money was involved in that motion. The point was how to do away not only with mere "charity" donations but with dependence on union leaders. Approving this motion signified establishing labor solidarity from below. Three days later, this motion was implemented at an area-wide meeting of local unions.

The miners elected two committees, one to go East and the other West. It was to become the turning point of the whole strike. You have read in Andy Phillips' account[3] how our comrades at the university got the idea of picketing the basketball game. It was their way to try to break down the division between the miners and the students. As one of our comrades put it, looking back to the magnificent caravan of food, clothing and money from the auto and steel rank and file workers:

> Let's face it. There was something about the deep philosophic probing that helped get results, and wonder of wonders, it even got the main red-baiter to stop referring to us as "fly-by-nights, running around town" and to ask people to leave us alone as we were doing a good job.

It was on February 15—the day after the miners had taken the first action to establish that new Miners' Relief committee—that James, Lee and I held the first meeting on the book at which a worker was present. (He [John Zupan] happened to be the one who would soon arrange the largest meeting in Detroit to raise a caravan of help for the miners.) Here is the way I began my presentation:

> Just as the 1945–46 General Strike transformed the abstract Russian Question on property forms into one of actual production relations, so at present the struggle of the miners and the new content they have infused into 'No contract, No Work' is what gave me the impulse to go into the essential dialectical development of Marx himself.[4]

I then proceeded to trace Marx's own development 1843–73. It made clear Marx's new historic points of departure that occurred in the 1860s. Ever since John Brown's attack on Harper's Ferry, Marx had been talking about a new epoch that was dawning, which was sure to bring about a civil war in the U.S. In discussing how Marx began once more to rework *Capital* in 1865–67, I said:

---

3   "A Missing Page from American Labor History," by Andy Phillips, Part I of the pamphlet *The Coal Miners' General Strike of 1949–50 and the Birth of Marxist-Humanism in the U.S.* —Editor.

4   The minutes of this meeting are included in the Archives collection, pp. 1585–1594.

There is the Jamaican Negro revolt in 1865. There was the Polish revolution, 1863. Then there are the Factory Reports. Marx asks Engels for a pamphlet on Machinery. He works out the average working wage. The whole history now becomes the history of production, not the history of theory.

I concluded, "Dialectically, the problem of form is the problem of the contract today."

1   Lenin's Philosophic Notebooks

As for the second new vantage point that I proposed for the book—Lenin's Abstract of Hegel's *Science of Logic*—I began this way: "Lenin was, of course, a revolutionary long before he read *Logic*." But, I stressed, he now felt the compulsion to re-evaluate his whole methodology in analyzing subjective as well as objective events. The shocking simultaneity of the war and the collapse of the Second International resulted in a break with his own philosophic past of mechanical materialism. Now Lenin saw in the Hegelian dialectic of negativity the need for a concept of goal, the future that revolutionaries were aiming at. As Lenin put it:

> Movement and self-movement... Who would believe that this is the core of 'Hegelianism,' of abstract and abstruse (difficult, absurd?) Hegelianism? We must disclose this core, grasp it, save, shell it out, purify it....[5]

As this discussion of Lenin further highlighted his preoccupation with the Doctrine of the Notion—that is, with the subjective as well as the objective paths to liberation—the worker we had invited to the discussion summed it up: "When you don't have a notion of the future, you just counter-pose essence to form. Is that what all this means?" Clearly, the worker's presence at this first meeting on the "Marx book" went a great deal further than "the class question." The worker was grappling with the question of concepts as well as the relationship of subjective to objective.

The new form for the book which I was presenting and the discussion around it, as well as the ongoing strike, convinced me that the ground was now cleared for me to finish the book, which I now began to call "the Lenin

---

5 *Russia: From Proletarian Revolution to State-Capitalist Counter-Revolution,* p. 84; Lenin, *Collected Works,* Vol. 38, p. 141. —Editor.

Book." However, upon my return to Pittsburgh, I found that the Socialist Workers Party (SWP) was sufficiently worried about the red-baiting taking place and distrustful enough about the West Virginia branch and my activity with them that they called a tri-state meeting of the members from Pittsburgh, West Virginia and Ohio—where they would have a majority. We were confident that we would be vindicated when they heard the miners' own reports.

By the end of that February 26 meeting,[6] their leader, Harry Braverman, said:

> I believe the Morgantown comrades have done one of the finest jobs of any of our trade union fractions. Morgantown has pushed the situation from a local question and made it into a national one, and in extending the strike they also seized upon another basic issue: relief, which is the center of the question now. Everything else is set—the men have determined not to go back to work. And now in getting the relief issue and getting the backing of the district, they have seized the center of the problem again.... The important thing is now to get aid from steel and other unions and to make a success of this venture.... once we act with caution and have mass backing, then we can proceed.

When Frank [Monico] asked whether it would be possible for me to come down to West Virginia for several days, permission was quickly granted. This time I was there with the official approval of the SWP. Indeed, the Militant published my March 6 report of the jubilation that greeted the arrival of the caravan from the UAW Local 600 workers.[7] You have read it in Andy's report.

One point which concerns the miners' reaction when they came to hear the debate between Harry Braverman and me on the "Russian Question" (which was then going full blast in preparation for the 1950 SWP convention) is important to record, although it is not directly related to the strike. As Frank reported the incident:

> When the two miners who came up with Andy and me to hear what to them was a very abstract debate, they nevertheless recognized more clearly than we did where it was all going. The conclusion they drew was: "This means split." They were happy about it.

---

6   See Minutes of Tri-State Meeting included in the Archives collection, pp. 1485–1491.

7   F. Forest, "Auto Union Relief Caravan Hailed in Coal Mining Town," *The Militant*, Vol. 14, #11, March 13, 1950, RDC, p. 1479. Also available at https://www.marxists.org/history/etol/newspape/themilitant/1950/v14n11-mar-13-1950-mil.pdf. —Editor.

What, however, is more important to record, to show why the miners felt so close to us, was that many of the packages sent in the relief caravan contained the name and address of the worker who had sent it and who was asking for correspondence with the miner who received it. One miner summed up the feelings of many when he said: "We have never seen anything like this before. We have never had relief operate this way." It was the rank and file to rank and file development that likewise opened a new stage in the consequences of this great movement from practice. I was anxious to continue my correspondence with some of the miners and was wondering whether I should not also work out a new essay on coal. Here are the two letters sent out on March 14, one to "Red" and the other to James:

March 14, 1950

Dear J [C.L.R. James]:

My dear Marx is always on the spot. Yes, he was in the very latest mine strike. It now turns out that among the additions in the 1872 edition [of *Capital*] was the transposition of a long footnote on miners into the text itself; you will find it on pp. 541–51 [MCIK, pp. 541–51; MCIP, pp. 626–34]. As soon as I get down at least some notes on the literally dozens of books I have read on coal in these past two weeks, I will put it away for a while since there seems to be no chance for an article. Or I may decide to write a rough (very rough first) draft anyway and then just let it lie with you and me in that condition until we get ready to rework. In the meantime I will return to work on *Capital*. (You can keep the minutes as I am being permitted the branch copy; but please do find JB's MS. Will see you get all current material possible.)

Meanwhile some gossip. You noted in the minutes that the initiative for the tri-state discussion was not from Pittsburgh, but from Youngstown, where people with higher trade union status than either El or me reside. Frank had to come to town about his leg yesterday and so dropped in and told me that they now have a letter from Youngstown asking "Red" to come down there to speak to the Ohio branches, and P'gh. would be invited too. Naturally he accepted. There is no doubt that both "Red" as a new member and the importance of the strike and relief actions has made Youngstown more than wish it was closer to Morgantown; an actual tie-up that-a-way is being built up....

Back to coal for a minute; I could deal with it either in the context of a full century, 1849–1949 (the first strike and union occurs in U.S. 1849), or restrict myself to the two World Wars, when all the technological changes occur. The crisis in coal, you know, began in 1924, not 1929. It seems many "friends" of miners as well as the coal barons thought that technology would eliminate the union since it would eliminate that independence of the miner and make him a button pusher even as it did the factory operative who was not organized (1925). The interlude of newness however lasted but a couple of years and the strikes recurred ever more sharply and in fact the initiative comes from the most mechanized mines, as it came in this very latest one. There is no richer mine for Johnsonism than a real mine.

    R.

• • •

March 14, 1950

Dear "Red":

Sorry that I had not gotten a chance to see more of you, but of course when the class struggle is active nothing else has precedence. However, the magnificent job you did plus the nearness to the masses just when both a great strike and an independent action such as relief was being accomplished ought not to be allowed to pass without some very precise and elaborate notes of every detail of the action and the reaction for future use. Always, at the end of such an action one finds how much one has grown in stature and experience, and how much more he will know the next time. The point is now not to let it disappear as the past, but to write it down carefully and reexamine later.

No doubt Frank has told you that I am working on a big article on coal. Although I have read literally dozens of books and know the history of miners for a full century, nothing will be as valuable in that article as the actual talks with rank-and-filers on their specific attitudes. All theory, you know, to Marxists is but the conscious expression of the "instinctive strivings of the proletariat to reconstruct society on Communist beginnings,"[8] as Trotsky pointedly put it. Moreover, the workers themselves have been the ones to "invent" new *forms* of organization. Take the Soviets in the good days of Lenin and Trotsky. The workers spontaneously established them and when the great Marxist theoreticians saw them, they said, "That's it" and they made their theories more concrete.

All this is merely to lead up to the necessity to make of theory and practice one, not two separate departments. Hence, when I get a rough draft down in a month or so, I most definitely want you to read it and give me your comments. Also, at some later stage I will want to come down to Morgantown and I hope

---

8 Leon Trotsky, *In Defense of Marxism: Against the Petty-Bourgeois Opposition* (New York: Pioneer Publishers, 1942), p. 104. —Editor.

it will be possible for you to arrange for me to meet some of the miners and talk to them....

Do let me know what you think of the idea of the article (perhaps 9,000 words) on coal; what notes you have of the recent experience and in general what comments you have to make.

COMRADELY,

R.

I didn't get to see "Red" then and I gave up the idea of the article on coal, as I had to engage in the debates on state-capitalism as the SWP was preparing for its convention. Although the rank-and-file miners who were direct participants when I debated with Harry Braverman in Pittsburgh correctly predicted split, we didn't actually go through with it then. Just as 1950 was not over when the miners went back to work in March 1950 but re-emerged the next year when they wildcatted over seniority in September 1951, so, though the Johnson-Forest Tendency had not left the SWP when we submitted our document on "State-Capitalism and World Revolution"[9] in August 1950, we did finally leave Trotskyism for good and all in August 1951.

2   Beginning of the End of the Johnson-Forest Tendency

The shock was that it was also the beginning of the end of a united Johnson-Forest Tendency. Where I proposed that the first issue of the new paper we planned to issue should be devoted to the new miners' seniority strike, Johnson (James) opposed. He insisted that

> our membership and their friends is the only audience I have in mind for the paper.... If a mighty bubble broke out, 500,000 miners vs. John L. [Lewis], and shook the minefields, I would not budge an inch from our program.[10]

We then went "underground," publishing only a mimeographed paper until 1953. It was during this period, 1951–52, that I continued my work on both

---

9   RDC, pp. 1333–1412. Recently published as C.L.R. James, *State Capitalism and World Revolution: Written in Collaboration with Raya Dunayevskaya and Grace Lee* (Oakland, Calif.: PM Press, 2013). —Editor.

10   Letter of C.L.R. James to "Irv," September 17, 1951, RDC, p. 9315. —Editor.

philosophy and the book, writing a 54-page outline,[11] which I developed on the basis of the February 15, 1950 meeting.

The differences that developed between Forest [Dunayevskaya] and Johnson [James] occurred, after all, in a most critical period both internationally and nationally—1950–1953. The Korean War and McCarthyism were raging and the death of Stalin brought it to a climax.

The death of Stalin lifted an incubus from my brain, and it was inconceivable to me that it wouldn't do that for the Russian and East European workers. I looked forward to great explosions. Charles Denby (the Black production worker who was to become editor of *News & Letters* when finally the break between me and Johnson occurred) called as soon as his shift ended to tell me of the excitement in his factory as the radio blared the news of Stalin's death. Each worker was saying that he had just the person to take Stalin's place—his foreman. I asked Denby to come over for a discussion.

When he came over, we spent several hours talking about both Stalin's death and the affinity the American workers felt with the Russian workers, especially on the trade union question. The discussion made it clear to me that, far from the American workers considering this a "Russian Question," they were relating it to their own working conditions in the shop and their relationship to their own bosses and union bureaucrats. Denby asked me whether I remembered the chapter he had written on the UAW in his autobiography,[12] where he had described the ever-widening gulf between leaders and ranks. The conclusions he had drawn had been intensified by his run-in with those bureaucrats when the rank-and-file miners had come to his local to ask for the autoworkers' help during the Miners' General Strike. The miners, too, had learned how crucial it was to deal directly with the rank and file, who forced the bureaucrats to triple the amount they had intended to give.

Denby felt the workers he knew would not only understand the problems the Russian workers faced, but that they would find lessons for their own struggles against both the union bureaucrats and the company. He raised the question I had been discussing with him sometime before, on the 1920–21 Trade Union debate between Lenin and Trotsky. He said that if I could put that story in the framework of what the workers were experiencing right then, he would

---

11   This second draft of the book, which I was then calling "the Lenin book," is included in the Archives collection, pp. 1735–96.

12   *Indignant Heart* was written under the pen name of Matthew Ward, and was published in 1952. This became Part I of the new edition published in 1978 under the title *Indignant Heart: A Black Worker's Journal,* in which Charles Denby included a whole new Part II that began with the events around the Montgomery Bus Boycott in 1955, the year *News & Letters* was born and he became its Black worker-editor.

be happy to distribute it to his fellow workers and tell me their comments. Outside of the two days it took me to write the political analysis of Stalin's death, I spent the next few weeks writing the essay on that debate, which I called "Then and Now."[13] I decided also to send it to West Virginia and asked that our comrades there should try to get the reactions of the miners to both Stalin's death and the trade union debate.

Once again I felt the compulsion to return to work on the Hegelian dialectic. What had begun in 1948 with the translation of Lenin's *Philosophic Notebooks,* and continued through 1951,[14] made me go this time directly to the Absolute Idea itself, six weeks before the actual first rebellion from under totalitarianism did erupt in East Germany on June 17, 1953, to be followed very shortly by revolt within Russia itself, in Vorkuta.

In a letter on Hegel's *Science of Logic,* I wrote to Grace on May 12, 1953:[15]

> I am shaking all over for we have come to *where we part from* Lenin. I mentioned before that although in the *approach* to the Absolute Idea Lenin had mentioned that man's cognition not only reflects the objective world but creates it, *within the chapter* he never developed it.

In disagreeing with Lenin for telling us that the last half of the final paragraph of Hegel's *Logic* is unimportant, I argued:

> But, my dear Vladimir Ilyitch, it is not true; the end of that page *is* important; we of 1953, we who have lived three decades after you and tried to

---

13   These articles are both included in the Archives collection, pp. 2180–2199. "Then and Now" appeared in the mimeographed Correspondence of April 16, 1953. A greatly edited version of my articles on Stalin's death had appeared in the March 19, 1953, issue and initiated a dispute with Grace Lee, who had edited it. It was printed as I wrote it in the issue of April 30, 1953.

14   A letter I wrote to James on June 16, 1951, shows how detailed was my study of Lenin's *Philosophic Notebooks,* in relation both to the specific sections in Hegel that Lenin was commenting on, and to the political repercussions of his study. Because I have just rediscovered it, this letter has not been included in the Archives collection as of this date, and is therefore reproduced here as Appendix B. [This letter has since been placed in the Archives, RDC, p. 9312, and is not included in this volume. —Editor.]

15   My "Letters on the Absolute Idea" of May 12 and May 20, 1953, were published along with my translation of Lenin's *Philosophic Notebooks* as the very first publication of News and Letters Committees. They are part of my pamphlet, *Dialectics of Liberation,* available from *News & Letters.* [After Dunayevskaya's death, the letters were published in *The Philosophic Moment of Marxist-Humanism: Two Historic-Philosophic Writings by Raya Dunayevskaya* and *The Power of Negativity: Selected Writings on the Dialectic in Hegel and Marx.* —Editor.]

absorb all you have left us, we can tell you that.... You didn't have Stalinism to overcome, when transitions, revolutions seemed sufficient to bring the new society. Now everyone looks at the totalitarian one-party state; *that* is the new which must be overcome by a totally new revolt in which everyone experiences "absolute liberation." ...

I concluded the letter of May 12 by insisting that I agreed with Lenin's interpretation of Nature as practice and could see why he was so attracted to it and stopped there, but that I would continue, as Hegel advised, to the other "sciences" where he first concludes his view of the Absolute, Nature and Mind. The next week, on May 20, I concentrated on the final three Syllogisms of Hegel's *Philosophy of Mind*—paragraphs 575, 576 and 577. Where ¶575 at once established that practice, too, is "implicitly the Idea," and in ¶576 Hegel still says "philosophy appears as a subjective cognition," it is only in ¶577 that the unification of the two—theory and practice, subjective and objective—takes place. And while I was excited enough to then say: "We have entered the new society," *the* new for our age was the fact that practice, as "implicitly the Idea," meant to me that mass practice is itself a form of theory.

3   *The Birth of a New Humanism for Our Age:* Marxism and Freedom, from 1776 until Today

Silence on the part of my co-leader became intolerable once I had written those letters—that is to say, once I had written out all that had been churning in me ever since 1948 and my translation of Lenin's Abstract of Hegel's *Science of Logic*; once I had experienced in the post-World War II period what Lenin had undergone at the simultaneity of World War I and the collapse of the *established* (Second) International; once I had grasped the concept of philosophy as action, as giving action its direction, and the following year had experienced that magnificent Miners' General Strike; once spontaneity appeared in an altogether different form in 1953 in East Germany, where the first revolt ever from under the heel of Stalinism raised the new slogan of "Bread and Freedom."

I tried not just philosophically but concretely to work out what these new movements from practice signified. I didn't fear the "Absolute" once I saw it as so new a unity of theory and practice as to signify *both totality and new beginning*. It was, indeed, this new conception of *the movement from practice that was itself a form of theory* that dictated the form in which I cast the work on which I had been laboring for some ten years. The book I had variously referred to as "Marxism and State-Capitalism," "the Marx book," and "the Lenin book,"

I now (in 1957, when I was free of Johnsonism and no longer restricted by factionalism) called *Marxism and Freedom, from 1776 Until Today*.

I could then openly dialectically declare: "This book aims to reestablish Marxism in its original form, which Marx called 'a thoroughgoing Naturalism or Humanism.'" Moreover, the Introduction proceeded to explain the new way of writing:

> No theoretician, today more than ever before, can write out of his own head. Theory requires a constant shaping and reshaping of ideas on the basis of what the workers themselves are doing and thinking.... At least, it dictated the method by which this book was written.... This work is therefore dedicated to the autoworkers, miners, steelworkers and student youth who have participated so fully in the writing of this book. They are its co-authors.

So many new voices and revolutionary actions by Blacks, women and youth erupted in the 1960s that the very recording of them led to many new discoveries. Thus, in Mississippi, where the first Freedom Riders filled the jails, a totally new organization called "Woman Power Unlimited" was formed (years before the Women's Liberation Movement of today arose) to bring human comfort to those in the jails and give them a place to stay when they were released.[16] Thus, the Freedom Schools raised a whole new concept of education which not only made life and learning one, but taught the Northern white youth who had come down to participate in the freedom struggles of the Southern Blacks what history really is: human beings shaping their own destinies.[17] Thus, "Black is beautiful" was not only an emotional manifestation of pride but the actual history of the U.S. in which Black masses in motion have always been the touchstone.[18]

When new developments brought forth a worldwide, massive, anti-war movement, a new generation of revolutionaries, and a whole new Third

---

16   See the News & Letters pamphlet, *Freedom Riders Speak for Themselves,* by Mary Hamilton, Louise Inghram, and others, published in 1961.

17   See especially "Robert Moses on Education in the South" in the 1965 *News & Letters* pamphlet, *The Free Speech Movement and the Negro Revolution* by Mario Savio, Eugene Walker and Raya Dunayevskaya.

18   The first edition of *American Civilization on Trial* appeared in 1963, three months before the famous civil rights March on Washington led by Martin Luther King, Jr. In 1983, on its 20th anniversary, a new, fourth edition was published by *News & Letters,* expanded to include my essay on "A 1980s View of the Two-Way Road Between the U.S. and Africa." [See Chapters 24 and 25 of this volume. —Editor.]

World, it seemed to many that we were, indeed, on the threshold of revolution. The youth who thought so, however, and who had very nearly dismissed theory as something that can be "picked up en route," found their revolution aborted at the very highest point of action—Paris, May 1968. Activities by themselves are as one-sided as theory by itself. Only in their unity—in a new relationship that is rooted where the action is—can we rise to the challenge of the times.

There did, indeed, arise in the 1970s a search for a philosophy of revolution. It is these new passions and forces that led us to spell out what we had been working on ever since 1953 when we broke through on the Absolute Idea. It was a return to the Hegelian dialectic "in and for itself," as well as working it out for our age. We called it *Philosophy and Revolution, from Hegel to Sartre and from Marx to Mao.* The 200 years since the birth of the machine age, which had been spelled out in *Marxism and Freedom* as a movement from practice, was now spelled out as a movement from theory. What was distinctive was the fact that the last chapter—entitled: "New Passions and New Forces: The Black Dimension, the Anti-Vietnam War Youth, Rank-and-File Labor, Women's Liberation"—was seen as inseparable from the very first chapter: "Absolute Negativity as New Beginning: The Ceaseless Movement of Ideas and of History."

That the movement from practice was, indeed, showing itself to be a form of theory had come to the fore in the 1970s as the Women's Liberation Movement was searching for a decentralized form of organization that would be founded on an organizing Idea. It inspired new digging into Rosa Luxemburg's concept of spontaneity and the relationship of Marx's philosophy of revolution to his organizational practice.

The 1970s also saw, for the first time, a transcription of Marx's last writings, his *Ethnological Notebooks,* which disclosed the new moments Marx experienced in the last decade of his life. It was in that decade—1873–1883—that Marx spelled out: (1) in his *Ethnological Notebooks,* a new concept of pre-capitalist societies and what he called the Asiatic Mode of Production (which we now refer to as the Third World); (2) in drafts of a letter to Vera Zasulich as well as in a new Preface to the Russian edition of the *Communist Manifesto,* the possibility of revolution coming first in the technologically underdeveloped East before the West; (3) in his *Critique of the Gotha Program,* the principles of a revolutionary organization that must not be separated from a total philosophy of revolution.

These so illuminated our state-capitalist age and its total opposite, the new passions and forces for creating a new society, that we rushed to complete our latest theoretical work, *Rosa Luxemburg, Women's Liberation, and Marx's Philosophy of Revolution,* for the Marx centenary.

Heretofore, Marxists have acted as though Marx had no concept of organization, as though there had been no theory of organization until Lenin. Since the rise of Stalinism had likewise been analyzed as mere bureaucratization rather than as a class transformation of a workers' state into its opposite—a state-capitalist society—no fundamentally new foundation was laid for the next generation of revolutionaries.

What became imperative for revolutionaries in the state-capitalist age was to recognize the class nature of state-capitalism and not to limit the discussion of organization to "democracy" vs. "bureaucracy." What was needed was not just a political rejection of the "party to lead" but a whole philosophy of revolution as it related to organization.

In focusing on the last decade of Marx's life, *Rosa Luxemburg, Women's Liberation, and Marx's Philosophy of Revolution* challenged all post-Marx Marxists, beginning with Engels, not only on what they couldn't have known (the *Ethnological Notebooks* had not yet been transcribed) but on the separation they all introduced between spontaneity, organization and philosophy.

• • •

As Andy Phillips put it at the end of his account of the unfolding of the Miners' General Strike of 1949–50:

> To some, many of the things the miners did seemed spontaneous, as though the actions came from nowhere. Just the opposite is true. The spontaneity of the miners flowed from their own repeated collective thought and action that preceded their "spontaneous" activity.[19]

It is long past time that the full story be told, and it must be recorded both as it happened and as the crucial relationship of theory to practice illuminates it.

The impulse to finally record this missing page of American labor history, as the preface states:

> was born when Raya Dunayevskaya began her Marx centenary tour with a lecture at West Virginia University which linked Marx's American roots directly to West Virginia in his hailing of John Brown's raid on Harper's Ferry as "the signal" that had been given for a whole new epoch—*and* Marxist-Humanism's roots directly to the 1949–50 Miners' General Strike

---

19   *The Coal Miners' General Strike of 1949–50 and the Birth of Marxist-Humanism in the U.S.,* p. 32. —Editor.

which had pointed to a whole new movement from practice to theory which is itself a form of theory.[20]

But that does not tell the whole story. The telling of it today shows that it was in our activities in that historic 1949–50 strike—where our theoretical and practical work were inseparable—that we find the roots of what became the whole body of ideas we call Marxist-Humanism which has been developed over the full thirty-five-year period since. As the News and Letters Committees perspectives for 1984–85 states:[21]

> Marx's Marxism, from the very beginning of his break with bourgeois society, disclosed that no concept of his was separate from that of permanent revolution—from 1843 to 1883. Our projection of Marx's Marxism as a totality disclosed that Marx's philosophy of "revolution in permanence" was ground also for organization, a concept we consider most pertinent for our age.

---

20   Ibid., p. 5. —Editor.

21   All Perspectives Draft Theses of News and Letters committees have been printed directly in *News & Letters* since 1975. This 1984–85 Thesis appears in the May 1984 issue, and is entitled: "Where are the 1980s Going? The Imperative Need for a Totally New Direction in Uprooting Capitalism-Imperialism."

CHAPTER 22

New Stage of Production, New Stage of Cognition, New Kind of Organization

Reflecting Dunayevskaya's new thoughts on revolutionary organization in response to the new moments of Marx's last decade, which became central to her work on the projected book on Dialectics of Organization and Philosophy, this chapter originally appeared as the prologue to the pamphlet A History of World-wide Revolutionary Developments: 25 Years of Marxist-Humanism in the U.S. *(Detroit: News and Letters, 1980).*

Ever since I began preparing for the celebration of May 5 as the birth-time of history—Marx's new continent of thought—I have been rethinking the birth of Marxist-Humanism in the U.S. There was no way to sum up twenty-five years of the birth and development of the News and Letters Committees, as well as *News & Letters* as newspaper, without taking account of the *philosophic* breakthrough on the Absolute Idea as containing a movement *from practice* as well as from theory. That occurred in 1953. Once the split in the State-Capitalist Tendency, known as Johnson-Forest,[1] was complete in 1955, our very first publication reproduced my May 12–20, 1953, Letters on the Absolute Idea along with the first English translation of Lenin's *Philosophic Notebooks*.

In a word, while 1955 saw the birth of News and Letters, both as Committees and as our paper, 1953 saw, at one and the same time, the emergence, *in* the Johnson-Forest Tendency, of open divergences towards objective events (be it Stalin's death. the East German revolt, the Beria purge, *or* McCarthyism), as well as towards the subjective idea of what type of paper *Correspondence* was to be and what was its relationship to Marxism.

In reaching back to 1953, a new illumination disclosed that we were really talking, not about a single year, but about the period 1949–1954. After all, nothing short of the second Industrial Revolution had emerged with the introduction of Automation in the mines. The actual word, Automation, was not invented until five years later during the wildcats in auto in Detroit. *The truth, however, is that Automation did initiate a new stage in industrial production.*

---

1 Johnson (C.L.R. James) broke with Forest (Raya Dunayevskaya), co-founder of the State-Capitalist Tendency, in March 1955. News and Letters Committees began functioning at once as Marxist-Humanists.

And since our age refuses to keep the objective and the subjective in totally separate compartments, it was during that period that I was working on three things ...: (1) I was active in the Miners' General Strike of 1949–50 during the day and evening; (2) late at night I was translating Lenin's Abstract of Hegel's *Science of Logic,* sending these translations with covering letters to Johnson (C.L.R. James); (3) I was working on a book on "Marxism and State-Capitalism." These three activities led to a three-way correspondence between myself, Johnson, and Lee (Grace Lee Boggs).

Furthermore, insofar as the year 1953 is concerned, something new has just emerged in re-examining that year. Although we had long ago known that Lee and I had totally different analyses of the March 5th death of Stalin and what we were to do about it, it is only now that I can see the link that connects those differences in 1953 to the period 1949–51. Because philosophic beginnings, the native ground for Marxist-Humanism which emerged in 1949, didn't become manifest until 1953, and because the Letters, in turn, contained what politically didn't come to fruition until the actual split of the Johnson-Forest Tendency in 1955 (at which time they were first mimeographed), it is necessary to begin at the beginning in 1949–51.

It is important that we look at the new stage of production, Automation, and the form of the workers' revolt against it—the 1949–50 Miners' General Strike—in the same way as, in 1953, we looked at the first revolt against state-capitalism and its work-norms in East Berlin. The point is that both stages of production and both forms of revolt were every bit as crucial for the re-emergence of Marx's Humanism in our age, as had been the outbreak of World War II for the birth of the State-Capitalist Tendency. To grasp the divide *within* the State-Capitalist Tendency as it grappled with the Hegelian dialectic and the historic rebirth of Marx's Humanism, it is necessary to look at the three-way correspondence on Lenin's Abstract of Hegel's *Science of Logic* as Lenin grappled with the Hegelian dialectic at the outbreak of World War I. Let's follow the sequence of letters that accompanied the various sections of Lenin's work I was sending to Johnson and Lee:[2]

On February 18, 1949 I sent the translation of Lenin's notes on the Doctrine of Being. The covering note refers to the "Notes on Dialectics"[3] Johnson had written in 1948, which had then impressed me very much, but which in 1949

---

2   The letters from November 2, 1948, through November 27, 1951, are included in RDC, pp. 1595–1734, with a descriptive chronology Dunayevskaya on pp. 1595–96; and RDC, pp. 9209–9327. A descriptive chronology of the latter is included in the Guide to The Raya Dunayevskaya Collection, which can be found at www.rayadunayevskaya.org. —Editor.

3   C.L.R. James, *Notes on Dialectics: Hegel, Marx, Lenin* (Westport, Conn.: Lawrence Hill & Co., 1980). —Editor.

made me call attention to the fact that Johnson "practically skipped over the first book." The same note focused on Lenin's new appreciation of the "self-development of the concept," no matter how "idealistic" that sounds. Lenin had written:

> Hegel analyzes concepts which usually appear dead, and he shows that there *is* movement in them. The finite? That means *movement* has come to an end! Something? That means *not what Other is*. Being in general? That means such indeterminateness that Being = Not-Being....[4]

It is with this new appreciation I felt for Lenin's *Philosophic Notebooks* that a philosophic division started to emerge between the two founders of the State-Capitalist Tendency—Johnson and Forest. My letters to Johnson continued all the way to June 10 before I ever got an acknowledgement of the receipt of any part of the translation. The silence did not stop me from continuing either with the translation or the covering notes.

Thus, on February 25, I sent him a translation of Lenin's notes on the Doctrine of Essence, singling out three new points for a "historical materialist" to be concerned with: (1) Suddenly Lenin was emphasizing very strongly the sequence of dates of publication which showed Hegel's *Logic* (1813) to have preceded Marx's *Communist Manifesto* (1848), and that to have preceded Darwin's *Origin of the Species* (1859); (2) Furthermore, Lenin was now emphasizing the genius of *Hegel's* appreciation, not just of Essence but also of Appearance as against the Kantian impenetrability of the "thing-in-itself"; (3) Lenin was breaking fully with his previous stress on the theory of the primacy of "Causality," now seeing that what is cause becomes what is effect, and vice versa. Instead, he was stressing totality, insisting that: "totality, wholeness, is richer than law." At that point he was underlining the language of certain "definitions" of totality by Hegel, such as *"sundered completeness,"* and the definition of Identity as "unseparated difference."

When, on March 12, I concluded the translation of Lenin's work and sent Johnson the section on the Doctrine of the Notion, my covering note for it no doubt shocked him:

> Let me say at the start that although you have entered into this "conspiracy" with Lenin, the outstanding difference between the two "versions"

---

4 *Russia: From Proletarian Revolution to State-Capitalist Counter-Revolution*, p. 82; Lenin, *Collected Works*, Vol. 38, p. 110. —Editor.

(of the Dialectic) is striking. You will note that Lenin's notes on the Notion are as lengthy as those on the Introduction and Doctrines of Being and Essence combined ... although you spent that much time on Notion, and included its practice, the thing you chose most to stop at and say: *hic Rhodus, hic salta* to was the Law of Contradiction in Essence ... (but Lenin) chooses to single out the section on the Idea.

I concluded that Lenin no longer "feared" the Absolute, seeing it both as unity of theoretical and practical idea, as the *method* of absolute cognition, and as criticism of all Marxists, including himself. Here is how Lenin had put it:

> Aphorism: Marxists criticized the Kantians and Humists at the beginning of the 20th century more in the Feuerbachian (and Buchnerian) than in a Hegelian manner.

Contrast this to what Johnson and Lee drew from my translation when they discussed it between themselves on May 27:

> Previous to 1914 the whole revolutionary movement, the Second International and all the rest of them, were essentially in the Realm of Being. Even Lenin before 1914 was not very conscious of Essence, although the objective situation in Russia drove him to the *Logic.* The key to Lenin's notes on *Logic* is this relation to Essence. We today have not only to do Essence, but also Notion, the dialectic of the party.

Lenin, they claimed, "is more concerned with self-movement than he is with Notion."

It is very nearly beyond comprehension to find how they could make such a claim in the face of the fact that Lenin's commentary on the Doctrine of the Notion was more comprehensive than what Lenin had written on all the rest of the *Logic* combined. In truth, as early as the Preface and Introduction, before he ever got into the *Science of Logic* "proper," Lenin called attention to the fact that the three categories of Notion—Universal, Particular, Individual—were precisely where Marx "flirted" with Hegel, especially in Chapter 1 of *Capital.* Which is why, when Lenin made his own leaps, he insisted that no Marxist had understood *Capital,* "especially Chapter 1," unless he had studied the *whole* of *Logic.*

Perhaps we can understand part of the reason why when we read the letter in which Johnson finally (on June 10, 1949) first acknowledged the translation of Lenin's *Philosophic Notebooks* and my commentaries. He wrote:

> You are covering a lot of ground and it is pretty good. But after conversations with G [Grace Lee] & reading (carefully, this time) your correspondence, I feel that we are still off *the* point....

Clearly, it is not I with whom they disagreed as hotly as they did with Lenin. Indeed, they had not the slightest notion of what Lenin was talking about until July 9, when finally Lee did get down to the Doctrine of Notion as Lenin worked it out. They continued to be preoccupied with their own great philosophic knowledge, Johnson stressing to Lee, "After weeks of painful back and forth, in and out, *you and I bearing the burden....*"[5]

Whatever "burden" they were bearing, it certainly wasn't comprehension of Lenin's Abstract of Hegel's *Science of Logic,* though Johnson continued to tell me precisely how many words I was to write on *Capital,* how many on *Logic* (1,000 words on each topic!). I plunged into a concrete study of differences in Lenin pre- and post-1914, and then into how the dialectic affected the varying structural changes in *Capital,* as well as the objective development of capitalist production from the end of the 19th century to the present.

Finally, on July 9, 1949, Lee began seriously to go at Lenin's *Notebooks* as well as Hegel's Doctrine of the Notion:

> In the final section on Essence (Causality) and the beginning of the section on Notion, Lenin breaks with this kind (Kantian) of inconsistent empiricism. He sees the limitations of the scientific method, e.g., the category of causality to explain the relation between mind and matter. Freedom, subjectivity, notion—those are the categories by which we will gain knowledge of the objectively real. [RDC, p. 1675]

Except for several letters by me on the changes in the structure of *Capital* (see those dated January 24, January 30, June 7, 1950, and January 15, 1951), the three-way philosophical correspondence stopped at 1950, as we prepared to face a new (and last) convention with the SWP by writing the document *State-Capitalism and World Revolution.*[6] It is true that that document, dated August 1950, had, for the first time, a section directly on philosophy, written by Lee. Peculiarly enough, it centered, not on the Absolute Idea—which we had reached (but not completed) in our three-way correspondence—but on Contradiction.

---

5 Quoted from letter of C.L.R. James to Grace Lee, June 19 (?), 1949, RDC, p. 1630. —Editor.

6 RDC, pp. 1333–1412. Recently published as C.L.R. James, *State Capitalism and World Revolution: Written in Collaboration with Raya Dunayevskaya and Grace Lee* (Oakland, Calif.: PM Press, 2013). —Editor.

The following year, the Johnson-Forest Tendency left the SWP for good and all, but we did not at once declare ourselves publicly as an independent Marxist tendency. The Korean War and McCarthyism were still raging, and we were experimenting with a decentralized form of organization and a new form of paper—*Correspondence*—but only in mimeographed form.

By 1953, it was decided to come out with a printed, public paper, and towards that end we were preparing for the first (and what turned out to be the last) convention of what had been the united Johnson-Forest Tendency. *Everything changed with the death of Stalin on March 5, when suddenly, it wasn't only the objective situation that had so radically changed, but divergences appeared between Lee and me within the Tendency.* Let us look at the sequence of events that followed Stalin's death.

That very same day I wrote a political analysis which stressed that an incubus had been lifted from the minds of both the masses and the theoretician; and that, *therefore,* it was impossible to think that this would not result in a new form of revolt on the part of the workers. Secondly, when Charles Denby (the Black production worker who was to become the editor of *News & Letters* after the split) called me upon hearing of Stalin's death, I asked him to inquire about other workers' reactions to the event. When he reported these conversations, I suggested a second article that would reproduce the 1920–21 Trade Union debate between Lenin and Trotsky within the context of both Russia and the U.S., 1953. Denby not only approved both ideas but the very next day brought me a worker's expression: "I have just the one to take Stalin's place— my foreman." It was that expression which became the jumping-off place for my analysis of the 1920–21 debate, on the one hand, and Stalin's death in 1953, on the other. The article was called "Then and Now."

Lee (who was then on the West Coast and acting as editor that month) had a very different view of what kind of analysis of Stalin's death was needed, because—far from seeing any concern with that event on the part of American workers—she made her point of departure the fact that some women in one factory, instead of listening to the radio blaring forth the news of Stalin's death, were exchanging hamburger recipes. She so "editorialized" my analysis and so passionately stressed the alleged indifference of the American proletariat to that event, that the article became unrecognizable. It was included in the mimeographed *Correspondence* of March 19, 1953 (Vol. 3, No. 12), as "Why Did Stalin Behave That Way?"

In Detroit, I was preparing a "Special Feature" for the issue of *Correspondence* of April 16, 1953 (Vol. 4, No. 2), devoted to the 1920–21 debate, which carried the subtitle: "An Historical Event and an Organizational Incident." The following issue, April 30 (Vol. 4, No. 3), likewise had a "Special Feature," which described the dispute over the political analysis, holding that it wasn't possible to substitute a description of the indifference of a few women in a single factory exchanging hamburger recipes for the political analysis of the ramifications of a world event such as Stalin's death. That issue then reproduced the article on Stalin's death as originally written.

Clearly, the whole month of April was taken up with this dispute and the polemical letters that accompanied it, by which time I was so exhausted that I asked for a week off. It was during that week that I wrote two things: One was a critique of Isaac Deutscher—whom I called a Stalinist parading as a Trotskyist—saying of his analysis of the "collectivity of leadership" that it had, in fact, always been the course toward totalitarianism's single maximum leader, and at no time more so than when Stalin arose out of his so-called "collective leadership."

The other was the May 12 Letter on the Absolute Idea. I returned to Detroit, and though I plunged into organizational activity, I couldn't resist going from *Science of Logic* and *Phenomenology of Mind,* with which the May 12 letter was concerned, to the *Philosophy of Mind* on May 20. The point that was singled out by Lee, who had called them nothing short of "the equivalent of Lenin's Notebooks for our epoch," was the fact that I had discerned a movement from practice. Johnson refused to discuss the Letters, sent Lee to Detroit with the promise that he would comment after he returned to England and after we had finished with our convention, to be held in July.

As we know, the subjective movement—*not* of intellectuals debating, but of millions of masses in motion—transforms the objective scene totally. In this case, the June 17 East German Revolt which erupted was followed, within two weeks, by a revolt from inside Russia—the slave labor camp of Vorkuta. Both events so electrified the world that this time there was no way to narrow the question to an "internal matter." The July convention, however, proceeded without any reference to those Letters on the Absolute Idea. Thus, no one knew either that they contained an anticipation of a movement from practice, or that they had fully worked out a logical conclusion of all that three-way correspondence from 1949 to 1951. The convention proceeded to vote for preparing the first printed *Correspondence* in September and datelining it October 3, 1953.

What was happening objectively in the world, however, had little regard for the fact that Lee and I had agreed to stop the polemic. The East German revolt had so shaken up the Russian bureaucracy that it brought about the first form of deStalinization. Though it was not yet designated as deStalinization, the truth is that Stalin's heir tried hard to disassociate himself from the immediate causes of the totality of the Russian crisis. Thus, the post-Stalin rulers stopped the Korean War; shot Lavrenti P. Beria, the head of the Secret Service and the most hated man of the totalitarian bureaucracy; and instituted some mild reforms, such as a turn to consumerism—without, however, demurring to Georgy Malenkov as the one allegedly chosen by Stalin.

In my analysis of the Beria purge, though I called attention to the fact that when thieves fall out, the one who was "not to be forgotten, although little known at present" was Nikita Khrushchev, my main point was:

> We are at the beginning of the end of Russian totalitarianism. That does not mean the state-capitalist bureaucracy will let go of its iron grip. Quite the contrary. It will shackle them more.... What it does mean is that from the center of Russian production, from the periphery of the satellite countries oppressed by Russia, and from the insides of the Communist Parties, all contradictions are moving to a head and the open struggle will be a merciless fight to the end.[7]

What I stressed was: "There is no getting away from it, the Russian masses are not only ill-fed, ill-clad, and ill-housed. *They are rebellious.*"

There was no way of keeping this article out of the Lead of the first issue of the printed *Correspondence,* because that was what was happening in the objective world and we were now public. That did not, however, mean that Johnson and Lee greeted it enthusiastically. Quite the contrary. It was met with the same hostility as was my analysis of Stalin's death, and the critique of it by followers of Johnson and Lee continued for several issues.

The analyses of both Stalin and Beria were written while McCarthyism was raging in the country. All three events brought about a sharp conflict between Johnson and Lee on the one side, and me on the other. It was clear that in the two years between leaving the SWP and the appearance of *Correspondence* there had developed in the followers of Johnson a great diversion from Marxism as well as from the American revolution. Just as Lee said Marxism was Europe's responsibility, not ours, so now Johnson said that the union stewards' movement in Britain rather than the American workers here could dissipate the war clouds over Formosa.

The truth is that they were not prepared to fight McCarthyism, once the war clouds began to form and we were listed in December 1954.[8] When Johnson could not win a majority of the organization, he broke it up.[9] War and

---

7 "The Beria Purge" (unsigned), *Correspondence,* 1:1, October 3, 1953. —Editor.

8 Correspondence Committees was put on the list of "subversive organizations" by the U.S. federal government. —Editor.

9 See "Johnsonism: A Political Appraisal" by O'Brien, a 1956 Bulletin which is included in the Archives. [RDC, pp. 2467–75].

revolution have always constituted the Great Divide between Marxist revolutionaries and escapists.

Within a short month, we held our first Conference, which decided that our new publication, *News & Letters,* would appear on the second anniversary of the June 1953 East German revolt; that it would be edited by a production worker; and that I should complete the work on Marxism, now known as *Marxism and Freedom, from 1776 until Today.* At the same time that we singled out the four forces of revolt—rank-and-file labor, Blacks, women and youth—we projected the calling of a Convention within a year to create, for the first time, a Constitution for the committee form of organization we were working out as against a "vanguard party to lead." In November 1955 we published as our first pamphlet the translation of Lenin's Abstract of Hegel's *Science of Logic,* along with my Letters on the Absolute Idea.

CHAPTER 23

The Dialectic of Absolute Idea as New Beginning

This text is excerpted from a transcript of Dunayevskaya's April 18, 1976, speech to a News and Letters Committees leadership body. The speech was titled, "Our Original Contribution to the Dialectic of the Absolute Idea as New Beginning: In Theory, and Leadership, and Practice." The full document can be found in The Raya Dunayevskaya Collection, *pp. 5622–30.*

We have to begin with what is new in our contribution, because we have been so anxious to stress we are a *continuity* from Marx and Lenin (and we certainly are), and we've been so anxious to stress that we couldn't possibly have been without Marx and Lenin (again, we couldn't have been), that we have underplayed what is absolutely new, not just in relationship to a lot of nobodies who call themselves Marxists, but in relationship to our founders themselves. And because we have overemphasized their contribution, without which we couldn't possibly have been, it is necessary to then think backwards right now.

No one was greater than Marx. No one needs to be convinced of that fact. However, when it comes to the Absolute Idea, it isn't only that the young Marx got so thoroughly disgusted with Absolutes by the time he discovered his new continent of thought, that he said that's the end of that, I'll return to it some other time.[1] It is that when he did return—and in his greatest work he did—it was already as practice, and not as something that would help us grasp it by having a foundation.

For example, at the height of *Capital*, we see him breaking up the Absolute Idea by speaking about the absolute general law of capitalist accumulation. But its opposite was always taken to be only the unemployed army—and not the absolutely, totally opposite which we take it to be now. Marx only mentioned it as "the new passions and new forces for the reconstruction of society." The negation of the negation at that point certainly wasn't spelled out [MCIK, pp. 835–37; MCIP, pp. 928–29].

Lenin certainly paid a lot more attention to Absolute Idea. We have that chapter commented on more than any other chapter in *Science of Logic*. But he, too, had to concentrate, as all of us have to concentrate, on what is concrete

---

1 This refers to the end of Marx's "Critique of the Hegelian Dialectic" (included in the appendix of this book), where Marx breaks off his 1844 *Economic-Philosophic Manuscripts* before getting to the "Absolute Mind" section of Hegel's *Philosophy of Mind.* —Editor.

for our age. What was concrete for his age was, as we know, the transformation into opposite. But he threw out the last half of the last paragraph of Absolute Idea and said, That doesn't make any difference. It did make a difference, and my Letters on the Absolute Idea of 1953 spend something like 12 pages arguing against him for leaving out that last half paragraph.

Even more important, Chapter 1 of *Capital* was always in Lenin's mind as he was reading.[2] We have stressed that Lenin says that Universal, Particular, Individual was exactly what Marx had in mind when he wrote *Capital*. But Lenin never says anything about *fetishism*. When he was referring to Universal, Particular, and Individual, he was referring to the section just before the fetishism of commodities, when Marx explains how we came from barter to sales to money to capital.

In other words, the fetishism of commodities, as the dead labor sucking the living labor, and as the fact that you not only were exploited, but you actually had become an appendage to a machine—that was not concrete for Lenin. In fact, at one point—even though it wasn't at the stage where he was working with the Absolute Idea—he was "taken in," so to speak, by the Taylor system.[3] He wondered whether that was just capitalistic, or whether it could be used if you had soviets and you saw that it wasn't exploitative, and so forth.

So that whether we take our very founders, Marx and Lenin, or any of the Hegelian Marxists: Lukács when he was at his best, Marcuse when he was at his best, Adorno when he was at his best, the East Europeans when they were at their best—in an actual revolution—no one, *no one,* had formulated or even given us any indication that if you are going to break your head over Absolute Idea, *it would be as a new beginning. That's our original contribution.*

It isn't only that we did this great thing by saying Absolute isn't absolute in the ordinary sense of the word—it's the unity of theory and practice; Absolute isn't absolute in the bourgeois sense of the word—it's the question of the unity of the material and the ideal. But who ever said Absolute was a new beginning? None but us. And if we don't understand that original contribution—*that we have to begin with the totality*—then we won't know what a new beginning is. A new beginning could just be that we discovered the four forces of revolution.[4] We're certainly very proud of that—but that isn't all we're saying.

---

2 Lenin's notes on Hegel frequently refer to Marx's *Capital.* —Editor.

3 Frederick Taylor developed a system of scientific management based on time-motion studies, which became widely used for efficient exploitation of workers in industrial production. In another context, Lenin referred to the Taylor system as "man's enslavement by the machine." See Lenin's *Collected Works*, Vol. 20, pp. 152–54, and Vol. 27, pp. 258–59. —Editor.

4 Since its beginning in 1955, News and Letters Committees singled four forces of revolution in the U.S.: workers, Blacks, women, and youth. —Editor.

In fact, I would say that if there's anything we do understand, it's the movement from practice. We certainly have that embedded in our being. We do understand that part of the Absolute. We do not understand the other part, Absolute Idea as second negativity. And until we do understand it, we will not be able to project. Therefore we must return to Chapter 1 of *Philosophy and Revolution*, and read it with altogether new eyes. It is not just that we're challenging, or threatening, or saying something that sounds great and philosophic, but all the ramifications of that.

Hegel died in 1831. He was the greatest philosopher that ever lived. It is now 1976, and it was 1953 when I broke through on the three last syllogisms in Hegel's *Philosophy of Mind*. I never bothered to look up the philosophic scholars. I was sure they had dealt with it in their bourgeois way. I found out that nobody in the world had done it. It was then I found out that Hegel himself hadn't put them in until 1830, the year before he died. He had left it at ¶574 in 1817.[5] I think the first time I saw anything written about it was in the 1960s and that was a whole decade after I developed it.

¶574 says, "This is a summation of what I did, and what I did explains my conclusions, Absolute Idea."[6] So why did he suddenly decide to add three paragraphs? To say "a summation" evidently didn't satisfy him the year before he died. In the first of the three, ¶575, Logic, Nature, Mind (the three volumes of Hegel's *Encyclopedia of the Philosophical Sciences*) are not simply the names of what Hegel wrote. Nature, the center part, is not just the second book. The center part, the middle, contains the whole; it looks both forward and backward, and therefore, that is really the key point.

Marx said that any proletarian could have told Hegel that he should have begun with material things first. Everyone says it's a good thing Lenin didn't know that's what Marx said, because he wouldn't have dared say, "Isn't that great that Hegel goes from Logic to Nature—he's extending a hand to historical materialism. Therefore, that chapter is the most central. The most ideal is really the most practical—terrific and magnificent!"[7]

I came to this part and said, if it turns both backward and forward, it isn't just the remembrance of things past, but Hegel's also seeing the future embedded in there. That means there must be a movement from practice to theory that is itself a form of theory. This was on May 12, 1953. There hadn't yet been

---

5   The 1817 first edition of *Philosophy of Mind* contained a different version of the last three paragraphs, #575–77. They were dropped in the 1827 edition and appeared in their final version in the 1830 edition. —Editor.

6   This is not a quotation but a paraphrase of ¶574. —Editor.

7   From Lenin's Abstract of Hegel's *Science of Logic*. See Dunayevskaya's English translation in *Russia: From Proletarian Revolution to State-Capitalist Counter-Revolution*, p. 105. —Editor.

the June 17, 1953, revolt [in East Germany]. Everybody thought I was crazy—all this worry about what Stalin's death meant and that it wasn't going to stand still. It is the period from March to June when Stalin died and when the East German revolt broke out that we're concerned with—these few months. When I broke through on the Absolute Idea, May 12 and 20, it was in anticipation of what was actually occurring.[8]

In the next paragraph, #576, Nature becomes first, Mind becomes second, and Logic is the end. So now Mind is the middle, the mediation, the center, the greatness from which the whole flows. What did that mean to us in the Johnson-Forest Tendency? I said it meant we had to dig deeper into philosophy; we couldn't stop with state-capitalism. We must see that this was new—this movement *from practice* and this movement *from theory* are a unity.

¶577 is even crazier than #575 and #576 were. Hegel has lived all his life on Logic, but when he comes to #577, instead of turning it to let Logic now become the center, Hegel just throws it out altogether. He says what we're dealing with is *Self-Thinking Idea*. In the whole thing, he has one single tiny sentence on eternity *after* the Self-Thinking Idea which has thrown out, replaced, Logic.

Now if that's what it means—and Hegel throws out his Logic—what could be greater? He says the Self-Thinking Idea is the self-bringing forth of liberty. That's when we already have it, the revolution is here, and everything is ready for not putting things off for the day after. It's right here and you better go do it and think it and everybody be part of the dialectic.

• • •

What do we mean by the cogency of dialectics of negativity for our period of mass revolutions? What do we mean by Absolute Idea as new beginning? When we keep stressing, correctly, that it's a unity of theory and practice, we do not know the double negation as being within each one.... I have stated many, many times that second negativity is not just when you come to the Absolute Idea, but that you experience second negativity at every single stage—and since everybody's always saying, "Don't give your first reaction, wait for second negativity," you would think we certainly understand second negativity. But until it becomes concrete, we don't.

There is one thing that I want to include here, in relationship to Jean-Paul Sartre and Frantz Fanon on the question of Particular. We've always talked

---

8 Dunayevskaya's "Letters on Hegel's Absolutes" of May 12 and 20, 1953, are available in *The Philosophic Moment of Marxist-Humanism* and *The Power of Negativity*. —Editor.

against the fixed Particular, nationalized property = socialism.[9] But Universal, Particular and Individual are the three main categories of the Doctrine of the Notion.[10] Particular is your first negation of the Universal when it's abstract, and Individual is the total concretization when it's Individualism which lets nothing interfere with its Universalism, that is, Freedom.[11]

The idea is that when it's *not* fixed, Particular is the way to get to the second negativity; there is no other way to get to it. And what Fanon expressed so passionately was that he did not mean that Negroes are not a Particular. He meant that Negritude is the Particular which is Universal. That is what he meant by "national consciousness that is not nationalism but is a form of internationalism."[12] He certainly did some very beautiful things on the difference between national consciousness that makes you proud of the heritage or makes you realize that this is a contribution, and nationalism, which he absolutely rejected because he was a total internationalist and revolutionary.

... The fixed particular is absolutely wrong and will kill you. But when it's not fixed, when it's a stage in the development of the concretization, that is the only way to get to second negativity.

What I'm trying to stress here are certain stages in Chapter 1 [of *Philosophy and Revolution*] which must be grasped as concrete. You have to say to yourself: If Absolute Idea means new beginnings, it means that in talking to such and such a person, I have to present the whole of philosophy and Marxist-Humanism. It is not enough to say, "We agree with you on the question of welfare or whatever." The question of welfare or whatever becomes a way not only of you learning something from them, but of them having an awful lot to learn from you, because they get an entirely new interpretation of the problem that had been bothering them....

---

9   Dunayevskaya argued that Leon Trotsky made an "abstraction of the Russian state, even after Stalinism had transformed it into its opposite, a state-capitalist society," thereby making a fixed particular of Russia's nationalized property, equating it to a "workers' state." See *Philosophy and Revolution*, pp. 139–45. —Editor.

10   This refers to Book Three, "The Doctrine of the Notion," in Hegel's *Science of Logic*. —Editor.

11   In Paragraph 481 of *Philosophy of Mind*, Hegel wrote of "individuality ... purified of all that interferes with its universalism, i.e., with freedom itself." —Editor.

12   In *The Wretched of the Earth*, Frantz Fanon wrote: "National consciousness, which is not nationalism, is the only thing that will give us an international dimension" (p. 247). —Editor.

SECTION B

Black Liberation and Internationalism

∵

CHAPTER 24

Abolitionism and the American Roots of Marxism

American Civilization on Trial, excerpted here, was first published in May 1963, signed by the National Editorial Board of News & Letters, with the subtitle "The Negro as Touchstone of History, 100 Years After the Emancipation Proclamation." It was written by Dunayevskaya, who poured into it a lifetime of work and activity, from her work with the Negro Champion *as a teenager through her 1940s arguments within Trotskyism for the validity of independent Black struggles, to the founding of News and Letters Committees, when she hailed the Montgomery Bus Boycott and singled out Black masses as one of the "four forces of revolution" in the U.S.* American Civilization on Trial *had four printings in Dunayevskaya's lifetime, with the subtitle changed to "Black Masses as Vanguard" in 1970. It proclaims a pathbreaking theoretical perspective, showing how Black masses have been the vanguard in U.S. history, whose turning points arose when white labor coalesced with Black masses in motion. It demonstrated the two-way road between Africa and America and the relationships of Marx and Lenin to the Black dimension in the U.S.* American Civiliation on Trial, *along with another* News & Letters *pamphlet,* Freedom Riders Speak for Themselves, *was used as a textbook in the Freedom Schools of Mississippi Freedom Summer (1964) in Jackson, Gulfport, McComb, and Canton, Miss.*

1   The Compelling Issue at Stake

American Civilization is identified in the consciousness of the world with three phases in the development of its history.

The first is the Declaration of Independence and the freedom of the thirteen American colonies from British Imperial rule.

The second is the Civil War.

The third is technology and world power, which are presently being challenged by the country that broke America's nuclear monopoly—Russia.

So persistent, intense, continuous, and ever-present has been the self-activity of the Negro, before and after the Civil War, before and after World War I, before, during, and after World War II, that it has become the gauge by which American Civilization is judged. Thus, Little Rock reverberated around the world with the speed of Sputnik I, with which it shared world headlines in 1957, and which gave the lie to American claims of superiority.

The Civil War remains the still unfinished revolution 100 years after, as the United States is losing the global struggle for the minds of men.

President Kennedy asked that this entire year, 1963, the centenary of the Emancipation Proclamation, be devoted to its celebration. Clichés strutted out for ceremonial occasions cannot, however, hide today's truth. Because the role of the Negro remains the touchstone of American Civilization—and his struggle for equal rights today belies their existence—paeans of praise for the Emancipation Proclamation can neither whitewash the present sorry state of democracy in the United States, nor rewrite the history of the past. Abraham Lincoln would not have issued the Proclamation had the Southern secessionists not been winning the battles *and* the Negro not been pounding down the doors of the Northern Armies demanding to fight.

By 1960, the year when no less than 16 new African nations gained their independence, the activities of the American Negroes had developed from the Montgomery, Alabama, Bus Boycott in 1956, the year of the Hungarian Revolution, to the Sit-Ins, Wade-Ins, Dwell-Ins, North and South.

In 1961 they reached a climax with the Freedom Rides to Mississippi. This self-activity has not only further impressed itself upon the world's consciousness, but also reached back into white America's consciousness. The result has been that even astronaut Walter Schirra's 1962 spectacular six-orbital flight became subordinate to the courage of James Meredith's entry into the University of Mississippi.

In a word, the new human dimension attained through an *oppressed people's* genius in the struggle for freedom, nationally and internationally, rather than either scientific achievement, or an individual hero, became the measure of Man in action and thought.

1.1   *Negroes' Vanguard Role*

The vanguard role of an oppressed people has also put white labor in mass production to the test. *And* it has put a question mark over the continuous technological revolutions, brought to a climax with Automation and nuclear power. For, without an underlying philosophy, neither the machine revolutions nor the splitting of the atom can produce anything but fear—fear of unemployment in the one case and fear of war in the other.

As was evident by the Negro's attitude in World War II, nothing can stop him from being the bitterest enemy of the existing society. In the midst of war, the Negro broke out in a series of demonstrations in Chicago, Detroit, New York as well as at army camps. Along with the miners' general strike that same year, these were the first instances in United States history when both labor, white and Negro, and the Negro as discriminated-against minority, refused to call a halt either to the class struggle or the struggle for equal rights. *Both* forces challenged their own State *as well as* Communist propagandists who had declared the imperialist war to have become one of "national liberation" which demanded subordination to it of all other struggles.[1]

Fully to understand today's activities—and that is the only meaningful way to celebrate the centenary of the Emancipation Proclamation—we must turn to the roots in the past. This is not merely to put history aright. To know where one has been is one way of knowing where one is going. To be able to anticipate tomorrow one has to understand today. One example of the dual movement— the pull of the future on the present and its link to the past—is the relationship of American Negro to the African Revolutions. Because it is easy enough to see that the United States Supreme Court which, in 1954, gave its decision on desegregation in schools[2] is not the Court which, 100 years before, proclaimed the infamous Dred Scott decision,[3] there are those who degrade today's self-activity of the Negro. Instead, they credit Administration policy with changing the status of the American Negro.

They point to the Cold War and the need for America, in its contest with Russia, to win "the African mind." There is no doubt that the Cold War influenced the decision of the Supreme Court. Neither is there any doubt that the African Revolutions were a boon to the Negro American struggles. But this is no one-way road. It never has been. For decades, if not for centuries, the self-activity of the American Negro preceded and inspired the African Revolutions, its leaders as well as its ranks, its thought as well as its actions. The relationship is *to and from* Africa. It is a two-way road. This too we shall see more clearly as we return to the past. Because both the present and the future have their roots in a philosophy of liberation which gives action its direction, it becomes imperative that we discover the historic link between philosophy and action.

1.2   *Birth of Abolitionism*

Despite the mountains of books on the Civil War, there is yet to be a definitive one on that subject. None is in prospect in capitalist America. Indeed it is an impossibility so long as the activity of the Negro in shaping American Civilization remains a blank in the minds of the academic historians. The bourgeois

---

1   *The Negro and the Communist Party*, by Wilson Record (Chapel Hill: University of North Carolina Press, 1951), is a useful book on all the changes in the Communist Party line for the period of 1941–45. Many of the quotations here are obtained from that book.

2   The Supreme Court's decision in *Brown v. Board of Education of Topeka*, 1954, declared laws establishing segregated public schools unconstitutional. —Editor.

3   The Supreme Court's decision in *Dred Scott v. Sandford*, 1857, declared essentially that Black Americans were not citizens and had no rights. —Editor.

historian is blind not only to the role of the Negro but to that of the white Abolitionists. Mainly unrecorded by all standard historians, and hermetically sealed off from the power of comprehension, lie three decades of Abolitionist struggle of whites and Negroes that preceded the Civil War and made that irrepressible conflict inevitable. Yet these are the decades when the crucible out of which the first great independent expression of American genius was forged.

The historians who dominate American scholarship have only passing references to the Abolitionist movement. Clearly no unbridgeable gulf separates this type of history writing from Russia's infamous rewriting of its revolutionary history. Only Negro historians such as W.E.B. Du Bois, Carter G. Woodson, and J.A. Rogers have done the painstaking research to set the record of American history straight by revealing the Negroes' great role in its making. With few exceptions, however, their work is ignored by the dominant white academicians. Literary historians, like Vernon L. Parrington in his *Main Currents in American Thought*, did, it is true, recognize that the soil which produced Ralph Waldo Emerson produced also a William Lloyd Garrison.

Essayists like John Jay Chapman go a great deal further than Professor Parrington. He sides with the Abolitionists against the great literary writers comprising the Transcendentalists. "The Transcendentalists," writes John Jay Chapman,

> were sure of only one thing—that society as constituted was all wrong. The slavery question had shaken man's faith in the durability of the Republic. It was therefore adjudged a highly dangerous subject.... Mum was the word ... from Maine to Georgia.

To this he contrasts William Lloyd Garrison's ringing proclamation:

> I will be as harsh as truth and as uncompromising as justice. On this subject [slavery] I do not wish to think, speak or write with moderation. I am in earnest—I will not equivocate—I will not capitulate—I will not retreat a single inch—AND I WILL BE HEARD!

In the 1921 preface to his biography of Garrison, Chapman boldly claims "that the history of the United States between 1800 and 1860 will someday be rewritten with this man as its central figure." This certainly separates Chapman decisively from established historians who "analyze" Abolitionism as if it comprised a small group of fanatics removed from the mainstream of American Civilization. Chapman certainly believed the Abolitionists to be the true molders of history. Such writing, however, remains a history of great men instead of great masses of "common men."

The Abolitionists, however, saw themselves differently. The great New Englander, Wendell Phillips, was fully aware of the fact that not only Negro leaders like Frederick Douglass or Harriet Tubman, but white Abolitionists like himself and even the founder of the *Liberator*, William Lloyd Garrison, were "so tall" because they stood on the shoulders of the actual mass movement of slaves following the North Star to freedom. Without the constant contact of the New England Abolitionists with the Negro mass, slave and free, they would have been nothing—and no one admitted it more freely than these leaders themselves. *The Abolitionists felt that strongly because they found what great literary figures like Emerson, Thoreau, Hawthorne, Melville and Whitman did not find—the human force for the reconstruction of society.*

This is what armed them 100 years ago, with a more accurate measure of "the Great Emancipator" [Abraham Lincoln] than most of today's writers, though the latter write with hindsight. This is what gave the Abolitionists the foresight to see that the Civil War may be won on the battlefield but lost in the more fundamental problem of reconstructing the life of the country. This is what led Karl Marx to say that a speech by Wendell Phillips was of "greater importance than a battle bulletin." This is what led the great Abolitionist, Phillips, after chattel slavery was ended, to come to the labor movement, vowing himself "willing to accept the final results of a principle so radical, such as the overthrow of the whole profit-making system, the extinction of all monopolies, the abolition of privileged classes ... and best and grandest of all, the final obliteration of that foul stigma upon our so-called Christian civilization, the poverty of the masses...."

1.3   *American Roots of Marxism*

The *spontaneous* affinity of ideas, the *independent* working out of the problems of the age as manifested in one's own country, and the common Humanist goal made inevitable the crossing of the paths of Karl Marx and the Abolitionists.

Deep indeed are the American roots of Marxism. Since Marxism is not only in books but in the daily lives of people, one must, to grasp its American roots, do more than inhabit an ivory tower. Far, however, from heeding Wendell Phillips' admonition that "Never again be ours the fastidious scholarship that shrinks from rude contact with the masses," American intellectuals have so adamantly sought escape from reality that they have become more conservative than politicians. To use another expression of the great Phillips, "There is a class among us so conservative, that they are afraid the roof will come down if you sweep the cobwebs."

This characterizes our age most accurately. It applies just as appropriately to the end of the nineteenth century when the country turned from populism to rampant racism because capitalism found it "simply liked the smell of empire."[4] By then Phillips and Marx were long since dead.

Fortunately, however, Marxism being a theory of liberation, its Humanism springs ever anew in today's activities.[5]

2   Part i: From the First through the Second American Revolution

The African, brought here as a slave against his will, played a decisive role in the shaping of American civilization.

Some[6] there are who feel it is wrong to begin the Negro's story in America with his arrival here as a slave in 1619 since he had reached these shores long before then—with the discovery of the new world, in fact, mainly as servants or, in some cases, in the entourage of the explorers themselves.

It is certainly true that in the first quarter of the 17th century there were as many as 10,000 free Negroes in the United States. This is not the point, however. The point is that in slave revolts, first and foremost, in appeals of free Negroes, in the runaway slave being "conducted" North via the Underground Railway by fugitive ex-slaves, the Negro, free or slave, but especially slave, was decisive in the course American development followed.

The Ambivalence of the Declaration of Independence

It was the Negro's will to be free, not his alleged docility, that inspired the first draft of the Declaration of Independence, in which Thomas Jefferson lashed out against King George iii for conducting a

> cruel war against human nature itself, violating its most sacred rights of life and liberty in the persons of a distant people who never offended him, captivating and carrying them into slavery in another hemisphere....

Upon the insistence of the Southern delegation at the Continental Congress, this paragraph was stricken from the Declaration. *In this first burial of full freedom's call lies imbedded the social conflicts of today.*

---

4 *American Diplomacy, 1900–1950*, by George F. Kennan (Chicago: University of Chicago Press, 1951).

5 For the Humanism of Marxism in its American setting see *Marxism and Freedom* by Raya Dunayevskaya.

6 See *The Negro Revolt*, by Louis L. Lomax (New York: Harper Collins Publishers, 1962).

Though the section which specifically aimed at the abolition of slavery was expunged from the Declaration of Independence so that the abstractions of freedom could fit into the context of a slave society, so overpowering were its *implications* that it "sounded the tocsin"[7] for the European revolutions that followed. From the very birth of the nation there was a great divide between the leaders in government and the rank-and-file masses. It wasn't limited to the slave revolts in the South. It showed itself in unrest and repressions of the free farmers in Massachusetts and New York in their first strikes and formations of workingmen's parties.

1793, the year Eli Whitney invented the cotton gin that transformed cotton into a lush cash crop, was the year in which the House of Representatives refused to pass a law abolishing slavery. It was the year the first Fugitive Slave Act was passed against the runaways. A short five years later, the Alien and Sedition Law that was passed was aimed at all opposition to the ruling Federalists. The so-called Jefferson revolution which put an end to the odious Alien and Sedition Law did not, however, do anything to reverse the first Fugitive Slave Act, which was soon to be followed by others more repressive.

The cotton gin had signaled not only the continuance of slavery in the 1790s, but the grafting upon it, at the turn of the 19th century, of all the added evils of commercial capitalism. The decade of 1820–1830 marked the birth of industrial capitalism, so that Cotton was now King not only in plantation economy and in trade, but in New England textile and industry and politics in general. Cotton as King made and unmade presidents and induced so great a national conspiracy of silence that it poisoned the young democracy. The stream of runaways played a key role in impelling civil war. Ross Barnett's[8] predecessor in office 100 years back, Governor John Quitman, complained that between 1800 and 1860 the South had lost more than 10,000 slaves, valued at $30 million.

Yet, by sharpening antagonisms and social conflicts, "the cotton fiber" produced the most glorious page in American history, that written by the Abolitionists.

3   Abolitionism, First Phase: From "Moral Suasion" to Harpers Ferry

Negro slave revolts had reached a certain stage with Denmark Vesey in 1824 which led to a new approach to the attempts to gain freedom. An Underground

---

7   Preface to *Capital* by Karl Marx [MCIK, p. 14; MCIP, p. 91].
8   Ross Barnett was the Democratic governor of Mississippi from 1960 to 1964. A rabid segregationist and white supremacist, he was known for having the Freedom Riders jailed in 1961 and trying to block desegregation of the University of Mississippi and public schools. —Editor.

Railway, which was neither underground nor a railway, was organized in 1825 to conduct runaway slaves to freedom in the North and in Canada. The following year the free Negroes organized the Massachusetts General Colored Peoples Association. Its paper, appropriately called *Freedom's Journal*, appeared in 1827, with its first editorial announcing, "Too long have others spoken for us."

3.1   *David Walker's Appeal*

The most sensational response, however, was achieved by a single Negro named David Walker, who, in 1829, published *Walker's Appeal, in Four Articles; Together with a Preamble, to the Coloured Citizens of the World, but in Particular, and Very Expressly, to those of the United States of America.*

David Walker was a free Negro from North Carolina who had settled in Boston, where he earned a living by collecting rags. His *Appeal* was addressed to the free Negroes. He took them to task for their meekness. He urged them to make the cause of the slave their own because the wretchedness of the free Negroes' conditions was due to the existence of slavery.

Walker urged them to make freedom their business. He pointed to the superiority of Negroes, in numbers and in bravery, over the whites. He took the great to task as well. In response to Thomas Jefferson, who had referred to the Negroes' color as "unfortunate," David Walker shouted

> My Colour will yet root some of you out of the very face of the earth ! ! ! America is more our country, than it is the whites'—we have enriched it with our *blood and tears*.

So extraordinary was the impact of this pamphlet that legislatures in the South were called into special sessions to enact laws against free Negroes as against the slaves for reading it. They put a price of $3,000 on the head of its author. Nevertheless, 50,000 copies of this 76-page pamphlet were sold and circulated hand to hand. Those who could not read had others read it to them. The South trembled at the simple words of an obscure Negro.

The vanguard role of the Negro in the struggle for freedom helped bring onto the historic stage the most extraordinary of all phenomena of American Civilization: New England Abolitionism. The year that William Lloyd Garrison[9]

---

9   For a modern biography of William Lloyd Garrison, see the one by John J. Chapman in *The Selected Writings of John Jay Chapman* (New York: Farrar, Strauss and Cudahy, 1957). For a more detailed biography, see *William Lloyd Garrison—The Story of His Life* (New York: Century Co., 1885–89) written by his children.

founded the *Liberator*, 1831, was the year also of the last and greatest of Negro slave revolts—that of Nat Turner. *The Cambridge Modern History* tells us:

> The insurrection was at once attributed to Negro preachers and "incendiary publications" such as Walker's pamphlet and the *Liberator*. To attack the *Liberator* now became habitual in all slave-holding States. The corporation of one city forbade any free Negro to take a copy of it from the post office. A vigilance committee in another offered $1,500 for the detection and conviction of any white person found circulating copies. The governors of Georgia and Virginia called on the mayor of Boston to suppress it; and the legislature of Georgia offered $5,000 to any person who should secure the arrest and conviction of Garrison under the laws of the State.
>
> Undeterred by these attacks, Garrison gathered about him a little band of Abolitionists, and towards the close of 1831 founded at Boston the New England Anti-slavery Society, and in 1833, at Philadelphia, the American Anti-slavery Society.

3.2 *Abolitionism: A New Dimension of American Character*

Nothing since has superseded this merger of white intellectual with the negro mass with the same intense devotion to principle, the same intimacy of relations of white and Black, the same unflinching propaganda in face of mob persecutions—and even death—the same greatness of character which never bent during the three long decades of struggle until the irrepressible conflict occurred, and even then did not give up the fight but sought to transform it—and succeeded—from a war of mere supremacy of Northern industry over Southern cotton culture to one of emancipation of slaves.

The movement renounced all traditional politics, considering all political parties of the day as "corrupt." They were inter-racial and in a slave society preached and practiced Negro equality. They were distinguished as well for inspiring, aligning with and fighting for equality of women in an age when the women had neither the right to the ballot nor to property nor to divorce. They were internationalists, covering Europe with their message, and bringing back to this country the message of the Irish Freedom Fighters.

They sought no rewards of any kind, fighting for the pure idea, though that meant facing the hostility of the national government, the state, the local police, and the best citizens who became the most unruly mobs. They were beaten, mobbed and stoned.

These New England Abolitionists added a new dimension to the word *intellectual*, for these were intellectuals whose intellectual, social, and political creativity was the expression of precise social forces. They gloried in being "the means" by which a direct social movement expressed itself, the movement of slaves and free Negroes for total freedom.

Pacifist though they were in philosophy, they lined up with John Brown. Perhaps that explains why, despite the great native tradition of Abolitionism, some of today's Negro leaders have traveled instead to India in search of a philosophy of non-violence.

Wendell Phillips eloquently explains why the pacifists came to the defense of the great martyr:

> Harpers Ferry is the Lexington of today.... Suppose he did fail. There are two kinds of defeat. Whether in chains or in laurels, Liberty knows nothing but victories. Soldiers call Bunker Hill a defeat; but Liberty dates from it....[10]

4   Abolitionism, Second Phase: The Unfinished Revolution

On January 11, 1860, Marx wrote to Engels:

> In my opinion, the biggest things that are happening in the world today are, on the one hand, the movement of the slaves in America started by the death of John Brown, and, on the other, the movement of the serfs in Russia.... I have just seen in the [*New-York Daily*] *Tribune* that there has been a fresh rising of slaves in Missouri, naturally suppressed. But the signal has now been given.[11]

When the young Marx first broke from bourgeois society and elaborated his philosophy of Humanism in 1844, he paid little attention to the remains of chattel slavery. Now, however, Marx kept his eyes glued on the movement of the Negro slaves. When the Civil War broke out, and "the Great Emancipator" did all in his power to limit it to a white man's war for Union, Marx began

---

10   For a modern biography of Wendell Phillips see *The Prophet of Liberty* by Oscar Sherwin (New York: Bookman Associates, 1958). Otherwise, see his own *Speeches and Writings* (Boston: Lee and Shepard, 1872). These also illuminate the role of women in the Abolitionist movement and its connection with the start of the suffragette movement.

11   *Selected Correspondence of Marx and Engels* [MECW 41, pp. 4–5]. Most of the other quotations from Marx's correspondence can be found easily in his writings from the dates given.

to popularize the speeches and analyses of the Abolitionists, especially those Wendell Phillips wrote against the Northern conduct of the war: "The President has not put the Confiscation Act into operation.... He has neither insight nor foresight...."

Because Lincoln's main strategic concern was to conciliate the so-called "moderate" border slave states that remained in the Union, he wanted neither to free the slaves nor allow them to participate in the war as soldiers. Lincoln nullified the few attempts by generals on the spot (John C. Fremont in Missouri, David Hunter in Georgia, Florida and South Carolina, and Ben Butler in Virginia) to issue their own emancipation proclamations. As late as 1862, when Horace Greeley as the editor of the *New-York Daily Tribune* published "A Prayer of 20 Millions" for the abolition of slavery, Lincoln replied: "My paramount objective *is* to save the union, and is *not* either to save or destroy slavery."

This denotes the first phase of the long Civil War, which lasted four years and cost the lives of a million men. Phillips maintained that if it had been fought as a war of liberation—and the Negroes were pounding at all the doors, North and South, to let them fight—it could be easily won in a few months. When military expediency, however, dictated a change in course, Phillips maintained that

> In this war mere victory on a battlefield amounts to nothing, contributes little or nothing toward ending the war.... Such an aimless war I call wasteful and murderous.

When Engels too feared that things were going so badly for the North that it would lose the war, Marx wrote:

> A single Negro regiment would have a remarkable effect on Southern nerves.... A war of this kind must be conducted on revolutionary lines while the Yankees have thus far been trying to conduct it constitutionally.[12]

Finally, on January 1, 1863, Abraham Lincoln issued his Emancipation Proclamation. It was no ringing declaration; his compromisist words moved gingerly to free only those slaves in the rebellious states. As one historian recently put it, it was "as emotional as a bill of sale."[13]

---

12   Ibid. August 7, 1862 [MECW 41, p. 400].
13   "Lincoln and the Proclamation," an article in *The Progressive*, December 1962, by Richard N. Current, author of many works on Lincoln.

4.1   *Turning Point*

Nevertheless it is the turning point. This second stage of the war altogether transformed its character. The passing of *this* year in the Civil War outlines the contrast of centuries. Negroes flocked into the Army, battles began being won. Wendell Phillips declared: "I want the blacks as the very basis of the effort to regenerate the South!"

On the other side of the Atlantic, English workers, whose livelihood as textile workers depended on Southern cotton, held mass demonstrations to prevent their ruling class from intervening on the side of the Bourbon South, whose cotton kingdom supplied Britain's textile barons raw materials for their world-dominating industry.

A new decade had indeed dawned in the world with the outbreak of the Civil War in the United States, the insurrection in Poland, the strikes in Paris, and the mass meetings of English workers who chose to starve rather than perpetuate slavery on the other side of the Atlantic. The actions culminated in the establishment of the International Working Men's Association, headed by Karl Marx.

From the first, Marx took the side of the North, though, naturally, as we saw, he was with Phillips' criticism of the conduct of the war, rather than with the President, of whom he had written to Engels:

> All Lincoln's acts appear like the mean pettifogging conditions which one lawyer puts to his opposing lawyer. But this does not alter their historic content.... The events over there are a world upheaval.[14]

He therefore separated himself from some[15] self-styled Marxists in the United States who evaded the whole issue of the Civil War by saying they were opposed to "all slavery, wage and chattel." In the name of the International, Marx wrote Lincoln,

---

14   *The Civil War in the United States*, by Marx and Engels (New York: International Publishers, 1970) [Letter of Marx to Engels, October 29, 1862, MECW 41, p. 421].

15   Just as Marx in his day separated himself, so Engels after Marx's death wrote: "The Social-Democratic Federation here shares with your German-American Socialists, the distinction of being the only parties that have managed to reduce Marxian theory of development to a rigid orthodoxy, which the workers are not to reach themselves by their own class feelings, but which they have to gulp down as an article of faith at once and without development. That is why both of them remain mere sects and come, as Hegel says, from nothing through nothing to nothing" (*Letters to Americans* by Marx and Engels, p. 263 [Letter of Engels to Friedrich Adolph Sorge, May 12, 1894, MECW 50, p. 301]).

While the workingmen, the true political power of the North, allowed slavery to defile their own republic; while before the Negro mastered and sold without his concurrence they boasted it the highest prerogative of the white-skinned laborer to sell himself and choose his own master; they were unable to attain the true freedom of labor or to support their European brethren in their struggle for emancipation, but this barrier to progress has been swept off by the red sea of civil war.

As Marx later expressed in *Capital,*

In the United States of North America, every independent movement of the workers was paralyzed so long as slavery disfigured a part of the Republic. Labor cannot emancipate itself in the white skin where in the black it is branded. But out of the death of slavery a new life at once arose. The first fruit of the Civil War was the eight hours' agitation, that ran with the seven-leagued boots of the locomotive from the Atlantic to the Pacific, from New England to California. The General Congress of Labor at Baltimore (August 16, 1866) declared: "The first and great necessity of the present, to free the labor of this country from capitalistic slavery, is the passing of a law by which eight hours shall be the normal working-day in all States of the American Union. We are resolved to put forth all our strength until this glorious result is attained." [MCIK, p. 329; MCIP, p. 414]

Soon after the war and the abolition of slavery, Abolitionism as a movement vanished from the scene. Of all its leaders, Wendell Phillips alone made the transition to the labor movement. The four million freedmen remained tied to cotton culture and therein lies imbedded the roots of the Negro question.

CHAPTER 25

Marx and the Two-Way Road between the U.S. and Africa

Dunayevskaya wrote the essay excerpted here as an "Introduction/Overview" for the expanded edition of American Civilization on Trial *published in 1983. It was originally titled, "A 1980s View of the Two-Way Road between the U.S. and Africa."*

What was won through the last two decades was inseparable from the intense new forms of revolt. The turbulent 1960s witnessed the birth of a whole Third World, central to which was the Black Revolution both in the U.S. and in Africa. Secondly, inseparable from and simultaneous with that, was the Marxist-Humanist banner that *American Civilization on Trial* raised in the context of the whole 200-year history of the U.S., whose civilization had been put on trial and found guilty.

In a word, to separate a philosophy of liberation from the struggle for freedom is to doom us to yet one more unfinished revolution such as has characterized the U.S. from its birth, when the Declaration of Independence was meant for white only and left the Black enslaved. It was because this history, not only as past but as present, remained racist on the 100th anniversary of the "Emancipation Proclamation" that the Introduction to *American Civilization on Trial* was entitled: "Of Patriots, Scoundrels and Slave Masters."

1   Historic Turning Points: Slave Revolts, Women's Dimension, Anti-Imperialism

What *American Civilization on Trial* disclosed was that, at each historic turning point of development in the U.S., it was the Black masses in motion who proved to be the vanguard. Take the question of the slave revolts leading to the birth of Abolitionism, which had created a new dimension of American character. It is not only, as we pointed out, that:

> They were inter-racial and in a slave society preached and practiced Negro equality. They were distinguished as well for inspiring, aligning with and fighting for equality of women in an age when the women had neither the right to the ballot nor to property nor to divorce. They were

internationalist, covering Europe with their message, and bringing back to this country the message of the Irish Freedom Fighters.

It is that the vanguard nature of the Black dimension in the Abolitionist movement has much to say to us today—even when it comes to Women's Liberation.

Take so simple a matter as a name, specifically Sojourner Truth's name. Keep in mind what the question of choosing a name means in today's Women's Liberation Movement, which has discussed widely the question of not bearing one's husband's name. But did anyone other than Sojourner Truth include a whole philosophy of freedom in a chosen name? Listen to her story. She said she "talked with God," told him she refused to bear a slave name, and asked what should she do? "He" answered her as follows: Sojourn the world over and tell everyone the truth about American democracy, that it doesn't exist for Blacks. That was how she decided to call herself "Sojourner Truth."

Woman as Reason as well as Force has always been hidden from history, not to mention philosophy. Yet, as early as 1831, the very year Nat Turner led the greatest slave revolt, Maria Stewart spoke up in public—the first American-born woman, white or Black, to speak publicly. Her appeal was to:

> O ye daughters of Africa, awake! awake! arise! no longer sleep nor slumber but distinguish yourselves. Show forth to the world that ye are endowed with noble and exalted faculties.... How long shall the fair daughters of Africa be compelled to bury their minds and talents beneath a load of iron pots and kettles? ... How long shall a mean set of men flatter us with their smiles, and enrich themselves with our hard earnings: their wives' fingers sparkling with rings and they themselves laughing at our folly?

Total deafness to women shaping history extended into the 20th century, even when it wasn't a question of the rights of any single person, but when whole masses in motion fought—and won!

In Africa, in 1929, tens of thousands of Igbo women had self-organized against both British imperialism and their own African chiefs, whom they accused of carrying out the new British edict to tax women. It took our age and a new Women's Liberation Movement to bring forth just such pages of history.[1]

---

1   See Judith Van Allen's "Aba Riots or Igbo Women's War" in *Ufahamu,* 6 no. 1 (1975). An elaborated version also appeared in *Women in Africa,* Nancy Hafkin and Edna Bay, eds. (Stanford, Calif.: Stanford University Press, 1976). See especially a global view of revolutionary women in *Rosa Luxemburg, Women's Liberation, and Marx's Philosophy of Revolution,* pp. 79–112.

The vanguard nature of the Black dimension is seen also in the struggle against imperialism at its earliest appearance. Take the question of the Spanish-American War. Blacks sensed its imperialist nature and became the very first force in the world outside of Latin America itself to organize an Anti-Imperialist League in 1899. In a word, whether the focus is on the Civil War in the U.S. or the world anti-imperialist struggles, the Black masses in motion showed their multi-dimensionality.

In the very same year that the Anti-Imperialist League was formed, in a different part of the world the revolutionary Marxist, Rosa Luxemburg, wrote:

> At present, Persia and Afghanistan too have been attacked by Russia and England. From that, the European antagonisms in Africa too have received new impulses; there, too, the struggle is breaking out with new force (Fashoda, Delagoa, Madagascar). It's clear that the dismemberment of Asia and Africa is the final limit beyond which European politics no longer has room to unfold. There follows then another such squeeze as has just occurred in the Eastern question, and the European powers will have no choice other than throwing themselves on one another, until *the period of the final crisis sets in within politics ... etc., etc.*[2]

The birth of a whole new Third World in our age cast a new illumination both on Luxemburg's flash of genius on imperialism's rise and on the little-known page of Black history concerning its early anti-imperialist struggles. The struggles today have reached a new intensity, and they are multi-dimensional. As we witnessed in the anti-Vietnam War struggles, it was the Black youth who first articulated the defiance as "Hell, no! We won't go!" Yet it has become clear since the 1960s that even the greatest actions need the direction that comes from a total philosophy of freedom. What is needed now is to concretize such a philosophy of freedom as the reality for our age.

2   Emergence of the Third World as Marx Foresaw it

What *American Civilization on Trial* reveals is both Marx's deep American roots and his Promethean vision. Take the succinct way in which Marx pinpointed the situation in the Civil War at its darkest moment, as the war dragged on and the Southern generals were winning so decisively as to produce a defeatist attitude in the North. Where others looked at the military forces, Marx looked at the forces of revolution: "A single Negro regiment would have a remarkable

---

2 Letter of Rosa Luxemburg to Leo Jogiches, January 9, 1899, *Rosa Luxemburg Reader,* p. 381.

effect on Southern nerves.... A war of this kind must be conducted along revolutionary lines ..." (Letter from Marx to Engels, August 7, 1862 [MECW 41, p. 400]).

From his very first break with capitalism, as he discovered a whole new continent of thought and of revolution which he called "a new Humanism," capitalism is what Marx critiqued and fought against throughout his life. Here is how he described the origins of European capitalism:

> The discovery of gold and silver in America, the extirpation, enslavement and entombment in mines of the aboriginal population, the beginning of the conquest and looting of the East Indies, the turning of Africa into a warren for the commercial hunting of black skins, signalized the rosy dawn of the era of capitalist production. [MCIK, p. 823; MCIP, p. 915]

The unmasking of Western civilization's racism by its Black dimension in revolutionary moments of mass upsurge makes imperative a most serious return, on this centenary of Marx's death, to his critical, revolutionary unmasking of Western civilization's capitalist foundations. Just as in the U.S., so in Britain, Western civilization has been put on trial by the Black dimension. This became especially sharp with the April 1981 Brixton rebellion. Like the famous Kerner Commission Report following the 1967 rebellions in the U.S. and the current investigations into the Miami rebellions, the British government has produced its own Scarman Report on the Black British rebellions. While the tone of the British report is more outraged than its American counterpart at the stripping away of Britain's fetishism about its vaunted "civilization," Lord Scarman nevertheless found that

> the disorders, like so many riots in British history, were a protest against society by people, deeply frustrated and deprived, who saw in a violent attack upon the forces of law and order their one opportunity of compelling public attention to their grievances.

Being in the business of empire longer than the Americans, however, the British authorities are more expert in recognizing historic continuities in the new forms of revolt against their rule. Thus, in its very first paragraph, the Scarman Report observed that "the petrol bomb was now used for the first time on the streets of Britain (the idea, no doubt, copied from the disturbances in Northern Ireland)."[3]

---

3 Marx often singled out the deep relationship between Irish revolutionaries and all other minorities. A new projected 11-volume documentary study covering the impact of Garveyism on the U.S., Africa and the West Indies, reveals the revolutionary relationship between

Frantz Fanon was absolutely right when, in our age, he wrote: "Two centuries ago, a former European colony decided to catch up with Europe. It succeeded so well that the United States of America became a monster...." The extreme urgency of dealing with that global monster today demands that the struggles be tightly woven together with a total philosophy. As we work it out for our age, what is needed is a concentration, at one and the same time, on (1) the trail to the 1980s from Marx's last decade, and (2) revolutionary Black thought.

It was in his last decade that Marx discovered still newer paths to revolution. Present-day existing state-capitalisms calling themselves Communist, like Russia and China, have totally abandoned both the philosophy and the actuality of Marx's "revolution in permanence." Marx, on the other hand, began introducing fundamental changes in his greatest theoretical work, *Capital*, which disclosed his new perceptions of the possibility of a revolution in technologically underdeveloped lands before the technologically advanced West. Take the simple word "so-called" placed by Marx in the title of the final part of *Capital*: "The So-Called Primitive Accumulation of Capital." Though that word has been disregarded by post-Marx Marxists, it touches the burning question of our day—the relationship of technologically advanced countries to the technologically underdeveloped Third World. What Marx was saying with that word, "so-called," was that it simply wasn't true that capitalism's carving up of the Asian and African world characterized only the primitive stage of capitalism.

To further stress that technologically advanced capitalism has not at all left behind the so-called primitive stage of turning Africa into "a warren for hunting black skins" and forcing them into slavery in "civilized" countries ... Marx added a whole new paragraph to the 1875 French edition of *Capital*, which showed that this continued outreach into imperialism "successively annexed extensive areas of the New World, Asia and Australia" [MCIP, p. 786 ftn.][4]

As Marx then turned to study pre-capitalist societies—be it of the Native Americans, the Indians in Morgan's *Ancient Society,* or the Australian Aborigine designated by Marx as "the intelligent Black"—he hit out against anyone trying to transform his chapter, "The Historical Tendency of Capitalist Accumulation"

Garveyism and the Irish struggles in the early part of the 20th century. Vol. I (1826–1919) and Vol. II (1919–1920) are due off the press in November, 1983, edited by Robert A. Hill (Berkeley, Cal.: Univ. of. California Press). See also "British Civilization on Trial," in the May-June, 1981, issue of *Marxist-Humanism*, journal of British Marxist-Humanists, available from *News & Letters*.

4   This paragraph was left out of Engels' English and German editions. It is discussed in Chapter 10 of *Rosa Luxemburg, Women's Liberation and Marx's Philosophy of Revolution*, "A Decade of Historic Transformation: from the *Grundrisse* to *Capital.*"

into a "Universal." Marx insisted that he had been describing the particular, historic stage of Western capitalism; that other societies need not follow that path. If they did, they would "lose the finest chance ever offered by history to a people and undergo all the fatal vicissitudes of the capitalist regime."[5]

3   Revolutions in Philosophy and in Fact

Marx's projection of the possibility of a revolution coming first in technologically underdeveloped lands achieved a new meaning for our age with the emergence of a whole new Third World, as well as new mass struggles and the birth of new revolutionary forces as reason. The Black dimension in the U.S. as well as in Africa showed that we had, indeed, reached a totally new movement from practice to theory that was itself a new form of theory. It was this new movement from practice—those new voices from below—which we heard, recorded, and dialectically developed. Those voices demanded that a new movement from theory be rooted in that movement from practice and become developed to the point of philosophy—a philosophy of world revolution.

Our very first major theoretical work, *Marxism and Freedom,* cast in the context of that movement from practice, was followed by a series of pamphlets in which the voices of all the revolutionary forces—workers, Blacks, women and youth—could be heard: from *Workers Battle Automation* to *Freedom Riders Speak for Themselves,* and from *The Free Speech Movement and the Negro Revolution* to *Working Women for Freedom.*[6] Indeed, it was not only the voices of the Freedom Riders we heard in 1961, but the story of the magnificent Black women in Mississippi who called themselves "Woman Power Unlimited" and came to the aid of the jailed Freedom Riders.

American Civilization on Trial cast a new illumination on the two-way road between Africa and the U.S. via the West Indies by showing that what, to the capitalists, was the triangular trade of rum, molasses and slaves, was, to the Blacks, the ever-live triangular development of internationalism, masses in motion and ideas. This triangular development remains the dominant force to this day.

---

5 Marx's letter [MECW 24, pp. 196–201] to the journal which had published a critique of his work by the Russian Populist, Mikhailovsky, was written in November, 1877, but not published in Russia until 1886, after Marx's death in 1883.

6 The full development of Marxist-Humanist philosophy in the U.S., under the title "Marxist-Humanism, 1941 to Today, Its Origin and Development in the U.S." is on file and available on microfilm at the Archives of Labor and Urban Affairs, Walter Reuther Library, Wayne State University, Detroit, Mt 48202.

In our epoch, the dynamism of ideas in Africa comes out in sharp focus as we contrast it to the weary American bourgeois ideologues who declared the 1950s to be "the end of ideology" just when a whole new Third World emerged. As against what the capitalist ideologues wrote then, consider the 1959 speech by Leopold Sédar Senghor to the Constitutive Congress which united Mali and Senegal:

> A nation that refuses to keep its rendezvous with history, that does not believe itself to be the bearer of a unique message—that nation is finished, ready to be placed in a museum. The Negro African is not finished even before he gets started. Let him speak; above all, let him act. Let him bring like a leaven, his message to the world in order to help build a universal civilization. Let us recapitulate Marx's positive contributions. They are: the philosophy of humanism, economic theory, dialectical method.[7]

It is true that Africa, too, has since undergone many retreats, as the Union of Mali and Senegal has broken up and Senghor has retrogressed in thought, as well. It is not true that the mass freedom struggles have abated. Nor is it true that Senghor represents all of African thought. Frantz Fanon was the opposite both in thought and in act, and it is his philosophy that is alive as far as South Africa is concerned and, indeed, can become a foundation for today's freedom struggles worldwide. It was this new stage in the two-way road that we presented in our 1978 pamphlet *Frantz Fanon, Soweto, and American Black Thought.*

If we return to the year 1959, when Senghor made the Address to his Congress, we find that to be the same year that Frantz Fanon addressed the Second Congress of Black Artists and Writers meeting in Rome, where he said:

> The consciousness of self is not the closing of a door to communication. Philosophic thought teaches us, on the contrary, that it is its guarantee. National consciousness, which is not nationalism, is the only thing that will give us an international dimension.[8]

Furthermore, this was not philosophy for its own sake or history as past, because Fanon was contrasting the Black worker to the Black intellectual in that battle against colonialism:

---

7 Léopold Sédar Senghor, *On African Socialism* (New York: Praeger, 1968), p. 65.
8 Fanon addressed the Congress on "The Reciprocal Basis of National Cultures and the Struggles for Liberation." This quotation appears in *Wretched of the Earth,* p. 247. —Editor.

> History teaches us clearly that the battle against colonialism does not run straight away along the lines of nationalism.... It so happens that the unpreparedness of the educated classes, the lack of practical links between them and the mass of the people, their laziness, and, let it be said, their cowardice at the decisive moment of the struggle will give rise to tragic mishaps. (*Wretched of the Earth,* p. 148)

In this, too, Fanon's vision saw far. Which is why the final chapter of the 1973 work *Philosophy and Revolution*—"New Passions and New Forces: The Black Dimension, the Anti-Vietnam War Youth, Rank-and-File Labor, Women's Liberation"—quoted the American Black autoworker who gave the philosophy of Humanism its sharpest edge:

> There is no middle road anymore. The days we accepted "we have to take the lesser of two evils" are gone. You have to go to the extreme now. Racism is the issue here, and to rid ourselves of that, to be Humanist, we need a revolution.

The Black Consciousness Movement today recognizes Fanon as a great Third World theorist, at the same time that they recognize Steve Biko's unique creativity in the Soweto uprising in 1976 and in founding their great new movement. This is precisely why South Africa's barbaric apartheid system murdered Biko in September 1977.

It was no accident that Charles Denby, the Black production worker-editor of News & Letters since its birth, felt impelled in 1978 to add a new Part II to the story of his life, which had been published in 1952 as *Indignant Heart.* Thus, Part II of *Indignant Heart: A Black Worker's Journal begins* with the Montgomery Bus Boycott in the very year News and Letters Committees were born and *ends* with a chapter on "The Worldwide Struggle for Freedom," which discusses "the American Black identification with Soweto and Biko, with Fanon and Caribbean thought." It becomes clear why this story of Denby's life, North and South, which sums up a half century of freedom struggles, from the struggles of rural Blacks in the South to the wildcat strikes of Black workers in the North, concludes with this Black worker's declaration, "I consider my story as part of the worldwide struggles for freedom."

It is in Azania (South Africa) that the most exciting events are now unfolding, revealing how the mineworkers there are both organizing and thinking their own thoughts. A simple word—"Amandla!" (Power)—tells how new a stage they have reached. It is this word which Teboho Noka, an organizer for the National Union of Mineworkers, used in order to stress that not only are they fighting for different conditions of labor and higher wages, but for "Amandla"—adding: "It shall be ours." It is that feeling of fighting for nothing less than freedom which transforms the struggle from a mere trade union battle to one for a whole new society.

Like Marx in his day, Frantz Fanon, in our age, declared his philosophy to be a "new humanism," as he developed it most originally in his *Wretched of the Earth*:

> Comrades, let us flee from this motionless movement where gradually dialectic is changing into the logic of equilibrium. Let us reconsider the question of mankind. (p. 314)
>
> For Europe, for ourselves, and for humanity, comrades, we must turn over a new leaf, we must work out new concepts, and try to set afoot a new man. (p. 316)
>
> This new humanity cannot do otherwise than define a new humanism both for itself and for others. (p. 246)

4   Mass Unrest Today and the Need for Truly Human Foundations

Just as it was the Black dimension which sounded the alarm against U.S. imperialism's first adventure in the Philippines and the Caribbean at the turn of the century, so today it is the Latino dimension which is opposing Reagan's imperialist actions in Central America and the Caribbean. The gunboat diplomacy which saw the United States invade again and again—from Cuba and Nicaragua to Panama and Honduras in the period from the turn of the century into the 1930s—has returned in a vicious new form under Reagan. His policies of installing right-wing dictatorships and attacking the nascent Nicaraguan revolution seemed aimed at engulfing all of Central America in a "regional" war—that is, getting the Latin American countries to fight each other for the benefit of U.S. imperialism. The revolutionary opposition arising from within Central America—indeed, all of Latin America—extends to the Latino dimension right here within the U.S. At one and the same time, all are united in working to stay Reagan's counterrevolutionary hand, and by seeking out and expressing the dimensions of national minorities, sex and class are creating new pathways toward social revolution, in Latin America and in the U.S. itself.

The mass unrest today throughout the world, the deep recession we are in, and the many political crises we face compel intense new activities—whether on the production line or in the massive anti-nuke campaign or in the Black revolutionary movements—unseparated from a new passion for philosophy and revolutionary direction.

That revolutionary direction can be seen as we sum up how Marx worked it out concretely for his philosophy of "revolution in permanence" in relation to the Black world.

Marx's reference in the *Ethnological Notebooks* to the Australian Aborigine as "the intelligent Black" brought to a conclusion the dialectic he had unchained when he first broke from bourgeois society in the 1840s and objected to the use of the word "Negro" as if it were synonymous with the word "slave." By the 1850s, in the *Grundrisse*, he extended that sensitivity to the whole precapitalist world. By the 1860s, the Black dimension became, at one and the same time, not only pivotal to the abolition of slavery and victory of the North in the Civil War, but also to the restructuring of *Capital* itself. In a word, the often-quoted sentence: "Labor cannot emancipate itself in the white skin where in the Black skin it is branded" [MCIK, p. 329; MCIP, p. 414], far from being rhetoric, was the actual reality *and* the perspective for overcoming that reality. Marx reached, at every historic turning point, for a concluding point, *not* as an end but as a new jumping-off point, a new beginning, a new vision.

In the specific case of the Civil War in the U.S., it was not only a question of theory or of national action, but one of international organization as Marx established the International Workingmen's Association to come to the aid both of the North, especially the Abolitionists, in that Civil War, and of the European working class struggles, especially the Polish revolt against Russian tsarism. As Poland shows us all over again today, freedom fighters do not give up their struggle even when compelled to work under the whip of the counterrevolution.

There is no doubt that we are on the threshold of new revolutionary beginnings in the Black world in this Marx centenary year. The 20-year history of *American Civilization on Trial* and world development has seen not only capitalism's drive to war threaten the very existence of civilization as we have known it, but also its absolute opposite; revolutionary masses in motion. The Reagan retrogression—and the ceaseless struggles against the attempts to push back all the gains of the past two decades—give urgency to this new fourth, expanded edition (and fifth printing) of *American Civilization on Trial*.

The absolute challenge to our age is the concretization of Marx's concept of "revolution in permanence." The Black dimension is crucial to the total uprooting of existing, exploitative, racist, sexist society and the creation of new, truly human foundations.

RAYA DUNAYEVSKAYA FOR THE NATIONAL EDITORIAL BOARD OF
NEWS & LETTERS, AUGUST, 1983

CHAPTER 26

Black Intellectuals in Dilemma

In 1944 in the midst of World War II, An American Dilemma: The Negro Problem and Modern Democracy *by Gunnar Myrdal was published. The November 1944 issue of the Workers Party's journal* The New International *(Vol. X, No. 11) published Dunayevskaya's critique of both Myrdal and the role of Black intellectuals who worked with him, counterposed to the revolutionary role of Black masses. Its original title was "Negro Intellectuals in Dilemma: Myrdal's Study of a Crucial Problem," with the signature Freddie Forest. It is included in* The Raya Dunayevskaya Collection, *pp. 271–74.*

Over four years were needed to complete this study.[1] It is a product not only of the Swedish scholar Gunnar Myrdal and his two associates, Richard Sterner and Arnold Rose, but of some seventy-five intellectuals, both white and Negro, who gave full or part time to the gathering and analysis of data. Some of these supplementary studies were elaborated and published separately. The outstanding of these are: *The Negro's Share* by Richard Sterner, *Patterns of Negro Segregation* by Charles S. Johnson, and *Organized Labor and the Negro* by Herbert R. Northrup. Other manuscripts prepared for the larger study have remained unpublished, but have been placed on file at the Schomburg Collection, where they are available to the public. Even without these more detailed studies of separate aspects of the Negro problem, the Myrdal work comprises the most comprehensive thus far produced on the subject, and makes it possible to clear our shelves of many of the earlier volumes on this topic. This assertion, which has been made by the Negro intellectuals in their reviews of *An American Dilemma,* is not, however, repeated by the present reviewer as unqualified praise of the book. On the contrary, that this work makes such a clearing possible is only further testimony as to the paucity of adequate books on the subject. There is not a single outstanding work dealing with the Negro problem "in general," although there are good studies of specific facets of the Negro problem. In the present research we get an overall view of the entire field.

However, in some instances, as on the Reconstruction period, it is a retrogression. I speak of retrogression because, whereas Myrdal states that no comprehensive scientific study of the Reconstruction period has yet been written

---

1 *An American Dilemma: The Negro Problem and Modern Democracy.* By Gunnar Myrdal, with the assistance of Richard Sterner and Arnold Rose (New York: Harper & Bros., 1944); 2 volumes, 1,483 pages, $7.60.

by American historians, and urges that such a study be made, he is not helping the case along by more or less dismissing the Negro studies of the Reconstruction period as mere counter-balances to the prejudiced reports by the whites. W.E.B. Du Bois' *Black Reconstruction,* which is a first-class piece of research and analysis in a field barely touched by our venerable white historians, can in no way be dismissed so cavalierly.

One of the most serious shortcomings of the Myrdal book arises from the fact that in those cases where no study of a field had ever before been made, as on the Negro role in the Populist movement in the South, those unexplored fields are not only further neglected but are ignored. At the very height of the prejudice-ridden post-Reconstruction period, when the South was supposedly solidly white in thought and action, the Populist movement that was sweeping the country found its most radical expression in the South. The National Colored Farmers' Alliance alone numbered one and one-quarter million members and, although separately organized from the white agrarians, waged their class battles as one. It was a power to be reckoned with in both state and national politics, and was instrumental in the elections of Populist governors as well as national and state representatives. There have not been many Negro organizations with so large a membership. Any "social scientists" seriously studying the Negro problem, as Mr. Myrdal surely did, could not have escaped becoming interested in and probing to the end this outstanding example of class solidarity across racial lines. However, Prof. Myrdal seems to be ignorant of this movement. In a bibliography of thirty-five pages, no reference is made even to such popular works as the scholarly and sympathetic study, *Tom Watson, Agrarian Rebel*, by C. Van Woodward, or the scholarly but prejudiced study, *The Populist Movement in Georgia*, by A.M Arnett. The bibliography does include John D. Hicks' standard *The Populist Revolt*, which contains one reference to the Negro Farmers' Alliance. If that left any impression on Mr. Myrdal, however, it was insufficient to induce him to pursue the study of this phenomenon through primary sources.

This failure must be analyzed. It was surely not due to lack of money or unavailability of scholars to undertake such a study, if an awareness of the need for such research had been felt. Mr. Myrdal neither searched this field nor even indicated that it should be searched because his outlook could not encompass the possibility of such a movement. Mr. Myrdal emphatically rejects the Marxian concept of the class struggle. He writes:

> Our hypothesis is that a society where there are broad social classes and, in addition, more minute distinctions and splits in the lower strata, the *lower class groups will to a great extent take care of keeping each other subdued*, thus relieving, to that extent, the higher classes of this otherwise

painful task necessary to the monopolization of the power and the advantages. (p. 68)

Clearly, this means that Mr. Myrdal thinks that the white and Negro masses, rather than turn against their common oppressor, will fight each other. "The Marxian scheme," he argues further,

assumes that there is an actual solidarity between the several lower class groups against the higher classes, or, in any case, a potential solidarity which as a matter of natural development is bound to emerge. (p. 68)

Mr. Myrdal maintains that that "scheme" has influenced Negro intellectuals, and has thus evidently blurred *their* vision. As an example of this he calls attention to Du Bois' *Black Reconstruction,* where it is stated:

The South after the [Civil] war presented the greatest opportunity for a real national labor movement which the nation ever saw or is likely to see for many decades.

Mr. Du Bois is wrong. No such possibility existed then for the simple reason that the industrial development in the South was of insufficient scope to allow the proletariat in heavy industry to become the leading social force and act as a bridge for the whole area with the more developed industrial North. Mr. Myrdal, however, is entirely wrong when he attributes the failure of a national labor movement to have arisen then to racial differences.

From our point of view such a possibility did not exist at all and the negative outcome was neither an accident nor a result of simple deception or delusion. These two groups, illiterate and insecure in an impoverished South, placed in an intensified competition with each other, lacking every trace of primary solidarity, marked off from each other by color and tradition could not possibly clasp hands. (p. 69)

The fact, however, is that the "negative outcome," that is, the first appearance of the Solid South, was shattered but a few years after it was instituted due to the onslaught of the Southern agrarian movement in which white and black fought together against the planter-merchant-railroad vested interests. In the previously cited work on Tom Watson, Mr. Van Woodward traces this period of white and black unity, and comments: "Never before or since have the two races in the South come so close together as they did during the Populist struggles." Yet Mr. Myrdal, in a sum total of 1,483 pages on the "Negro problem," finds no space for so much as a footnote to refer to the Negro role in this tremendous mass movement. This is the result of his "non-class struggle" approach. In this respect it is not devoid of interest to note that the sponsor of this study is the Carnegie Corporation.

1   Myrdal Justifies His Selection

The present study was projected by this corporation, which sank over a quarter of a million dollars into the venture. So prejudiced are the American "social scientists" that, in order to get the facts on the Negro problem impartially set down, the corporation found that it would need to engage a foreign scholar. Not accidentally, however, its search for one unprejudiced in racial questions ended when it found one who was anti-Marxist in political outlook. Mr. Myrdal's anti-Marxism colors his approach to the entire work as well as to his co-workers. Mr. Myrdal's insistence on the invalidity of the Marxian theory shows that he knows quite well where the "main enemy" is and who his sponsor is.

Mr. Myrdal denies that "the economic factor" is the primary one in the development of society, or rather, in the existence of the Negro problem. To him the Negro problem is a moral problem arising out of the conflict between the "American creed," that all men are created equal, and the American reality, in which the Negro minority is so unjustly treated. However, it is clear from the 1,000-odd pages of text, that, if the Negro problem is in the "mind and heart" of America, it has nevertheless a most solid economic foundation, and it is precisely the chapters that deal with the economic foundation that are the best in the two volumes. A particularly admirable job was done with the section on the Negro laborer. That section was under the general direction of Mr. Sterner, who also is the author of the appendix relating to this section. This appendix is entitled "Pre-War Conditions of the Negro Wage-Earner in Selected Industries and Occupations." It deals both with the industries in which the Negroes are the predominant labor force, lumber milling, fertilizer manufacturing, turpentine farming, etc., and with the industry which practically excludes any Negro labor, the major Southern industry, textiles. From it we also get a glimpse of the difference between the conditions in a non-unionized industry and a unionized one. In turpentine farming the Negro earns little more than $200 a year and some forms of peonage are still extant. In mining, however, the worker gets comparatively high wages, being unionized in the United Mine Workers, where no discrimination exists. In fact, even in Alabama, the Negro union member talks as freely as the white union member, and the local union itself is generally administered by a white president and a Negro vice-president.

The study of the Negro worker is preceded by an examination of the plight of the Negro sharecropper. The chapters on Negro and Southern agriculture are on as competent a level as those on the Negro in industry. Anyone who has entertained any illusions as to what the New Deal meant to the poor farmers, white and Negro, in the semi-feudal conditions of the South, will have them quickly dispelled by the accumulated weight of evidence. This shows that the governmental agricultural policies had graver consequences in uprooting the Negro farmer than soil erosion, the boll weevil and the Southwestern shift of cotton culture combined.

The above citations indicate that the value of *An American Dilemma* does not reside in its "value premises" but in the fact that it offers up-to-date informational summaries of the economic, legal and social status of the Negro in America.

No criticism of Mr. Myrdal's "value premises," however, could have dealt them so fatal a blow as was struck by the author himself. This occurs when his thesis reaches the South, where, after all, four out of five Negroes still live, where the Negro problem was created, where it still has its roots. It is there that the contradiction between the "American creed" and the economic reality is sharpest. It is therefore not at all surprising that it is there that the contradiction between Mr. Myrdal, the scholar with "value premises," and Mr. Myrdal, the "social scientist," becomes not only acute but ludicrous.

Mr. Myrdal, the scholar, writes that with the entrenchment of slavery in the South, the blackout on independent thinking was so overwhelming that Southern thought to this day suffers from lack of free intercourse with the varied currents of thought since the early nineteenth century. "... The region is exceptional in Western non-fascist civilization since the Enlightenment in that *it lacks every trace of radical thought*. In the South all progressive thinking going further than mild liberalism has been practically non-existent for a century" (p. 469).

Mr. Myrdal, the scholar, further demonstrates that the war, which has increased the militancy of the Negro, has scared these Southern white liberals into an outright reactionary position. They would not continue their cooperation with the Negro intellectuals against discrimination unless the latter accepted, nay, avowed, social segregation. So benighted is that region that the following passed for the words of a liberal! It is Mark Etheridge, ex-chairman of the Fair Employment Practices Committee, who writes in July, 1942:

> There is no power in the world—not even the mechanized armies of the earth, the Allied and the Axis—which can now force the Southern white people to the abandonment of social segregation. It is a cruel

disillusionment, bearing germs of strife and perhaps tragedy, for any of their [Negroes'] leaders to tell them that they can expect it, or that they can exact it, as the price of their participation in the war.[2]

This, then, is the "American creed" when expressed in Southern lingo. What happens now to the scholar's "value premise," that the Negro is entitled to full participation in American democracy? Overboard goes the scholar and out emerges the "social scientist," who turns out to be a bourgeois politician. Mr. Myrdal, the "social scientist," begins to appeal to his Southern bourbon class brethren. Since, says Mr. Myrdal, the good bourgeois, *"changes should, if possible, not be made by sudden upheavals but in gradual steps"* (p. 518), the South had better start enfranchising its Negro citizens now. Mr. Myrdal pleads that this "is truly a conservative" conclusion. And just to prove to the Southern bourbons that it is not a wild-haired Marxist who is asking them to take this plunge, he writes that they can, to begin with, start enfranchising *"the higher strata of the Negro population"* (p. 519). The appeal of the "social scientist" is not a challenge; it is a whimper.

Here you have the political formula of this massive work in a nutshell! Here is a scholar who has digested the major part of the available literature on the subject of the Negro problem, who has conducted field studies and case histories, all of which lead him to uphold "value premises" that demand the full participation of the Negro in all aspects of American life, who holds no brief for intellectual Uncle Tomism of either Negro or white variety, who says the South is as backward intellectually as economically, that its ignorance is, in fact, unique in non-fascist Western civilization, and yet so bourgeois is he that his class instinct prevails upon him to produce so impotent, so ludicrous a "solution" as to turn the American tragedy into a Swedish farce! What is so elementary that even British imperialism has granted it to a colony like Jamaica—universal suffrage—Mr. Myrdal, "the social scientist from non-imperialist Sweden," is not yet ready to demand from the Southern bourbons!

2   "The Treason of the Intellectuals"

One might have supposed that the Negro intellectuals would arise one and all in criticism of *An American Dilemma*. But any such supposition is, unfortunately, quite unfounded. Mr. Du Bois, for example, who considers the

---

2 Cf. *The Virginia Quarterly Review* (Autumn, 1942) for view of Southern "liberalism" ("The Southern Negro and the War Crisis").

"acculturation of the masses" to be the task of the "talented tenth,"[3] did not consider it the task of the "talented tenth" to criticize a work saddled with so much high-brow talk and so little high- or low-brow action. On the contrary, he considered it to be a "monumental and unrivalled study" whose scientific approach should be emulated (*Phylon*, second quarter, 1944). In general, the Negro press met the work with paeans of praise. A sadder commentary yet on the state of the Negro intelligentsia than the Negro press is the manner in which Mr. Myrdal got from it its staff members. These intellectuals were at his beck and call at all times, although some of them seem to be so far to the left of him as to be on the opposite side of the fence. Mr. Myrdal's chief complaint against them is that they have been influenced by Marxism. Consider, then, the case of Charles S. Johnson, who has been so influenced and who considers the Negro problem to be rooted in economic factors. During the extensive Negro migrations northward in the period of World War I, Mr. Johnson saw the solution to the Negro problem in the urbanization and proletarianization of the Negro, which, more or less automatically, would shift the problem from a racial to a class plane. When the depression interrupted the continuity of this development, Mr. Johnson seemed to rely upon the impact of the crisis to cause such an upheaval in the Southern economy as to unseat King Cotton. When the Agricultural Adjustment Act pumped some subsidies into cotton culture and propped up the collapsing regime of cotton tenancy, Mr. Johnson still had his eyes on some "automatic" economic revolution to be caused by the introduction of the mechanical cotton picker. Mr. Johnson the scholar seemed blissfully unaware of the significance of the political alliance of the New Deal-Wall Street North with the bourbon semi-feudal South. Or perhaps not so much unaware as unwilling to give up the quiet of an academic chair for the hubbub of mass activity which would "induce" the "economic" revolution. Yet he continued to write radical words:

> The acuteness of the industrial and relief situation in the cities of the North will find white and Negro unemployed making their demands together. There is, however, one disturbing possibility. It is that the anti-Semitism generated in Europe, in response to a hopelessly depressed economic situation, will find in the urban Negro an emotional scapegoat. In this event anything can happen.

---

3   In connection with this section of the review, the reader should consult *The Journal of Negro Education*, July, 1939, the entire issue of which was devoted to "The Position of the Negro In the American Social Order," and to which Messrs. Du Bois, Bunche and Johnson made contributions.

Every so often in the works of Mr. Johnson one finds a situation described so lucidly that the revolutionary answer to "anything can happen" seems clear enough. But it is never stated in so many words. The reason lies partly in the fact that the majority of the research projects or economic and social analyses regarding the Negro have white guardian angels in the form of some bourgeois fund, whether it is Carnegie, or Rockefeller or Rosenwald or the government. It is only natural that the studies stop short of their implicit conclusions, if indeed the professors ever breathe the conclusions even to themselves and thus jeopardize the comfort of the academic chair. Researchers, of course, are paid to indulge in "educational treatises," not to carry on revolutionary propaganda. Thus it happens that the attacks of the "radicals" on Uncle Tom Negroes do not encompass them, and the struggle against Booker T. Washington's philosophy of "cast down your bucket wherever you are" does not get far beyond the academic hall, while the Negro masses continue to be ground beneath the millstone of class and racial oppression.

The sorriest spectacle of the Negro "talented tenth" is presented by Ralph Bunche. Mr. Bunche is critical not only of the economic, political and social status of the Negro, but of all existing Negro organizations that strive to ameliorate this condition. He calls them "philosophic and programmatic paupers." He is critical likewise of all Negro leaders who, he says, "think and act entirely in a black groove." In his pamphlet, *A World View of Race*, he even comes up with a solution to the Negro problem:

> The Negro must develop, therefore, a consciousness of class interest and purpose and must strive for an alliance with the white working class in a common struggle for economic and political equality and justice.

Yet this most radical of radicals found it permissible to shelve his more radical conclusions in the Schomburg collection, while his research data is used by Mr. Myrdal for his own conservative ends. This is not at all accidental. Mr. Bunche's revolutionary thunder is no more than radicalism of the chair. Mr. Bunche may not attack Mr. Myrdal, but Mr. Myrdal does not hesitate to attack Mr. Bunche:

> In passing it should be observed that the academic radicalism of Negro intellectuals exemplified by the citation from Mr. Bunche, can easily come to good terms with the type of liberal but skeptical *laissez-faire* [do nothing] opinion so prevalent among white social scientists, writing on the Negro problem.... Since neither party is very active in trying either to induce or prevent an economic revolution, it does not make much

difference if the Negro radicals look forward to an economic revolution and the white sociologists do not. (p. 1398, ftn. 13)

3   The Proletarian Way

Of the Negro intellectuals who have reviewed the Myrdal volumes, the only critic so far has been L.D. Reddick, curator of the Schomburg collection. Mr. Reddick has written two reviews, one for the *Journal of Negro Education*, spring, 1944, and the other for Opportunity. In both reviews he offers three criticisms of the book. He rejects Mr. Myrdal's sociological concept of caste. He shows himself aware of the weaknesses of the historical sections of the book; and he is critical of Mr. Myrdal's solution. The best thing in the reviews is his recognition that the ultimate solution of the Negro question is along class lines. However, the way in which Mr. Reddick phrases this is extremely significant. He writes: "Finally, Dr. Myrdal is unduly pessimistic over the possibilities of Negro and white workers uniting and struggling together for common goals." If Mr. Myrdal is unduly pessimistic, it is clear that Mr. Reddick is not unduly optimistic.

Thus far we have not considered George S. Schuyler, who in the past has done one of the finest reportorial jobs in popularizing the CIO to the Negro workers and the Negro community as a whole. Mr. Schuyler for some time has shown himself a believer in managerial society. He condemns both sides of the war as imperialist. He has turned away from the revolutionary movement, but retains some Marxism. It is not surprising that, although he considers the Myrdal book a superior work, he is cynical of any solutions. In his review of the book in the July issue of *Politics,* he writes: "He [Mr. Myrdal] is modest enough to predict no solution, for the problem may well be insoluble."

This brings us to one of the most significant omissions of this book. If even Mr. Myrdal is unaware of the Populist movement, no one who thinks of the Negro question at all is unaware of the Garvey movement. This is the most remarkable phenomenon in the history of the Negro in the United States. Mr. Myrdal recognizes its importance. He writes:

> For one thing it proves that it *is* possible to reach the Negro masses if they are appealed to in an effective way. It testifies to the basic unrest in the Negro community. It tells of a dissatisfaction so deep that it mounts to hopelessness of ever gaining a full life in America. (p. 749)

Mr. Myrdal himself does not analyze the Garvey movement, although he states that this, along with a thorough study of the movement, ought to be done:

> Negro intellectuals, for understandable reasons, show certain inhibitions in dealing with the topic, as do the white students of the Negro problem. But it is worthy of intensive historical investigation and careful reflection. (p. 749)

Why Mr. Myrdal has not done so in a study lasting four years and covering 1,400 pages of text remains inexplicable. Mr. Myrdal further observes that the

> Negroes are beginning to form a self-conscious "nation within the nation," defining ever more clearly their fundamental grievances against white America.
>
> *America can never more regard its Negroes as a patient, submissive minority.* Negroes will continually become less well "accommodated." They will organize for defense and offense. (p. 1004)

To anyone who is concerned about the Negro question today, this neglect of the Garvey movement has just about reached its end. There is stirring in the Negro people in the United States today a racial consciousness which has at present found its most extreme expression in the writings of Richard Wright. Wilfred H. Kerr, co-chairman of the Lynn Committee to Abolish Segregation in the Armed Forces, has noted the phenomenon, which he calls "Negroism." These are portents on the horizon which can be ignored only to the peril of the labor movement. But they must be approached upon the indispensable basis of the revolutionary struggle for socialism and of the proletariat as that social class which will solve the Negro problem along with all other major problems that capitalist society cannot solve. From the very fact that scholars like Mr. Johnson and Mr. Myrdal make such valuable contributions to the Negro question, it is necessary for Marxists to attack and expose without mercy their false philosophical premises.

F. FOREST

Women's Liberation and the Dialectics of Revolution

Marx's "New Humanism" and the Dialectics of Women's Liberation in "Primitive" and Modern Societies

Marx's treatment of the Man/Woman relationship in his works—at every period from his youth in the 1840s through to the end of his life—is traced in this essay, illuminating how total the uprooting of society needs to be. It began as a paper delivered to an International Conference on "Ideology, Bureaucracy and Human Survival" in September 1983, during the centenary of Marx's death, at the New School for Social Research, New York. A slightly edited version was published in Praxis International, *an international-Yugoslav dissident philosophic journal, in January 1984 (Vol. 3, No. 4). It was reprinted as a* News & Letters *pamphlet in April, 1984 (RDC, pp. 8066–87). This chapter is based on the text as edited by Dunayevskaya for* Women's Liberation and the Dialectics of Revolution.

I

Bureaucracy, as the focal point of this year's international conference, gains a special significance because it takes place in the year of the Marx Centenary when, for the first time, we have a transcription of Marx's last writings—*The Ethnological Notebooks of Karl Marx* (transcribed and edited, with an Introduction, by Lawrence Krader and published by Van Gorcum in 1972). This allows us to look at Marx's Marxism *as a totality* and see for ourselves the wide gulf that separates Marx's concept of that fundamental Man/Woman relationship (whether that be when Marx first broke from bourgeois society or as seen in his last writings) from Engels' view of what he called "the world historic defeat of the female sex" as he articulated it in his *Origin of the Family, Private Property and the State* as if that were Marx's view, not alone on the "Woman Question" but on "primitive communism."

To this day, the dominance of that erroneous, fantastic view of Marx and Engels as one[1] (consistently perpetuated by the so-called socialist states) has

---

1 In a letter to Engels in 1856, Marx commented on the attitude of the journalist who had written about them: "What is so very strange is that he treats the two of us as a singular, '*Marx and Engels says*,' etc."

by no means been limited to Engelsianisms on women's liberation. The aim of the Russian theoreticians, it would appear, has been to put blinders on non-Marxist as well as Marxist academics regarding the last decade of Marx's life, when he experienced new moments in his theoretic perception as he studied new empiric data of pre-capitalist societies, in works by Lewis Henry Morgan, Maxim Kovalevsky, John Budd Phear, Henry Sumner Maine, John Lubbock. In Marx's excerpts and comments on these works, as well as in his correspondence during this period, it was clear that Marx was working out new paths to revolution, not, as some current sociological studies[2] would have us believe, by scuttling his own life's work of analyzing capitalism's development in West Europe, much less abrogating his discovery of a whole new continent of thought and revolution, which he called a "new Humanism." Rather, Marx was rounding out 40 years of his thought on human development and its struggles for freedom, which he called "history and its process," "revolution in permanence."[3]

What was new in Marx's Promethean vision in his last decade was the diversity of the ever-changing ways men and women had shaped their history in pre-capitalist societies, the pluri-dimensionality of human development on a global scale. Marx experienced a shock of recognition in his last decade as he studied the new empiric anthropological studies and saw positive features—be it of the role of the Iroquois women or the agricultural commune and resistance to capitalist conquest—which bore a certain affinity to what he had articulated when he first broke with capitalist society and called for "a human revolution."

The result was that in that decade, 1873–1883, he, at one and the same time, introduced new additions to his greatest theoretical work, *Capital*, and projected nothing short of the possibility of a revolution occurring first in a backward country like Russia ahead of one in a country of the technologically advanced West. Clearly, there was no greater "empiricist" than the revolutionary dialectician, Karl Marx! Marx did not live long enough to work out in full those paths to revolution he was projecting, but we can see, in the correspondence he carried on at that time, the direction in which he was moving. Thus, we read his

---

2   See Mikhail Vitkin, *Vostok v Philosophico-Historicheskoi Kontseptsii K. Marksa y F. Engelsa* (Moscow: 1972). Those who do not read Russian can get the essence of his view in several articles which have appeared in English, among which are: "The Problem of the Universality of Social Relations in Classical Marxism," *Studies in Soviet Thought* 20 (1979); "The Asiatic Mode of Production," *Philosophy and Social Criticism*, Vol. 8 (1) 1981; and "Marx Between West and East," *Studies in Soviet Thought* 23 (1982).

3   Marx's "revolution in permanence" is not to be confused with Trotsky's theory of permanent revolution, which had always subordinated the peasantry as any sort of vanguard revolutionary force; indeed, not even granting them a "national consciousness."

sharp critique of the Russian Populist, Mikhailovsky, who attempted to attribute to Marx the making of a universal out of his "The Historical Tendency of Capitalist Accumulation."[4] Marx insisted that it was a particular historic study of capitalist development in West Europe, and that, if Russia continued on that path, "she will lose the finest chance ever offered by history to a people and undergo all the fatal vicissitudes of the capitalist regime."[5]

That letter was unmailed, but one of the four drafts he had written on the same subject to Vera Zasulich, who had written to him in the name of the Plekhanov group which was moving to Marxism, was mailed. And the most important of all his written statements on this subject is the Preface to the Russian edition of the *Communist Manifesto*.

What the post-Marx Marxists have made of all this can be challenged by our age, not because we are "smarter" but because we now have Marx's Marxism as a totality, and because of the maturity of our age when a whole new Third World has emerged and Women's Liberation has moved from an idea whose time has come to a movement. The challenge to post-Marx Marxists to do the hard labor needed to work out Marx's new moments in that last decade is occasioned, not as a minor "demand" for an explanation as to why the unforgivable 50-year delay in publishing what had been found by Ryazanov in 1923, nor is the challenge limited to what the post-Marx Marxists did not do about the *Ethnological Notebooks*. The point is that even when the unpublished works of Marx, such as the *Economic-Philosophic Manuscripts of 1844*, did come to light soon after they were retrieved from the vaults of the Second International by Ryazanov, under the impulse of the Russian Revolution—and even when they did create lengthy international debates—certain limitations of the historic period in which those commentaries on the work appeared point up the greater maturity of our age.

Take Herbert Marcuse's analysis of those Essays.[6] It was certainly one of the first, and a most profound analysis "in general," but he managed to skip over a crucial page on the Man/Woman relationship. On the other hand, Simone de Beauvoir, who does not approach Marcuse's Marxist erudition and is not a Marxist but an Existentialist, singled out precisely that Man/Woman relationship from Marx in her *The Second Sex*: "The direct, natural, necessary relation of human creatures is the *relation of man to woman*," she quotes on the very

---

4 This is the title of Chapter 32 of *Capital*, Vol. I. —Editor.

5 Marx's November 1877 letter to the editor of the Russian journal which had printed Mikhailovsky's critique is included in Marx-Engels *Selected Correspondence*, Moscow, 1955.

6 The 1932 essay by Marcuse, "The Foundation of Historical Materialism," was translated and included in *Studies in Critical Philosophy* (London: New Left Books, 1972).

last page, and stresses its importance by writing: "The case could not be better stated."

Unfortunately, what follows that sentence and completes her final paragraph runs counter to Marx's thrust: "It is for man to establish the reign of liberty.... It is necessary, for one thing, that by and through their natural differentiation men and women unequivocally affirm their brotherhood."[7] In a word, de Beauvoir's high praise of Marx notwithstanding, the conclusion she draws from the essay of Marx as well as all her data over some 800 pages fails to grasp the reason Marx singled out the Man/Woman relationship as integral to alienation, not only under capitalism but also what he called "vulgar communism." His "new Humanism" stressed: "We should especially avoid re-establishing society as an abstraction, opposed to the individual. The individual *is the social entity*" [Appendix, p. 334]. Which is why he concluded with the sentence, "... communism as such is not the goal of human development, the form of human society" [Appendix, p. 340].

Let us now reread that sentence that de Beauvoir quoted (except that I want to use a more precise translation[8]):

> The infinite degradation in which man exists for himself is expressed in this relation to the *woman*.... The direct, natural, necessary relationship of man to man is the *relationship of man to woman*. [Appendix, p. 332]

Women's Liberation had to develop from an Idea whose time has come to an actual Movement before either Simone de Beauvoir or Herbert Marcuse could see the need to grapple with Marx's Promethean vision on Man/Woman relationships.

Marx's concept of the Man/Woman relationship arose with the very birth of a new continent of thought and of revolution the moment he broke from bourgeois society. Before that decade of the 1840s had ended, Marx had unfurled a new banner of revolution with the *Communist Manifesto*, where he explained how total must be the uprooting of capitalism, the abolition of private property, the abolition of the state, the bourgeois family, indeed, the whole "class culture" [MECW 6, p. 501]. This was followed immediately by his becoming a participant in the 1848 Revolutions. Far from retreating when those revolutions were defeated, Marx greeted the new 1850s by calling for the "revolution in

---

7   Simone de Beauvoir, *The Second Sex*, translated by H.M. Parshley (New York: Bantam, 1961), p. 690.

8   There have been several translations by now of the 1844 *Manuscripts*. The best known are those by Martin Milligan, Erich Fromm, T. Bottomore, and Loyd Easton and Kurt Guddat. I am using my own translation, however, which is the first one that was published in English, as an appendix to my *Marxism and Freedom* (New York: Twayne Pub., 1958).

permanence." Once again, in that decade, as he now came to view other pre-capitalist societies and analyzed anew human development, he further deep-ened his concepts as well as aims by concretizing it as the "absolute movement of becoming" [*Grundrisse*, p. 488].

The *Grundrisse* is the mediation, on the one hand, both to Marx's greatest theoretical work, *Capital*, and to his activity around and writings on the Paris Commune; and, on the other hand, to the *Ethnological Notebooks*. One can see, imbedded in the latter, a trail to the 1980s. At least, that is what I see; and it is for this reason that I chose as my subject the relationship of Marx's philoso-phy to the dialectic of women's liberation throughout the whole 40 years of his theoretic development. My emphasis on the last decade of his life—which until now has been considered hardly more than "a slow death"—is because it is precisely in that last decade that he experienced new moments, seeing new forces of revolution and thought in what we now call the Third World and the Women's Liberation Movement. The new return to and recreation of the Hegelian dialectic as he developed the *Grundrisse* was the methodology that determined all his works.

What never changed was his concept and practice of criticism of all that exists, defined as follows: "Ruthless criticism of all that exists, ruthless in the sense that the critique is neither afraid of its own results nor of conflicting with the powers that be" [MECW 3, p. 142]. Which is exactly why Marx never sepa-rated criticism from revolution, and such total uprooting of all that is, sparing no bureaucracies either in production or in education, that he counterposed to the old his concept of "revolution in permanence."

And how very today-ish is his early attack on bureaucracy in education:

> Bureaucracy counts in its own eyes as the final aim of the state.... The aims of the state are transformed into the aims of the bureaux and the aims of the bureaux into the aims of the state. Bureaucracy is a circle from which no one can escape. Its hierarchy is a hierarchy of knowledge. The apex en-trusts the lower echelon with insight into the individual while the lower echelon leaves insight into the universal to the apex, and so each deceives the other.
>
> MECW 3, pp. 46–47

This sharp critique of the bureaucracy in education under capitalism, like the singling out of the alienated Man/Woman relationship, was but the be-ginning of his critique of what is an exploitative, sexist, racist, capitalist society. It remains most relevant for our nuclear age, whether our preoccupa-tion is that of the Third World or the very survival of civilization as we have known it.

A concentration on Marx's last decade makes it necessary for me to greatly abbreviate the two decades that followed the 1840s. The abbreviation will not, however, be at the expense of discussing one of Marx's greatest works, the *Grundrisse*, because I will consider that work together with the *Ethnological Notebooks* of Marx's last decade. Here, I mention the *Grundrisse* only to point out that it was when Marx was working on it, in 1857, that he concluded that there were more than three periods of human development—slavery, feudalism, and capitalism. He saw a whole new era of human development which he then called "Asiatic mode of production." "Asiatic" did not mean only "Oriental." He was talking about a primitive communal form of development in the West as well as in the East, whether it was among the Celts or in Russia. For anthropologists of our era to disregard Marx's sensitivity to that "Asiatic mode of production" in the 1850s beginning with the Taiping Revolution, and act as if he was totally Euro-centered then, is on the level of their disregard of his concept of the Man/Woman relationship in 1844.

II

Indeed, what I do wish to single out from the 1850s are two events, both of which relate precisely to women. The first was the 1853–54 strike in Preston, England, where no less than 15,000 workers were on strike against the despotic conditions of labor, about which Marx wrote in great detail for the *New York Tribune*, paying special attention to the conditions of the women workers. The second was the support he gave to Lady Bulwer-Lytton, the author of a novel, *Cheveley, or the Man of Honour*, who, in 1858, had dared not only to differ with the views of her conservative, aristocratic-politician husband, but to wish to make her views public. Because she dared to leave the hustings and attempted to rent a lecture hall for her views, her husband and son had her thrown into a lunatic asylum! In his article, "Imprisonment of Lady Bulwer-Lytton," Marx defended her and attacked not only the Tory press for its sexism, but also "the Radical press, which more or less receives its inspirations from the Manchester School."[9]

As for the articles on the Preston strike, Marx went into detail about both the special exploitation women were subjected to and the fact that even these monstrous conditions did not limit women to fighting those exploitative

---

9   See Marx's August 4, 1858 article in the *New York Daily Tribune*, "Imprisonment of Lady Bulwer-Lytton," in Saul K. Padover, ed., *The Karl Marx Library Vol. VI: On Education, Women, and Children* (New York: McGraw-Hill Book Co., 1975), pp. 76–80 [MECW 15, pp. 596–601].

conditions of labor but challenged the educational system. Marx's Chartist activities and his studies, not only for his books but for agitational writings on behalf of labor, were never written as if only male workers were involved. Quite the contrary. And, in writing: "The factory operatives seem resolved to take the education movement out of the hands of the Manchester humbugs," Marx hit out against child labor and the extremities to which capitalists resorted. He cited the case of "a little girl of nine years of age (who) fell on the floor asleep with exhaustion, during the 60 hours; she *was roused and cried, but was forced to resume work!!*" (Emphasis is Marx's.)[10]

Marx never separated his theoretic works from his actual activities, and it is the activities of the workers in particular that he followed most carefully both in the "blue books" of the factory inspectors and what was actually happening that did reach the press. In April 1856, he summarized the whole question of capitalism and its technology in his speech at the anniversary of the Chartists' paper: "All of our inventions and progress seem to result in endowing material forces with intellectual life, and in stultifying human life into a material force" [MECW 14, p. 656].

The battle of ideas Marx was engaged in was so inseparable from both class and all freedom struggles (what Marx called "history and its process") that he hailed John Brown's attack on Harpers Ferry in 1860 as signaling the beginning not only of the end of slavery, but of a whole new world epoch. It is impossible in this age to deny the facts. The Civil War in the U.S. did break out the following year; the intensification of the class struggle in Great Britain reaching out for international labor solidarity affected the outcome of the Civil War in the U.S. in a revolutionary way; the 1863 uprising in Poland against tsarist Russia, followed by the intense class struggles in France with its labor leaders coming to London, did culminate in the founding of the First International, with Marx as its intellectual leader.

What ideologues do deny, and even some post-Marx Marxists question, is that these objective events (and Marx's activities related to them) led Marx to break with the very concept of theory. How otherwise to account for the total restructuring of *Grundrisse* as *Capital*? After all, *Grundrisse* (and the correspondence around it) reveals that Marx was so glad about his re-encounter with Hegel's dialectic that he credited it with helping him work out the "method of presentation" of all those massive economic studies. Yet, as great as was the change when Marx decided to prepare part of *Grundrisse* for publication in 1859 as *Contribution to the Critique of Political Economy*, he began it, not with

---

10   This article is included in Karl Marx and Frederick Engels, *Collected Works*, Vol. 12, pp. 460–463.

Money or Value, but wrote a whole new first chapter on the Commodity. It was, indeed, a great innovation, which would be retained as a new beginning for all drafts and for the finally edited *Capital*. Nevertheless, that wasn't all that determined the content and structure of *Capital*. What did determine the totality of the restructuring was Marx's decision to put away both the *Grundrisse* and the *Critique* and start *"ab ovo."*

His *re*-creation of the Hegelian dialectic *in the historic framework of the turbulent 1860s is what led to his break with the very concept of theory*. This becomes clear not simply from his 1877 "confession," but from the actuality of what *is Capital*; but here is his "confession" as he put it in a letter to Sigmund Schott, November 3, 1877:

> Confidentially speaking, I in fact began *Capital* in just the reverse (starting with the third, the historic part) of the order in which it is presented to the public, except that the first volume, the one begun last, was immediately prepared for publication while the two others remained in that primitive state characteristic of all research at the outset.

Marx's battle of ideas with bourgeois theoreticians had so expanded at the beginning of the 1860s that the manuscript numbered nearly 1,000 pages. This "History of Theory" made up three books and we know it as *Theories of Surplus Value* (*Capital*, Vol. IV). But what is most historic and crucial about these magnificent, profound studies is that Marx relegated them to the very end of his three volumes of *Capital*. Instead of continuing with his critique of classical political economy "on its own," what Marx did was to turn to what the workers were doing and saying at the point of production.

The first great innovation Marx introduced, as he was preparing the first volume for the printer, was an addition to the very first chapter on "The Commodity" of the section, "Fetishism of Commodities." To this day, none—either Marxist or non-Marxist—question the *today-ness*, as well as the uniquely Marxian unity of theory and practice, that characterizes Marx's historical materialist view of human development through the ages and the different types of societies. How, then, can those critics still hold on to the contention that Marx was totally "Euro-centered"; that this, indeed, was so-called "classical Marxism"; that Marx, "the economist," failed to grasp "the Asiatic mode of production" as totally different from what he allegedly made into a universal—West European economic development? Wouldn't it be more correct (even when these critics did not yet know of the *Grundrisse*, much less the *Ethnological Notebooks*) to take serious note of Marx's brief view of pre-capitalist societies right in that first chapter of *Capital?* Marx not only specified the existence of primitive communal forms "among Romans, Teutons, and Celts," but held that a "more exhaustive study of Asiatic ... forms of common property would show how, from the different forms of primitive common property, different forms of its dissolution have been developed" [MCIK, p. 89, ftn. 1; MCIP, p. 171, ftn. 32]. Clearly, that is exactly what Marx himself had embarked upon; and, still, few study seriously his *Ethnological Notebooks*.

One great economist, Joseph Schumpeter, who was most impressed with the profundity of Marx's critique of classical political economy and didn't shy away from acknowledging that economists owe much to Marx's analysis of the economic laws of capitalist development, was, nevertheless, so antagonistic to philosophy that he held it was impossible to have a truly genuine economic argument with him, because, as philosopher, he was forever "transforming historic narrative into historic reason."[11] That *is* the dialectic of Marx's seeing, not merely the statistics he had amassed, but the live men and women reshaping history. Nowhere is this more true than concerning the so-called "Woman Question." Having turned away from further arguments with theoreticians to follow instead the happenings at the point of production and their political ramifications on the historic scene, Marx came up with the second great innovation in *Capital*—his chapter on "The Working-Day."

That chapter had never appeared in Marx's theoretical works before—be it the *Grundrisse* or *Critique of Political Economy* or *History of Theory*. Although, as a revolutionary activist, Marx had always been involved in the struggle for the shortening of the working day, it was only when his analysis covered it in such detail (seventy-six pages, to be exact) that Marx devoted that much space to women in the process of production and arrived at very new conclusions on new forms of revolt. Where bourgeois theoreticians held that Marx, in detailing the onerous conditions of labor (and especially the degrading form of female labor), was writing not theory but a "sob story," Marx, in digging into those factory inspectors' "blue books" which the ideologues dismissed, did more than single out the inhuman attitude to women when he wrote: "In England women are still occasionally used instead of horses for hauling canal boats...." Marx now concluded that the simple worker's question, When does my day begin and when does it end?, was a greater philosophy of freedom than was the bourgeois Declaration of the Rights of Man that Marx now designated as "the pompous catalogue of the 'inalienable rights of man.'"

Even were one opposed to Marx's description of the capitalists' "were-wolf hunger" [MCIK, p. 268; MCIP, p. 353] for ever greater amounts of unpaid labor

---

11   Joseph A. Schumpeter, *Capitalism, Socialism and Democracy* (London and New York: Routledge, 1994), p. 44.

and looked only at the machine and at Marx's description of that instrumentality as a "mechanical monster" with its "demon power" organized into a whole system to which, Marx said, "motion is communicated by the transmitting mechanism from a central automaton ..."—wouldn't the today-ness of it strike our age of robotics? It certainly struck the miners on General Strike against the first appearance of automation in 1950. They thought that description was written, not by a mid-19th-century man, but by someone who must have been right there in the mines with them and the continuous miner, that they called "a man-killer."

Marx didn't separate his "economics" in *Capital* from its social and political ramifications, and thus he saw one and only "one positive feature"[12]—allowing women to go "outside of the domestic sphere." However, he warned at once against factory labor "in its brutal capitalistic form," which is nothing other than a "pestiferous source of corruption and slavery." But the collective labor of men and women, under different historic conditions, "creates a new economic foundation for a higher form of the family and of the relation between the sexes."

Marx continued: "It is, of course, just as absurd to hold the Teutonic Christian form of the family to be absolute as it would be to apply that character to the ancient Roman, the ancient Greek, or the Eastern forms.... "Marx ends by pointing to the fact that other historic conditions where both sexes work collectively could "become a source of human development."

That, of course, is not what capitalism aims at, and therefore Marx intensifies his attack as he lashes out also against the whole bureaucratic structure, not just in the state, but in the factory. There the despotic plan of capital has a form all its own: the *hierarchic structure of control over social labor*, which he further concretizes as requiring a whole army of foremen, managers and superintendents. This planned despotism, Marx points out, arises out of the *antagonistic* relation of labor and capital with its bureaucracy, which Marx likens to the military, demanding "barrack discipline" at the point of production. That is why Marx calls the whole relationship of subject to object, machines to living labor, "perverse." He has concretized what the early Marx had warned would be the result of the division between mental and manual labor: "To have one basis for life and another for science is *a priori* a lie" [Appendix, p. 338].

Marx, the activist philosopher of revolution, was completing Volume I of *Capital* in the same period when he was most active in the First International:

---

12   All quotes from *Capital* in this and the following paragraph are found on p. 536, Kerr edition [MCIK, p. 536; MCIP, pp. 620–21].

(1)   It is that organization that records, on July 19, 1867, that Marx proposed
       to the General Council that at its forthcoming Congress a discussion be
       held on the practical ways the International could "fulfill its function of
       a common center of action for the working classes, male and female, in
       their struggle tending to their complete emancipation from the domina-
       tion of capital" [MECW 20, p. 203].
(2)   On December 12, 1868 Marx wrote Ludwig Kugelmann:

       Great progress was evident in the last Congress of the American "La-
       bor Union" in that, among other things, it treated working women with
       complete equality.... Anybody who knows anything of history knows
       that great social changes are impossible without the feminine ferment.
       [MECW 43, pp. 184–85]

(3)   Marx again called Dr. Kugelmann's attention to the fact that, of course,
       the First International was not only practicing equality where women
       were concerned, but had just elected Mme. Harriet Law into the General
       Council.

Marx's sensitivity to women both as revolutionary force and reason held true
in his individual relations as well as organizational relations—and on an international level. It took all the way to the end of World War II before women's
revolutionary activities in the Resistance Movement finally inspired one woman Marxist to undertake a study of women in the Paris Commune. Edith Thomas' work, *Women Incendiaries*, is the first to give us a full view of women in the
greatest revolution of Marx's time—the Paris Commune. It is there we learn of
Marx's role—for it was he who had advised Elizabeth Dmitrieva to go to Paris
before the outbreak of the Civil War—and it was she who organized the famed
Union des Femmes pour la Défence de Paris et les Soins aux Blessés, the independent women's section of the First International. Moreover, the relationship between Marx and Dmitrieva had developed earlier when she was sending Marx
material on Russian agriculture, which was also her preoccupation.

       III

"The weak points in the abstract materialism of natural science, a materialism that excludes history and its process," Marx wrote in *Capital* [MCIK,
pp. 406–07, ftn. 2; MCIP, p. 494, ftn. 4], "are at once evident from the abstract
and ideological conceptions of its spokesmen, whenever they venture beyond
the bounds of their own specialty." As we can see from this, Marx's turn, in his
last decade, to the study of empiric anthropology was made under no illusion

that he would there find other historical materialists who would be dialectically analyzing the new findings on pre-capitalist societies, a question he had posed to himself as he was working on the *Grundrisse* and asked himself what preceded capitalism, and concluded from his studies that human development was an "absolute movement of becoming" [*Grundrisse*, p. 488]. Marx's ever-continuing confrontation with "history and its process," as much as his Promethean vision, disclosed not only how different were his views from bourgeois theoreticians but how his views on anthropology differed from those of his very closest collaborator, Frederick Engels.

With hindsight, it is not difficult to see that Engels did not rigorously follow what Marx had asked him to do—to make sure that all further editions and translations of Volume I of *Capital* followed the French edition. Whether he was in any way responsible, with his overemphasis on the materialist aspects, the point is that it was not only the Populist, Mikhailovsky, who tried to attribute to Marx the making of "The Historical Tendency of Capitalist Accumulation" into a universal for all human development. As we showed, Marx had written a very sharp critique of Mikhailovsky's article. Post-Marx Marxists, however, continued to express similar views to Mikhailovsky's and to base themselves on Engels' editions of Volume I of *Capital.*

What mainly concerns us here is the superficial (if not outright chauvinist) attitude of post-Marx Marxists to the last decade of Marx's life. Especially shocking is the attitude of David Ryazanov, who first discovered the *Ethnological Notebooks* and, without reading them, declared them to be "inexcusable pedantry." What was more damaging, however, to future generations of Marxists was the very first book that Engels wrote after Marx's death, *The Origin of the Family, Private Property and the State*, presenting it as a "bequest" from Marx. But the simple truth tells a different story. It is true that Marx had asked Engels to be sure to read *Ancient Society* [by Lewis Henry Morgan], which had just come off the press and interested him greatly. We have Engels' word for it, however, that he was too busy with other matters to read it and got it only after Marx's death when he found Marx's notes on it. It is not clear whether Engels had by then found in those unpublished manuscripts of Marx either the *Grundrisse* or much of what we now know as the *Ethnological Notebooks*, except the notes on Morgan and perhaps Kovalevsky. Because he presented this as a "bequest" from Marx, we were all raised on this concept of women's liberation as if it were, indeed, a work of Engels and Marx. Now that we finally have the transcription of the *Ethnological Notebooks*—and also have Marx's commentaries on Kovalevsky[13] and correspondence on Georg Maurer,[14] as well as the

---

13   Published in Lawrence Krader's *The Asiatic Mode of Production: Sources, Development and Critique in the Writings of Karl Marx* (Assen: Van Gorcum, 1975). —Editor.

14   See letters of Marx to Engels of March 14 and March 25, 1868 [MECW 42, pp. 547–49, 557–59]. —Editor.

Grundrisse—it shouldn't be difficult to disentangle Marx's views on women and dialectics from those of Engels.

It is true that Engels was Marx's closest collaborator, whom he had entrusted to "make something out of" the massive material he had accumulated for Volumes II and III of *Capital*, but did not live to edit. What Marx had also entrusted him with was to make sure that the French edition of Volume I, which is the only definitive edition Marx himself edited, should be the one used for all other editions.[15] What is most relevant to us now is what exactly Engels had done on that, since the most important changes Marx had introduced there concerned the accumulation of capital. They have become crucial since the emergence of a Third World.

So little attention had been paid to that little word, "so-called," as used for Part VIII ("The So-Called Primitive Accumulation of Capital"), that Marx evidently felt that, in order to stress both the concentration and centralization of capital and the dialectical development of Part VII ("The Accumulation of Capital"), he should subordinate Part VIII to that Part VII,[16] thereby showing that the so-called primitive accumulation wasn't at all limited to the beginnings of capital. The key to the ramifications of the concentration and centralization of capital, and its extension to what we now call imperialism, was one of the most significant paragraphs in that French edition. Unfortunately, that is precisely the paragraph Engels omitted as he edited the English edition. It is the one which stresses the creation of a world market when capitalism reaches its highest technological stage. It is at that point, says Marx, that capitalism "successively annexed extensive areas of the New World, Asia, and Australia" [MCIP, p. 786 ftn.].[17]

When we come to Engels' *The Origin of the Family* it is necessary to keep in mind that it wasn't only a quantitative difference between what Engels quoted from Marx's "Abstract"—some few pages—and the actual excerpts and commentary that Marx had made, which amounted to some 98 pages....

What was a great deal more important in tracing historic development and seeing other human relations was that it allowed for seeing new paths to revolution and the multidimensionality of human development. For example, as early as the *Grundrisse* (but then, Engels did not know the *Grundrisse*), Marx called attention to the "dignity" of the guild, commenting: "Here labor itself

---

15 For a critical discussion see Kevin Anderson, "The 'Unknown' Marx's *Capital*, Vol. I: The French Edition of 1872–75, 100 Years Later," *Review of Radical Political Economics*, 15:4 (1983).

16 In fact, what became Parts VII and VIII were combined in the first edition of *Capital* and were split apart in the 1872–75 French edition and the 1873 German edition. —Editor.

17 For the full paragraph which Engels left out, see my *Rosa Luxemburg, Women's Liberation and Marx's Philosophy of Revolution* (New Jersey: Humanities Press, 1982), p. 148.

is still half the expression of artistic creation, half its own reward. Labor still belongs to a man" [*Grundrisse,* p. 497].

What was crucial to Marx in seeing the great freedom of the Iroquois women was to show how great was the freedom the women had before American civilization destroyed the Indians. Indeed, first, it was true throughout the world that "civilized" nations took away the freedom of the women, as was true when British imperialism deprived the Irish women of many of their freedoms when they conquered Ireland. Marx's hatred of capitalism as he studied precapitalist societies grew more intense....

Secondly, and that is inseparable from the first, was the resistance of the women, the "feminine ferment" [MECW 43, pp. 184–85] Marx saw in every revolution. Thus Marx criticized Morgan on some of his statements about ancient Greece and the degraded status of women. Marx held that the Greek goddesses on Olympus were not just statues, but expressed myths of past glories that may, in fact, have reflected a previous stage, and/or expressed a desire for a very different future....

If I may divert for a moment, I'd like to cite the fact that in my national lecture tour this year on the Marx Centenary, I found the greatest interest in that subject when I addressed the Third World Women's Conference held in Urbana, Illinois, from April 9 to 13. I was especially impressed with the fact that there seemed to be no separation in their minds between the question of Third World and the question of women's liberation. As impressive, also, was the audience at my lecture in Salt Lake City, where I found that a woman anthropologist, Patricia Albers, had just co-edited with Beatrice Medicine *The Hidden Half: Studies of Plains Indian Women* (Washington, D.C.: University Press of America, 1983). In her introductory essay, Albers points out that the views of the Plains Indian women as "chattel, enslaved as beasts of burden" in which the creativity and struggle of these women is ignored, "tell us more about the attitudes of the Euro-Americans who studied Plains Indians than about the actual conditions under which these people lived."

One of the most important differences between Marx and Engels is that Marx drew no such unbridgeable gulf between the primitive and the civilized as Engels did. The pivotal point, to Marx, always was "the historical environment in which it occurs." Instead of seeing human development unilinearly, he pointed to the variety of paths which led from the primitive commune to a different world—never, however, without a revolution. Thus, when, in his last year, his trip to Algiers led him to become so excited with the Arabs that he praised not only their resistance to authority but even their "elegant and graceful dress," he ended his description of the experience: "Nevertheless, they will go to the devil without a revolutionary movement" [MECW 46, pp. 231, 242].

As Paul Lafargue reported the end of Marx's trip: "Marx has come back with his head full of Africa and the Arabs."[18]

The new moments he was experiencing as he intensified his studies of pre-capitalist society, on women, on the primitive commune, on the peasantry, illuminate Marx's works as a totality. Thus it isn't a question of a mere return to the concept of women which he first expressed in the *Economic-Philosophic Manuscripts of 1844*, nor, as some anthropologists would have it, simply a move from a philosophic to an empiric anthropology. Rather, as a revolutionary, Marx's hostility to capitalism's colonialism was intensifying to such a degree that his emphasis was on how deep must be its uprooting. His latest studies enabled Marx to see the possibility of new human relations, not as they might come through a mere "updating" of primitive communism's equality of the sexes, as among the Iroquois, but as Marx sensed they would burst forth from a new type of revolution.

The economist Schumpeter was not the only one who saw Marx turning historic narrative into historic reason. The great anthropologist, Sir Raymond Firth, who is certainly no Marxist, focuses on the fact that *Capital* is not so much an economic work as "a dramatic history designed to involve its readers in the events described."[19] I heartily agree with Professor Stanley Diamond's editorial in the first issue of *Dialectical Anthropology* in 1975:

> The Marxist tradition can be taken as an anthropology which was aborted by the rise of academic social science, and including academic Marxists, and the stultifying division of intellectual labor involved in the very definition of a civilized academic structure, whether right, left, or center.[20]

Marx, of course, was not limiting his critique to "stultifying division of intellectual labor," but to the division between mental and manual labor. However, he never underestimated the creativity of hard intellectual labor once the intellectual related himself to the labor movement. What post-Marx Marxists have failed to do with his legacy and their near disregard of his *Ethnological*

---

18   These letters are included in Saul K. Padover, *Karl Marx: An Intimate Biography* (New York: McGraw-Hill, 1978) [p. 372]. [Lafargue's letter to Engels of June 16, 1882, can be found in Frederick Engels, Paul and Laura Lafargue, *Correspondence,* Vol. I (Moscow: Foreign Languages Publishing House, 1959), p. 83.].

19   See Raymond Firth, "The Sceptical Anthropologist? Social Anthropology and Marxist Views on Society," in *Marxist Analyses and Social Anthropology* (London: Malaby Press, 1975).

20   Stanley Diamond, "The Marxist Tradition as a Dialectical Anthropology," *Dialectical Anthropology,* Vol. 1, No. 1, January 1975, pp. 1–5.

Notebooks is no reason for us not to do the hard labor required in hearing Marx think.

Marx's historic originality in internalizing new data was certainly worlds apart from Engels' being overwhelmed by it. And in each case Marx saw economic crises as "epochs of social revolution." The Taiping Revolution led him to an interest in pre-capitalist society. Not only did the *Grundrisse*, the impulse for which has always been attributed to the British economic crisis in 1857, have that magnificent part on pre-capitalist societies; but Marx remembered the Taiping Revolution in *Capital* itself.

In the 1860s, it was not only the Civil War in the United States which ended slavery and opened new doors of development, but all the actual struggles of women were seen at their highest point in the greatest revolution of Marx's day—the Paris Commune. Marx's new studies in the 1870s until his death meant a return to anthropology, not as concept alone, nor as empiric studies in and for themselves, but as a movement of "absolute becoming" through his philosophy of "revolution in permanence."

CHAPTER 28

Marx's and Engels' Studies Contrasted: Relationship of Philosophy and Revolution to Women's Liberation

This essay contains an extended commentary on Marx's Ethnological Notebooks, *relating them to the difference between Marx and Engels and to the contemporary Women's Liberation Movement, which Dunayevskaya contends was given little direction by Engelsian Marxism. It was originally published in the January-February 1979 issue of* News & Letters *as the first draft chapter of* Rosa Luxemburg, Women's Liberation, and Marx's Philosophy of Revolution. *This chapter is based on the text as edited by Dunayevskaya for* Women's Liberation and the Dialectics of Revolution.

1   Why a Century to Publish Marx?

Because Marx had discovered a new continent of thought as well as revolution, and because both concept and fact have ever been rigorously tied together in Marx's Marxism, his works carry a special urgency for our age. More relevant than the ceaseless question of private vs. collective (or state property that calls itself Communism) is Marx's articulation of Man/Woman as the fundamental relationship, at the very moment (1844) when he first laid the philosophic foundation for what became known as Historical Materialism. The new continent of thought Marx discovered soon issued its indictment of the past—"The history of all hitherto existing society is the history of class struggles" [MECW 6, p. 482]—and its call for a new world, new human relations, a classless society.

What has an imperativeness for today is the fact that, at the very end of his life (1880–1882)—after the French edition of his greatest theoretical work, *Capital*, which was published after the defeat of the greatest revolution he had witnessed, the Paris Commune—Marx returned to the pivotal Man/Woman relationship, as, at one and the same time, he excerpted Lewis H. Morgan's *Ancient Society*[1] and wrote to Vera Zasulich about the needed Russian Revolution.

---

1 In 1972, Marx's Notebooks, under the title *The Ethnological Notebooks of Karl Marx* (Assen, The Netherlands: Van Gorcum, 1972), were finally transcribed by Lawrence Krader

It has taken nothing short of a series of revolutions to bring out the un-published writings of Marx.[2] The *Economic-Philosophic Manuscripts of 1844* were not published until after the Russian Revolution. The 1857–58 *Grundrisse* was not published until after the Chinese Revolution. Unfortunately, Women's Liberationists of the mid-1960s to mid-1970s exercised no revolutionary prod to wrest Marx's notes on anthropology from the Archives, much less dialectically work out, on that ground, all the new from the ongoing Movement. Quite the contrary. The Women's Liberation Movement, which *had* helped create a new interest in Engels' *The Origin of the Family, Private Property and the State*, only served to provide new loopholes for Marxists, "orthodox" and so-called inde-pendent alike, to rush in and try to have *that* work be the ground, the direction the Movement would take.

Though there had always been a Party, and, indeed, an International (the Second) that laid claim to the heritage of Marx, the truth is that it took the Russian Revolution of November 1917 to prod even Marxist scholars to discov-er the now famous *Economic-Philosophic Manuscripts of 1844*. And once the early workers' state became transformed into its opposite—a state-capitalist society—these continued to gather dust until the 1956 Hungarian Revolution brought them onto the historic stage.

To bring about a serious study of the next unpublished work, the *Grundrisse*,[3] in the 1950s, it took nothing short of the Chinese Revolution of 1949. It took still another decade before even the single most discussed chapter of that work—"Forms Which Precede Capitalist Production"—was published in English as *Pre-Capitalist Economic Formations*. Because, however, the discussion was focused mainly on feudalism, or, rather, the transition from feudalism to capi-talism, many lacunae gaped open as to its relationship to Engels' *The Origin of the Family*, with all Marxists, Eric Hobsbawm included, claiming: "This was a work which Marx wanted to write, and for which he had prepared

---

and painstakingly footnoted, with quite a profound 90-page Introduction. It is necessary to emphasize the word, transcribed. It is not a translation. The Notebooks were written by Marx in English but include many phrases and full sentences in French, German, Latin, and Greek.

2   Not all have been brought out even now! There is no dearth of scholars who are happy to jump at such an excuse in order not to grapple seriously with that which is available, es-pecially on *Capital*. See Ernest Mandel's introduction to the Pelican edition of vol. 1 of Karl Marx's *Capital* (Middlesex: Penguin Books, 1976; New York: Vintage Books, 1977), p. 29 and again p. 944. And see my critique of Mandel, "Today's Epigones Who Try to Truncate Marx's *Capital*," in my *Marx's "Capital" and Today's Global Crisis* (Detroit: News & Letters, 1978) [Chapter 6 in this book].

3   The *Grundrisse* was not published in full in English until 1973, when the Pelican Marx Library published it in London. (London: Penguin Books; New York: Vintage Books).

voluminous notes, on which Engels based himself so far as possible."[4] Was that really so?

The year which finally saw the publication of Lawrence Krader's transcription of Marx's *Ethnological Notebooks*, 1972, was the year also when Eleanor Burke Leacock wrote a new Introduction "updating" Engels' work. She perpetuated the myth that *The Origin of the Family* is a product of Marx as well as Engels.[5] In 1974, Charnie Guettel, in her pamphlet *Marxism and Feminism*, makes Leacock's Introduction "mandatory reading for any serious Marxist."[6]

1972 is also the year that saw the publication of a most serious independent work on the history of women's resistance from the 17th century to the present, *Women, Resistance and Revolution*, by Sheila Rowbotham, who likewise not only acts as if Marx and Engels were one, but singles out Hal Draper's "Marx and Engels on Women's Liberation" thusly: "This is a very useful summary of what Marx and Engels wrote about women."[7] While she is independent

---

4 Karl Marx, *Pre-Capitalist Economic Formations*, with an Introduction by Eric J. Hobsbawm (New York: International Publishers, 1965), p. 51, ftn. 2. There is no indication anywhere that Hobsbawm had seen these "voluminous notes," which dealt with Morgan, Phear, Maine, and Lubbock.

5 Frederick Engels, *The Origin of the Family, Private Property and the State* (New York: International Publishers, 1972, 1975.) All pagination is to this edition. In her 66-page Introduction, Leacock writes: "The book was written after Marx's death, but was drawn from Marx's as well as Engels' own notes" (p. 7). Neither the 1972 nor 1975 edition has any reference to *The Ethnological Notebooks*, nor does Leacock show any awareness of the fact that Marx's notes on Morgan had been available in Russia since 1941.

6 Charnie Guettel, *Marxism and Feminism* (Toronto: The Women's Press, 1974): "Leacock's introduction is the most valuable current study of Engels available and mandatory reading for any serious Marxist" (p. 14, n. 8).
   As for Evelyn Reed's *Woman's Evolution* (New York: Pathfinder Press, 1975)—the pretentious "product of over 20 years of research," glorifying a "matriarchal age" "comprising more than 99 percent of human existence"—its emptiness of any revolutionary socialism is seen in the studied elimination of any and all reference to Marx. This is further emphasized by the fact that none of Marx's works are listed in the bibliography. Consider the fact that Evelyn Reed's subject is "woman's evolution," and both Morgan's and Engels' studies do play an acknowledged, important part in her analysis, but there is not one word about *The Ethnological Notebooks of Karl Marx*. Whether that is out of sheer ignorance or out of studied omission, one must question what is her purpose. A little bit of dialectics, of course, would have gone a long way to soften her complaint that the "wealth of data on the question of anthropology and archeology has not been matched by an equivalent expansion in theoretical insight" (p. xvi). Evelyn Reed explains her methodology to be "evolutionary and materialist." All one can say about that is that it certainly isn't revolutionary or historical.

7 Sheila Rowbotham, *Women's Liberation and Revolution* (Bristol, England: Falling Wall Press, March 1972, expanded in 1973), p. 6. This is the "extensive, descriptive bibliography" to which Rowbotham refers in *Women, Resistance and Revolution*.

enough of Marx to call Marx and Engels "a couple of bourgeois men in the 19th century,"[8] she has but one criticism of Draper's "summary": "It doesn't really point out problems and inadequacies of what they wrote."

Hal Draper, the author of the article Rowbotham recommends was then (1970) working on a book pretentiously[9] entitled *Karl Marx's Theory of Revolution*. It is first now (1978) seeing the light of day and still not in toto. Clearly, however, eight years back, Draper was so very anxious to bring his views to bear on the Women's Liberation Movement, subjected to "less-than-knowledgeable summaries that have seen the light recently," that he chose that chapter for separate publication.[10] Neither then, nor now, has he shown any knowledge of the finally available *Ethnological Notebooks of Karl Marx*. The pretentious scholar who so heavily roots himself in Engels' *The Origin of the Family*—not only in the chapter on "Women's Liberation" but throughout his projected six-volume work—should surely have known about these Notebooks, and I'm not referring only to 1972, when they were finally transcribed in their original English, but to the first mention of them in the early 1920s when David Ryazanov discovered them and had them photographed.[11] In 1941, the Marx-Engels Institute published a Russian translation.[12] And therein lies a tale.

It is true that Engels did think he was carrying out a "bequest" of Marx in writing *The Origin of the Family*.... But Engels was not Marx, as he, himself, was the first to admit, and *The Origin of the Family* was *his* version, in which the select quotations from Marx gave the impression that he was reproducing Marx's "Abstract." ...

Far from that being true, we now know that not only is the "Abstract"— that is to say, Marx's actual Notebook on Morgan—148 pages long, but also that it is not the whole of Marx's Notebooks on anthropology. The whole is

---

8   Sheila Rowbotham, *Women, Resistance and Revolution* (New York: Vintage Books Edition, 1974), p. 62.

9   Draper explains his goal to have been "a full and definitive treatment of Marx's political theory, policies, and practice," but since that is "unattainable," since politics has come to have a narrow meaning, and since there is a need to go "beyond the indispensable 'grand theory' ... It is to bend the stick the other way that this work is titled *Karl Marx's Theory of Revolution* rather than *Political Theory*, which might be interpreted too narrowly." See Hal Draper, *Karl Marx's Theory of Revolution* (New York and London: Monthly Review Press, 1977), pp. 11, 12.

10   Hal Draper, "Marx and Engels on Women's Liberation," *International Socialism*, July/August 1970. All pagination in the text is to this article.

11   See "New Data about the Literary Legacy of Marx and Engels (Report of Comrade Ryazanov Made to the Socialist Academy on Nov. 20, 1923)," in *Bulletin of Socialist Academy*, book 6, October-December 1923 (Moscow and Petrograd: State Publishing House, 1923).

12   *Arkhiv Marksa y Engelsa*, vol. 9, 1941 (Leningrad).

254 pages—and even that is not the whole.[13] It will be sufficient to focus first on a fairly minor matter—how important even a mere excerpt is in Marx's hands—through the way in which he emphasized certain words that were not emphasized in Morgan. Here is one excerpt on women of the Iroquois:

> The *women allowed to express their wishes and opinions through an orator of their own election. Decision* given by the Council. *Unanimity was a fundamental law of its action among the Iroquois. Military questions* usually left to the *action of the voluntary principle.*[14]

Secondly, and this is the critical point, the Russians took liberties when they, in 1941, did translate the Marx text on Morgan. Engels, naturally, cannot be blamed for this mistranslation. Nor can the Russians excuse themselves on the basis that the inspiration for using the words "private" and "hallowed" came from Engels. Here is how Marx excerpted a part of Morgan:

> When *field culture* bewiesen hatte, dass d[ie] *ganze Oberfläche der Erde could be made the subject of property owned by individuals in severalty* u[nd] [das] *Familienhaupt* became *the natural center of accumulation,* the *new property career of mankind* inaugurated—fully done *before the close of the Later Period of Barbarism,* übte einen grossen *Einfluss auf* [the] *human mind,* rief *new elements of character* wach....
>
> *Ethnological Notebooks,* pp. 135–136

Here is how the Russian translation reads:

> When field agriculture had demonstrated that the whole surface of the earth could be made the *object* of property of separate individuals and the head of the family became the natural center of accumulation of wealth, mankind entered the new *hallowed path of private property.* It was already fully done before the later period of barbarism came to an

---

13   Marx's notes on Kovalevsky, which the Russians published in 1958, were reproduced by Lawrence Krader in *The Asiatic Mode of Production* (Assen, The Netherlands: Van Gorcum, 1975), available from Humanities Press.

14   *The Ethnological Notebooks,* p. 162. In the edition of *Ancient Society* I am using (Chicago: Charles H. Kerr Pub. Co., 1907, the reproduction of the original 1877 edition), this appears on p. 118. Not only is there no underlining in Morgan, but in Marx the role of the women is not limited by "even," nor is the word "decision" limited by a "but" as in Morgan: "Even the women were allowed to express their wishes and opinions through an orator of their own selection. But the decision was made by the council ..."

end. *Private* property exercised a powerful influence on the human mind, awakening new elements of character....

> *Arkhiv Marksa y Engelsa*, 9:52. Emphasis is mine to stress what was neither in Morgan nor in Marx's excerpt

Here is the original Morgan excerpt:

> When field agriculture had demonstrated that the whole surface of the earth could be made the subject of property owned by individuals in severalty, and it was found that the head of the family became the natural center of accumulation, the new property career of mankind was inaugurated. It was fully done before the close of the Later Period of barbarism. A little reflection must convince any one of the powerful influence property would now begin to exercise upon the human mind, and of the great awakening of new elements of character it was calculated to produce.

Now, the Russians have very concrete, *class*—state-capitalist class—interests that inspire them to translate "the career of property" as "private property" and repeat the word twice. But why should independent Marxists who are not statist-Communists likewise narrow the subject to collective vs. private property, when Marx's point is that the "property career" i.e., accumulation of wealth, is that which contains the antagonisms of the development of patriarchy and later class divisions?

2   Hal Draper Misconstrues

Hal Draper no sooner opens his chapter on women's liberation than he at once starts sniping at today's Women's Liberationists' "social psychology and attitude (like 'male chauvinism')," contrasting it to the view of "Marx and Engels" who, he claims, rooted the "Woman Question" in the "primordial division of labor" between the sexes, and warning us that since that preceded "capitalism, or the state, or the division between town and country, or even private property ... *this* division of labor will be most resistant to uprooting" (p. 20, col. 2).

To help us in this tortuous task, it would seem he would at once plunge into Marx's whole new continent of thought. No. Draper, instead, chooses to roll Marx's views back to his "pre-socialist" days. This at once makes it clear that the "Woman Question" is not the only theme of which Draper is oppressively aware; the other apparition is Hegel. He blames Marx for casting his views "in typically Hegelian-idealist terms" (p. 21, col. 1). By no accident, what then manifests itself is that these two preoccupations, in turn, take second place to the overwhelming drive to do *nothing short of transforming into opposite Marx's concept of that most fundamental relationship of Man/Woman as measure of just how deep a revolution is needed to uproot this exploitative alienating social order.*

Bent on that goal, Draper begins his task by trying to reduce Marx's concept to that of Charles Fourier, frothing at the mouth about the first "lucubrations of this newfledged socialist, his 'Paris manuscripts.'" He is talking about the epochal Humanist Essays of Marx, holding that they are a product of the fact that Marx's view that the Man/Woman relationship is a measure of humanity's development is only due to the fact that Marx "enthusiastically" adopted Fourier's view.[15]

So anxious is Draper to force Marx's Promethean concept of the Man/Woman relationship into the Procrustean attitude of Draper's view of Fourier that he embarks on yet another bold leap downward to his *reductio ad absurdum* thesis by skipping the years between 1844 and 1868, though he is still dealing with the first section, "Marx's Early Views (1842–1846)." Obviously not all that confident that he has succeeded in obfuscating the year before Marx broke with bourgeois society (1842) with the year after (1844), as he presents the years 1842 to 1846 as a single unit, Draper now decides to devise a different scenario in jumping to 1868. First he refers to Engels in *Anti-Dühring* (1878) as again paying "homage to Fourier."[16] Then Draper divines that Marx is also paying homage to Fourier in 1868. Proof? It takes strange ears to hear it in Marx's letter to Ludwig Kugelmann (December 12, 1868):

> Great progress was evident in the last Congress of the American "Labour Union" in that, among other things, it treated working women with complete equality ... Anybody who knows anything of history knows that great social changes are impossible without the feminine ferment. Social

---

15   Contrast this to Simone de Beauvoir's *The Second Sex*, where she shows that Fourier "confused the emancipation of women with the rehabilitation of the flesh, demanding for every individual the right to yield to the call of passion and wishing to replace marriage with love; he considered woman not as a person but only in her amorous function" (p. 103). As total opposite to Fourierism, the penultimate paragraph of de Beauvoir's entire work is that very paragraph from Marx on the Man/Woman relationship.

16   What is especially telling about all these references to Fourier and the homage paid to him is that the bulk of the quotations are from *The Holy Family*. This happens to be the work where Marx and Engels defended Flora Tristan's *Union Ouvrière* as against the bourgeois philistine, Eugène Sue, who attacked her in his best-selling novel, *The Mysteries of Paris*. There is not a single reference to that in Draper's article, although one would think that anyone writing on Women's Liberation in 1970 would know that that would hold great interest for the movement.

progress can be measured exactly by the social position of the fair sex
(the ugly ones included).

MECW 43, pp. 184–85

If you failed to hear that "echo" of enthusiasm for Fourier in Marx's 1868 letter, you are obviously not as adept as Draper in "the exercise in excavation."[17]
To hear it where it isn't, you need the presumptuousness of Draper's divina-
tions that Marx, "perhaps without thinking of the source" (p. 21, col. 2), nevertheless achieved that "echo."

Please remember that Draper is not at this point writing about "the lucubrations of the newfledged socialist." No, the Marx he is talking about here is
the Marx who, the year before, finally published his greatest theoretical work,
Capital. Marx had devoted no less than 80 pages of *Capital* to the struggles for
the shortening of the working day, and the bulk of that chapter dealt with the
oppression of women and children.[18] Now Marx sees something happening
across the ocean on the subject, and he calls Dr. Kugelmann's attention to the
women being invited to join the First International. That letter does have another sentence Draper chose to leave for later. Marx was stressing that they had
elected Madame Harriet Law to the highest ranking body, the General Council.
Wouldn't that have been something to shout to the skies about, that in mid-
19th century Victorian England, Marx organized the First International which
had women not only as members but in decision-making positions?[19]

The question of sexual relations, forms of marriage, the family, are certainly
pivotal, and even if one, like Draper, wishes he could skip over the *Economic-
Philosophic Manuscripts of 1844*, especially so on the question of that fundamental relationship of Man/Woman, there nevertheless has been plenty of
other evidence about Marx's disgust with bourgeois monogamy and its double
standard, all of which needed total uprooting in any new society. After all, the
very next year, 1845, there was the joint work of Marx and Engels, *The German
Ideology*, which is recognized as the first statement of Historical Materialism,

---

17   The phrase Draper uses here is what appears in his *Karl Marx's Theory of Revolution* as *the*
      method that will govern the whole work. See pp. 20–23 of that work.

18   See the section on "The Working Day and the Break with the Concept of Theory" in my
      Marxism and Freedom.

19   In the U.S., the first national trade union organization, the National Labor Union, joined
      the First International and elected many women to decision-making positions. Two of
      the best known were Kate Mullaney, president of the Troy Collar Laundry Workers, who
      was appointed assistant secretary and national organizer for women, and Augusta Lewis,
      a leader in the typographical union. See Joyce Maupin's *Working Women and Their Orga-
      nizations* and *Labor Heroines*, both published in 1974 by Union WAGE, Berkeley, California.

and which Draper quotes at length on these questions. And in that famous year, there is Marx's *Theses on Feuerbach* that again Draper quotes, even calling attention to the fact that where Marx wrote that "the family" had to be "destroyed in theory and in practice," Engels had edited it to read that the family "must be criticised in theory and revolutionized in practice" [MECW 5, pp. 4, 7]. Nor did one have to search for heretofore unpublished documents, since the most famous of all of Marx's works—the *Communist Manifesto*—made no bones about the fact that it was "self-evident" that with the "abolition of private property" would come "the abolition of the family" [MECW 6, pp. 501–02].

Whether it's out of Draper's sheer ignorance of Marx's Notebooks (he refers only to an "Abstract" that Engels supposedly reproduced more or less in full), or because the erudite Draper decided to invent new categories of his own, one thing his footnote to Karl Kautsky does disclose is the smug attitude of Draper on Women's Liberation. He clings to Engels' designation about "*the world historic defeat of the female sex*," which, in turn, he is always relating, with great emphasis, to the "primordial division of labor between the sexes." And, of course, both are deeply rooted in the transition from matriarchy, or at least matrilineal descent, to patriarchy. No matter how hard Draper tries to insinuate that "the world historic defeat of the female sex" is a view that Marx shares with Engels, *that is no expression of Marx's*. What is true of both Marx and Engels is that they were constantly driving at the "etymology" of the word, family. Far from the word bearing a reference to a married couple and their children, it was the word for slaves. *Famulus* meant domestic slave, *familia* referred to the total number of slaves one man owned. (See *The Origin of the Family*, p. 121.) And Marx's stress is on the *social* and not only the "sexual division of labor."

Of course, Marx strongly opposed patriarchy, calling for the "abolition" of the patriarchal family. He held that: "The modern family contains in embryo not only slavery (*servitus*) but serfdom also, since from the very beginning it is connected with agricultural service. It contains within itself, *in miniature*, all the antagonisms which later develop on a wide scale within society and its state."[20] And "all the antagonisms" extended from "ranks" that begin in

---

20   Quoted by Engels in *The Origin of the Family*, pp. 121–122. Incidentally, and not so incidentally, Engels omitted the sentence that preceded this paragraph. It reads: "Fourier characterizes the Epoch of Civilization by Monogamy and private Property in land" (*The Ethnological Notebooks*, p. 120). From the manner in which Engels had worked the omitted single sentence into an entire paragraph that he placed prominently in a note at the very end of his work (p. 236) on how we find already in Fourier "the profound recognition that in all societies which are imperfect and split into antagonisms, single families (*les familles incoherentes*) are the economic unit," Draper would have learned a great deal about the difference between Marx and Engels on the "acceptance" of Fourier.

communal life and lead to the division between chieftain and the masses, class divisions in embryo, *"in miniature."*

It is not true, as Draper would have it, that Engels devoted "one" chapter to "The Family," so entitled; in truth, very nearly one-third of the book is devoted to that subject. Engels appears to have a unilinear instead of a multilinear attitude to the question of the development of Man/Woman.

Marx, on the contrary, showed that the elements of oppression in general, and of woman in particular, arose from *within* primitive communism, and not only related to change from "matriarchy," but beginning with establishment of ranks—relationship of chief to mass—and the economic interests that accompanied it. Indeed, in Volume 3 of *Capital*, as Marx probed in his chapter, "Genesis of Capitalist Ground Rent," "the economic conditions at the basis" of class "individuality," you can see the actual dialectical foundation for his stress, in the Notebooks on anthropology, on property as the material base for changing social relations. He was not using Morgan's phrase, "career of property," as if it were a synonym for historical materialism.

Engels' uncritical acclaim of Morgan notwithstanding, Morgan had not "discovered afresh in America the materialist conception of history discovered by Marx forty years ago."[21]

Marx emphasized Morgan's great contribution on the theory of the gens and its early egalitarian society, but he certainly didn't tie it, alone, to the precedence of matriarchy over patriarchy as did Engels in the Preface to the Fourth Edition, 1891:

> This rediscovery of the primitive matriarchal gens as the earlier stage of the patriarchal gens of civilized peoples has the same importance for anthropology as Darwin's theory of evolution has for biology and Marx's theory of surplus value for political economy.

Marx didn't take issue with Morgan's findings about the Iroquois society and especially singled out the role of women in it. But he did not stop there. He called attention to other societies and other analyses, and brought new illumination to the writings of Plutarch with his own commentaries in his *Ethnological Notebooks*:

> The expression by Plutarch, that "the lowly and poor readily followed the bidding of Theseus" and the statement from Aristotle cited by him,

---

21   Engels' Preface to the First Edition of *The Origin of the Family*.

that Theseus "was inclined toward the people" appear, however, despite Morgan, to indicate that the chiefs of the gentes, etc., already entered into conflict of interest with the mass of the gentes, which is inevitably connected with the monogamous family through private property in houses, lands, herds.[22]

Then, Marx demonstrates that, long before the dissolution of the primitive commune, there emerged the question of ranks *within* the egalitarian commune. It was the beginning of a transformation into opposite—gens into caste. That is to say, within the egalitarian communal form arose the elements of its opposite—caste, aristocracy, different material interests. Moreover, these weren't successive stages, but coextensive with the communal form. As Marx observed of the period when they began changing the names of the children to assure paternal rather than maternal rights (a paragraph Engels did reproduce in *The Origin of the Family*):

Innate casuistry! To change things by changing their names! And to find loopholes for violating tradition while maintaining tradition, when direct interest supplied sufficient impulse.

In a word, though Marx surely connects the monogamous family with private property, what is pivotal to him is the antagonistic relationship between the Chief and the masses.

Marx's historic originality in internalizing new data, whether that be in anthropology or "pure" science, was a never-ending confrontation with what Marx called "history and its process."[23] That was concrete. That was ever-changing. And that ever-changing concrete was inexorably bound to the universal, because, precisely because, the determining concrete was the ever-developing Subject—self-developing men and women.

---

22   I'm using Krader's translation in his article, "The Works of Marx and Engels in Ethnology Compared," *International Review of Social History,* Vol. XVIII, Part 2, 1973. This is really an extension of his magnificent transcription and editing of Marx's *Ethnological Notebooks,* and I am greatly indebted to the seminal introduction he wrote for it.

23   *Capital,* Volume 1 (Chicago: Charles H. Kerr, 1909; reprinted New York: International Publishers, 1967), p. 406, n. 2: "The weak points in the abstract materialism of natural science, a materialism that excludes history and its process, are at once evident from the abstract and ideological conceptions of its spokesmen, whenever they venture beyond the bounds of their own specialty" [MCIK, pp. 406–07, ftn. 2; MCIP, p. 494, ftn. 4]. See also Chapter 2, "A New Continent of Thought," in my *Philosophy and Revolution* (New York: Dell, 1973).

The whole question of transitions is what is at stake between Marx's and Engels' views. Marx is showing that it is *during* the transition period that you see the duality, the beginnings of antagonisms, whereas Engels always seems to have it only at the end, as if class society came in very nearly full blown *after* the communal form was destroyed and private property was established. *Moreover, where, to Marx, the dialectical development from one stage to another is related to new revolutionary upsurge, Engels sees it as a unilateral development.*

In the 1850s, for example, what inspired Marx to return to the study of pre-capitalist formations and gave new appreciation of ancient society and its craftsmen was the Taiping Revolution.[24] It opened so many new doors on "history and its process" that "materialistically" a stage of production wasn't just a stage of production—be it the Western or the Asiatic mode of production—but a question of revolutionary relations. Whether that concerned the communal form or the despotic form of property, the development of [the relationship of] the individual to society and to the state was crucial. It was no accident, on the other hand, that Engels, who certainly agreed with Marx's singling out the Asiatic mode of production, nevertheless happened to skip over the question of the Oriental commune in *his* analysis of primitive communism in *The Origin of the Family.*

Hal Draper, on the other hand, not only continues to act as though Engels' *The Origin of the Family* was written also by Marx, but as if he, Draper, is speaking for them, as he reaches the last part of his chapter, entitled "Problems of Women's Liberation." Thus, in returning to Marx's December 12, 1868, letter to Kugelmann, this time citing that the First International had elected "Madame Law to be a member of the General Council," Draper presents that fact with the same attitude that he has towards the statement of Engels that became such a favorite of Clara Zetkin and the whole Social Democratic women's movement: "In the family, he [man] is the bourgeois; the wife represents the proletariat." Draper's comment is that that was meant "as a strong metaphor, of course" (p. 24, col. 2).

No wonder that the stress, as he goes to the actual women's movement, is on Engels' and August Bebel's role in encouraging the establishment of women's organizations with their own "autonomous leadership" (p. 27, col. 1), rather than the women's autonomous leadership itself. No wonder Clara Zetkin rates hardly more than a couple of paragraphs, and whereas he does say she was the head of the movement, whose organ, *Gleichheit*, reached a circulation of 100,000, he acts as if all they discussed was the "Woman Question." Not a word

---

24   It is not clear whether Engels knew Marx's *Grundrisse*, but he did know the articles in *The New York Tribune* on the Taiping Revolution.

comes into it about the fact that women played the greatest revolutionary role in opposing the First World War.

Why should Eleanor Marx, who is finally recognized "as a revolutionary organizer and agitator" as well as "extraordinarily effective political activist" be listed only as "the ablest woman trade union organizer in the *New Union-ism*," when, in fact, it wasn't only "as a woman" that she was a great organizer. She was the one who took seriously Marx's urging, after the fall of the Paris wwCommune, that revolutionaries should go "lower and deeper"[25] into the proletariat, away from the skilled toward the unskilled and the most exploited, not to mention the newly arrived peasants and the doubly exploited Jew of London's East End. Draper does give her credit for playing "an active role in the building of the new-type Gas Workers' and General Laborers Union" (p. 27, col. 1) and says she "co-authored a pamphlet for England on *The Woman Question*." But he doesn't single this out as something significantly new both for her, and the Movement.[26]

Most important and relevant for our age, however, is not what Engels wrote in 1884, much less whether there was or wasn't a matriarchal stage. Nor is it the "Woman Question" as Bebel saw it at the beginning of the 20th century, though both men's writings had a great influence on the development of the social-ist women's movement, which was likewise way ahead of the times, not just theoretically, but in the actual mass organization of working women. What is cogent today is whether the ground laid helps or doesn't help today's Women's Liberation Movement. Draper's doesn't.

Even without knowing (or perhaps just not caring) about Edith Thomas' *The Women Incendiaries*,[27] there was no way of his not knowing about the most famous woman revolutionary, Louise Michel, and about the young woman Marx advised to go to Paris, Elizabeth Dmitrieva, to organize a women's section of the International. What was necessary, to make the women's participation in the Paris Commune, as both force and reason, come alive, required more

---

25   It took World War I before Lenin found that phrase of Marx, made to the 1871 Congress of the International Workingmen's Association, and first then made a category of it. See Chapter X, "The Collapse of the Second International and the Break in Lenin's Thought," in Marxism and Freedom.

26   Contrast this to what has since been developed by a young woman revolutionary, Terry Moon, in an essay on "Eleanor Marx in Chicago," published by *News & Letters* for Interna-tional Women's Day, March 1984.

27   Draper published, edited and wrote a Foreword to a whole book, *Karl Marx and Friedrich Engels: Writings on the Paris Commune* (New York: Monthly Review Press, 1971), which likewise failed to take into account any of the material on what actually happened, un-covered by this magnificent book, *The Women Incendiaries*, written by Edith Thomas and published in France in 1963, and in New York in 1966 (New York: George Braziller, 1966).

space than the single paragraph Draper devoted to it. Let us see what he does when he finally reaches the culmination of his subject with the thunderous "Social Revolution Comes First."

It focuses on *counter*revolution, with the apex of the whole—the very, very final sentence—narrowing the question to the "division of labor between the sexes":

> But in the last analysis the historic forms of the division of labor between the sexes could be uprooted for good and all only by as profound an up-heaval as it had originally taken to impose "the world-historic defeat of the female sex" of which Engels had written.

The nonsense of talking about the "division of labor between the sexes" as if that "primordial" state is the burning question of the day, when even for the primitive stage it was part of the *social* division of labor, is not only forgetting what was at stake, but what *is* pivotal and underlies all class societies—the division between mental and manual labor. There is not a whiff of *that Great Divide*, and that is of the essence for our age.

Is the totality of that "primordial" counterrevolution the ground for Women's Liberation today? And can we possibly disregard Draper's cynicism as he feels compelled to add, parenthetically, of course, that the totality of the change needed in the Man/Woman relationship holds under "all" circumstances: "(That would be so even without the Pill.)"? Does he consider it mod to keep stressing, when he refers to "the world-historic defeat of the female sex," that it "cannot be changed basically simply by ideological (including psychiatric) exhortation" (p. 24, col. 2)? What idiocy, first to reduce today's fight for total liberation to the merely "ideological," and then further to reduce ideology to "psychiatric exhortation"!

3   Marx's Notebooks: Then and Now

Marx died before he could write up his Notebooks on anthropology either as a separate work, or as part of Volume 3 of *Capital*. There is no way for us to know what Marx intended to do with this intensive study, much less the concrete manner in which he would have dialectically related the external to the internal factors in the dissolution of the primitive commune. What is clear, however, is that the decline of the primitive commune was not due just to external factors, nor due only to "*the world historic defeat of the female sex*." (That was Engels' phrase, not Marx's.) Just as there was conquest, even when the commune was at its height, and the beginning of slavery when one tribe defeated another, so there was the beginning of commodity exchange between the communes as well as emergence of conflict within the commune, within the family, and not only between the family and the gens. All these conflicts coalesced during the dissolution, which is why Marx's Notebooks keep stressing the duality in primitive communism.

Take, for example, the question of the division of labor. Though, in 1845, in *The German Ideology*, he called attention to the fact that the first division of labor was sexual, he now stresses the twofold nature in the division of labor: (1) physiological as well as inter-tribal conflict; (2) the *social* division of labor based both on exchange of surplus products between communities and on the mode of labor. As the family develops as an *economic unit* and gets separated out of the gens, the focus changes again to the different material interests that are developing both internally and externally, including development of technology and agriculture. Which was why, in the paragraph that Engels did quote in *The Origin of the Family*, Marx emphasized that not only slavery but also serfdom was latent in the family, indeed, that all conflicts that were developing in the transition to class society were present in the family *"in miniature."*

Finally, what Marx called "the excrescence of the state" in class-divided society—and he uses that in his reference to a period during the dissolution of the commune—is introduced into the question of transition from primitive communism to a political society. The point at all times is to stress a differentiation in the family, both when that is part of the gens and as it evolves out of the gens into another social form, at which point Marx again differentiates between the family that is in a society that already has a state and the family before the state emerged. The point at all times is to have a critical attitude both to biologism and uncritical evolutionism.

It was by no means simple, unitary development, and it cannot under any circumstances be attributed to a single cause like patriarchy winning over matriarchy and establishing thereby nothing less than some sort of "world historic defeat of the female sex." Marx, by taking as the point of departure not the *counter*-revolution, but new stages of revolution, was enabled to see, even in the Asiatic mode of production, the great resistance to Western imperial encroachments, contrasting China to India, where British imperialism won.

Throughout Marx's Notebooks, his attack on colonialism, racism, as well as discrimination against women, is relentless, as he refers to the British historians, jurists, anthropologists, and lawyers as "blockheads" who definitely didn't appreciate what discoveries were being made and therefore often skipped over whole historic periods of humanity. Listen to the criticisms included in Marx's Notebooks on Maine: "Herr Maine als blockheaded Englishman geht nicht von gens aus, sondern von Patriarch, der später Chief wird etc."[28] And a little later:

> Nach dem *Ancient Irish Law* women had some power of *dealing with their own property without the consent of their husbands,* and this was one of the institutions *expressly declared by the English blockheaded Judges to be illegal at the beginning of the 17th century.*[29]

As against Engels, who was so overwhelmed with all the new data on forms of marriage and the development of a family, in and out of the gens, that it very nearly subsumed the question of property, i.e., economics, Marx, in assembling new data, never fails to criticize the major writers he is excerpting. He does this, not just "politically," i.e., calling attention to the fact that they are bourgeois writers, but calling attention to the fact that their method is empiric, and nowhere is empiricism as method as vacuous as when gathering new facts. What Marx was doing, instead, was following the empiric facts dialectically, relating them not only to other historic facts, but tracing the development of each fact, its petrifaction and transformation into opposite, caste. Which is why he kept his eye on the differences in rank in the gens, emergence of conflict within it, both in changing material interests and in relations between Chief and ranks. And yet, Marx drew no such unbridgeable gulf between primitive and civilized as Engels had. As he was to write to Zasulich, in the year he was working most intensively on Morgan's *Ancient Society*, the pivotal point was that everything "depends on the historical environment in which it occurs."

While there was no difference between Marx and Engels on such a conclusion—indeed, the expression "Historical Materialism" was Engels', not Marx's—the relationship of concrete to universal always remains, with Engels, in two totally separate compartments. Put differently, "knowing" Historical Materialism, and having that always at the back of his mind, and recognizing Marx as "genius" whereas he and the others were "at best, talented," did not impart to Engels' writings *after Marx's death,* the totality of Marx's new continent of thought. Engels' *The Origin of the Family,* as his first major work after the death of Marx, proves that fact most glaringly today, because Women's

---

28   *The Ethnological Notebooks,* p. 292: "Mr. Maine, as a blockheaded Englishman, doesn't proceed from *gens,* but rather from Patriarch, which later becomes Chief, etc."

29   Ibid, p. 323. It should be noted also that Marx had an extensive library on matriarchal laws.

Liberation is an Idea whose time has come, and for that, *The Origin of the Family* sheds little direction.

As Marx, in the last years of his life, was turning to anthropology, it was neither as the philosophic anthropology which ran through his 1844 Essays, nor just as the latest empiric data in the 1880s. Rather, whether it's a question of the description of the equality of women during primitive communism or the question of Morgan's theory of the gens, what Marx was focusing on was the self-development of humanity from primitive communism to the period in which he lived, through revolutionary praxis. That is what kept him enthralled as he dug deep into the latest in anthropology, in early history, technology, and agriculture, craftsmanship and primitive human relations. Truly, we see here that *no greater empiricist ever lived than the great dialectician, Karl Marx.* And Marx wasn't hurrying to make easy generalizations, such as Engels' on the future being just a "higher stage" than primitive communism. No, Marx envisioned a totally new man, a totally new woman, a totally new life form (and by no means only for marriage): in a word, a totally new society.

Suddenly, Marx found it difficult to answer a simple question from Vera Zasulich on the future of the Russian commune, in the manner in which it was debated between the Narodniks and the Marxists—that is to say, whether it could lead to communism without needing to go through capitalism and evidently without a revolution! He wrote no less than four different versions of his answer, the first of which was fully ten pages long. From that first draft until the very much abbreviated one that he finally sent, what is clear is that his preoccupation is not "the commune" but the "needed Russian Revolution": "In order to save the Russian commune a revolution is needed."[30]

The second draft manifests also what he had developed with the Asiatic mode of production:

> The archaic or primary formation of our globe contains a number of strata of different ages, one superimposed on the other ... [isolation] permits the emergence of a central despotism above the communities. ... I now come to the crux of the question. We cannot overlook the fact that the

---

[30] The 1970 edition of the three-volume *Karl Marx and Frederick Engels: Selected Works* (Moscow: Progress Publishers) finally published the first draft of Marx's reply, pp. 152–163. Peculiarly enough, the explanatory note (p. 522, n. 113) refers to the fact that Marx was working on the third volume of *Capital* at this time, without referring to the fact that he was then studying Morgan's *Ancient Society*, though Marx himself refers to it and they have to footnote the actual title of Morgan's book.

archaic type to which the Russian commune belongs, conceals an internal dualism.[31]

The third draft, which in part was quoted above on the question of the historical environment being the crucial point, was a conclusion Marx reached as he
emphasized "the dualism within it [the commune] permits of an alternative:
either the property element in it will overcome the collective element, or the
other way."

This is always the key to the whole. We must remember that just as, in 1844,
Marx was projecting not just the overthrow of the old but stressing that a new
society must change human relationships totally, actually as well as philosophically, so, once the 1848 Revolutions were defeated, Marx developed a new
concept—the "revolution in permanence." In a word, it was in the March 1850
Address to the Communist League that Marx first projected both the deepening
of the concrete revolution as well as the world revolution, the interrelatedness
of both.

As we saw, it was the Taiping Revolution in the 1850s which led, at one and
the same time, to his probing of pre-capitalist forms of society and seeing the
Chinese Revolution as "encouraging" the West European proletariat, which
was quiescent at the moment, to revolt. The *Grundrisse*, which contained that
most brilliant chapter on pre-capitalist formations, also contained the projection of a totally new society wherein man, wrote Marx, "does not seek to
remain something formed by the past, but is in the absolute movement of becoming" [*Grundrisse*, p. 488].

And here—*after* the great "scientific-economic" work, *Capital* (which, however, likewise, projected "human power is its own end"[32]); *after* the defeat of
the Paris Commune; and *after* four full decades from the start of Marx's discovery of a whole new continent of thought, first articulated in 1844—we see that

---

31   Excerpts from the second and third drafts are included in *Pre-Capitalist Economic Forma-
     tions.* All four drafts are included in full in *Arkhiv Marksa y Engelsa,* vol. 1. They are also
     included in the Russian *Collected Works of Marx and Engels,* vol. 19. Actually, Marx wrote
     all the drafts in French. [All four drafts were published in English translation in Teodor
     Shanin, ed., *Late Marx and the Russian Road: Marx and "the Peripheries of Capitalism"*
     (New York: Monthly Review Press, 1983), pp. 99–124.

32   *Capital,* Vol. 3 (Chicago: Charles H. Kerr, 1909; reprinted New York: International Publish-
     ers, 1967), p. 954 [MCIIIK, p. 954; MCIIIP, p. 959]. One erudite anthropologist, who is cer-
     tainly no Marxist, Sir Raymond Firth, also focuses on the fact that *Capital* is not so much
     an economic work as "a dramatic history designed to involve its readers in the events
     described." See "The Sceptical Anthropologist? Social Anthropology and Marxist Views of
     Society," by Raymond Firth in *Marxist Analyses and Social Anthropology* (London: Malaby
     Press, 1975).

Marx returns to probe "the origin" of humanity, *not* for purposes of discovering "new" origins but for perceiving new revolutionary forces, *their* reason, or as Marx called it in emphasizing a sentence of Morgan, "powers of the mind." How total, continuous, global must the concept of revolution be now? One culminating point in this intensive study of primitive communism and in the answer to Vera Zasulich[33] can be seen in the preface Marx and Engels wrote for the Russian edition of the *Communist Manifesto*, which, without changing a word in the Manifesto itself,[34] projected the idea that Russia could be the first to have proletarian revolution:

> If the Russian Revolution becomes the signal for a proletarian revolution in the West, so that both complement each other, the present Russian common ownership of land may serve as the starting point for a communist development.

The preface was dated January 1882. Marx continued his work in ethnological studies for the rest of the year. The last writer he excerpted—Lubbock—was studied but four months before his death. He did not abate his criticism of either the writers or their reports. Thus, in excerpting Lubbock's statement, "Among many of the lower races relationship through females is the prevalent custom...." and noting that Lubbock still continues to talk of "a man's heirs," Marx contemptuously noted "but then they are not the man's heirs; these civilized asses cannot free themselves of their own conventionalities."[35]

How can anyone consider that what Engels was writing in *The Origin of the Family* was the equivalent of Marx's accumulated depth and breadth of thought and revolutionary experience? The dialectic of all the developments, subjective and objective, in Marx's day (1843–1883) has a great deal to tell us,

---

33   Her letter to Marx is included in *The Russian Menace to Europe*, edited by Paul W. Blackstock and Bert F. Hoselitz (Glencoe, Illinois: Free Press, 1952), but the liberties they take by trying to create a one page composite of the four drafts of Marx's answer leave a great deal to be desired.

34   In that 1882 preface, signed by both Marx and Engels, Marx saw no reason for making any changes, although he was then intensively studying primitive communism, something they knew little about in 1847 when the Manifesto was first written. Engels, on the other hand, in the 1888 English edition, felt called upon to offer a demurrer to the epoch-making statement: "All history is a history of class struggles" [MECW 6, p. 482]. He claimed in a footnote that this meant all *"written"* history, but that since the publication of Morgan's *Ancient Society*, much more had been learned about primitive communism [MECW 6, p. 482, ftn.]. To this writer, Engels thereby modified the dialectic structure of Marx's historic call to revolution.

35   *The Ethnological Notebooks*, p. 340.

but we will not get it from Draper's "summation" of what "Marx and Engels" wrote on women's liberation, or from the socialist women who accept that summation.

I began this chapter by focusing on the fact that, though Marx's discovery of a new continent of thought signaled, as well, an epoch of revolution, it nevertheless took a whole series of revolutions to bring out his unpublished works. The fact that the mid-1960s also gave birth to a new Women's Liberation Movement, as both force and reason, makes it necessary to study the finally published notebooks of Marx on Morgan, Maine, Phear, and Lubbock.[36] As theoretic preparation for the American Revolution, it is of more than passing interest that what preoccupied Marx in his last years was a study by an American anthropologist, Morgan, centering on the Iroquois Confederacy. Of course, each generation of Marxists must work out its own problems. But Marx's philosophy of revolution is so total a concept that it cannot be just heritage. Rather, it is the type of past that is proof of the continuity of Marx's philosophy for our age. We will continue to grapple with it throughout this projected work, *Rosa Luxemburg, Today's Women's Liberation Movement and Marx's Philosophy of Revolution*.

---

36   Marx's *Ethnological Notebooks* include his studies of Lewis Henry Morgan's *Ancient Society*, John Budd Phear's *The Aryan Village*, Henry Sumner Maine's *Lectures on the Early History of Institutions*, and John Lubbock's *The Origin of Civilization*.

CHAPTER 29

Letter to Adrienne Rich on Women's Liberation, Gay Liberation, and the Dialectic

Responding to Adrienne Rich's very serious review of Dunayevskaya's four books (Adrienne Rich, "Living the Revolution," The Women's Review of Books Vol. 3, No. 12, September 1986), this letter expands on the reason for being of Philosophy and Revolution, and on the concepts of "woman as revolutionary reason as well as force" and "new forces and new passions" of revolution, especially in relation to Women's Liberation and the Dialectics of Revolution: Reaching for the Future, and Dunayevskaya's work-in-progress, Dialectics of Organization and Philosophy. In doing so, the letter illuminates her view of multilinearity in Marx's late writings as a dimension of his concept of revolution in permanence concerning not only class but all social relations, including questions of sexuality and women's liberation. Rich's review, this letter, and additional correspondence are included in the Supplement to the Raya Dunayevskaya Collection, pp. 11293–11309.

September 18, 1986

Dear Adrienne Rich:

Your review of my four major works[1] created an adventurous journey for me. It was an adventure because it showed that not only does the uniqueness, the newness of today's Women's Liberation Movement no longer stand in the way of its appreciation of Rosa Luxemburg, the great revolutionary Marxist feminist, but it poses as well other critiques of today's Marxism.

The simultaneity of the appearance of Women's Liberation—that had developed from an Idea whose time had come to a *Movement*—and the appearance of the transcription of Marx's *Ethnological Notebooks* led me to think (evidently wrongly) that the work I was rushing to completion—*Philosophy and Revolution*—with its final chapter tackling "new passions and new forces," would result in a veritable union of radical feminism and Marxist-Humanism.

---

1 Rich's review took up *Marxism and Freedom, from 1776 until Today; Philosophy and Revolution, from Hegel to Sartre and from Marx to Mao; Rosa Luxemburg, Women's Liberation, and Marx's Philosophy of Revolution;* and *Women's Liberation and the Dialectics of Revolution: Reaching for the Future.* —Editor.

Instead, as you so cogently expressed it in your review, "... a term like 'Marxist-Humanism' would, in the late sixties and early seventies, have sounded like a funeral knell," to the Women's Liberation Movement at that time.

From the reception (mostly the lack of it) of my works by so-called orthodox Marxists, on the one hand, and by radical feminists, on the other hand, I felt that both the radical feminists and the post-Marx Marxists lack a philosophy of revolution needed for total revolution. It became clear to me that the Marxists were raised on *Engelsian* Marxism, not *Marx's* Marxism, i.e., what Marx from the very start called "a new Humanism."

How could women, I asked myself, skip over history and act as if nothing happened before the 1960s? After all, it meant skipping over integral, crucial periods of their own history, be it of the 19th century or the 1930s.

In Yenan [China] in those 1930s and 1940s, some women were critiquing Mao Zedong himself. The great writer and revolutionary Ding Ling had written "Thoughts on March 8," declaring the wives of the Communist leaders as "Noras who came home." Yet U.S. radical feminists not only dismissed the 1930s as "counterrevolutionary," but never addressed the significance of the battles of the housewives driven into the factories to become those "Rosie the Riveters," only to be thrown out of the factories at the end of World War II and told to go back to the kitchen.

It seemed to me that not only was a critique of the Women's Liberation Movement needed, but it was also necessary to draw up a balance sheet about that missing link—philosophy—not only in the Women's Liberation Movement, but among even the great Marxist revolutionaries.

Pardon me for smiling at the word "academic" in your description of *Philosophy and Revolution* as "the most academic." What is true is that way back in 1950 when I was active in the Miners' General Strike and writing the dispatches also on the miners' wives, I also dug deep into a study of Hegel's works. Having never been part of academia (I'm 76), I was not even aware that when, in 1953, I first broke through to a new concept of Hegel's Absolutes,[2] I had broken with the whole Hegelian tradition which saw Hegel's Absolutes as a hierarchical system. Instead, I saw in the Absolute, new beginnings, a movement from practice as well as from theory.

---

2   Over a decade after those Letters on the Absolute Idea were written (see my Archives, *The Raya Dunayevskaya Collection* at Wayne State University, pp. 2431–66 and pp. 5041–5109), as I began writing my draft chapters of *Philosophy and Revolution*, I found that Hegel scholars had left the three final syllogisms of Hegel's *Encyclopedia of the Philosophical Sciences* (paragraphs 575, 576, 577) fairly untouched, without realizing that it was not Logic, but Nature that had been the mediation, the ground for the self-movement of the Idea, from *Phenomenology of Mind, Science of Logic, Philosophy of Nature, Mind,* i.e., the whole *Encyclopedia*.

This is why Marx never let go of the Hegelian dialectic, which he saw as "the source of *all* dialectics" [MCIK, p. 654; MCIP, p. 744; emphasis added]. Marx held Absolute Negativity—"the negation of the negation"—to be an active creativity that Feuerbachian materialism's critique of Hegel's idealism had not matched.[3] Marx's dialectical, historical materialism did not depart in its critique of Hegel, though Marx had discovered a whole new continent of thought and revolution, of class struggles, of the Man/Woman relationship— in a word, "revolution in permanence."

It was only when the turbulent 1960s ended with Charles de Gaulle winning in Paris, 1968, without firing a shot, at the very height of that massive activity that had relegated theory to something that could supposedly be caught *"en route,"* that I finally felt compelled publicly to delve into that missing dimension of philosophy—the Hegelian dialectic that Marx had been rooted in. To tackle the dialectics of thought and revolution was, I held, what all the new passions and new forces needed to have as their ground. I knew I was treading uncharted waters, not only among Women's Liberationists, but among orthodox Marxists, but I did not expect the response to my findings would be such total silence.

You have hit the nail on the head when you wrote: "If, indeed, Marx was moving in such a direction, we can't leap forward from Marx without understanding where he left off and what he left to us." That's what I thought I was doing when I concretized the task as the need to work out the *new* signaled by the 1950s that I had designated a movement from practice that is itself a form of theory. I involved myself in the recording of those new voices, beginning with the miners on general strike, and their wives, in those activities against that machine, the "continuous miner," which they called a "man-killer." With it they had posed the question: "What kind of labor should man do?"

In the 1960s we recorded the voices from below in *Freedom Riders Speak for Themselves* (from Mississippi and Louisiana jails), as well as the voices and thoughts from the Mississippi Freedom Schools and the Free Speech Movement. This last pamphlet, *The Free Speech Movement and the Negro Revolution,* by Mario Savio, Eugene Walker, and Raya Dunayevskaya, as well as the pamphlet *Notes on Women's Liberation: We Speak in Many Voices,* were issued along with *Nationalism, Communism, Marxist-Humanism and the Afro-Asian Revolutions.* I had hoped that the essence of all these new voices and new worlds was articulated in *Philosophy and Revolution.*

Passions, I might add—and Marx was a great one to talk about "new forces and new passions"—were not restricted to what Audre Lorde calls the "erotic

---

3 See appendix, pp. 341–44, 349–54. —Editor.

as power." Any struggle for new human relations required not only philosophy and revolution, but *self*-development, and that both the day of revolution and the day after. That nothing new, much less a totally new society, could be achieved cold-bloodedly shows that the creative urge demanded passion. That is what brought forth from Marx such new *language* as "time is space for human development"[4]—and that in an article on economics.

Towards the end of your review of my books, you place a whole new series of problems before me. You single out "the edges of struggle," asking me to expand on the question of Women's Liberation's relationship to revolution, since sexuality—"neither sexual purity nor sexual liberation"—has established any relationship to revolution. What remains

> still unclear [is] how, and by what historical forces heterosexuality has been socially constructed; the degree to which lesbian and gay liberation has been a revolutionary force; how actual sexual practice informs theory; the conditions under which sex is work, recreation, or, in Audre Lorde's phrase, "the erotic is power."

My problem is: how can I answer the specificity of sexuality in the sense it is now used without seeming to slough it off if I reply: You are the one who must do it; workers work out their own emancipation and Blacks theirs, so must all other forces of revolution—youth, women, and women not just in general, but the very concrete question of lesbianism, or, for that matter, all of homosexuality.

It is true that women revolutionaries in the 19th and early 20th century referred to sexuality (if they used the word at all), and meant by it only the discrimination against women in labor and wages, never bringing the topic into the "Party," as if it had no relation to men in the movement. And it is true that by the mid-20th century, when we began posing the subject, we were still referring, not to specific practices, but using the word sex as if it encompassed homosexual as well as heterosexual, and thus leaving the impression that we actually narrowed sexism to conditions of labor, class struggle, or race, rather than different sex practices. What was true was that as revolutionaries we were always putting the priority on the dialectics of revolution.

I believe that where I have had the greatest experience with a specific force of revolution demanding proof of the concreteness of freedom for itself is with the Black Dimension. I have been active there from literally the first moment I, a Ukrainian, landed on these shores, the first time I saw a Black man. I asked

---

4   See MECW 33, p. 493; see also MECW 20, p. 142; MECW 32, p. 390; *Grundrisse*, p. 708. —Editor.

who was that? I took myself from the Jewish ghetto to the Black ghetto in the 1920s. In the 1960s, on the 100th anniversary of the Emancipation Proclamation, we embarked on a short history of the whole Black Dimension in American history, *American Civilization on Trial*, which had as its subtitle, "Black Masses as Vanguard."[5] I was questioned by a Black woman in the late 1960s about what the concept of freedom in Marxist-Humanism means to Black women.

Without feeling that I was evading her question, my answer stressed the fact that, far from Marxist-Humanist philosophy limiting us in the fight for total freedom for all, it led me to the creation of the category, "Woman as Revolutionary Reason as well as Force," and that before Women's Liberation had moved from an Idea to a Movement. I pointed to Black women speaking for themselves in *News & Letters* not only as activists, but as columnists such as Ethel Dunbar in "Way of the World" and the development of a "Woman as Reason" column. I had to respond that each revolutionary force does have to concretize the question for what it considers, holds, as the proof that freedom is here and does relate to them. *No one can do it for Other.*

I then embarked on collecting 35 years of my writing for *Women's Liberation and the Dialectics of Revolution: Reaching for the Future.* Clearly, dialectics of revolution was still my preoccupation. This time, however, I wanted to single out women as the subject. The aim was to show how total the uprooting of the old must be, be it in work, or culture, or leisure, or self. And with it, how total freedom must be, which was the meaning of Marx's "revolution in permanence," that is, to continue *after* the overthrow of the old, at which point the task becomes most difficult, as it involves nothing short of such full *self-development* that the division between mental and manual is finally abolished.

The Introduction/Overview to that book, *Women's Liberation and the Dialectics of Revolution*, tried to spell out that dialectic of revolution, whether it dealt with labor, Black, women (Part I), or, as in Part II, all women, whether leaders, or ranks, or whatever, and in whatever period, designated "Revolutionaries All." At the same time, I had been developing the indispensability of theory by speaking on "Not by Practice Alone: The Movement from Theory."[6] Where, in Part III, I spoke of "Sexism, Politics and Revolution" in various parts of the world, I posed the question without answering it: "Is There an Organizational

5   See Chapters 24 and 25. —Editor.
6   See "Not by Practice Alone," published in both *The Marxist-Humanist Theory of State-Capitalism* and in *The Power of Negativity*, originally part of "The Movements from Theory as Well as from Practice vs. the Great Artificer, Ronald Reagan, for whom the Whole World Is a Stage," July 7, 1984, Perspectives Report, RDC, pp. 8193–8218. —Editor.

Answer?"[7] I deliberately didn't answer it there because I feel very strongly that without that missing link—philosophy—there is no answer to the question of organization, which of course means relationship to revolution.

This is exactly what I am in the process of working out in my book-to-be, *Dialectics of Organization and Philosophy: The "Party" and Forms of Organization Born out of Spontaneity*. As you saw from Part IV of my last book, I traced Marx's New Humanism together with the Dialectics of Women's Liberation in Primitive and Modern Societies.[8] Here is how I phrased it in my new working papers:

> Put briefly, Women's Liberation is the first dialectic of revolution *when* it is relationship—when it comes out of—the new epoch itself, which we declared philosophically to be a movement from practice that is itself a form of theory, and absolutely inseparable from revolution. It is those three elements—the epoch, the philosophy, and a new force of revolution—which we, and we alone, named when we saw Women's Liberation not only as Force, but as Reason.[9]

My point was that before Marx learned all those great things about the Iroquois that excited him so much as to create still "new moments" for him, he wrote the first draft of *Capital* (which the Marx-Engels Institute, a belated century later, called the *Grundrisse*), where he analyzed pre-capitalist society and became sufficiently enamored of those societies that he used a most Hegelian phrase to designate human development—"the absolute movement of becoming" [*Grundrisse*, p. 488].

This *dis*continuity of epochs becomes creatively original rather than being just an "update" when it is deeply rooted in *con*tinuity. The new continent of thought and of revolution that Marx had discovered when he broke with capitalism, as well as with what he called "vulgar communism," and critiqued Hegelian dialectics, he called a "new Humanism." That will remain *the* ground needed until there has been total uprooting of all forms of capitalism, state as well as private, including capitalist-imperialism. That is first when the

---

7   The first three parts of *Women's Liberation and the Dialectics of Revolution* are titled "Women, Labor and the Black Dimension"; "Revolutionaries All"; and "Sexism, Politics and Revolution—Japan, Portugal, Poland, China, Latin America, the U.S.—Is There an Organizational Answer?" —Editor.

8   See Chapter 27. —Editor.

9   From "Responsibility for Marxist-Humanism in the Historic Mirror: A Revolutionary-Critical Look," presentation to the Expanded Resident Editorial Board of News and Letters Committees, December 30, 1984, RDC, pp. 8334–47. —Editor.

Self-Bringing Forth of Liberty brings the Self-Determination of the Idea to maturity and the dialectic is unchained. The Universal and the Individual become one, or, as Hegel put it: "Individualism which lets nothing interfere with its Universalism, i.e., Freedom." We cannot tell in advance what a fully new human being is because we are not.

I would very much like to talk more with you. Is Chicago on your calendar? Would you be interested in commenting on any of the sections of what I am now working on, *Dialectics of Organization and Philosophy*?

YOURS,

RAYA DUNAYEVSKAYA

SECTION D

Dialectics of Organization and Philosophy

∵

CHAPTER 30

Spontaneity, Organization, Philosophy (Dialectics)

Dunayevskaya's work on Dialectics of Organization and Philosophy began during the writing of Rosa Luxemburg, Women's Liberation, and Marx's Philosophy of Revolution *and continued throughout the rest of her life. This "Rough Draft of Chapter 7"* (Supplement to the Raya Dunayevskaya Collection, *pp. 14866–83*) *for the Luxemburg book contains material on dialectics and organization never before published. Here and in the following chapter she begins to draw out the connection of the theory of revolutionary organization to Marx's last decade and his concept of revolution in permanence.*

> ... cause is the highest stage in which the concrete Notion as beginning has an immediate existence in the sphere of necessity; but it is not yet a subject....
>
> HEGEL, *SCIENCE OF LOGIC*, VOL. 2, P. 172

Rosa Luxemburg was so consistent throughout her life in her belief in the Party, that even when she called the Second International a "stinking corpse" she opposed the building of a Third International and, at the time she broke with Karl Kautsky over nothing short of the General Mass Strike, it appeared as if it were only personal because she not only did not leave the [German Social Democratic] Party, she did not create a Left faction, which she only built in the Independent Social Democratic Party of Germany, and when she finally did in the outright revolution of 1918, it was the Communist Party of Germany; in a word, it still was "the Party."

And yet, not only was that point not stressed, it is hardly even mentioned except when Marxists do defend her as not having been a "total" spontaneist. What she is known for, and rightly so (i.e., rightly if you understand the multifacetedness and complexity of her), is her confidence in the proletariat's actions, her praise—very nearly glorification—of, and surely giving her priority to, spontaneity over not only Party but also leadership. And that remained true even when she did in the [1919 German] Revolution not only create a Communist Party in Germany, but consented to that which she had fought all her life, to a unity of her Polish tendency with that of the Left Polish Socialist Party to construct the Communist Party of Poland.

How to explain so many contradictions in which there likewise exists a unifying force—the Party—and so tightly a unifying force that unity, unity, unity, unfortunately in the full Social Democratic concept, [meant] that she opposed splits even at the point where there wasn't a single point of affinity between the tendency her thought represented and the dominant tendency in the German Social Democratic Party?

It is the overriding concept of unity which has given so many false interpretations of what Luxemburg's concept of organization as well as concept of spontaneity truly was. Let's begin with her first and most famous and most misused article—misused to the point of the "West" not even allowing her to name the title of her article. The title she gave was "Organizational Questions of Russian Social Democracy." The title the "West" gave it was "Leninism or Marxism?"[1] The different historic periods likewise led to one-sided interpretations. Thus the German Social Democrats *before* World War I were forever quoting and attacking both her writings on spontaneity during the first Russian Revolution, specifically *The Mass Strike, the Political Party, and the Trade Unions*, while the post-World War II Social Democrats, West or otherwise, were always stressing the 1904 critiques of Lenin. In both cases two opposites that *weren't* genuine opposites to Luxemburg—democracy/dictatorship regarding the 1904 writing—and two opposites—spontaneity/organization for 1906— were stretched out to make her say what she did not say.

Thus, "Organizational Questions of Russian Social Democracy"[2] was a critique not of *What Is to Be Done?* which everyone including J.P. Nettl attributed it to[3] but was a critique of Lenin's *One Step Forward, Two Steps Back*. Because of her disagreement with the Bolsheviks on the National Question, Luxemburg's tendency never attended that famous 1903 Congress [the subject of *One Step Forward*]. It was Lenin's critique of the behavior of the Mensheviks at that congress that she criticized. She was asked for the article by *Iskra*—not the *Iskra* that Lenin edited but the one appropriated by the Mensheviks at that 1903 Congress even though they had been outvoted.

---

1   The title "Leninism or Marxism?" was first imposed on the article by the Anti-Parliamentary Communist Federation in Glasgow, Scotland, which published an English translation in 1935. That title was kept in the more widely available *The Russian Revolution and Leninism or Marxism?* first published in 1961 by the University of Michigan Press, with no editor specified but an introduction by Bertram D. Wolfe, who considered "the Glasgow title as the most attractive and best known in English" (p. 11). —Editor.

2   The new translation with the correct title appears in Dick Howard, *Selected Writings*, pp. 283–306.

3   Norman Geras [Apparently, Dunayevskaya intended to write a footnote on Norman Geras, *The Legacy of Rosa Luxemburg* (London: NLB, 1976). See RDC, pp. 14248–50, 14288–89. —Editor.].

She doesn't mention that fact, since, as far as she was concerned, the SDP of Russia was still one. It is important to keep this in mind, even as it is important to be as rigorous as she was in paying strict attention to the objective situation, to the fact that Russia was indeed a "police state," that you truly had need for centralism, and that in fact it wasn't only the Russian Social Democracy but the German Social Democracy that practiced centralism as a principle.

What she objected to was what she called Lenin's ultracentralism.[4] This criticism of the Russian Social Democracy was, indeed, implicitly likewise a criticism of the German Social Democracy. To sharpen that aspect of her critique, she made it clear that she did not think that when a Social Democratic Party is not as big as the German, it is in any way "underdeveloped"; *each* Marxist party was, historically, equal. To illuminate the differences and again to give due credit to the Russian Social Democracy wanting to establish a national organization, she stressed that it was indeed necessary to have done with the "circle and local club atmosphere" that had pervaded the Russian attempt to build a unified organization and required a full three-year campaign, 1900–03, to prepare for that congress. "However," she continued (p. 286),

> at the Party Congress, and even more so after it, it became evident that centralism is a slogan which does not completely exhaust the historical content and the particularity of the Social Democratic organization.

She leveled her severest attack on Lenin's formulation that a Social Democrat is "a Jacobin indissolubly connected with the organization of the class-conscious proletariat" (p. 288). And it is at that point when she developed her opposition to Jacobinism and Blanquism in so detailed a form that she left no room whatever for the concrete happenings of the congress, which led to the split (which was the preoccupation of Lenin). One could say that the minute she reached "history," her critique was so full of generalizations that it was hard to see anything concrete relating to the congress, and even be inclined to overpraise Lenin, who stuck only to the concrete, and thus "proved" her wrong. *Which with hindsight, absolutely is not true, that is to say, some of the generalizations are so very relevant to our day, that we must go into them.*

For example, there is absolutely no doubt that there is ground for a great deal more of democracy, more need for different tendencies to express themselves,

---

4 Lenin's denial that he was ultracentralist in his reply to her was never published; it was rejected by Kautsky and even in the Russian it was first published ... [Dunayevskaya notes elsewhere that it is doubtful Luxemburg ever saw Lenin's reply. —Editor.].

and surely it is imperative not to make a virtue of necessity, which leads one living under tsarism to overstress the need for centralism to oppose it. Furthermore, whereas her expression, "No rigid formulas for organization will do to express Marx's conception of socialism" (p. 286), may have left elbow room for opportunism to continue functioning in a Marxist organization—as witness the fact that the first expression of reformism, Eduard Bernstein, was not expelled—it is even truer that Lenin's concept of centralism had even more need of decentralization.

Where it seems to this writer that Luxemburg wrongly almost makes do with spontaneity, if not sans organization, certainly without philosophy, is in her singling out the 1896 strike in St. Petersburg, the student agitation of 1901, and the mass strike in Rostov-on-Don, as if their arising spontaneously had also meant that they had no need for a Marxist party. The fact was that it was precisely these strikes and great spontaneous actions which led Lenin to conclude that if Marxists are going to act only as economists, there will be a gap between political work and the development of an actual revolution.

It was no accident that Luxemburg's hammering away at Lenin's supposed exaggeration of "factory discipline" (p. 291), which he insisted the intellectuals lacked, in turn, led her to defend intellectuals. Where she shone brilliantly was in the dialectical relationship of spontaneity to organization:

> What is always important for Social Democracy is not to prophesy and to preconstruct a ready-made recipe for the future tasks. Rather, it is important that the correct historical evaluation of the forms of struggle corresponding to the given situation be continually maintained in the party, and that it understand the relativity of the given phase of the struggle, and the necessary advancement of the revolutionary stages toward the ultimate goal of the proletarian class struggle. (p. 294)

While Luxemburg was absolutely correct in her emphasis that the Marxist movement was the "first in the history of class society which, in all its moments, in its entire course, reckons on the organization of the independent, direct action of the masses" (p. 288), she is not correct in holding that that very nearly automatically means so total a conception of socialism that a *philosophy* of Marx's concept of revolution could be likewise left to spontaneous action. Far from it. And nowhere is this seen more clearly than when we get to the 1905 revolution, where spontaneity is absolutely the greatest but fails to achieve its goal. The question of class consciousness does not exhaust the question of cognition, of Marx's philosophy of revolution, of second negation, that is to say, not alone the destruction of the old, but the creation of the new, has still to be tested, and we cannot here skip from 1904 to 1917 and 1919. So within the context of that debate, it is sufficient to end where she ended, stressing the right of the working class

> to make its own mistakes and to learn the historical dialectic by itself. Finally, we must frankly admit to ourselves that errors made by a truly revolutionary labor movement are historically infinitely more fruitful and more valuable than the infallibility of the best of all possible "central committees." (p. 306)

As we have seen in the chapter on the 1906 pamphlet on the General Strike, as well as the one on the 1910 split with Kautsky,[5] Luxemburg's making a category of spontaneity was in the first case exactly in the same period as Lenin modifying his rigid concept in *What Is to Be Done?* and stressing instead spontaneity. It wasn't merely the fact that she had written this in Kuokkala,[6] but that the revolution itself sharpened their view historically, as well as actually. On the other hand, she was way ahead of Lenin in 1910 in judging the deep opportunism of Kautsky. At the same time, however, the inversion of the relationship between organization and action once again meant the disregard of philosophy.

It is absolutely true, as Luxemburg expressed it in *What Next?* that "any mass action, once unleashed, must move forward." It is not true that a forward movement by the masses cannot be reversed or stopped by a leadership which uses the rhetoric of revolution but practices *counter*-revolution. In a word, where Luxemburg saw the opportunism in Kautsky, she by no means expected outright betrayal and indeed did not conceive that counterrevolution can arise from within revolution. It is that dialectic, that transformation into opposite, that Lenin, who had not seen as clearly as she the nature of the German Social Democracy, saw when he leapt far beyond her once World War I showed the betrayal, in issuing the slogan, "Turn the imperialist war into civil war," and in his critique of even his own Bolsheviks [in April 1917], threatening to resign the Central Committee and "go to the sailors" if they did not pose the question of the conquest of power.

---

5 Chapter 2 of *Rosa Luxemburg, Women's Liberation, and Marx's Philosophy of Revolution* as published is "The Break with Kautsky, 1910–11: From Mass Strike Theory to Crisis over Morocco—and Hushed-Up 'Woman Question.'" —Editor.

6 Luxemburg wrote *The Mass Strike, the Political Party, and the Trade Unions* during a month's stay in Kuokkala, Finland, in 1906 after the first Russian Revolution. During that time she met with Lenin, who was also there. —Editor.

Bertram D. Wolfe mistitled her work because his title was more "attractive," and thus gave her 1904 critique so anti-Leninist a twist that he attributes to her a persistent anti-Leninism not only in 1904 but also in 1917.

Between 1904 and 1917 there was first and foremost nothing short of the Russian-Polish Revolution of 1905–07. So close were Lenin and Luxemburg in that period and directly after, both on revolution *and* organization, that the Polish Party actually joined the Russian Party. Moreover, though in 1906 when [the Polish Party] joined, there was also a joining of Mensheviks and Bolsheviks, it was by no means the Mensheviks she related to. It was the vote of "the Poles" that helped Lenin get a majority at the 1907 Russian congress. Theoretically, their interpretation of the Revolution extended beyond Russia and Poland. That same year, 1907, there was also the International Socialist Congress [in Stuttgart], where again Lenin and Luxemburg gave the direction to the amendment on the anti-war drive (while Trotsky and [Yurii] Martov likewise associated with the amendment, there is no doubt whatever where the closeness lay, theoretically and practically even to the point of specific formulations).

(Interestingly enough, it was also at that congress that Luxemburg introduced Lenin to Clara Zetkin—Zetkin was both a member of the International and the head of the German Social Democracy women's conference, which also met during that period. The point was that Lenin's own reports of the Stuttgart Congress were heavily and openly based on Zetkin's and her articles about that Congress in *Gleichheit*.)

By the time the disputes with Kautsky on her demand that her position on the general strike be applied to Germany 1910 reached a climax, they were so absolutely at opposite ends that she broke with him completely. Bertram Wolfe has his reasons for skipping all these world-historic events, not to mention betrayal on the part of the Social Democracy in World War I and Luxemburg's final break with that organization. In a word, when we come to her intransigent revolutionary anti-war stand, there is certainly not one whiff of affinity between her and the Social Democratic organization, German or international, which she declares to be a "stinking corpse." And certainly there is again not a single grain of affinity between her critical position on the Russian Revolution and the Social Democratic position on the *counter*-revolution against it. She hailed that Revolution as the greatest world-historic event, which, even if it failed, would remain a beacon for all, and for which failure the German Social Democracy would bear the greatest responsibility.

What then was her criticism? We wish here to focus strictly on organization (later we will deal with the theoretical differences). The main point of difference organizationally—and in that she was certainly not only correct as against Lenin, but actually foresaw what became the Stalinist degeneration—was her demand for greater democracy not only for the masses but within the state and government, with a multiplicity of parties and tendencies.

She warned against making "a virtue of necessity," that is to say, Marxists must be careful that even when an absolute necessity, because the counterrevolution is at the door, requires the curtailing of freedom, at no time should one give in to the temptation to make the temporary relapse into a general principle.

Surely her critical contribution to the question of proletarian democracy and democracy within the Marxist party was of great merit and far outdistanced any of the Bolsheviks who were directly in the fray in foreseeing what was to become bureaucratization. But how can that possibly be made to have any affinity whatever with Social Democracy? How can that criticism, which was definitely of a technical type, be raised to the level of her break with the International, her leadership of the Spartacus League,[7] and, above all, the leadership of the actual German Revolution? Then, regarding one of the very things she had criticized in Russia, i.e., the dismissal of the Constituent Assembly, she declared in the most unequivocal terms on the German scene that this type of assembly was a bourgeois institution to which she counterposed workers' democracy as contained only in actual workers' councils, so that very nearly all of the main slogans of the Russian Revolution were exactly what she herself called for in what turned out to be the last two months of her life.

No, what she criticized in 1904 and what she criticized in 1917 bear very little resemblance to each other, either in principle or in tactic, either in theory or in practice, either in the different historic periods or the different goals in 1905 and in 1917. And her greatest contribution, both in relationship to rooting the concept of the party in spontaneity and internal democracy, was not without its own philosophic weakness.

Nor was her philosophic weakness limited to organization. When you rethink what the contradiction seems to be, the genuine genius in the prescience of catching imperialism before it was ever recognized or even seen by either bourgeois scholars or Marxists, and yet one would think she would have immediately singled out as Subject the colonial masses oppressed by imperialism as its gravediggers; when you recognize that back in 1899 soon after the

---

7   The Spartacus League began in 1915 as a revolutionary, anti-war faction within the German Social Democratic Party, basing itself on Luxemburg's Junius pamphlet (*The Crisis of German Social Democracy*, published under the pseudonym "Junius"). It was part of those who were purged from the Party in 1917 and formed the Independent Social Democratic Party of Germany. After revolution broke out in Germany in November 1918, the Spartacists split to form an independent party, which was renamed the Communist Party of Germany. —Editor.

Sino-Japanese War she was already sensing a global shift in powers and had not let go in her critiques of the German Social Democracy, be it in not articulating opposition to the Japanese War in China or the Morocco Incident,[8] and being so aroused over the opportunism in not fighting the very first sign of imperialism, that she made you literally listen, *hear* the cries of the Herero women and children as they tried to escape the savagery of General Trotha and his army pursuing them;[9] and when you see how deep was her internationalism as relates to race that even when there was a world war and Mathilde Wurm bemoaned the condition of the Jews she replied:

> What do you want with this particular suffering of the Jews? The poor victims on the rubber plantations in Putumayo, the Negroes in Africa with whose bodies the Europeans play a game of catch, are just as near to me. Do you remember the words written on the work of the Great General Staff about Trotha's campaign in the Kalahari desert? "And the death-rattles, the mad cries of those dying of thirst, faded away into the sublime silence of eternity."
>
> Oh, this "sublime silence of eternity" in which so many screams have faded away unheard. It rings within me so strongly that I have no special corner of my heart reserved for the ghetto; I am at home wherever in the world there are clouds, birds and human tears....[10]

She always was looking for root causes and always speaking of class consciousness; and yet not jamming the two up against each other so that they would result in a new unity. Instead, she let them lie side by side. We have seen when Lenin argued against her position on the "National Question," which she couldn't see as revolutionary in World War I, this imperialist war, he used the term "halfway dialectical" [Lenin, *Collected Works*, Vol. 19, p. 210]. It came from his own philosophic reorganization during that war. It is the very period when Lenin, when approaching the Absolute Method in Absolute Idea, shows that "when *opposite* determinations ... come before consciousness without mutual contact (the object)—that is the essence of anti-dialectics" [Lenin, *Collected Works*, Vol. 38, p. 228].

---

8   After Germany sent a gunboat to Morocco in 1911, Luxemburg attacked the party leadership for its lack of a serious Marxist analysis and any serious struggle against the *"internal development of German militarism ... and Germany's urge for world power"* ("Our Morocco Leaflet," in *Leipziger Volkszeitung*, August 26, 1911). —Editor.

9   The German army massacred both fighters and civilians in a 1904–07 uprising by the Hereros and Nama in Namibia against German colonial rule. —Editor.

10   Letter of February 16, 1917, *The Letters of Rosa Luxemburg*, ed. Stephen Bronner (Boulder, Colo.: Westview Press, 1978), p. 178. —Editor.

Lenin's point, as in this case Hegel's, was to show that only second negativity is the solution, because there is no other way to transcend "the opposition between Notion and Reality, and that unity which is the truth," except to see that they "rest upon this subjectivity alone." In a word, the fact that only the proletariat, only the oppressed, only the Subject who is being oppressed, is the one for the overthrow, cannot possibly be kept apart from the objective situation which drives them in that direction.

Dialectically speaking, why should a revolutionary stop at causality? A sort of one-to-one relationship is thereby explained, and one must get rid of explaining as if cause isn't but one moment and effect the next; and since cause and effect interrelate in a way that at separate times Luxemburg did see as part of a totality, why should the totality have been so mechanical as not to see subject? Without subject there can be no total uprooting. Without subject revolutionary action is hardly more than contemplation, that is to say, you look at an object—in this case, imperialism—and say that it causes something else, i.e., impossibility otherwise of continued accumulation; inevitably then you go to markets and even colonialism instead of subject. No wonder those objects don't move. The market can't produce its own negativity, but the subject could.

You never look at people, the exploited, except as suffering subjects, which is why they remain as if they are only objects. There is no duality, no deep contradiction. Instead Luxemburg shifts back to home and says long before this type of collapse will happen, the proletariat will [overthrow capitalism].

If, however, you look not just at the root cause but at new beginnings that will themselves determine the ends, there would be no way to avoid subject.

What has been unnoticed until this day is that early on, back in 1899, long before Luxemburg hit out against Marx for his rococo style even in the first volume [of *Capital*], Luxemburg had always excluded Vol. II from the consideration of the totality of Marx's economic views. Thus she wrote:

> The Marxist formula for crises as presented by Engels in *Anti-Dühring* and by Marx in the first and third volumes of *Capital* applies to all crises only in the measure that it uncovers their international mechanism and their general basic causes.

As we saw when we dealt with Luxemburg's interregnum,[11] which led her to critique not so much Kautsky as Marx, it became clear that just as her

---

11   This refers to 1911–13, the period between Luxemburg's break with Kautsky and her dismissal of the whole Second International as a "stinking corpse" after it collapsed at the outbreak of World War I, with most of its consituent parties betraying their principles and supporting the war. Dunayevskaya discarded the term "interregnum" shortly after this,

Accumulation of Capital diverted from Marx's analysis, but Lenin's did not, so, ironically enough, on the question in which Luxemburg and Lenin seemed to be on totally opposite points—the Party—both *alike* did not integrate philosophy with organization: (1) Luxemburg, because she paid very little attention to philosophy, and (2) Lenin, because with all the profound attention he gave philosophy to the extent even of reorganizing himself, as well as the nature of imperialism and the national question, the national question and revolution, dialectics themselves, and the state, it nevertheless was not extended to the Party. Thus, no one gave an answer, and we naturally cannot assume after the event that if they had integrated philosophy, there would have been the correct answer. We do, however, start with a clean slate, that is, nobody has the answer. Nevertheless, precisely because Marx and Marx alone had discovered a new continent of thought and had a philosophy of revolution from the very start of his break from capitalism, he will also have the ground for a philosophic concept of organization, even if he had "no theory of organization."

Let's review, though very briefly, what he did say in addition to the fact that the proletariat must have a party of its own, from which he never departed, be it 1848, 1871, 1875, or 1882.[12] Where it became concretized or broadened, as you wish, is in the philosophic conception. Thus, the 1848 Revolutions ended with the need for an independent working-class party but also a philosophy of permanent revolution.

Thus, the Paris Commune had a new reason—"its own working existence" [MECW 22, p. 339].

Thus, the Gotha Program was criticized mercilessly, comprehensively, theoretically, point by point, precisely because his position was that, whereas a movement is greater and more important than any set of programs, if you cannot have unity on principled ground, then it is best not to unite but to limit united action to specifics only. It also had yet a newer vision extending all the way to communist society where "working would not just be a means to life, but the very first necessity of living" [MECW 24, p. 871]. Put otherwise, it meant that if there really is an end to division between mental and manual work, then that is your life, that is to say, there is no division between life and science and thought, etc. He insisted that children, in play, actually labor and discover many things through breaking things.

---

concluding that, far from an "interregnum," it was the period of Luxemburg's development of her theoretical magnum opus, *Accumulation of Capital*. —Editor.

12   These dates refer to the 1848 revolutions and the activity of the Communist League; the 1871 Paris Commune and activity of the First International; Marx's 1875 *Critique of the Gotha Program* (see next chapter); and his final works, including *Ethnological Notebooks* and preface to the Russian edition of the *Communist Manifesto*. —Editor.

Finally, what is most exciting about his very last years is that in returning to the Man/Woman relationship, which is traced through from gens, matrilineal society, to the savagery and retrogression in progressive capitalism when it comes to the position of women, he was critical also of primitive communism, insisting that it was not an outside force that overthrew it, but that it came from within through the development of chiefs, etc. Thus, above all else what was new was this: the multilinear development of humanity, be it from primitive communism, or the Asiatic mode of production, or Western capitalism, proved that it is impossible to have but one answer to all the multitude of developments. On the contrary, a backward country like Russia could have a revolution before an advanced country *if* new forces and relations, including even the peasant commune, made its revolution or rather related its revolution to the technologically, industrially advanced nations, and if, with the new countries like the USA, it had a global not a national view, and if.... Precisely because we have so many more new grounds for philosophy, even when it is only on the subject of organization, we better finally learn Marx's philosophy of revolution.

$$\bullet\;\bullet\;\bullet$$

[The remainder of this chapter consists of fragments, some of which were placed earlier in Dunayevskaya's manuscript. —Editor.]

(2) At the same time, when the causal relationship of theory is class consciousness, which is what makes materialism not mechanical and not just a matter of trade union goals but class power, and live people therefore holding destiny in their own hands, there suddenly manifests itself root cause as purpose, which enables the intellectual to be there with the proletariat.

(3) On the other hand, causality is used to rid the leadership of its opportunism, parliamentarism, and routine-like work to bring in the spontaneous action of the proletariat who would *push* the leadership forward. It is true she again uses the word revolution as the only answer to Kautsky's "Strategy of Attrition" [which is the] sheerest opportunism to evade the actual class actions of the general strike (which is both political and economic), but it stops short of subject.

(Work out the relationship to Lenin's remark that the end of teleology [handwritten: (?)] just before we enter the Notion says: "N.B. Freedom = Subjectivity, on the threshold of the Idea ('or' goal, consciousness, striving, N.B.).")[13]

$$\bullet\;\bullet\;\bullet$$

---

13   *Russia: From Proletarian Revolution to State-Capitalist Counter-Revolution,* p. 89. —Editor.

(NOTES TO MYSELF)

Check whether the question of party was taken up not only as relationship of spontaneity to organization but as leadership to mass, and as philosophy to organization, so that Luxemburg must answer what is meant by "pushing" the leadership forward.

Moreover, with Luxemburg making a special category of general strike as both political and economic, she still naturally sees that it must go to insurrection, then how could that be without subject?

The tragedy in Lenin is not only that he didn't reorganize on the question of the party, but that his great philosophic leap forward is not made available to the masses. Again, raise Luxemburg and party: she certainly wasn't as hostile to the peasantry as Leon Trotsky, and yet she is so opposed to the Bolsheviks' giving land to the peasantry, as if that meant immediate parceling out the national land to private property.

Finally, the proof of error was not only that the Spartacus League should have been independent long before, but why the opposition to the timing of the Third International because it would be dominated by Russia?[14]

• • •

The origin of the Idea in the notion of Teleology throws immense light on Hegel's philosophy. The Idea does not explain things by being their cause, or their underlying Substance, or the Whole of which they are the parts: it explains them by being the End towards which they must be thought of as tending....

We should be able to see what Hegel means by "the Notion" by seeing how its concept develops out of the three concepts of Substance, Causality, and Reciprocal interaction. Necessity there "swung over" into Freedom....[15]

• • •

Quotations appended to Organization chapter

14   While Lenin called for the creation of a new international shortly after the beginning of World War I, Luxemburg opposed it, although she designated the Second International a "stinking corpse." She continued to oppose the immediate creation of a new international even when the Spartacus League split to become an independent party. —Editor.

15   J.N. Findlay, *The Philosophy of Hegel: An Introduction and Re-Examination* (New York: Collier, 1962), pp. 253, 222.

Causality according to natural laws is not the only one from which all the phenomena of the world may be derived; it is necessary to assume another causality through freedom in order to explain them.

The antithesis is:—There is no freedom, but everything in the world happens solely according to natural laws....

It is said that this proposition is self-contradictory because natural law consists just in this, that nothing happens without a cause sufficiently determined *a priori*, which cause thus contains an absolute spontaneity;— that is, the assumption which is opposed to the thesis is contradictory because it contradicts the thesis.

In order to prove the antithesis it has to be posited that there is a freedom as a particular kind of causality—a freedom to initiate a state and hence also a series of consequences of the state.

HEGEL'S *SCIENCE OF LOGIC*, VOL. II, pp. 377–78

(It's the page in which Lenin calls attention to the fact that Hegel is talking against Kant.)

(Hegel says "because self-determination is applied to them only externally" (p. 391) or what we would call intellectual planning, they are only means to an end, not an end in themselves.)

CHAPTER 31

Philosopher of Permanent Revolution and Organization Man

This draft of Chapter 11 of Rosa Luxemburg, Women's Liberation, and Marx's Philosophy of Revolution (*Supplement to the Raya Dunayevskaya Collection, pp. 14922–40*), *and the chapter in the published book, contain Dunayevskaya's most comprehensive discussions of Marx's concept of revolution in permanence and his* Critique of the Gotha Program, *in relationship to the new moments Marx developed in his last decade.*

1   Critique of the Gotha Program (*of a United Workers' Party of Germany*)

> The international activity of the working classes does not in any way depend on the existence of the International Working Men's Association. This was only the first attempt to create a central organ for that activity; an attempt which was a lasting success on account of the impulse which it gave but which was no longer realizable in its first historical form after the fall of the Paris Commune.
>
> KARL MARX, CRITIQUE OF THE GOTHA PROGRAM, 1875

The fetish of a vanguard party to lead is very nearly beyond comprehension when it affects as great a revolutionary as Rosa Luxemburg, who had such overpowering confidence in the spontaneous action of workers that she was considered as simply a spontaneist. It is true that that is wrong, because her passionate conviction about the creativity and spontaneity of the masses did not keep her from being a member of a strictly Marxist party, a strictly Marxist International. Indeed, the fetish of unity kept her from breaking with the party to the point of building a new one, even at the outbreak of war and the betrayal of *established* Marxism, though she had called that Second International a "stinking corpse." Nevertheless, she was still working to "reconstruct" it rather than to call for a new International. So all-pervasive was the idea of a vanguard party that, though she functioned as an independent revolutionary tendency—the Spartacus League—she remained with the Independent Social Democratic Party of Germany until the very eve of the 1919 Revolution; and at that point, when the Spartacus League did transform itself into a new and separate Communist Party, she still had instructed it to vote against the establishment of a new Third International.

Luxemburg herself may not have seen the great contradiction in the manner in which she projected, even hallowed, spontaneity, and the way she clung to the party even though she was always calling for (and was convinced that the leadership needed a hefty push from) the spontaneous mass actions to move forward. She certainly didn't attribute the breakup of her passionate and complex relationship with Leo Jogiches to the strains of organization in a period of open revolution. Yet a serious look back to that highest point of her activity in the 1905–06 Russian Revolution will disclose the sharp dualism in the two aspects of organization and spontaneity, not to mention the other silent feature—the Man/Woman relationship for one as independent as Luxemburg. Yet it became ground for the heart-breaking separation, though they never separated for a single instance as revolutionaries, as Marxist activists. They had the same perspective of world revolution, and Jogiches met his death shortly after hers in the struggle to find her murderer and to continue with the revolutionary work.

In the 1905–06 Revolution, too, the exultation that came with their joint activity never wavered. The fact that she was also with her lover, who was an organization man, par excellence, in those 24-hour-a-day whirlwind activities, seemed to have reached the highest point of all. Yet another fact is likewise indisputable. Becoming witness to a small organization being transformed overnight into a mass party in the midst of masses in motion, did modify her appreciation for what Jogiches never left out of his view in this activity—the need also for secrecy, oppressive awareness of the strength of the powers that be, working night and day to achieve a counterrevolution.

In our search for illumination on this burning question of the relationship of spontaneity to organization, three very different dates and one totally different subject—a philosophy of revolution—are needed: (1) Luxemburg's analysis of Ferdinand Lassalle that she wrote in 1904 as celebration of the March 1848 Revolution; (2) Marx's 1875 *Critique of the Gotha Program,* which was a critique of Lassalle's doctrines; and (3) Lenin's transforming that *Critique* into ground for 1917.

Long after his death, Lassalle remained a pervasive force and not only for reformists but for revolutionaries, and specifically on the point of organization. We would be in an entirely different period, on the eve of the 1917 Revolution, before a single Marxist, Lenin, took Marx's *Critique of the Gotha Program* so seriously as to build his whole *State and Revolution* on it. On the eve of the first Russian Revolution that was not the case, and everyone from Luxemburg to

Trotsky extolled Lassalle, not only very nearly on the same level as Marx, but in fact "when it comes to organization," admitted or otherwise, he stood on a higher, that is, more concrete level. Thus, in the year 1904 Luxemburg wrote of "Lassalle and the Revolution." Its centerpoint was that—though Lassalle had committed many errors, and though Marx's criticism of him was valid—nevertheless, he enters into history because

> it was Lassalle who transformed into deed the *most important historical consequence* of the March revolution in finally liberating the German working class, fifteen years later, from the levy-in-arms of the bourgeoisie and organizing it into an independent class party.

As if that weren't clear enough praise, it is further called "immortal work" and that remark is made though it is followed by a reference to Marx's 1868 critique of Lassalle.[1] In a word, the critique is made subordinate to Lassalle's great deed, which does "not diminish but grows more and more with the historical perspective from which we view it."

Why did it grow "more and more with the historical perspective" of forty years? Wasn't this due to the fact that Marx's *Critique of the Gotha Program* was never fully internalized? Could a duality between the concept of organization and a philosophy of revolution have arisen without awareness if one had not separated Marx's concept of revolution from his concept of organization? Isn't it a fact that the need for and the building of organization so preoccupied all Marxists except Marx that a fetish was made of it? It is a fact that the fetish was at the very innards of the German Social Democratic Party (SPD). From its very birth, that was so overwhelming a factor that although the SPD was preparing to replace the Gotha Program of its predecessor with a new one, the Erfurt Program, they balked at publishing Marx's *Critique,* even fifteen years after the event. Not only that. They seemed to have disregarded the fact that it was Marx, not Lassalle, who founded the first International Working Men's Association. Worse still, it wasn't only disregarded. It was the greater appreciation of a *national* organization, the German party.

The innumerable articles written about the fact that Marx had no theory of organization obscured, if they did not totally cover up, the fact that Marx was indeed conscious of organization, helped found organizations—from the International Communist Correspondence Committees to the First International. Because that mediation—proletarian organization, an independent

---

1   See letter of Marx to Johann Baptist von Schweitzer, October 13, 1868, MECW 43, pp. 132–35.
    —Editor.

proletarian organization, and one that would be both international and have the goal of revolution and a new society—was so central to his views, Marx kept referring to "the Party" when all that was involved was himself and Engels.

What Marx called "party in the eminent historical sense"[2] was alive to Marx throughout the entire decade when no organization existed in the 1850s with which he could associate. Once a mass movement emerged, he left the British Museum to help establish the International Working Men's Association. And when at its height—the Paris Commune—the International was disintegrating, he did not consider that its end. On the contrary, he sent it away to make sure, however, that it would not "suddenly" get a totally new philosophy—in this case, anarchism—which was waiting in the wings. But he also was ready to hail the slimmest possibility of another organization which he was sure would result from a new mass movement. This was the case in the United States, when the great class struggles of the mid-1870s in railroads and in the mines, culminating in the first General Strike in the United States, in St Louis, would result, he hoped, "in an independent working class party."[3]

To underline its significance, Marx said that the First International was but a form of organization suited to the time, and that the creativity of the masses would discover another form. Marx at no time made a fetish of organization, which is why, in the covering letter of the *Critique,* he wrote:

> Every step of real movement is more important than a dozen programmes. If, therefore, it was not possible—and the conditions of the time did not permit it—to go *beyond* the Eisenach programme, one should simply have concluded an agreement for action against the common enemy.
>
> MECW 24, p. 78

How inseparable were theory and organization will not only be present throughout the modestly entitled "critical marginal notes" but even in his covering note, which includes the fact that he is sending "in the near future the last parts of the French edition of *Capital*" [MECW 24, p. 78]. And there were also references to a new edition of the 1852 *Revelations Concerning the Communist Trial in Cologne.* In a word, 1875 was a most active year politically, philosophically, and organizationally, none of which was separable from both a philosophy of revolution and the perspectives for the future.

The *Critique* itself is, of course, not just a criticism of a program, but a comprehensive analysis of Lassalle's doctrines. It contains a theory of the state and,

---

2   Letter from Marx to Ferdinand Freiligrath, February 29, 1860, MECW 41, p. 87. —Editor.
3   Letter from Marx to Engels of July 25, 1877, MECW 45, p. 251.

more importantly, of the non-state-to-be (as he called the Paris Commune), which was to be the model for the future breakup of the capitalist state and establishing a commune form of non-state. Furthermore, not only was capitalism a transient stage, but so was "the revolutionary dictatorship of the proletariat" (p. 28),[4] which was to replace it. These two fundamental principles were to become the basis for the 1917 Revolution and Lenin's *State and Revolution.*

Unfortunately, the great transformation in Lenin, both on philosophy and the revolutionary dictatorship of the proletariat, did not extend to Lenin's concept of the party, which, despite all modifications in actual revolutions, remained essentially what it was in 1903. And since by now that tactical work [Lenin's *What Is To Be Done?*] had been made into a fetish—a universal fetish at the very time that the first workers' state was transformed into its opposite, a state-capitalist society—the relevance of Marx's *Critique of the Gotha Program* gains a special urgency for our age.

Paragraph by paragraph, beginning with the first paragraph of the program [MECW 24, p. 81], Marx analyzes how totally wrong (and when not wrong quite imprecise) is the program's analysis of labor, its subordination to "the monopoly of the means of labor" [MECW 24, p. 83]. Where, for the First International, the class of monopolists included both capitalists and landowners, Lassalle spoke as if it were only the capitalist class, thus letting the Prussian landowners, by no accident, off scot-free.

Along with this came the point that was most objectionable to Marx, that "the working-class strives for its emancipation first of all *within the framework of the present day national state...*" (p. 18), to which Marx asks: how could socialists "conceive the workers' movement from the narrowest national standpoint ... after the work of the International!" (p. 21) [MECW 24, p. 89]. Marx naturally considered it the greatest retrogression to go back from the international to a national standpoint.

What must tower above all struggles against exploitation, nationally and internationally, must be the perspective of a totally classless society, and that the vision of its ground would be "from each according to his ability, to each according to his needs" (p. 14) [MECW 24, p. 87].

To this day, this remains the perspective for the future, and yet the Marxists who keep quoting it never bother to study just how concretely that arose from the *Critique* of the supposedly socialist program, and what would be required to make that real. The revolution that would overthrow capitalism would have to be a great deal more total in its uprooting of the old than just what it is

---

4 Dunayevskaya's page numbers refer to *Critique of the Gotha Program* (London: Lawrence & Wishart, n.d.). This quotation is found in MECW 24, p. 95. —Editor.

against. Thus Marx says that to reach the communist stage, there would have to be an end to the "enslaving subordination of the individual to the division of labor and therewith also the antithesis between mental and physical labor ..." (p. 14) [MECW 24, p. 87].

This is not the young Marx speaking. This is the mature author of *Capital,* the revolutionary who has experienced both the exciting 1860s reaching its climax in the historic Paris Commune, but one who has suffered through its defeat, and yet is projecting so totally new a concept of labor as the creative self-activity of humanity that he is now saying that we will reach communism only when "labor from a mere means of life, has itself become the prime necessity of life" (p. 14) [MECW 24, p. 87].

Now then, what had happened between the transfer of the First International to the United States and the attempts at unity between two different tendencies of the German workers' movement, and why was it that Lassalle, who founded the General Association of German Workers in the early 1860s as the first independent mass political organization, should still tower above Marx after he founded the International Working Men's Association? Was there a national strain from the start? How could Rosa Luxemburg, who was the greatest internationalist, not have seen any of this? It couldn't have been national vs. international. It could have only been activism vs. philosophy. That Marx's *Critique of the Gotha Program* couldn't win adherents among the new leadership of the German Social Democracy may be understandable considering their isolation at the time as against the birth of a new "mass party." What isn't understandable—in fact, is very nearly fantastic—is that no revolutionary studied these notes as not just a critique of a particular tendency, but as actual perspective for the whole movement. Let's remember that not only was it Eduard Bernstein, the reformist, who tried to revise Marx's principles; it was also Kautsky, then the "orthodox" Marxist. And not only that. No revolutionary took it as a point of departure for working out a theory of organization that would be inseparable from the theory of revolution. Any "orthodox" Leninist who tries to say that Lenin's statement that there could be no revolution without a revolutionary theory meant that his concept of organization was in any way related to Marx's theory in the *Critique of the Gotha Program,* rather than the immediate concrete of having to function under tsarism, would have to contend with both Lenin's own statement in the midst of the 1905 Revolution, when he moved far, far away from his own narrow position,[5] and the position Lenin had on the eve of the 1917 Revolution as he completed his *State and Revolution.* Unfortunately, neither Lenin's philosophic reorganization on the basis of the Hegelian-Marxian dialectic, nor the ground for *State and Revolution* gained from Marx's *Critique of the Gotha Program,* extended to Marx's concept of the party.

That means that Lenin's philosophic reorganization remained in a separate compartment from the concept of the party and the practice of vanguardism. Clearly, there is no substitute for the totality that was Marx as organization man, as political theorist, as visionary of a future social order, which is exactly the warp and woof of his theory of permanent revolution. The covering letter that Marx wrote with the *Critique of the Gotha Program,* which showed that he had just completed the 1875 French edition of *Capital,* also referred to the reissuance of the 1852 *Revelations of the Cologne Communist Trial.* What is significant about this is that this was the edition which reproduced the 1850 *Address to the Communist League.*[6] In turning to that projection of the permanent revolution, we should also keep in mind the fact that the 1848–49 revolutions had led to a restudy of the peasantry and its great revolts. Indeed, not only was Engels' *The Peasant War in Germany*—and Marx kept reminding us that that was the only revolutionary moment in German history, and its betrayal by Luther and feudalism, Marx held, accounted for Germany's backwardness—important in relation to the 1848 revolutions and the theory of permanent revolution for that period, but Marx clearly held it out for future perspectives. Here is what he wrote to Engels on April 16, 1856:

> The whole matter in Germany will depend upon the possibility of supporting the proletarian revolution with a sort of second edition of the peasant war. Then the thing will be excellent.
>
> MECW 40, p. 41

Once Marx finished with the *Critique of the Gotha Program* and returned to work on volumes II and III of *Capital,* he became interested, at one and the same time, in Russian agriculture and the study of the primitive commune— elements of which still existed in Russia—and in the possibility of a new independent workers' party in the United States as a result of the new heightened class struggles on the railroads. All of these will reconnect with the theory of the permanent revolution in a totally new, never-before-thought-of way, both in the letters to Vera Zasulich and in the Russian Preface to the 1882 edition of the *Communist Manifesto.* It is to this we need to turn.

---

6   According to Hal Draper, *Marx-Engels Register* (New York: Schocken Books, 1985), p. 2, the *Address* was published in the 1885, not 1875, edition of the *Revelations.* —Editor.

2   The Permanent Revolution: From 1843 to 1883

> Revolution is never practical until the hour of revolution strikes. *Then* it alone is practical, and all the efforts of the conservatives and compromisers become the most futile and visionary of human language.
>
> JAMES CONNOLLY, WORKSHOP TALKS

> The relation of the revolutionary workers' party to the petty-bourgeois democrats is this: it marches together with them against the faction which it aims at overthrowing, it opposes them on everything whereby they seek to consolidate their position in their own interests.... Their battle cry must be: The Revolution in Permanence.
>
> MARX, ADDRESS TO THE COMMUNIST LEAGUE, MARCH 1850

Luxemburg's internationalism was second to none in her thought, in her actions, indeed her whole life. As she put it on what turned out to be the last day of her life—the following day the counterrevolution beheaded the 1919 German Revolution, she was murdered:

> "Order reigns in Berlin!" You stupid lackeys! Your "order" is built on sand. Tomorrow the revolution will rear its head once again, and, to your horror, will proclaim, with trumpets blazing: *I was, I am, I will be*!

Clearly, her luminous mind, when it came to the question of revolution, was likewise second to none. The 1905 Revolution, which led to her exclamation that the revolution was "everything" and all else was "bilge,"[7] was the red thread that permeated all her writings. Yet when it came to philosophy, even when that was a philosophy of revolution, that was not the dominant factor. Quite the contrary.

To the extent that Marx's 1850 *Address* on the permanent revolution was a point of reference, it was most often a reference to the "mistake" of thinking after the defeat of 1848–49 that a revolution was still in the offing in 1850, as if the dating was the pivotal point rather than the philosophy of revolution and all that flowed from it, beginning with the fact of taking the highest point of any revolution as the point of departure for the next revolution. Even when, in her 1904 review of Franz Mehring's publication of some of Marx's early works, Luxemburg recognized "the original *conception* ... the hopes for the so-called 'revolution in permanence,'" the emphasis was on the "so-called" as she spelled out Marx's "anticipation that the bourgeois revolution would be only the first

---

7   Letter of Luxemburg to Emmanuel and Mathilde Wurm on 18 July 1906. —Editor.

act, immediately followed by the petty-bourgeois, alternately, in the proletarian revolution."

The truth, however, is that, in the very first year that he broke with bourgeois
society, 1843, and even when he was writing on a "mere" individual subject like
the "Jewish Question," Marx refused to leave it at merely "being for" civil rights
for Jews. Rather, he insisted that the question revolved around the inadequacy
of any bourgeois rights. And because his vision from the start was for totally
new human relations, he there—and that was the first time—projected the
concept of permanent revolution:

> At times of heightened self-confidence, political life seeks to suppress its
> own presumption, [namely] the civil society and its elements, and to set
> itself up as the real species-life of man without any contradictions. But it
> can do this only in *violent* contradiction with its own conditions of exis-
> tence, only by declaring the revolution to be *permanent* and hence the po-
> litical drama ends with the restoration of religion, private property and all
> the elements of the civil society just as inevitably as war ends with peace.
> MECW 3, p. 156

It is true that there were elements of the concept of permanent revolution
once Luxemburg was in the actual 1905 Revolution and judged that revolution
to be no mere extension of 1848 but rather initiation of 20th century European
revolutions. But it was not worked out as a theory, as Leon Trotsky had done
on what later became known as the theory of Permanent Revolution.[8] What
Luxemburg singled out was the General Strike, which did combine politics and
economics, but not only did not have a philosophy of revolution emerging out
of it, but even the totally new form of organization which had emerged spontaneously—soviets—was mentioned only in passing. It would remain so until
the very eve of the 1919 Revolution, when she rejected the reactionary call for a
Constituent Assembly and called for the creation of Workers' Councils.

To put it even more sharply, even when finally the Spartacus League did decide to transform itself into a separate and independent Communist Party, that
break with the fetish of "unity of party" preceded any concept of permanent
revolution, as was seen once again by the fact that even then she instructed
the German delegation to oppose the immediate establishment of a new Third
International.

---

8   See *Rosa Luxemburg, Women's Liberation, and Marx's Philosophy of Revolution,* afterword to
    Chapter 11, titled "Trotsky's Theory of Permanent Revolution," and "The Theory of Permanent
    Revolution," Section A of Chapter 4 of *Philosophy and Revolution.* —Editor.

Karl Marx, on the other hand, as we have seen, was grounded in a philosophy of permanent revolution as far back as 1843, kept developing the concept and the activities in revolutionary struggles culminating in the 1848–49 revolution, after which he worked it out, not just in passing, but in full in the March 1850 *Address to the Communist League*.

In reviewing "the two revolutionary years, 1848–1849" and the activities of the League "in the movement, in all places, in the press, on the barricades, and on the battlefields," Marx's report to the League stresses in the very next sentence that it was rooted in "the conception of the movement as laid down in circulars of the congresses and of the Central Committee of 1847 as well as in the *Communist Manifesto* ..." [MECW 10, p. 277]. In a word, not a single element of this *Address* to the League—whether it concerned the need for "reorganization" in a centralized way because "a new revolution is impending, when the workers' party, therefore, must act in the most organized, most unanimous, and most independent fashion" [MECW 10, p. 278], or whether it concerned the outright declaration "Revolution in Permanence" [MECW 10, p. 297]—is in any way separated from the total conception of philosophy *and* revolution. The most important conclusion for the movement then and now was that never again will a workers' movement be tied to the bourgeois democratic movement, even when they fight together against feudalism:

> The relation of the revolutionary workers' party to the petty bourgeois democrats is this: it marches together with them against the faction which it aims at overthrowing, it opposes them in everything whereby they seek to consolidate their position in their own interests.
>
> MECW 10, p. 280

Marx kept stressing the fact that "far from desiring to revolutionize all society," the democratic petty bourgeois were striving to work within the bourgeois framework and in fact showed themselves to he a more deadly enemy than the liberals [MECW 10, p. 280]. The search for revolutionary allies, therefore, must include the "rural proletariat" [MECW 10, pp. 284–85]. The stress on achieving the workers' own class interests was made the centerpoint of everything, even as the international outlook would mean that the German workers look upon not only their country but "the direct victory of their own class in France" [MECW 10, p. 287]. In developing the strategy and tactics for a continuous revolution, this *Address* that was actually distributed in illegal leaflet form ended as follows:

> But they themselves must do the utmost for their final victory by clarifying their minds as to what their class interests are, by taking up their

position as an independent party as soon as possible and by not allowing themselves to be seduced for a single moment by the hypocritical phrases of the democratic petty bourgeois into refraining from the independent organization of the party of the proletariat. Their battle cry must be: The Revolution in Permanence.

MECW 10, p. 287

Far from that *Address* being something Blanquist that Marx discarded afterwards, it was followed with another *Address* in June where he reviewed the concrete activities in five of the countries—Belgium, Germany, Switzerland, France, England. And the Minutes of the Central Committee meeting on September 15, 1850, pointed to the possibility of defeats. There was no letting go of what was needed for total uprooting of this society, even if that needed "15, 20, 50 years of civil war to go through in order to change society" [MECW 10, p. 626]. In a word, what remained in the statutes of the Communist League was:

The *aim* of the Communist League is to bring about the destruction of the old order of society and the downfall of the bourgeoisie—the intellectual, political and economic emancipation of the proletariat, and the communist revolution, using all the resources of propaganda and political struggle towards this goal.

MECW 10, p. 634

For that matter, it wasn't the phrase, Permanent Revolution, that was the proof of the concept, but the fact in the constant search for revolutionary allies the vision of the revolutions to come was in no way changed. Thus—whether it was a question of the organization itself, i.e., the Communist League, which was in fact disbanded in 1852, and Marx kept referring to the party "in the eminent historical sense"; or whether it was the search for historic roots and, with it, the projection of a revolutionary role for the peasantry, and Engels in that very same period wrote the magnificent work *The Peasant War in Germany,* which was published in the *Neue Rheinische Zeitung Revue*[9]—Marx was concluding:

---

9   The *Neue Rheinische Zeitung. Politisch-ökonomische Revue* was the bimonthly revolutionary journal Marx edited from exile in London in 1850, following up on the daily revolutionary newspaper he ran from Cologne from 1 June 1848 to 19 May 1849. The writings by Marx and Engels published in the *NRZ-Revue* are included in MECW 10. —Editor.

> Everything in Germany will depend upon whether it will be possible to support the proletarian revolution by something like a second edition of the Peasant War. Only then will everything proceed well.
>
> MECW 40, p. 41

It should not need to be said that this philosophy of revolution, far from diminishing in the mid-1850s, was intensified with his original study of "Economics." But, since the fact that Marx was "closeted" in the British Museum has been interpreted as "a scientific period," it does need to be stressed that it is precisely the work on the *Grundrisse* and its relationship to what Marx called "epochs of social revolution" which gave him a new appreciation of the Asiatic mode of production and the Oriental society's resistance to British imperialism. In a word, the dialectics of economic development and the dialectics of liberation led to a further development of the concept of permanent revolution, world revolution, under no matter what name. The establishment of the First International, on the one hand, and the final structuring of *Capital* on the other hand, in the 1860s, revealed, at one and the same time, not only the break with the concept of theory as a debate with theoreticians, and the development of the concept of theory as a history of class struggles, but a concept also of a new revolutionary force—Black.[10] The culmination of all these theories and activities was, of course, the historic appearance of the Paris Commune of 1871, and there, too, we saw—along with the great discovery of an historic form for working out the economic emancipation of the proletariat—a new force of revolution, women.[11]

The greatest concretization of the philosophy of revolution, and its reconnection with the deep roots of the concept of permanent revolution first developed in the 1850 *Address*, came in the last years of Marx's life and the study of the pre-history as well as the history of humanity.

It is that March *Address* which is to this day still a point of debate. The first revisionists began not only attacking it but trying to attribute the thought not to Marx but to Auguste Blanqui.[12] Whether it was the Mensheviks' slanders that the concept of permanent revolution was Blanquist; or revolutionaries like Trotsky, who had developed the theory of permanent revolution but one that was hardly rooted in Marx's (see Afterword [to Chapter 11 of *Rosa Luxemburg, Women's Liberation, and Marx's Philosophy of Revolution*]); or even Lenin, who certainly did ground the whole theory of *State and Revolution* in Marx's

---

10   See Chapter 24. —Editor.
11   See Chapter 27, Section 2. —Editor.
12   See Hal Draper, *Karl Marx's Theory of Revolution*, Vol. 2, pp. 591–95. —Editor.

Critique of the Gotha Program, none seemed to have made a special category of Marx's 1882 preface to the Russian edition of the *Communist Manifesto.* There the concept was worked out anew as the relationship between advanced and underdeveloped countries, where the latter rather than the former might spark the revolution. No doubt part of this was due to the fact that the *Ethnological Notebook*s were unknown and so was the letter to Vera Zasulich, all of which would have shown how deep were the roots of a seemingly wild statement for 1882. But we do have that advantage.

Let us keep the following quotation from the preface to the Russian edition in mind as we turn to the final section:

> If the Russian Revolution becomes the signal for a proletarian revolution in the West, so that both complement each other, the present Russian common ownership of land may serve as the starting point for a communist development.
>
> MECW 24, p. 426

A Post-World War II View of Marx's Humanism, 1843–1883; Marxist Humanism, 1950s–1980s

Completed on May 1, 1987, this was the last article written by Raya Dunayevskaya for publication in a book before her sudden death on June 9, 1987. It includes some of the themes of her work toward the book she had tentatively titled "Dialectics of Organization and Philosophy: 'The Party' and Forms of Organization Born out of Spontaneity." This essay was intended for the Encyclopedia of Contemporary Socialism, *a Yugoslav project that was never completed.*

> Don't talk to me about space ships, a trip to the moon, or Marx, about life in the atomic age....
>
> We live like this. In darkness, in mud, far away...
>
> Don't tell me it is worse in Africa. I live in Europe, my skin is white. Who will embrace me to make me feel that I am human?
>
> KAROLY JOBBAGY
>
> BUDAPEST, APRIL 1956

The two-fold problematic of our age is: (1) What happens *after* the conquest of power? (2) Are there ways for new beginnings when there is so much reaction, so many aborted revolutions, such turning of the clock backward in the most technologically advanced lands?

Self-emancipatory movements, both from the emergence of a whole new Third World which had won its independence from imperialism—Africa, Asia, Latin America, Middle East—as well as revolts within the Western world itself, articulated themselves as what I have called "a movement from practice that was itself a form of theory." The ambivalence in the theoretical developments persisted though they reached for a total philosophy.

The world had hardly caught its breath from the devastation of World War II when already it was confronted with the birth of the nuclear age in the form of the atomic bomb. Nor was the "high-tech" confined to war: it at once moved into production, first in the mines and then soon invading all of industrial production. The very first to battle automation were the U.S. miners on General Strike in 1949–50 against the introduction of the continuous miner, which they called the "man-killer." What was new in this proletarian revolt was that, instead of just fighting unemployment and demanding better wages, the miners were posing totally new questions about what *kind* of labor man should do, and why there was an ever-widening gulf between thinking and doing.[1]

Three years later, we witnessed the first ever uprising from within the Communist world, which had been preceded by Yugoslavia's first act of national independence from Russia, and which was followed by revolts within the Vorkuta forced labor camps in Russia itself. The East European revolts seemed to be continuous. They expressed themselves most luminously in one form or another of Marxist Humanism: in Poland there appeared a work in 1957 called *Toward a Marxist Humanism;*[2] in Yugoslavia there was a tendency that called itself "Marxist Humanist";[3] in 1968 in Czechoslovakia it was termed "Socialism with a Human Face."[4] The revolt has continued to this day in ever new forms, such as Solidarność in Poland today. Multi-forms of struggles for new human relations to free us from the limited choice of East or West circled the world.

In the United States, the first full theoretical declaration of Marxist-Humanism was my work *Marxism and Freedom,*[5] which declared the whole purpose of the work "as aiming to re-establish Marxism in its original form, which Marx called 'a thoroughgoing Naturalism or Humanism.'" [*Marxism and Freedom*, p. 21] This 371-page book has undergone five different editions, and been translated into French, Spanish, Japanese, and Italian, with some chapters translated and circulated underground by individuals in Russia, Poland, China, and South Korea.[6]

In Latin America, the young Fidel Castro embraced Humanism in 1959. He said at that time,

> Standing between the two political and economic ideologies being debated in the world, we are holding our own position. We have named

---

1 See Chapter 21. —Editor.

2 Leszek Kolakowski, *Toward a Marxist Humanism* (New York: Grove Press, 1969). —Editor.

3 Marx's Humanism began to be studied seriously in Yugoslavia in the 1950s and led to the birth of the journal *Praxis*, which was published in Serbo-Croat and in English in an international edition. —Editor.

4 "Socialism with a Human Face" was an opening created by the Communist government of Czechoslovakia in January 1968 in response to mass disaffection. New forms of self-organization and expression in a movement called Prague Spring went far beyond the set limits and it was crushed by a Russian invasion in August 1968. See also *Czechoslovakia: Revolution and Counter Revolution* (Detroit: News and Letters, 1968). —Editor.

5 The first edition of *Marxism and Freedom, from 1776 until Today* (New York: Bookman Associates, 1958), actually published in 1957, had appended the first English translation of Marx's 1844 Humanist Essays and the first English translation of Lenin's Abstract of Hegel's *Science of Logic*.

6 Since Dunayevskaya's death, *Marxism and Freedom* has also been translated into Chinese, Farsi, Russian, and Arabic. —Editor.

it Humanism, because its methods are humanistic.... This is a humanist revolution, because it does not deprive man of his essence, but holds him as its aim.... This revolution is not red, but olive-green.[7]

I New Passions and New Forces: The 1950s' Rediscovery of Marx's 1844 Humanist Essays

Rather than a seeming accident, and far from being at best a remembrance of things past on the part of the Old Left, the 1950s' rediscovery of Marx's 1844 Humanist Essays was altogether new, todayish, precisely because it speaks to this age's problematic—"What happens after?" How could so great a revolution as the November 1917 Russian Revolution, the only successful proletarian revolution in the world, which established the first workers' state, degenerate into Stalinism? What happens after the conquest of power?

Nothing like that was facing Marx and yet, by discovering a whole new continent of thought and of revolution, which he had named "a new Humanism," Marx pointed to a direction beyond communism. In his break with capitalism, though he had singled out the proletariat as *the* revolutionary class, he expanded the need for totally new human relations by at once questioning the capitalistic alienated concept of the Man/Woman relationship. Not only that. It was clear that the overthrow of private property capitalism would not end by overthrowing private property; it was as necessary to break with "vulgar communism." Instead of either materialism or idealism, there would be a new unity of idealism and materialism:

> Just as atheism, as transcendence of God, is the becoming of theoretical humanism, and communism, as transcendence of private property, is the vindication of actual human living as its own property, which is the becoming of practical humanism, so atheism is humanism mediated by transcendence of religion, and communism is humanism mediated by the transcendence of private property. Only by the transcendence of this mediation, which is nevertheless a necessary presupposition, does there arise *positive* Humanism, beginning from itself. [Appendix, p. 352]

In 1950—when the workers battled automation and raised the question of "What *kind* of labor?"—a new stage of cognition appeared in the economic sphere. This, as we saw, was followed by political and social battles for truly new human relations. The emergence in our age of a new Third World, not only

---

7 See *New Left Review*, 7, January–February 1961, p. 2.

Afro-Asian but Latin American and Middle East, was no mere geographic designation, as massive and substantive as that was. Rather, Third World became synonymous both with new forces of revolution and with those new forces as Reason. These new revolutionary forces—peasants as well as proletarians, Women's Liberationists as well as youth anti-war activists—saw in that most exciting color, Black, so deep a revolutionary dimension and so intense an internationalism imbedded in their national liberation struggles, that, far from being a "Third" World, it encompassed the whole world.

The world of the 1960s, indeed, was aflame with rebellion, North and South, East and West. The depth of the revolt that freedom fighters in East Europe unleashed against the Communist totalitarians characterized, as well, the new generation of revolutionaries in the West, rebelling against the bureaucratic, militaristic, capitalist-imperialist world they did not make.

The African Diaspora meant not only South Africa but South USA, and Black meant not only Africa—South, West, East and North—but also Latin America, including the Caribbean. Whether it was the slogan, "Ready or not, here we come," which Kwame Nkrumah used as he led the general strike and the mass demonstrations that won independence for Ghana,[8] or whether it was the Africans who criticized the pre-independence intellectuals' concept of Negritude, the point was that the many voices of the Black Dimension used a single global word: "Freedom!" both in the Third World and in the U.S.

Black consciousness in the United States put American civilization on trial. There is very nearly no end to the varied forms in which the Black Dimension expressed itself. It was the Montgomery Bus Boycott,[9] where the *daily* revolutionary activity—taking care of transportation, organizing meetings, holding marches, creating their own direct democracy in mass meetings three times a week—helped launch the Black Revolution.

A look at another new force—Women's Liberation—will show that by the 1970s it had developed from an idea to a *movement*. Though it was itself faced with contradictions of class, race and culture, it had a determining effect on the whole emancipatory process, whether this came from East or West, North or South.

A penetrating look into the incomplete emerging Portuguese Revolution appeared even before the mass revolt against fascism burst forth, in a book called *The Three Marias*, which gave notice of an opposition that the authorities

---

8   See "The African Revolutions and the World Economy," Chapter 7 of *Philosophy and Revolution.* —Editor.

9   See especially Charles Denby, *Indignant Heart: A Black Worker's Journal* (Boston: South End Press, 1978), pp. 181–89.

thought they could silence by imprisoning its three authors.[10] So powerful was the protest pouring forth from the Women's Liberation Movement *internationally*, that not only did the authors gain their freedom, but an autonomous women's movement became integral to the revolution itself. Despite this fact, Isabel do Carmo—who headed the revolutionary group PRP/BR (Revolutionary Party of the Proletariat/Revolutionary Brigades), which had raised the historically urgent question of *apartidarismo* (non-partyism) for the first time within the Marxist movement—dismissed the autonomous Women's Liberation Movement as purely petty-bourgeois, that is to say, non-revolutionary. But as the revolution faltered and she was again arrested, she rethought the whole struggle of both the revolution and its incompleteness, while the Women's Liberationists continued their activity for her release. She concluded: "I'm beginning to think our whole struggle, the struggle of the Revolutionary People's Party, was really a fight carried on by women."[11] That extreme declaration, when you are talking of the revolution as a whole—and being mindful that the Portuguese Revolution really started in Africa—is as wrong as her previous denial of the Women's Liberation Movement; but the objectivity of that movement as a new revolutionary force and Reason is undeniable.

The Youth, who have always been what Marx called the energizing force of every revolution, are now showing themselves not only as the most courageous but as those who are developing new ideas, new forms of organization, and new relationships of theory to practice. Even the bourgeois press has had to note a new type of radical who goes from the classroom, whether in academia or in an underground discussion club on Marx, directly into the mass demonstrations and battles—as is true right now in South Korea, South Africa, Haiti and the Philippines.[12]

II   The Myriad Global Crises and Counterrevolutions

The counterrevolutions that we in the 1980s are now battling had been nurtured by the U.S. defeat in Vietnam, because the U.S. had been operating on the grand imperial illusion of the 1970s that they supposedly could have both

---

10   *The Three Marias: New Portuguese Letters* by Maria Isabel Barreno, Maria Teresa Horta, Maria Vello da Costa (Garden City, New York: Doubleday, 1975). —Editor.

11   See John Darnton, "Women Add a Certain Pizazz to Portugal's Politics," *The New York Times*, February 24, 1984.

12   See both Susan Chira, "Korea is Breeding a New College Radical," *The New York Times*, June 17, 1986; and June Kronholz, "A Year after Marcos, Celebration is Quirky as Coup Itself Was," *The Wall Street Journal*, February 26, 1987.

guns and butter. This was the lie; what the militarization actually produced was the global structural economic crisis of 1974–75.

Marx's greatest theoretical work, *Capital*, marched onto the present historic stage even among bourgeois ideologues, since there is no other way to understand today's global economic crisis. Thus, *Businessweek* (June 23, 1975) suddenly started quoting what Marx had said on the decline in the rate of profit as endemic to capitalism. It even produced official graphs from the Federal Reserve Board, the Department of Commerce, Data Resources, Inc., as well as its own data, all of which showed that the post-World War II boom had ended.[13]

The capitalists may not be ready to "agree" with Marx that *the* supreme commodity, labor-power, is the only source of all value and surplus value, but they do see the decline in the *rate* of profit compared to what *they* consider necessary to keep investing for expanded production in a nuclear world.

By now, in the 1980s, we are far beyond what the serious bourgeois economist, Simon Kuznets, wrote in the early post-war period when he said that

> the emergence of the violent Nazi regime in one of the most economically developed countries of the world raises grave questions about the institutional basis of modern economic growth—if it is susceptible to such a barbaric deformation as a result of transient difficulties.[14]

Reagan's retrogression started by turning the clock backward on all the gains won by the civil rights struggles,[15] the battles fought by the Women's Liberation Movement, by the Black Dimension, by the Youth. After six years of Reaganomics, nearly three million are now officially estimated as homeless in the U.S.—a number which exceeds that recorded in the Great Depression of the 1930s. What is new today is that within this class-divided society ever-larger segments of the working class are sinking so rapidly into pauperism that Marx's absolute general law of capitalist accumulation has moved to the realm of actual description.

---

13   See my pamphlet, *Marx's "Capital" and Today's Global Crises* (Detroit: News and Letters, 1978). [See Chapter 6. —Editor.].

14   Simon Kuznets, *Postwar Economic Growth* (Cambridge: Harvard University Press, 1964).

15   On the 100th anniversary of the Emancipation Proclamation, at the beginning of the Black Revolution in the U.S., the National Editorial Board of News and Letters Committees published *American Civilization on Trial* (Detroit: May 1963). A fourth, expanded edition was published in 1983, with a new Introduction on "A 1980s View of the Two-Way Road Between the U.S. and Africa," (Chicago: News and Letters, 1983). [See Chapters 24 and 25. —Editor.].

The over eight million who are officially listed as "unemployed" in the U.S. are "average," and do not reflect the situation in what are known as the "rust belts," depressed industrial centers where unemployment is 10 to 12 percent. When it comes to Black unemployment, the figure is as high as 20 percent. The statistic of eight million unemployed doesn't even mention the 1.3 million "discouraged" workers who no longer search for jobs regularly, or the six million part-time workers who want, but cannot find, a full-time job. The enormous lines that form in industrial cities whenever job openings are announced—10,000 in Detroit recently applying for 30 openings—are the proof of the severity of the crisis.

Women and children are the hardest hit. In Mississippi today more than one family in three is living below what even the Reagan administration calls the "poverty line." In Chicago, the infant mortality rate now exceeds that of Costa Rica. The Physicians' Task Force on Hunger recently called the situation in Chicago "as bad as anything in the Third World countries," and pointed to the soaring tuberculosis rate.[16]

Youth, Black youth especially, have before them a lifetime of unemployment or minimum-wage jobs. In Detroit, every high school student knows that he or she will never be able to get a job in the auto plants; in Pittsburgh it is the same for the steel mills. Even in that mecca of "high-tech," the Silicon Valley of California, where only a few years ago computer production was hailed as the answer to U.S. economic decay, there are now layoffs and fears of homelessness.

Inseparable from the continuing economic crises has been the extension of the U.S. imperialist tentacles, which came to a climax in the Spring 1986 imperial intrusion into the Gulf of Sidra and the actual bombing of the headquarters and the home of Col. Kadaffi. Without resting for a single instant, the U.S. continued with its raising of a counterrevolutionary army of mercenaries trying to overthrow the legitimate government of Nicaragua. This series of outright invasions of other countries began with the unprovoked invasion of Grenada in October, 1983.

The fact that the first shot of counterrevolution in Grenada was fired by the "revolutionaries" themselves—*its* Army, politically and militarily headed

---

16   *Hunger in America: the Growing Epidemic* by Physician Task Force on Hunger in America (Middletown, Connecticut: Wesleyan UP, 1985), p. 77, reports: "Cook County Hospital is located right in the middle of Chicago, the nation's third largest city. It is an unlikely place to find kwashiorkor and marasmus, the Third World diseases of advanced malnutrition and starvation.... Malnutrition has clearly gone up in the last few years. We have more low-birth-weight babies. We are seeing so much TB that my house staff is no longer excited by it." —Editor.

by Gen. Hudson Austin (plus [Deputy Prime Minister] Bernard Coard)—demands that we take a deeper look at the type of revolution that erupted in Grenada in 1979. It is impossible not to be moved by the last words spoken by the leader of that revolution, Maurice Bishop, as, in utter shock, he looked at the Army shooting into the masses who had just released him from house arrest: "My God, my God, they have turned the guns against the people."[17]

That does not free us from facing the stark fact that the first shot of counterrevolution came from *within* the revolutionary Party-Army-State. That first shot opened the road for the imperialist U.S. invasion that, it is true, lay in wait from Day One of the revolution. This, however, in no way absolves the "Party" of its heinous crime. The fact that Cuban President Fidel Castro—though an "internationalist" who spelled out his solidarity in concrete acts such as sending Grenada doctors and construction workers, teachers as well as military advisers—nevertheless failed to develop the ideas that were at stake, left the masses unprepared for ways to confront the divisions within the leadership that were to have gory consequences.

Instead of Castro focusing on a theory of revolution, he substituted and based himself on what he called the "principle of non-interference in internal affairs." He proceeded to praise Bishop for adhering to that "principle" by not asking for help in the leadership disputes—as if these were mere matters of "personality" and merely "subjective," rather than the result of the *objective* pull backward *because* the revolution itself was barren of a philosophy. Castro disregarded the dialectics of revolution—that is to say, the digging into what was coming *from below, the mass consciousness, its reasoning*. Instead, both he and the Grenadian leadership reduced the ideas of freedom to "subjective, personality" matters.

While the savage, unprovoked, long-prepared-for imperialist invasion and conquest of Grenada makes it imperative to never let go the struggle against U.S. imperialism until it is vanquished, it is urgent to face the retrogressive reality in the Left as well.

This is exactly why, in the whole post-World War II period, Marxist Humanists have been raising new questions on forms of battle, on the need for spontaneity, on the struggle against single-partyism; indeed, raising the whole question of what kind of philosophy can become *the* motivating force of all the contemporary struggles. The most acute expression of this was articulated by Frantz Fanon, who, while giving up his French citizenship to become an African revolutionary, at the same time critiqued the new leadership that arose with decolonization:

---

17   Quoted in BBC report, "1983: Grenada's prime minister 'assassinated.'" —Editor.

"Leader": the word comes from the English verb, "to lead," but a frequent French translation is "to drive." The driver, the shepherd of the people no longer exists today. The people are no longer a herd; they do not need to be driven.

Fanon further concretized his critique of the "Leader" and his cohorts who formed the dominant party: "The single party is the modern form of the dictatorship of the bourgeoisie, unmasked, unpainted, unscrupulous and cynical." His conclusion about the African revolutions was that: "This new humanity cannot do otherwise than define a new humanism both for itself and for others."[18]

III   Once Again, Marx—This Time with Focus on His Final Decade
       and on Our Age

The philosophy of *praxis* is consciousness full of contradictions in which the philosopher himself, understood both individually and as an entire social group, not merely grasps the contradictions, but posits himself as an element of the contradictions and elevates this element to a principle of knowledge and therefore of action.

ANTONIO GRAMSCI, "PROBLEMS OF MARXISM"

The newness of our age was seen in the whole question of Humanism, of the relationship of party to spontaneity, of mass to leadership, of philosophy to reality.

On October 23, 1956, a student youth demonstration in Budapest was fired upon.[19] Far from dispersing the young students, these were soon joined by the

---

18   Frantz Fanon, *The Wretched of the Earth* (New York: Grove Press, 1968), pp. 148, 133, 197, 246. See also my pamphlet *Nationalism, Communism, Marxist Humanism and the Afro-Asian Revolutions* (Cambridge University: The Left Group, 1961), and new edition (Chicago: News and Letters, 1984). Consult also *The Raya Dunayevskaya Collection, Marxist-Humanism, 1941 to Today*, held by the Archives of Labor and Urban Affairs, Walter Reuther Library, Wayne State University, Detroit, and available from them on microfilm, which includes my letters written from Africa, 1962. [See RDC, pp. 3034–50, 3061–76, 3184–3203, 9573–9677 —Editor.].

19   For a report from the Central Workers' Council of Greater Budapest, see *The Review*, Vol. II: 4, 1960, published in Brussels by the Imre Nagy Institute. See also an "Eyewitness Report of How the Workers' Councils Fought Kadar," *East Europe* (New York), April 1959; and Miklos Sebestyen, "My Experiences in the Central Workers' Council of Greater Budapest," *The Review*, Vol. III: 2, 1961. In my *Philosophy and Revolution, from Hegel to Sartre and from*

workers from the factories in the outlying suburbs. The revolution had begun in earnest. During the following 13 days, ever-broader layers of the population revolted. From the very young to the very old, workers and intellectuals, women and children, even the police and the armed forces—truly the population to a man, woman and child—turned against the top Communist bureaucracy and the hated, sadistic AVO/AVH (secret police). The Communist Party with more than 800,000, and the trade unions allegedly representing the working population, just evaporated. In their place arose Workers' Councils, Revolutionary Committees of every sort—intellectuals, youth, the army—all moving *away from* the Single Party State.

Overnight there sprang up 45 newspapers and 40 different parties, but the decisive force of the revolution remained the Workers' Councils. When 13 days of armed resistance was bloodily crushed by the might of Russian totalitarianism, the new form of workers' organization—the factory councils—called a general strike. It was the first time in history that a general strike *followed* the collapse of the revolution. It held the foreign imperialist as well as the "new government" at bay for five long weeks. Even János Kádár[20] said he was listening to the demands of the Workers' Councils for control over production and the "possible" abrogation of the single-party rule.

What none but Marxist-Humanists saw as the *transition point* between the East German Revolt of 1953, the outright Hungarian Revolution of 1956 and its philosophy was revealed in two seemingly unconnected events in 1955: (1) the Montgomery Bus Boycott opened the Black Revolution in the U.S. and inspired a new stage of revolution in Africa as well; (2) in Russia, there suddenly appeared, in the main theoretical Russian journal, *Questions of Philosophy* (No. 3, 1955), an academic-sounding article entitled "Marx's Working Out of the Materialist Dialectics in the Economic-Philosophic Manuscripts of the Year 1844." It was an attack on Marx's Humanist Essays, contending that the young Marx had not yet freed himself from Hegelian mysticism and its "negation of the negation." What the state-capitalist rulers calling themselves Communists had become oppressively aware of was the mass unrest, especially in East Europe. What they feared most was a new uprising.

Simply put, although the Russian theoreticians chose to shroud the philosophic phrase in mysticism, ever since Marx had materialistically "translated" the Hegelian dialectic of negativity as the philosophy of revolution, "negation

---

Marx to Mao (New Jersey: Humanities Press, 1982), see especially "Once Again, Praxis and the Quest for Universality," pp. 263–66.

20   Kádár was chosen by the Russian Communists as the Hungarian figurehead for the counterrevolution. —Editor.

of the negation" stood for an actual revolution. What the Russians fear most is exactly what erupted in Hungary in 1956. In all the changes since then, nothing truly fundamental has been altered. This is seen most clearly of all in the fact that it has always been the Single Party State that remained the all-dominant power. In this, China—Deng's China as well as Mao's China—has held to the same totalitarian principle.

This overriding fact makes it urgent to turn once again to Marx, this time not to the young Marx and his "new Humanism," nor to the mature Marx as a supposed economist, but to Marx in his last decade, when he discovered what we now call his "new moments" as he studied pre-capitalist societies, the peasantry, the women, forms of organization—the whole dialectic of human development.

Because politicalization has, in the hands of the Old Left, meant vanguard-ism and program-hatching, we have kept away from the very word. It is high time *not* to let the "vanguard party to lead" appropriate the word, politicaliza-tion. The return is to its original meaning in Marx's new continent of thought as the uprooting of the capitalist state, its withering away, so that new hu-manist forms like the Paris Commune, 1871, emerge. Marx himself was so non-vanguardist that, although the First International had dissolved itself, he hailed the railroad strikes spreading throughout the U.S. and climaxed in the 1877 St. Louis General Strike, as both an elemental "post festum" to the First International Workingmen's Association, and the point of origin for a genuine workers' party.[21]

For that matter, the whole question of pre-capitalist societies was taken up long before that last decade. In the 1850s, for example, what inspired Marx to return to the study of pre-capitalist formations and gave him a new apprecia-tion of ancient society and its craftsmen was the Taiping Revolution. It opened so many doors to "history and its process" that Marx now concluded that, *his-torically-materialistically* speaking, a new stage of production, far from being a mere change in *property form*, be it "West" or "East," was such a change in *produc-tion relations* that it disclosed, in embryo, the dialectics of actual revolution.[22]

What Marx, in the *Grundrisse*, had defined as "the absolute movement of becoming" [*Grundrisse*, p. 488] had matured in the last decade of his life as new moments—a multilinear view of human development as well as a

---

21   See letter of Marx to Engels, July 25, 1877 [MECW 45, p. 251]. See also Moon and Brokmeyer, *On the 100th Anniversary of the First General Strike in the U.S.* —Editor.

22   For a more a detailed discussion of the Taiping Revolution's influence on Marx's thinking see *Rosa Luxemburg, Women's Liberation, and Marx's Philosophy of Revolution*, pp. 133–39. —Editor.

dialectic duality within each formation. From within each formation evolved *both* the end of the old *and* the beginning of the new. Whether Marx was studying the communal or the despotic form of property, it was the human resistance of the Subject that revealed the direction of resolving the contradictions. Marx transformed what, to Hegel, was the synthesis of the "Self-Thinking Idea" and the "Self-Bringing-Forth of Liberty" as the emergence of a new society.[23] The many paths to get there were left open.

As against Marx's multilinear view which kept Marx from attempting any blueprint for future generations, Engels' unilinear view led him to mechanical positivism. By no accident whatever, such one-dimensionality kept him from seeing either the communal form under "Oriental despotism" or the duality in "primitive communism" in Morgan's *Ancient Society*. No wonder, although Engels had accepted Marx's view of the Asiatic mode of production as fundamental enough to constitute a fourth form of human development, he had left it out altogether from *his* analysis of primitive communism in the first book he wrote as a "bequest" of Marx—*Origin of the Family*. By then Engels had confined Marx's revolutionary dialectics and historical materialism to hardly more than Morgan's "materialism."

In Marx's revolutionary praxis, the germ of each of the "new moments" of his last decade was actually present in his first discovery. Take the question of the concept of Man/Woman, which he raised at the very moment when he spoke of the alienations of capitalist society and did not consider them ended with the overthrow of private property. This was seen most clearly in the way he worked during the Paris Commune, and in the motions he made to the First International. One such motion at the 1871 London conference recommended "the formation of female branches among the working class." The Minutes recorded:

> Citizen Marx adds that it must be noted that the motion states "without exclusion of mixed sections." He believes it is necessary to create exclusively women's sections in those countries where a large number of women are employed (since) they prefer to meet by themselves to hold discussions. The women, he says, play an important role in life: they work in the factories, they take part in strikes, in the Commune, etc. ... they have more ardor than the men. He adds a few words recalling the passionate participation of the women in the Paris Commune.[24]

---

23 This refers to the conclusion of Hegel's *Philosophy of Mind*. See Chapter 21. —Editor.

24 Quoted in Jacques Freymond, ed., *La Première Internationale, Receuil et documents*, Vol. II (Geneva: Librairie Droz, 1962), pp. 167–68 (my translation). [See also MECW 22, p. 413. —Editor.].

Nor was it only a question of the women. In a speech at this same London conference of the First International—September 20, 1871—Marx said:

> The trade unions are an aristocratic minority. Poor working people could not belong to them; the great mass of the workers who, because of economic development, are daily driven from the villages to the cities, long remain outside the trade unions, and the poorest among them would never belong. The same is true of the workers born in London's East End, where only one out of ten belongs to the trade union. The farmers, the day laborers, never belong to these trade unions.[25]

Or take the whole question of human development. Marx definitely preferred the gens form of development, where, he concluded, the communal form—whether in ancient society, or in the Paris Commune, or in the future—is a higher form of human development. The point is that individual self-development does not separate itself from universal self-development. As Hegel put it: "individualism that lets nothing interfere with its universalism, i.e. freedom."[26]

While Marx considered the gens a higher form of human life than class society, he showed that, in embryo, class relations actually started right there. Most important of all is that the multilinear human development demonstrates no straight line—that is, no *fixed* stages of development.

The difficulty is that post-Marx Marxists were raised not on Marx's Marxism, but on Engelsian Marxism—and that was by no means limited to Engels' *Origin of the Family*. Rather, Engels' unilinearism was *organic*—which is why we must start from the beginning.

Marx's Humanist Essays showed his multilinearism, his Promethean vision, whether on the concept of the Man/Woman relationship, or the question of idealism and materialism, or the opposition not only to private property capitalism but what he called "vulgar communism," which is why he called his philosophy "a new Humanism."

These motifs are the red thread through his final decade, as well. The Iroquois women, the Irish women before British imperialism, the Aborigines in Australia, the Arabs in Africa, Marx insisted in his *Ethnological Notebooks*,[27]

---

25 Quoted in Karl Marx, *On the First International,* edited by Saul K. Padover (New York: McGraw-Hill, 1973), p. 141 [MECW 22, p. 614].

26 Hegel, *Philosophy of Mind,* ¶481.

27 Lawrence Krader transcribed Marx's Notebooks, which were published as *The Ethnological Notebooks of Karl Marx* (Assen: Van Gorcum, 1972). For my analysis, see my *Rosa Luxemburg, Women's Liberation and Marx's Philosophy of Revolution* (New Jersey: Humanities Press, 1982).

have displayed greater intelligence, more equality between men and women, than the intellectuals from England, the U.S., Australia, France or Germany. Just as he had nothing but contempt for the British scholars, whom he called "rogues," "asses," and "blockheads," who were expounding "silliness," so he made a category of the intelligence of the Australian Aborigine, since the "intelligent black" would not accept the talk by a cleric about there being a soul without a body.

How could anyone consider the very limited quotations from Marx that Engels used in the *Origin of the Family* as any kind of summation of Marx's views? How could someone like David Ryazanov think that those *Ethnological Notebooks* dealt "mainly with landownership and feudalism"? In truth they contain nothing short of both a prehistory of humanity, including the emergence of class distinctions from within communal society, and a history of "civilization" that formed a complement to Marx's famous section in *Capital* on the historical tendency of capitalist accumulation, which was, as he wrote to Vera Zasulich, "only of Western civilization."[28]

One Russian scholar, M.A. Vitkin (whose work, *The Orient in the Philosophic-Historic Conception of K. Marx and F. Engels,*[29] was suddenly withdrawn from circulation), did try to bring the Marx-Engels thesis on the Asiatic Mode of Production, if not on Women's Liberation, into the framework of the 1970s. This original contribution had concluded that "it is as if Marx returned to the radicalism of the 1840s, however, on new ground." And the new ground, far from being any sort of retreat to "old age" and less creativity and less radicalism, revealed "principled new moments of his (Marx's) philosophic-historic conceptions."

It was in his last decade, as he finished the French edition of *Capital*, that Marx wrote his *Critique of the Gotha Program*, on which Lenin's profound revolutionary analysis of the need to break up the state was based. Lenin failed, however, to say a word about what in Marx's critique of the Gotha Program is the foundation of a principled proletarian organization, which led Marx to separate himself from the unity of the Eisenachists (who were considered to be Marxists) and the Lassalleans. Nor was there any reference by Lenin to his own critique of *What is To Be Done?*, Lenin's main organizational document.[30]

---

28   This is a paraphrase of a sentence from Marx's letter to Zasulich: "Hence the 'historical inevitability' of this process is *expressly* limited to the *countries of Western Europe*" [MECW 24, p. 370]. —Editor.

29   Mikhail Vitkin, *Vostok v Philosophico-Historicheskoi Kontseptsii K. Marksa y F. Engelsa* (Moscow, 1972) was available only in Russian. —Editor.

30   Lenin's many critiques of the concept of vanguardism and centralism during the development of Marxism in Russia were published in Russia as a pamphlet entitled *Twelve Years*.

He thus disregarded the twelve years of self-criticism during which he insisted that *What is To Be Done?* was not a universal, but a tactical question for revolutionaries working in tsarist Russia. Instead, it was made into a universal after the revolution. This set the ground for a Stalin—that is to say, for the problem that remains the burning question of our day: What comes after the conquest of power?

It gives even greater significance to the question that Rosa Luxemburg raised both before the 1917 Russian Revolution and directly after.[31] "The revolution," Luxemburg wrote,

> is not an open-field maneuver of the proletariat, even if the proletariat with social democracy at its head plays the leading role, but is a struggle in the middle of incessant movement, the creaking, crumbling and displacement of all social foundations. In short, the element of spontaneity plays such a supreme role in the mass strikes in Russia, not because the Russian proletariat is "unschooled," but rather because revolutions are not subject to schoolmastering.[32]

The dialectic of organization, as of philosophy, goes to the root of not only the question of the relationship of spontaneity to party, but the relationship of multilinearism to unilinearism. Put simply, it is a question of human development, be it capitalism, pre-capitalism or post-capitalism. The fact that Stalin could transform so great a revolution as the Russian Revolution of 1917 into a state bureaucracy tells more than just the isolation of a proletarian revolution in a single country. The whole question of the indispensability of spontaneity not only as something that is in the revolution, but that must

---

See his "Preface to the Collection *Twelve Years*," in Lenin, *Collected Works*, Vol. 13 (Moscow: Progress Publishers, 1978), pp. 94–113.

31 Lenin's philosophic ambivalence had become so crucial for our age that I wrote a chapter with that as its title for my work, *Philosophy and Revolution*; the chapter, indeed, was published separately even before the book itself was published. Its timeliness in the year 1970 opened many new doors for Marxist Humanism. Thus, I spoke to such widely different audiences as the Hegel Society of America and the first conference of the young radical philosophers of *Telos*. The chapter was also published by *Aut Aut* in Italy and by *Praxis* in Yugoslavia. The opening to so many different international forums was in great part due to the fact that, because 1970 was both the 200th anniversary of Hegel's birth and the 100th of Lenin's, there were all sorts of criss-crossings of those two events.

32 Quoted in my *Rosa Luxemburg, Women's Liberation and Marx's Philosophy of Revolution*, p. 18, where the whole question of Luxemburg as a revolutionary, as a theoretician, as an unknown feminist, is developed. [See Luxemburg, *Selected Political Writings*, p. 245. —Editor.].

continue its development after; the question of the different cultures, as well as self-development, as well as having a non-state form of collectivity—makes the task much more difficult and impossible to anticipate in advance. The self-development of ideas cannot take second place to the self-bringing-forth of liberty, because both the movement from practice that is itself a form of theory, and the development of theory as philosophy, are more than just saying philosophy is action. There is surely one thing on which we should not try to improve on Marx—and that is trying to have a blueprint for the future.

MAY 1, 1987

Raya Dunayevskaya's Translations from Marx's *Economic-Philosophic Manuscripts of 1844*

Editor's Note: Dunayevskaya began to draw on Marx's 1844 Economic-Philosophic Man- uscripts *when she concluded that the Russian "workers' state" had transformed into its opposite, to state-capitalism, and felt a need to re-establish Marxism on the basis of what she came to call Marx's Humanism. Her championing of the Manuscripts' importance resulted in her being the first to translate and publish selections in English in the 1958 first edition of* Marxism and Freedom, *from 1776 until Today. She wrote later (Chapter 3, above), "I had great difficulty in convincing either commercial publishers or university presses that they ought to publish Marx's Humanist Essays or Lenin's Philosophic Note- books. I succeeded in getting both these writings published only by including them as appendices to my* Marxism and Freedom." *Kevin O'Brien digitized her translations of "Private Property and Communism" and "Critique of the Hegelian Dialectic" as published there.*

1   Translator's Note by Raya Dunayevskaya

This is the first published English translation of Marx's essays—*Private Property and Communism,* and *Critique of the Hegelian Dialectic.* They form the central part of his *Economic-Philosophic Manuscripts, 1844,* which did not see publication until nearly a century later when they were bought by the famous scholar, David Ryazanov, for the Marx-Engels Institute in Moscow and published under his editorship (*Arkhiv Marksa-Engelsa,* Vol. Ill, Moscow, 1927). They were republished in the *Complete Works of Marx and Engels,* 1932, in the original German and in Russian translation. They were trans- lated for me from the German text (*Marx-Engels Gesamtausgabe, Bd. 1, Abt. 3,* Berlin, 1932). However, the American students (intellectuals and workers alike) in my classes on Marxian philosophy found these translations almost incomprehensible.

It is my belief that the knowledge of Marxian-Hegelian philosophy is greatly ob- structed by the available translations, which are evidently intended for philosophic circles exclusively. On the other hand, the average Russian reader has found the phi- losophy comprehensible in Russian translations, which indeed are the finest of all the translations of the work. The Russian language, it is true, does not have as precise a philosophic idiom as the German, but at the same time it loses none of the spirit and is more comprehensible to the lay public. I therefore made a new translation from the Russian text. I hope these translations will prove more comprehensible to the modern American and English readers, including workers whom, after all, Marx considered "the inheritors of German philosophy."

Because of the similarity of topics dealt with in these essays (which were unpublished in Marx's lifetime) with those in his book *The Holy Family, A Critique of Critical Critique,* Ryazanov concluded that they were "Preparatory Work for the *Holy Family*" and so listed them. In 1955, the official philosophical journal *Questions of Philosophy* (#3) suddenly stated that that was the wrong listing for these essays, that they were, instead, part of Marx's first work, *Critique of Politics and Political Economy,* which had remained unfinished and are unpublished to this day. Whether they are part of one work or the other does not in any way affect the text itself, although there is now some doubt as to whether all the texts have been published.

I took the liberty of eliminating the first four paragraphs of the essay *Critique of the Hegelian Dialectic* because they dealt with the "Critical Critique" (Young Hegelians with whom Marx had broken) and were not germane to Marx's critique of Hegel here. The English reader now has available to him Marx's complete work on that philosophic group. (See K. Marx and F. Engels: *The Holy Family, Or Critique of the Critical Critique,* 1956.) All footnotes, except where otherwise mentioned, are mine.

—R.D.

2   Private Property and Communism

Ad. pag. xxxix. But the opposition between the *lack of property* and *property* is still an undifferentiated opposition, an opposition that is not yet in an *active relation* to its own *inner* situation. So long as it is not conceived as the opposition between *labor* and *capital,* it is not yet a contradiction. In its *first* form it can express itself where the developed movement of private property is absent (for example, in ancient Rome, in Turkey, etc.). In this form it does not yet *appear* as the result of private property itself. However, labor, the subjective essence of private property as the moment excluding property, and capital, objective labor as the moment excluding labor—this is *private property* that has developed to the point of contradiction and, therefore, is the active form driving toward resolution.

(Ad. ibid.) The abolition of self-alienation follows the same course as self-alienation itself. At first, *private property* is regarded only from its objective aspect—but with labor as its essence. Therefore the form of its being appears to be capital, "which is to be annihilated as such" (Proudhon). Or a specific form of labor, for example, leveled down, fragmented and, therefore, unfree labor—is regarded as the source of *all* the pernicious characteristics of private property and of its alienation from human existence. Like the Physiocrats, Fourier also regarded *agricultural labor* as at least the best form of labor, while St. Simon, on the other hand, considered *industrial labor*, as such, as the essence of wealth, and desired the *exclusive* rule by the industrialists, and the improvement of the conditions of labor. Finally, *communism* is the *positive* expression of transcended private property, appearing to begin with as *universal* private property. Regarding private property in its universality, communism appears in its form only as its *generalization* and *completion*. As such, it has a twofold form: on the one hand, it overestimates the role and domination of *material* property to such a degree that it wishes to abolish *everything* which cannot be possessed by everybody as *private property*; it wishes by force to eliminate all talents, etc. In its eyes, the sole purpose of life appears to be direct and physical *possession*. The form of activity of the *worker* is not here abolished, but merely extended to all men.

The relation of private property remains the relation of the community to the world of things. Finally, this movement of counterposing universal private property to private property is expressed in the animal form that *marriage* (which, of course, is a *form of exclusive* private property) is counterposed to having *women in common*. Hence the woman becomes *communal* and *common* property. We might say that this idea of communal women expresses the secret of this quite vulgar and unthinking communism. In the same way that the woman is to abandon marriage for general prostitution, so the whole world of wealth, that is, the material essence of man, goes from the relation of exclusive marriage with the private property owner for the relation of universal prostitution with the community. Prostitution is only the *particular* expression of the universal prostitution of the *worker* and since prostitution takes in not only the prostituted but the prostitutor (the lowest of all) so the capitalist, etc., falls into this category. Since it completely negates the *personality* of man, this type of communism is only the logical expression of private property, which is just this negation. Universal *envy*, constituted as power, is only the secret guise in which *greed* asserts itself and is to be satisfied. The thought of every property owner, as such, is directed—*at least* against the *wealthier* one—as envy and a desire to reduce all to a common level, constituting even the essence of competition. The vulgar communist is only the consummation of this envy and this craving to level down, establishing a certain common denominator. He has a *definitely limited* standard. How little this type of abolition of private property is an actual appropriation and enrichment is proved precisely by its abstract negation of the entire world: it is only a retrogression to the *unnatural* simplicity of a *poor* and needy man who not only has not gone beyond the limits of private property, but has not even attained its level.

According to this theory, the community is only a community of *labor* and the equality of *wages* which the communal capital, or the community as the universal capitalist, pays out. Both sides of the relationship between capital and labor are elevated into a *sham* universality: *labor* as the lot of each member of the community; capital as the real universality and power of the community.

The infinite degradation in which man exists for himself is expressed in this relation to the *woman* as the spoils and handmaid of communal lust. For the secret of the relationship of man to man finds its *unambiguous*, definitive, *open*, obvious expression in the relationship of *man* to *woman*, and, in this way, the *direct, natural* relationship between the sexes. The direct, natural, necessary relationship of man to man is the *relationship of man to woman*. In this natural relationship of the sexes, the relationship of man to nature is immediately his relationship to man, just as the relationship of man to man is his relationship to nature, his own natural determination. Consequently, in this relation, there is *sensuously*, in an obviously *factual* way, disclosed to what extent the human essence of man has become that of nature, or to what extent nature has become the human essence of man. Therefore, on the basis of this relation we can judge the whole stage of the development of man. From the character of this relation it follows to what degree *man*, as a *species*, has become *human,* and has recognized himself as such. The relationship of man to woman is the *most natural* relationship of man to man. Consequently, in it is revealed to what degree the *natural* behavior of man has become *human*, or to what degree *human* essence has become his *natural* essence, to what degree his human nature has become his nature. To what degree the *needs* of man have become *human* needs is also seen in this relationship, i.e., to what degree *another* human being is needed as a human being; to what degree he, in his most individual existence, has at the same time become part of the community. Thus the first positive transcendence of private property, *vulgar* communism, is only a *form of appearance* of the baseness of private property, which seeks to assert itself as the *positive* social essence.

(2) Communism: (a) in its political nature, democratic or despotic; (b) transcending the state, but representing an uncompleted structure which still preserves private property, i.e., the alienation of man. In both these forms communism already appears as the reintegration, or return of man to himself, as transcendence of human self-alienation. But insofar as it has not yet grasped the positive essence of private property and to the same degree has little understood the *human* nature of needs, communism still remains under the influence of private property. It has, to be sure, caught hold of the concept of private property, but has not yet grasped its essence.

(3) Communism, as the *positive* abolition of private property, which is human self-alienation, and, therefore, as the actual *appropriation* of human essence by man and for man, is the return of man to himself as *social*, i.e., human man, complete, conscious and matured within by the entire wealth of developments to date. Just as completed humanism is naturalism, so this communism, as completed naturalism, is humanism. It is the *true* solution of the strife between man and nature, and between man and

man. It is the true resolution of the conflict between existence and essence, between reification and self-affirmation, between freedom and necessity, between individual and species. It is the solution of the riddle of history and it knows itself as this solution.

The whole movement of history is, therefore, on the one hand, its *actual* act of creation—the act by which its empirical being was born; on the other hand, for its thinking consciousness; it is the *realized* and *recognized* process of development. The former, still incomplete communism, evolving out of the historical cultures opposing private property, seeks a *historical* justification by seizing upon the particular moments in the process of development (Cabet, Villegarde, etc., especially ride this horse) and pointing to these as proof of its historical maturity. Thereby incomplete communism only demonstrates that the disproportionately greater part of the historical movement contradicts its assertions and that if it had once existed, the very fact that it is *past* refutes its pretensions of being essential.

It is not difficult to see the necessity of this, that in the movement of *private property*, there is to be found both the empirical and theoretical base not alone of political economy, but of the whole revolutionary movement.

Material, directly *sensuous* private property is the material, sensuous expression of *alienated human* living. Its movement, production and consumption, is the *sensuous* manifestation of the movement of all production up to now, i.e., the realization, or the actuality, of man. Religion, the family, the state, law, morals, science, art, etc., are only *particular* forms of production, and subordinated to its universal law. The positive transcendence of *private property*—of this element of human actuality—like the appropriation of *human* living, is, therefore, the positive abolition of every kind of alienation, i.e., the return of man from religion, the family, the state, etc., to his *human,* i.e., *social* existence. Religious alienation, as such, takes place only in the sphere of consciousness, the inner sphere of man, but economic alienation is that of *actual life.* It is self-evident that the question as to when the movement of different nations first made its appearance depends on how the real recognized life of the people occurs, whether more in consciousness or in the external world; whether it is more ideal or actual. Communism begins at first (Owen) with atheism, but atheism in its first stages is far from being communism as atheism in general is an abstraction. Therefore the philanthropy of atheism is at first only a *philosophically* abstract philanthropy while the philanthropy of communism is, from the very beginning, *really* and immediately directed toward *action.*

We have seen how, by presupposing the positive abolition of private property, man produces man, himself and other men: how the object, which is the immediate assertion of his individuality, is at the same time his own existence for other men; for their existence, and their existence for him. In the same way, both the material of labor and man as subject are equally the result and the starting point of the movement. (And it is precisely the historical *necessity* of private property that it must be this point of departure.) The social character of the whole movement means its *universal* character. Just as society itself produces *man as man*, so it is *produced by him*. The activity of labor and of spirit, both in content and in *origin*, is *social* activity and *social* spirit. The human essence of nature exists only for *social* man; only in the society of nature is there the *link* with man, his being for another; and the other for him, only in the society of nature is there the *basis* of his *human* existence. Only in society is his *natural* existence his *human* existence, and nature become human for him. Thus *society* is the complete, essential unity of man with nature, the true resurrection of nature, the achieved naturalism of man, and the achieved humanism of nature.

Social activity and social spirit by no means exist merely in the form of direct *community* activity and direct *community* spirit, although *community* activity and spirit, i.e., activity and spirit which are expressed and asserted directly in *actual society* with other men, are to be found wherever such a direct expression of sociality is based in the essential content of the activity and correspond to its nature.

However, whenever I am active *scientifically*, etc., engaged in activity which I myself can pursue alone, without any direct association with others, I act *socially* nevertheless because I am active as a *man*. Not only the material of my activity is given to me as a social product—as is the case even with language in which the thinker is active—but my *own* existence is social activity inasmuch as what I make for myself I make also for society and with the consciousness of myself as a social being.

My *universal* consciousness is only the *theoretical* form of the *living* form, which is the *real* communal, social existence inasmuch as nowadays universal consciousness is an abstraction from real life and, as such, is hostile to it. Hence also the *activity* of my universal consciousness, as such, is my *theoretical* existence as a social being.

We should especially avoid re-establishing society, as an abstraction, opposed to the individual. The individual *is the social entity*. Therefore his expression of life (although it may not appear in the direct form of a *communal*-type life carried out simultaneously with others) *is* an expression and assertion of *social living*. The individual and the species-life of man are not *distinct* from one another. Thus, also and of necessity, the mode of existence of an individual life is a more *particular* or more *universal* manner of existence of the species-life, or the species-life is a more *particular* or *universal* individual life.

As *species-conscious*, man asserts his real *social* life and only recapitulates in thought his actual existence, even as conversely the existence of the species affirms itself in the consciousness of the species, and exists, in its universality, as a thinking being, for itself.

Therefore, although man is a *particular* individual—and precisely his specificity makes him an individual and an actual, *individual* communal being—he is the *totality*, the ideal totality, the subjective existence of society, thought out and experienced for itself. Likewise, he exists in actuality, both in perception and in the actual spirit of social existence, as a totality of the human expression of life.

Thus, although thinking and being are distinguishable from one another, they are, at the same time, in unity with one another.

Death appears as a harsh victory of the species over the individual and as a contradiction of this unity. But the determinate individual is only a *determinate species-being* and, as such, mortal.

(4) *Private property* is only the sensuous expression of the fact that man at one and the same time becomes *objective* for himself, becomes an alien and inhuman object. In expressing his life, he alienates his life. His realization is a separation from reality, an *alien* reality. Hence, the positive transcendence of private property, i.e., the *sensuous* appropriation of human essence and living, of material things created by and for man is to be conceived not only in the sense of direct, one-sided enjoyments nor only in the sense of *possession*, a sense of *having*. Man appropriates himself as an all-sided essence in an all-sided way; hence, as a whole man. Each of his human relations to the world—seeing, hearing, smell, taste, feeling, thought, perception, experience, wishing, activity, loving—in short, all organs of his individuality, like the organs which exist directly in the form of communal organs, are in their objective relation or in their relation to the *object*, the appropriation of it. The appropriation of *human* actuality, its relation to the object, is the *affirmation of human actuality*. Therefore it is as all-sided as are the essence of man and the *forms of his activity*. Human activity and human *suffering*, regarded in a human way—this is self-enjoyment to man.

Private property has made us so stupid and one-sided that any kind of object is *ours* only when we have it, i.e., when it exists for us as capital, or when we possess it directly—eat it, drink it, wear it, live in it, etc.—in short, use it. But, from the point of view of private property, all these direct forms of possession, in their turn, exist only as *means to life*; and the life to which these serve as means is the *life of private property*— labor and capitalization.

Therefore, in place of all the physical and spiritual senses, there is the sense of possession, which is the simple alienation of all these senses. To such absolute poverty has human essence had to be reduced in order to give birth to its inner wealth! (Regarding the category of possession, see Hess, *21 Bogen*).[1]

The transcendence of private property is, therefore, the total *freeing* of all the human senses and attributes. However, it is this emancipation precisely because these senses and attributes have become *human*, both subjectively and objectively. The eye has become a *human* eye when its *object* is a social *human* object, created by man for man. Thus the *senses*, in their immediate practice, have become theoretical. They are related to the *thing* for the sake of the thing, but the thing itself is an objective human relation to itself, and to man, and *vice versa*. Therefore, to the extent that utility has

---

1 Moses Hess, *Einundzwanzig Bogen aus der Schweiz* [Twenty-One Printer's Sheets from Switzerland] (1843). —Editor.

become *human* utility, need or enjoyment have lost their *egoistic* nature in nature, have lost their bare utility.

In the same way the senses and spirit of other men have become my *own* appropriation. Therefore, besides these direct organs, social organs are developed in the *form* of society; thus, for example, activity directly in association with others, etc., becomes an organ of the *manifestation of life* and a method for appropriating *human* life.

It is self-evident that the *human* eye sees differently from that of the crude, non-human eye, that the *human* ear hears differently from that of the crude ear, etc.

We have seen that man is not lost in his object only if the latter becomes his as a human object or as *objective man*. This is only possible insofar as it becomes a *social* object for him, and he himself becomes a social being even as society exists for him in this object.

On the one hand, therefore, inasmuch as objective actuality becomes everywhere for man in society the actuality of human essential capacities, human actuality, and thus the actuality of his own essential capacities, all *objects* become for him the *objectification* of himself, objects affirming and realizing his individuality, *his* objects, i.e., the objects of *himself. How* they become his objects depends on the *nature of the object*, and the nature of the *essential capacity* corresponding to it. For just the *determinate character* of this relationship constitutes the specific *actual* manner of affirmation. For the *eye* an object has a different form than for the *ear*, and the object for the eye is different from that for the ear. The uniqueness of every sense is precisely its *own essence*. Likewise, the *unique form* of its objectification, its *objective, active* living being. Therefore, not only in thought, but with *all* his senses, man is thus affirmed in the objective world.

Let us express this differently, from the subjective point of view: just as music evokes the musical sensitivity of man, while for the unmusical ear the most beautiful music makes *no* sense, is not an object, because my object can only be the assertion of my own essential capacities; so an object has sense for me (only has sense for a corresponding sensitivity) only insofar as it is my essential capacity because the sense of an object for me goes just as far as *my* sensitivity goes. Therefore the *sensitivities* of the social man are *other* than those of the unsocial. Only thanks to the objectively unfolded wealth of human nature, does the wealth of subjective *human* sensitivity develop: a musical ear, eyes for the beauty of form, in short, for the first time there will develop *senses* which are capable of human appreciation, which will assert themselves as *human* essential senses. Not only the five senses but also the so-called spiritual senses, the practical senses (will, love, etc.), in a word, *human* sensitivity, the humanity of the senses will be achieved only thanks to the existence of *their* object, because of their *humanized* nature. The *cultivation* of the five senses is the work of the whole history of the world to date. *Sensitivity*, preoccupied with crude practical necessity, is only *limited* sensitivity. For the starved man the human form of food does not exist, it exists only in the abstract form of nourishment. It would be just as good placed before him in its crudest form, and it is impossible to say what distinguishes the human activity of nourishment from the animal activity of nourishment. The anxiety-ridden, needy man is incapable of appreciating the most beautiful drama. The tradesman in minerals sees only their monetary value, not the beauty and unique character of minerals; he has no mineralogical sensitivity. Thus, it would be necessary to objectify human essence, both theoretically and practically, in order to make the *sensitivity* of man *human* and thus create a corresponding human sensitivity for the appreciation of the whole wealth of *human* and natural essence.

Just as through the movement of private property and the wealth and poverty it creates—or material and spiritual wealth and property—the developing society finds the formation of all material things, so the developing society produces man as its permanent actuality, with the total wealth of his nature, creates the *rich* and *profoundly sensitive* man.

We see how subjectivism and objectivism, spiritualism and materialism, activity and passivity, first lose their character of opposites and therefore their existence as such opposites only under social conditions.

We see that the solution of theoretical oppositions can be accomplished only in a *practical way*, only through the practical energy of man. Their resolution is, therefore, by no means a task only for knowledge, but a task of actual life. *Philosophy* cannot solve them precisely because philosophy grasps them only as theoretical problems.

We see that the history of *industry* and the *objectively* developed existence of industry are the *opened book of human capacities*, which, sensuously considered, is human *psychology*. Up to now industry has not been regarded in connection with the essence of man, but has always been regarded only in terms of external relations, or *utility*. That is due to the fact that, moving within the framework of alienation, we have looked for the actuality of human essential capacities and activity of the human *species* only in the universal existence of man in religion, or history in its abstractly universal essence (politics, art, literature, etc.). In *ordinary, material* industry (which can be regarded both as part of the universal movement just mentioned, and also as the specific part of industry since all human activity has up until now been labor, i.e., industry alienated from self-activity) what we are dealing with is *sensuous, alien, useful objects* as seen within the framework of alienation, that is to say, the *objectification of the human capacities of man*.

For *psychology*, this book, i.e., precisely the sensuously most concrete, most accessible part of history, is closed. In general, what should we think of a science which *presumptuously* abstracts from this enormous section of human labor and does not feel its own inadequacy? What should we think of a science where such an extensive realm of human activity says no more to it than what can be said in one word: "Need," "common need"!

The *natural* sciences have developed an enormous activity and have appropriated for themselves a constantly expanding subject matter. But philosophy has remained an alien science to them even as they remained alien to philosophy. Their momentary unity was only a *fantastic illusion*. The will for such a unity was there, but not the capacity. Historical writing itself pays the natural sciences only cursory consideration, as moments of enlightenment, of utility, of individually great discoveries. But the more, *in practice*, there has been an invasion of human living by natural science through industry, transforming it, the more has there been a preparation for the liberation of humanity, although in its first instance it led to its complete dehumanization. *Industry* is the *actual* historical relationship of nature to man, and therefore of the natural sciences to man. Therefore, if it is regarded as the *exoteric* unfolding of human *essential capacities*, the human essence of nature and the natural essence of man can also be understood. Then natural science loses its abstract materialistic, or rather idealistic, direction and becomes the basis for *human* science. Today, it has already become— although in an alienated form—the basis of *actual* human life. To have one basis for life and another for science is *a priori* a lie.

Nature, developing in human history—by that act human society was born—is the actual nature of man. Therefore, nature as it develops through industry, even if in an *alienated* form, is real *anthropological* nature.

Sensuousness (see Feuerbach) must be the basis for all science. Science is real only when it proceeds from sensuousness in the dual aspect both of *sensuous* consciousness and *sensuous* needs; in other words, only when science proceeds from nature is it a genuine science. All of history is the history of preparation, the history of the development of this, that "man" becomes the object of *sensuous* consciousness, and the need of "man as man" becomes the basis of needs. History itself is the *actual* part of the *history of nature*, of nature's development into man. Afterwards, natural science will become the science of man, just as the science of man subsumes natural science under it: both become one. It will be a *single* science.

Man is the direct object of natural science because the direct *sensuous nature* for man is direct human sensitivity (or—which is the same thing—*another* man is sensuously present for him because his own sensitivity exists for him as human sensitivity only *through other* men). But if *nature* is the direct object of the *science of man*, the first object of man—namely, man—is nature. Just as sensitivity and the specifically human essential sensuous capacities find their objective realization only in natural objects, so, in general, they find their self-recognition only in the science of nature. Even the fundamental element of thinking, the element in which the life of thought is expressed—*language*—is sensuous nature. The *social* actuality of nature and human natural science, or the *natural* science of man—these are all identical expressions.

We see how the *wealthy man* and the *wealth of human needs* take the place of the wealth and poverty of political economy. The wealthy man is at the same time the man *in need* of an expression of a totality of human living, man who feels his own realization as inner necessity, as *need*. On the basis of socialism not only the *wealth*, but also the *poverty* of man likewise attains a *human*, and consequently, a social significance. It is the passive link which permits man to feel the need for his greatest wealth, that of *other* men. The mastery of objective essence in me, the sensuous outburst of my essential activity, is the *passion* which in this way becomes the *activity* of my being.

(5) Being first appears as independent in its own eyes as soon as it stands on its own feet, and it stands on its own feet only when it owes its *existence* only to itself. A man who lives by the grace of another regards himself as a dependent being. However, I live completely by the grace of another when I owe him not only the maintenance of my life, but when he has produced my life, when he is its source. My life necessarily has such a source outside itself whenever it is not my own creation. Therefore, it is very difficult to dislodge from the consciousness of people the concept of creation. Because it contradicts all the obvious facts of practical life, it is *inconceivable* to them that nature and man exist through themselves.

The theory of the *earth's* creation has received a powerful blow from *geology*, the science which presents the formation and development of the earth as a process of self-production. "Generatio Equivoca" is the only practical refutation of theories of creation.

Now it is certainly easy to say to a single individual what Aristotle has already said: Your father and mother gave birth to you. Hence you are the coupling of two people, i.e., you are the sex act of man, produced by man. You see that man owes his physical existence to man. Thus, you must not only bear in mind the *one* side, the interminable series which leads you to inquire further: Who has given birth to my father, my grandfather? You must also keep in mind the *circular* process which is sensuously observable in this progression, according to which a man recapitulates himself in procreation and, consequently, *man* thus remains the subject. You may reply: I'll grant you this circular process if you will grant me the interminable series which continually drives me further until I ask you who has produced the first man and nature in general. I can only answer you: Your question is itself the product of abstraction. Ask yourself how you arrived at this question; ask yourself whether your question does not occur from a point of view which I cannot answer because it is a senseless one. Ask yourself whether, for reasonable thought, progression exists as such. Whenever you ask about the creation of nature and man, you abstract from man and nature. You presuppose them as *non-existing* and yet you demand that I prove their existence to you. I now say to you:

Abandon your abstraction and you will give up your question. Or, if you hold fast to your abstraction, accept the consequence: Whenever you think of man and nature as *non-existent*, regard yourself, you who are natural and human, as non-existent. Think not, ask me not, for as soon as you begin to think and ask, your abstraction of nature and man from existence loses all sense. Or are you such an egotist that you recognize the non-existence of everything, wishing at the same time to save your own existence?

You can reply: I do not want to presuppose the non-existence of nature, etc. I ask you about the *act of its origin* in the same way as I ask the anatomist about the formation of bones, etc.

However, inasmuch as for socialist man, *all of history* is nothing else than the production of man through human labor, none other than the becoming of nature of man, to that extent he has the obvious, irrefutable proof of his *birth* through the process of his own birth. Insofar as the *essential* character of man and nature, that is the existence of man for man as the existence of nature, and of nature for man as the existence of man, has become *practical*, sensuous and observable, so the question of an *alien* being, a being beyond nature and man, is a question which involves the confession of the unessentiality of nature and man. *Atheism*, as the denial of unessentiality, makes no more sense because atheism is a negation of God and poses the existence of man through this *negation*. But socialism as socialism no longer needs such mediation. It begins from the *theoretical* and *practical* sensuous consciousness of man and nature as the *essence*. It is the *positive* self-consciousness of man no longer mediated by the transcendence of religion. Like real life, it is the positive *actuality* of man no longer mediated like *communism* by the transcendence of private property. *Communism* is positive affirmation as negation of the negation and, therefore, the *actual* moment, necessary for the immediate future historical development, the actual moment of human liberation and reconquest of humanity. Communism is the necessary form and the energizing principle of the immediate future. But communism, as such, is not the goal of human development, the form of human society.

3   Critique of the Hegelian Dialectic

... [Ludwig] Feuerbach is the only one who has a *serious, critical* relation to the Hegelian dialectic. He alone has made genuine discoveries in this sphere and, in general, has truly transcended the old philosophy. The greatness of the accomplishment, and the quiet simplicity with which Feuerbach has given it to the world, stand in striking contrast to the reverse behavior of the Critical Critique.[2]

Feuerbach's feat consists in the following:

---

2 See last paragraph of my prefatory note. —RD.

(1)   The proof that philosophy is nothing else than religion, translated into thought and worked out logically, that it is only another form and mode of existence of the alienation of human essence, and is, therefore, likewise to be condemned.

(2)   To the extent that Feuerbach made the social relation of "man to man" the basic principle of theory, he laid the foundation of *genuine materialism* and real science.

(3)   Feuerbach counterposes the positive, which rests on itself and is positively grounded in itself, to the negation of the negation, which declares itself to be the absolute positive.

Feuerbach explains the Hegelian dialectic (and thereby justifies the departure from the positive, from sense-certainty) in the following manner:

Hegel proceeds from the alienation of substance (logically: the infinite, the abstractly universal), from the alienation of absolute and fixed-absolute abstraction. Popularly speaking, his point of departure is Religion and Theology.

Secondly, he transcends the infinite, puts the actual, sensuous, real, finite, particular in its place. (Philosophy, the transcendence of Religion and Theology).

Thirdly, he again transcends the positive, again puts in its place the abstract, the infinite. Re-introduction of Religion and Theology.

Thus Feuerbach regards the negation of the negation only as the contradiction of philosophy with itself, as philosophy which affirms Theology (Transcendentalism) after it has denied it, and, accordingly, affirms it in opposition to itself.

The positive, or self-affirmation and self-confirmation which inheres in the negation of the negation, is here conceived as the positive which is not yet certain of itself, and therefore charged with its opposite, something which is doubtful of itself, and therefore in need of proof, something incapable of proving itself through its own existence, and hence unacknowledged. Consequently, he directly and immediately counterposes to it positive sense-certainty, positive affirmation which is based on itself.

But inasmuch as Hegel comprehends the negation of the negation in accordance with the positive relation, which is immanent in it, as the only truly positive, and in accordance with the negative relation which is immanent in it, as the only true act, an act of self-manifestation of all being, to that extent he has discovered only the *abstract, logical* and speculative expression for the movement of history. This is not yet the actual history of man as a presupposed subject, but only the act of generation, the history of the *origin* of man. We shall attempt to explain the abstract form of this movement in Hegel, as well as the difference between this process in Hegel and the same process in the modern criticism and in Feuerbach's *Essence of Christianity*. Or, more precisely, we shall attempt to explain the critical form of this movement which is still uncritical in Hegel.

A glance at the Hegelian system. We must begin with Hegel's *Phenomenology* [*of Mind*], the true source and secret of the Hegelian philosophy: *Phenomenology*:[3]

A.   *Self-consciousness*
   I.   *Consciousness*
       a)   Sense-certainty, or This and Meaning.
       b)   Perception, or the Thing with its characteristics and illusion.
       c)   Force and understanding, Appearance and the Supersensuous world.
   II. *Self-consciousness.* The Truth of Certainty of Itself.
       a)   Independence and dependence of self-consciousness, Lordship and Bondage.
       b)   Freedom of Self-consciousness. Stoicism, Scepticism, the Unhappy Consciousness.
   III. *Reason.* Certainty and Truth of Reason.
       a)   Observing Reason: Observation of Nature and of Self-consciousness.
       b)   Realization of rational self-consciousness through itself. Desire and Necessity. The Law of the Heart and the Delusion of Conceit. Virtue and the Course of the World.
       c)   Individuality which is real in and for itself. The Spiritual realm of animals and the fraud or the fact itself. The law-giving Reason. The law-testing Reason.
B.   *Spirit*
   I.   The *True* Spirit: Ethics.
   II. The Alienated Spirit, Culture.
   III. The Spirit sure of itself, Morality.
C.   *Religion. Natural* Religion in the *form of Art. Revealed* Religion.
D.   *Absolute Knowledge.*

Hegel's *Encyclopedia* [*of the Philosophical Sciences*] begins with *Logic*, with *pure, speculative thought*, and ends with Absolute Knowledge, self-conscious, philosophic, or absolute spirit grasping itself, as philosophic or absolute, i.e., superhuman abstract spirit, therefore the whole *Encyclopedia* is nothing but the *expanded essence* of the philosophic spirit. Feuerbach still regards the negation of the negation, concrete notion, as transcending in thought and, as thought, desiring to be direct contemplation,

---

3   *The Phenomenology of Mind.* The translation of this contents page is made from Marx's text, and does not agree in all particulars with the standard English translation. —RD.

nature, actuality, the objectification of thought. In an analogous manner, the philosophic spirit is nothing but the alienated spirit of the world, thinking within its self-alienation, i.e., grasping itself abstractly. *Logic* is the *money* of the spirit, the *abstract expression* of the speculative value of the thoughts of man and nature. It has become completely indifferent to all actual determinateness and is, therefore, unactual essence. It is *estranged thinking* and thus abstracted from Nature and actual man. It is *abstract thinking*. The *externality of this abstract thinking is Nature*, as it exists for this abstract thinking. Nature is external to this thinking, the loss of itself, and this thinking also grasps Nature merely in an external way, as abstract thought, but as estranged, abstract thought. Finally, there is *Spirit* returning to its own source. It first asserts itself as anthropological, then as phenomenological, psychological, ethical, artistic, religious spirit until it finally finds itself as *absolute* knowledge, and relates the now absolute, i.e., abstract spirit, to itself, and thus attains its conscious and appropriate existence. For its actual existence is *abstraction*.

There is a double error in Hegel:

The first appears most clearly in the *Phenomenology* as the source of the Hegelian philosophy. When, for example, Hegel considers Wealth, State Power, etc., as Essences alienated from *Human* Essence, he does so only in their alienated thought form. They are alienated essences and, therefore, merely an alienation of *pure*, i.e., abstract philosophical thought. The whole movement, therefore, ends with Absolute Knowledge. It is precisely abstract thinking from which these objects are alienated and to which they stand opposed with their pretension of reality. The *philosopher*, who is, himself, an abstract form of alienated man, establishes himself as the *yardstick* of the alienated world. Therefore the whole *history of estrangement*, the whole transcendence of this estrangement is nothing else than the history of abstract, that is, absolute thinking, logical, speculative thinking. Hence, the *alienation* which forms the real interest of this externalization, and the transcendence of this externalization, is the opposition between *Being-in-itself* and *Being-for-itself*, between consciousness and self-consciousness, between object and subject, i.e., the opposition between abstract thinking and sensuous actuality, or actual sensuousness, within the process of thinking itself. All other oppositions and movements of these oppositions are only the *semblance*, the *veil*, the *exoteric* form of these oppositions which are the solely interesting ones and which constitute the intrinsic meaning of the other profane oppositions. What is regarded as the essence of alienation, which is posed and to be transcended, is not the fact that human essence *materializes* itself in an *inhuman* manner in *opposition* to itself, but the fact that it materializes itself from, and in opposition to, abstract thinking. Thus the appropriation of the essential capacities of man which have become objects, and alien objects at that, is, in the first place, an *appropriation* which proceeds in *consciousness*, in *pure thinking*, that is, in abstraction. It is an appropriation of these objects as *thoughts* and as *movement of thought*. Hence, despite its thoroughly negative and critical character, and despite the criticism actually contained in it, which often far surpasses the later developments, there is already in the *Phenomenology*, hidden in embryo, the latent potentiality and secret of uncritical positivism and equally uncritical idealism of the later Hegelian works—philosophic disintegration and resurrection of extant Empiricism.

Secondly. The demand for the vindication of the objective world for men, e.g., the knowledge that the *sensuous* consciousness is no *abstractly* sensuous consciousness but a *humanly* sensuous consciousness, that Religion, Wealth, etc., are only the alienated actuality of deeds and, therefore, only the *road* to true *human* actuality—this appropriation, or the insight into this process, therefore, appears in Hegel in such a way that *sensuousness, religion, state power,* etc., are *spiritual* essences. For in Hegel only the *spirit* is the true essence of man, and the true form of the spirit is the thinking spirit, the logical speculative spirit. The *humanity* of Nature, and of the Nature produced by history, the products of men appear in it as *products* of the abstract spirit, and thus as *spiritual moments, alienated essences.*

The *Phenomenology* is, therefore, the hidden, still unclear even to itself, and mystifying critical philosophy. However, to the extent that it holds fast the *alienation* of Man—even if Man appears only in the form of Spirit—to that extent *all* elements of criticism lie hidden in it and are often already *prepared* and *worked out* in a manner extending far beyond the Hegelian standpoint. The sections on "Unhappy Consciousness," the "Honorable Consciousness," the fight of the noble and downtrodden consciousness, etc., etc., contain the critical elements—although still in an alienated form—of whole spheres like Religion, the State, Civic Life, etc. Just as the *essence* is the *object, alienated,* so the subject is always *consciousness,* or *self-consciousness.* Or, rather, the object appears only as abstract consciousness, man only as *self-consciousness.* The different forms of alienation which appear in the *Phenomenology* are, therefore, only different forms of consciousness and self-consciousness. Just as abstract consciousness in itself—as that by which the object is grasped—is merely a differentiating moment of self-consciousness, so the identity of self-consciousness with consciousness appears as the result of the movement, Absolute Knowledge, which no longer goes outside, but merely continues within its own process of abstract thinking. That is, the dialectic of pure thought is the result.

The greatness of Hegel's *Phenomenology*, and of its final result—the dialectic of negativity as the moving and creating principle—lies in this, that Hegel comprehends the self-production of man as a process, regards objectification as contra-position, as externalization, and as the transcendence of this externalization; that he, therefore, grasps the essence of *labor* and conceives objective man, true, actual man as the result of *his own labor.* The *true,* active relating of man to himself as species-essence, that is, as human essence, is possible only because man actually produces all the capacities of his *species*—and this again is only possible thanks to the collective activity of man, is possible only as a result of history—and he relates himself to it as well as to the objects, which is again at first possible only in the form of alienation.

We will now present in a detailed fashion the one-sidedness and the limitation of Hegel in the concluding chapter of the *Phenomenology*, in Absolute Knowledge, a chapter which contains both the summation and the quintessence of the *Phenomenology*, and contains the relation of the *Phenomenology* to the speculative dialectic, and the view of Hegel regarding their mutual and many-sided relationship.

In a preliminary way, we will remark only the following: Hegel stands on the basis of modern political economy. He regards *labor* as the *essence*, as the self-preserving essence of man. He sees only the positive side of labor and not its negative side. Labor—man's becoming-for-self within the limits of *externalization*—is *externalized* man. Hegel knew and acknowledged only one form of labor, that is, *abstractly spiritual labor*. Therefore, what Hegel recognized as the essence of philosophy, and it is this, in general, which constitutes its *essence*, is the externalization of man knowing himself, or externalized science thinking itself. And it is for this reason that he is capable of summarizing the preceding philosophy in terms of its particular moments and presenting his philosophy as *the* philosophy. From the very nature of the activity of philosophy Hegel knows what all other philosophers have done—viz., that they have conceived particular moments of Nature and of human life as moments of self-consciousness, or rather of abstract self-consciousness; therefore his science is absolute.

We will now proceed to the question of Absolute Knowledge—the last chapter of the *Phenomenology*.

The essence of the matter is that the *object of consciousness* is none other than *self-consciousness*, or that the object is only *objectified self-consciousness*, self-consciousness as object. (Man=self-consciousness.) Therefore, it is necessary to transcend the *object* of consciousness. *Objectivity*, as such, has the force of *alienated* relationship of man, not corresponding to the *human essence*, to self-consciousness. That means that the *re-appropriation* of the objective essence of man as alien and produced under the determination of alienation, serves not only to transcend *alienation*, but also to transcend *objectivity*, i.e., man is regarded as an *un-objective, spiritual* essence.

Hegel describes the movement of *transcending the object of consciousness* in the following way:

The *object* does not show itself only as *returning to the Self*. (That is, according to Hegel, a one-sided comprehension of that movement which grasps merely one aspect of it.) Man is equal to Self. The Self, however, is only man *abstractly* conceived and abstractly produced. Man is Self-ish. His eyes, his ears, etc., are *Self-ish*. Each of his essential capacities has in him the character of *Self-ishness*. But on this account it is now quite false to say: *Self-consciousness* has eyes, ears, essential capacities. Human nature is not a quality of *self-consciousness*. Self-consciousness is, rather, a quality of human nature, of the human eye, etc.

The Self, abstracted for itself and fixed, is man as abstract egotist, egotism in its pure abstraction, elevated to the level of thinking. (We will return to this point later.)

Hegel regards *human essence*, Man, as equal to *self-consciousness*. All alienation of human essence is, therefore, no more than *alienation of self-consciousness*. The alienation of self-consciousness is not regarded as an expression of the *actual* alienation of human essence. Rather, the *actual* alienation, which appears as real, is—according to its innermost concealed essence, first revealed through philosophy—nothing but the appearance of the alienation of actual human essence, of *self-consciousness*. The science which comprehends this is, therefore, called *Phenomenology*. All reappropriation of the alienated objective essence appears, therefore, as an incorporation into his self-consciousness. Man, insofar as he is taking possession of his essence, is only self-consciousness taking possession of the objective essence; return of the object to the self is, therefore, the reappropriation of the object.

If we are to express the all-sided transcendence of the object of consciousness, it consists of the following:

(1)   the object, as such, presents itself to the self as a vanishing factor;

(2)   the emptying of self-consciousness itself establishes thinghood;

(3)   this externalization of self-consciousness has not only *negative*, but *positive*, significance;

(4)   significance not merely *for us* or *per se,* but for *self-consciousness itself.*

(5)   The negativity of the object, or its cancelling its own existence, gets for self-consciousness a *positive* significance. Or self-consciousness *knows* this nothingness because self-consciousness externalizes itself, for, in doing so, it establishes itself as object, or, by reason of the indivisible unity characterizing its self-existence, sets up the *object* as *its* self.

(6)   On the other hand, there is also the other moment in the process, that self-consciousness has just really cancelled and superseded this externalization and objectification and, consequently, has resumed them into itself *as such.*

(7)   This is the movement of consciousness and is, therefore, the totality of its moments.

(8)   Consciousness, at the same time, must have taken up a relation to the object in all its aspects and phases, and have grasped its meaning from the point of view of each of them. This totality of its determinate characteristics makes the object *per se*, or inherently, a *spiritual essence*, and it becomes so in truth for consciousness when the latter apprehends every individual one of them as self, i.e., when it takes up toward them the *spiritual* relationship just spoken of.

ad. 1. That the object, as such, presents itself to consciousness as vanishing is the above-mentioned return of the object to the self.

ad. 2. *The externalization of self-consciousness* posits the category of *thingness*. Since man is self-consciousness, his externalized, objective essence, or *thingness*, equals externalized self-consciousness, and thingness is posited through this externalization. (Thingness is that which is object for him, and object is truly for him only what is essentially object, which is thus his objective essence. Since it is not actual man, and likewise not Nature as such—man is human nature—which is made the subject, but only the abstraction of man, namely, self-consciousness, thingness can only be externalized self-consciousness.)

What is absolutely true is that a living natural being, endowed and gifted with objective, i.e., material essential capacities, also possesses *actual* and *natural objects* of its own essence, and it is just as natural that his self-externalization should be the determination of an *actual* objective world, which appears under the form of *externality* and not belonging to his essence and is more powerful than the objective world. There is nothing inconceivable and perplexing in this. Rather the reverse would be perplexing. But it is just as clear that self-consciousness, i.e., its externalization, could only posit *thingness*, i.e., again only an abstract thing, a thing of abstraction, and not an *actual* thing. It is further evident that thingness, therefore, is not at all *independent* and *essential* over against self-consciousness, but is a mere creature, something *posited* by consciousness; and that which is posited, instead of being something which confirms itself, is only a confirmation of the act of positing, which momentarily fixes its energy in the form of a product and *in appearance* apportions to it the role—but only for one moment—of the independent actual being.

When actual corporeal Man, standing on firm and well-rounded earth, inhaling and exhaling all natural forces, posits—thanks to his externalization—his actual objective *essential* capacities as alien objects, it is not the act of *positing* which is the subject. It is the subjectivity of *objective* essential capacities, whose action must, therefore, also be *objective*. Objective essence works objectively, and it would not work objectively if objectivity did not inhere in the determination of its essence. It creates, posits only objects because it is posited through objects, because fundamentally it is *Nature*. That means that in the act of positing, it does not depart from its "pure activity" in order *to create the object*, but its objective product confirms merely its *objective* activity, its activity as an activity of an objective natural essence. We see here how thoroughgoing Naturalism, or Humanism, distinguishes itself both from Idealism and Materialism, and is, at the same time, the truth uniting both. We see, at the same time, how only Naturalism is capable of grasping the act of world history.

Man is directly a *natural* being. As a natural being, and especially as a living natural being, he is endowed partly with *natural* forces, with living forces, he is an *active*, natural being. These forces exist in him as dispositions and capabilities, as *instincts*. As natural, corporeal, sensuous, objective being, he is, like an animal and a plant, a *distressed*, conditioned, and limited being. That is, the *objects* of his instincts exist outside him, as *objects* independent of him. But these objects are *objects* essentially serving his needs, essential objects indispensible to the action and confirmation of his own essential capacities. That man is a *corporeal*, natural, living, actual, sensuous, objective being means that he has actual sensuous objects as objects of his essence of his expression of life, or that he is capable of *expressing* his life only in actual, sensuous objects. It is the same thing to be objective, natural and sensuous, or to have object, nature, sense outside oneself, or even to be object, nature, sense for a third being. *Hunger* is a natural necessity. Therefore, in order to satisfy and appease it, one requires a nature outside oneself, an object outside oneself. Hunger is the objective need of a body for another, for an *object* outside itself, indispensible to its integration and expression of his life. The sun is *object* for the plant, an object indispensible to it, confirming its life. In the same way, the plant is an object to the sun, as expression of the life-producing power of the sun, of the objective essential forces of the sun.

A being which does not have its nature outside itself is not a natural being, takes no part in the essence of nature. A being which has no object outside of itself is not an objective being. A being which is not itself object for a third being has no being for its object, that is, does not behave objectively; its being is not objective.

A non-objective being is a monstrous being.

Suppose there was a being neither itself an object nor having an object. Such a being would, first of all, be the only being. There would exist no other being outside of it. It would exist alone and solitary. For as soon as there are objects outside of myself, as soon as I am not alone, I am an *Other, another actuality* than the object outside of me. For this third object I am thus an actuality other than it, i.e., its object. A being which is not object to another being presupposes thus that no objective being exists. As soon as I have an object, this object has me for its object. But an *un-objective* being is an unactual, unsensuous being, merely thought, i.e., only a fancied, abstract being. To be sensuous, i.e., to be actual, is to be an object of sense, to be a *sensuous* object; therefore, to have sensuous objects outside oneself, to have objects for one's sensuousness. To be sensuous is to be *suffering*.

Therefore man as an objective sensuous being is a suffering being and since he is a being experiencing his suffering he is a passionate being. Passion is the essential power of man striving energetically toward his object.

However, man is not merely a natural being, but he is also a *human* natural being, i.e., a being which is for itself; therefore, a *species-being*. As such, he must confirm and affirm himself both in his being and in his knowing. *Human* objects are, therefore, not those objects of nature which offer themselves immediately. In the same way, *human* sense, insofar as it is direct and objective, is not *human* sensuousness, human objectivity. Neither Nature, taken objectively, nor Nature, taken subjectively, is immediately adequate to *human* essence. And just as all natural things must emerge, man also must have his act of emergence—*history*. This, however, is for him a known act of emergence and, therefore, an act of emergence which is transcended in consciousness. History is the true natural history of Man.

Thirdly. Since this positing of thingness is itself only an appearance, an act of contradicting the essence of pure activity, so it must also again be transcended. Thinghood must be negated.

ad. 3, 4, 5. 6.

(3) This striving toward consciousness has not only *negative*, but also *positive*, meaning; and (4) this positive meaning is not only *for us*, or, in itself, but for it itself, for consciousness. (5) The negativity of the object, its transcendence of itself, has, *for consciousness*, a *positive* meaning, that is, it *knows* this nothingness because it externalizes itself. For in this externalization, it knows its own self as object, or the object for the sake of the inseparable unity of its for-itselfness. (6) On the other hand, the other Moment is herein implied, namely, that it has also transcended and withdrawn into itself this externalization and objectivity, and that, accordingly, it is in *its own otherness, as such.*

We have already seen that, for Hegel, the appropriation of alienated objective essence, or the transcendence of objectivity under the determination of alienation—which is to develop from indifferent strangeness into actually hostile alienation—has, at the same time, or even mainly, the significance of transcending objectivity because the stumbling-block in the alienation is not the *determinate* character of the object, but its *objective* character. The object is, therefore, something negative, something transcending itself, a *nothingness*. For consciousness, this *nothingness* of the object has not only a negative, but also a *positive* meaning, for this nothingness of the object is the self-affirmation of un-objectivity, of *abstraction* of itself. For *consciousness* itself, the nothingness of the object has, therefore, a positive meaning, namely, that it knows this nothingness, the objective essence as its self-externalization, that it knows that it only exists through its self-externalization: The way in which consciousness exists and in which something exists for it is knowledge. Knowing is its sole act. Therefore, something exists for it to the extent it knows this thing. Knowledge is its single objective relation. Consciousness knows the nothingness of the object, i.e., the essence of distinction of the object from it, the not-being of the object for it, to the extent that it knows that the object is its self-externalization, i.e., it knows itself—knowledge as object—because the object is only the appearance of an object, an artificial vapor and, in its essence, no other than knowledge, which is counterposed to itself and therefore has counterposed to itself a nothingness, something which has no objectivity outside of knowledge. In other words, knowledge knows that only to the extent that it is related to an object is it outside of itself, does it externalize itself, that it itself appears to itself as object, or that what appears to it as object is only itself.

On the other hand, in the words of Hegel, there is also here contained the other Moment, namely, that it has likewise transcended and withdrawn into itself this externalization and objectivity. Hence, that in its otherness, it is as such by itself.

All the illusions of abstract, speculative thinking are concentrated in this judgment.

Firstly: consciousness, self-consciousness is with itself in its *otherness as such*. It is thus—or, if we abstract here from the Hegelian abstraction; and substitute for self-consciousness the self-consciousness of men—it is by itself in its *otherness* as such. In this is implied, on the one hand, that consciousness—knowledge as knowledge, thinking as thinking—pretends to be nothing else than the other of itself, pretends to be sensuousness, actuality, life. Thinking surpasses itself in thinking (Feuerbach). This aspect is here implied insofar as consciousness as mere consciousness meets an obstruction, not in alienated objectivity, but in *objectivity as such*.

Secondly, what is implied here is that self-conscious man, insofar as he has recognized the spiritual world—or, the spiritual universal existence of this world—nevertheless, confirms himself again in this alienated form and proclaims it to be his true existence, restores it and pretends to be with himself in his *otherness, as such*. Thus, after transcending, for example, religion, after the recognition of religion as a product of self-alienation, he still finds himself confirmed in *religion as religion*. Here we have the root of the false positivism of Hegel, or his only *apparently* critical position, which Feuerbach characterizes as positing, negating and the restoring of religion or theology—which is, however, to be conceived more generally. Thus reason is by itself in unreason as unreason. Man who has recognized that in law, politics, etc., he is leading an alienated life, pursues in this alienated life, as such, his true human life. In this way, true *knowledge* and *life* are self-affirmation and self-confirmation in contradiction with itself, both in regard to knowledge and to the essence of the object.

Thus nothing more need be said of Hegel's adaptation to religion, the state, etc., for this lie is the lie of his principle.

When I know that religion is alienated human self-consciousness, I therefore know that in it, as religion, I confirm, not my self-consciousness, but my alienated self-consciousness. I therefore know my self-consciousness, belonging to itself and to its essence, is confirmed not in religion but, on the contrary, in a religion that has *negated, transcended*.

In Hegel, the negation of negation is, therefore, not the confirmation of true essence, namely, through negation of apparent essence, but the confirmation of apparent essence, or of alienated essence in its denial, or the denial of this apparent essence as an objective essence existing outside man and independent of him, and its transformation into the subject. Therefore, transcendence plays a peculiar role, in which both negation, and preservation or affirmation are united.

Thus, for example, in Hegel's *Philosophy of Right*, transcended *private right* is *morality*; transcended morality is the same as *family*; transcended family the same as *civil society*; transcended civil society the same as the *state*; transcended state the same as *world history*. In *reality*, however, private right, morality, family, civil society, the state, etc., remain in existence. Only they have become *moments*, forms of existence of men, which are not valid in their isolation, which resolve and produce one another, etc. Moment of the movement.

In their actual existence their moving essence is concealed. It appears and is revealed only in thought, in philosophy. That is why my own true religious existence is my religious-philosophical existence, my true political existence my existence in the philosophy of right, my true natural existence my existence in the philosophy of nature, my true artistic existence my existence in the philosophy of art, my true human existence my philosophic existence. In the same way, the philosophies of religion, nature, the state, and art are the true existence of religion, state, nature, and art. If, however, the *philosophy of religion*, etc., is for me the only true existence of religion, I am truly religious only as a philosopher of religion, and thus I deny actual religiousness and the actually religious man. But at the same time I affirm them, partly within my own existence or within alien existence which I counterpose to them, for this is only their philosophic expression; partly, in their peculiar original form, for to me they are valid only as apparent otherness, as allegories, as configurations hidden under sensuous husks of their own true existence, which is my *philosophic* existence. In the same way, transcended quality is the same as *quantity*; transcended quantity the same as *measure*; transcended measure the same as *essence*; transcended essence the same as *appearance*; transcended appearance the same as *actuality*; transcended actuality the same as *notion*; transcended notion the same as *objectivity*; transcended objectivity the same as *absolute idea*; transcended absolute idea the same as *nature*; transcended nature the same as *subjective spirit*; transcended subjective spirit the same as *ethical, objective* spirit; transcended ethical spirit the same as *art*; transcended art the same as *religion*; transcended religion the same as *absolute knowledge*.

On the one hand, this transcendence is a transcendence of essence insofar as it is *thought*, and hence, private property, as *thought*, is transcended in *thoughts* of morality. And because thinking fancies itself to be directly the other of itself, sensuous actuality, therefore, its action seems to it also to be *sensuously actual*. Thus, this transcendence through thinking which permits its object to remain in actuality, believes it has *actually* overcome the object. And, on the other hand, because the object has now become for it a moment of thought, this object is also taken by it in its actuality, as the self-confirmation of itself, or self-consciousness, or abstraction.

In one respect, therefore, the existence which Hegel *transcends* in philosophy is not *actual* religion, the state, nature, but religion as an object of knowledge, as a dogmatism. The same is true of jurisprudence, the science of the state, the science of nature. On the other hand, he opposes both the *actual* essence and direct unphilosophic science, or the unphilosophic *notions* of this essence. He therefore contradicts their accepted notions.

In another respect, the religious, etc., man can find in Hegel his final confirmation.

Now we must try to grasp the *positive* moments of the Hegelian dialectic, within the limits of the category of alienation.

(a) *Transcendence*, as objective movement, *withdrawing* externalization *into itself.* This is the insight, expressed within alienation, of the *appropriation* of objective essence through the transcendence of its alienation, the alienated insight into the actual objectification of man, into the actual appropriation of his objective essence through the destruction of the *alienated* determination of the objective world, through its transcendence in its alienated existence. Just as atheism, as transcendence of God, is the becoming of theoretical humanism, and communism, as transcendence of private property, is the vindication of actual human living as its own property, which is the becoming of practical humanism, so atheism is humanism mediated by transcendence of religion, and communism is humanism mediated by the transcendence of private property. Only by the transcendence of this mediation, which is nevertheless a necessary presupposition, does there arise *positive* Humanism, beginning from itself.

Atheism and communism, however, are not a flight or abstraction from, nor a loss of, the objective world produced by man or of his essential capacities brought to objectivity. It is not a poverty returning to unnatural, undeveloped simplicity. Atheism and communism are rather the first actual process of becoming, the actualization of his essence become actual for man, and of his essence as actual.

Thus Hegel, insofar as he grasps the meaning of the *positive* sense of the negation related to itself, even if in an alienated way, conceives self-alienation, externalization of essence, contraposition and the separation of men from reality as a process of self-conquest, alteration, or essence, objectification and realization. Briefly, within an abstract framework, he considers labor to be the self-productive act of man, the relation of himself as an alien essence, and its manifestation as alien essence, as the developing consciousness and *life of the species.*

(b) In Hegel, apart from, or rather as a consequence of the perversity already described, this act appears *firstly* as *formal* because it is abstract, because human essence itself is regarded only as an abstract thinking essence, as self-consciousness.

Secondly, because the conception is *abstract* and *formal*, transcendence of alienation becomes confirmation of alienation. But as this movement of *self-production*, or *self-objectification*, as self-externalization and self-alienation is, for Hegel, the *absolute*, therefore its self-purpose, resting in itself and arrived at its essence, is the final *expression* of *human* life. This movement, in its abstract form as dialectics, is, therefore, regarded as *truly human living.* Yet, because it is an abstraction, an alienation of human life, it is regarded as a *divine* process, hence as the divine process of man, a process carried out, in distinction from himself, by its abstract, pure, absolute essence.

Thirdly, this process must have a bearer, a subject, but the subject emerges only as a result. This result, the subject knowing itself as absolute self-consciousness, is, therefore, *God, absolute spirit, the Idea knowing and affirming itself.* Actual man and actual nature become mere predicates, symbols of this concealed, unactual man, and this unactual nature. Subject and predicate, therefore, have a relation of absolute inversion to each other, mystical *subject-object*, or a *subjectivity extending beyond the object, the absolute subject as a process*, a subject alienating itself and returning to itself from this alienation, but returning it at the same time into itself and the subject as this process, the pure restless circling within itself. We have a *formal* and *abstract* conception of the human act of self-production or the act of self-objectification of man.

Since Hegel supposes man to be the same as *self-consciousness*, the alienated object, the alienated actual essence of man is nothing else than consciousness, is only the thought of alienation, its abstract and, therefore, empty unactual expression, negation. Therefore, the transcendence of this externalization is likewise only an abstract empty transcendence of the former empty abstraction, *the negation of the negation*. The full living sensuous, concrete activity of self-objectification, therefore, becomes its mere abstraction, *absolute negativity*, an abstraction which is, again, fixed as such and is thought as an independent activity, as simply activity. Because this so-called negativity is nothing but the abstract, *empty* form of the former actual living act, its content also can be merely *formal* content produced by the abstraction from all content. Therefore, the *abstract formulas*, forms of thought, logical categories torn away from *actual* spirit and from *actual* nature are the universal forms of abstractions, pertaining to every content and, therefore, indifferent to all content and for that reason applicable to any content. (Further down we will develop the logical content of absolute negativity.)

The positive contribution which Hegel has made in his speculative *Logic* is this: The *definite concepts*, the universal, *fixed* forms of thought represent, in their independence of nature and spirit, the necessary result of the universal alienation of human essence and, hence, also of human thinking. And therefore Hegel has presented and collected them together as moments of the process of abstraction. For example, transcended being is essence, transcended essence is notion, transcended notion is the Absolute Idea. But what, then, is the Absolute Idea? It, in its turn, transcends itself, if it is not going to carry out again the whole previous act of abstraction, and if it is not going to be satisfied with being a totality of abstractions, or the abstraction grasping itself. But the abstraction grasping itself as abstraction knows itself as nothing. It must abandon the abstraction and arrive at an essence which is its very opposite, i.e., *Nature*. The whole *Logic* is, therefore, the proof that abstract thinking is nothing for itself, that the Absolute Idea is nothing for itself until nature is something.

The Absolute Idea, the abstract Idea which "when viewed on the point of this, its unity with itself, is *Intuition*." (Hegel, *Encyclopedia*, 3, Ans. p. 22.)[4] Which, "in its own absolute truth ... resolves to let the 'moment' of its particularity or of the first characterization and other-being, the immediate idea, as its reflected image, go forth freely

---

4   Hegel, *Logic,* p. 379.—RD.

as Nature." This whole Idea, behaving in such a strange and baroque way, which has caused the Hegelians tremendous headaches, is nothing else than mere abstraction, i.e., the abstract thinker who, made clever by experience and enlightened beyond its truth, has decided under many false and still abstract conditions, to *abandon* himself and to substitute his otherness, the particular, the determined, for his self-contained being, his nothingness, his universality and his indeterminateness. It decides to release freely from itself Nature, which it had concealed within itself only as an abstraction, as a thing of thought, i.e., to abandon abstraction and to observe Nature free from abstraction. The abstract Idea which becomes immediate intuition is nothing but abstract thinking which abandons itself and decides to *intuit*. This whole transition from the *Logic* to the *Philosophy of Nature* is merely the transition from *abstraction* to *intuition*, a transition difficult for the abstract thinker to execute and, therefore, described by him in such a fantastic fashion. The *mystical* feeling which drives the philosophers from abstract thinking into intuition is boredom, the yearning for a content. Man, alienated from himself, is also the thinker who is alienated from his essence, i.e., his natural and human essence. His thoughts are therefore fixed spirits, residing outside Nature and Man. Hegel has gathered and imprisoned all these fixed spirits in his *Logic* and has conceived each of them first as negation, as externalization of human thinking, then as negation of negation, i.e., of transcendence of this externalization, as the actual expression of human thinking. But since it is still caught in the alienation, this negation of the negation is partly the restoration of this thought in its alienation, partly a remaining in the final act, the relation to itself to its externalization as the true existence of these fixed spirits. (That is, for the former fixed abstractions Hegel has substituted the act of abstraction, circling within itself.) Thereby, he has performed the service of tracing the origin of all these improper conceptions of the individual philosophies according to their standpoint. He has collected them and, instead of a determinate abstraction, has created the abstraction of its entire range as the object of the critical philosophy. We will see later why Hegel separates thinking from the subject. It is now, however, already clear that if there is no man, the expression of his essence can also not be human; hence, that thinking cannot be regarded as the expression of human essence, considered as a human natural subject with eyes and ears, living in society and in the world and in nature. Partly, insofar as this abstraction comprehends itself and experiences about itself an infinite boredom, there appears in Hegel the abandonment of abstract thought which only moves in thought, which is without eyes, without teeth, without ears, without anything, namely, as the decision to acknowledge *Nature* as Essence and to apply itself to intuition.

But also, *Nature*, taken in its abstraction, for itself, fixed in its separation from man, is *nothing* for Man. It is self-evident that the abstract thinker, who has decided to intuit Nature, serves it abstractly. Just as Nature remained enclosed by the thinker, in its concealed and mysterious form, as Absolute Idea, as a thing of thought, so the thinker in releasing it has in truth released only this *abstract Nature* from himself, only the abstraction of Nature, although with the conviction that it is the otherness of thought, that it is actual, observed nature, distinguished from abstract thinking. Or, to speak human language, the abstract thinker in his intuition of Nature experiences that the essences which he meant to create in the divine Dialectics out of nothing, out of pure abstraction, as pure products of the work of thought, weaving in itself and nowhere looking out into actuality, are nothing but *abstractions of the determinations of Nature*. The whole of Nature thus repeats for him the logical abstractions, except in a sensuous external form. He again analyzes it and these abstractions. Thus his conception of Nature is only the act which confirms his abstraction from the observation of Nature, the generative process of his abstraction consciously repeated by himself.

We will in a moment examine the Hegelian determination and the transition from Nature to Mind.

"Nature, as Idea, has resulted in the form of Otherness," the course of this abstraction.

In this way, for example, time is like the negativity which relates itself to itself (p. 238, 1.c.). Transcended becoming of a something corresponds in natural philosophy to the transcended movement as matter. Light is the natural form of reflection in itself. Body, as *moon* and comet, is the natural philosophical form of the *opposition* which according to the *Logic* is, on the one hand, the *positive* resting in itself, on the other, the *negative* resting in itself, etc. The earth is the *natural* philosophical form of logical *ground*, as the *negative* unity of opposites, etc.

Nature as Nature, i.e., insofar as it still distinguishes itself sensuously from the above-mentioned secret meaning hidden in it, Nature, separated and distinguished from these abstractions, is nothing, a nothing preserving itself as nothing. It is senseless or has only the sense of an externality which has been transcended.

"In the finite-*teleological* standpoint, we find the correct presupposition, that Nature does not contain in itself an absolute purpose" (p. 225). Its purpose is the confirmation of abstraction. "Nature has shown itself to be the Idea in the *form of otherness*. Since the Idea thus exists as the negative of itself or external to itself, Nature likewise is not external, except relative to this Idea, but Externality constitutes the determination under which the Idea is as Nature" (p. 227). *Externality* is here not to be understood as sensuousness expressing itself and revealed in light and to sensuous man. Externality is to be taken here in the sense of externalization, of a lack, of an inadequacy which ought not to be. For the true is still the Idea. Nature is only the *form of its otherness*. And since abstract thinking is the *essence*, whatever is outside of it is, according to its essence, only external. The abstract thinker acknowledges at the same time that sensuousness is the essence of Nature, externality in opposition to self-sufficient thinking.

But at the same time he expresses this opposition in the following way, that this externality of Nature is its opposition to thinking, the latter's deficiency, and thus that insofar as it is distinguished from abstraction, it is a deficient being, a being which is not only deficient for me, in my eyes, but a self-deficient being which has something outside itself which it lacks, i.e., its essence is something other than itself. Therefore, for the abstract thinker, Nature must transcend itself, since it is presupposed by him as an essence potentially transcended.

> From our point of view, Mind has for its *presupposition* Nature, of which it is the truth, and for that reason its *absolute prius*. In this, its truth, Nature has vanished, and mind has resulted as the "Idea" entered into possession of itself, whose object as well as subject is the concept. This identity is *absolute negativity*—because in Nature the concept has its completely external objectivity which has however transcended its externalization and it has in this become identical with itself. Thus at the same time it *is* this identity only so far as it is a return out of nature. (p. 392, ¶381)[5]
>
> *Revelation*, which as the *abstract* idea is an immediate transition, the *becoming* of nature, is as revelation of spirit, which is free, the *positing* of nature as its world; a *positing* which as reflection is at the same time presupposition of the world as independent nature. Revelation in the concept is creation of nature as its being, in which it gives itself the affirmation and truth of its freedom.
>
> The *Absolute* is spirit; this is the highest definition of the Absolute. (¶384)

---

5 *Philosophy of Mind.* Pars. 381 and 384 are the only reference in Marx's Essay to the *Philosophy of Mind.* It is clear that this essay of Marx's is unfinished.

Bibliography

Works by Raya Dunayevskaya

The most complete source for Dunayevskaya's works is The Raya Dunayevskaya Collection—Marxist-Humanism: A Half-Century of Its World Development and Supplement to the Raya Dunayevskaya Collection. The bulk of the Collection, the Supplement, and Guides to the Collection and Supplement are on the Internet at www.rayadunayevskaya.org. Originals are on deposit at Wayne State University Archives of Labor and Urban Affairs, Detroit, Michigan. The Raya Dunayevskaya Archive in the Marxist Internet Archives (http://www.marxists.org/archive/dunayevskaya/index.htm) contains many documents, some of which are not available elsewhere online. All the issues of News & Letters, the newspaper Dunayevskaya founded and regularly wrote for from 1955 to 1987, are online in pdf form at https://newsandletters.org/back-issues/. The issues up to December 2009 are also available at https://www.marxists.org/history/etol/newspape/news-and-letters/.

●●●

Dunayevskaya, Raya, *American Civilization on Trial: Black Masses as Vanguard.* Chicago: News and Letters, 2003. [Originally signed by the National Editorial Board of News and Letters Committees.]

Dunayevskaya, Raya, "Analysis of the Russian Economy," *New International*, December, 1942, January, 1943, February, 1943, December, 1946, and January, 1947.

Dunayevskaya, Raya, "A New Revision of Marxian Economics," The *American Economic Review,* September 1944.

Dunayevskaya, Raya [F. Forest], "Auto Union Relief Caravan Hailed in Coal Mining Town," *The Militant,* Vol. 14, No.11, March 13, 1950.

Dunayevskaya, Raya, "The Beria Purge" (unsigned), *Correspondence,* October 3, 1953.

Dunayevskaya, Raya, "Bureaucratie et capitalisme d'état," by Raya Dunayevskaya, *Arguments* No.17, Paris 1960.

Dunayevskaya, Raya, "The Case of Eugene Varga," RDC, pp. 12456–62, May 1949.

Dunayevskaya, Raya, "Critique of Althusser's Anti-Hegelianism," *News & Letters*, October, 1969.

Dunayevskaya, Raya, *Crossroads of History: Marxist-Humanist Writings on the Middle East by Raya Dunayevskaya.* Chicago: News and Letters, 2013.

Dunayevskaya, Raya, *Dialectics of Liberation.* Detroit: News and Letters, 1974.

Dunayevskaya, Raya, "Draft Perspectives Thesis, 1977–1978: Time Is Running Out" (signed "The Resident Editorial Board"), *News & Letters,* August-September, 1977.

Dunayevskaya, Raya, *A History of Worldwide Revolutionary Developments: 25 Years of Marxist-Humanism in the U.S.* Detroit: News and Letters, 1980.

Dunayevskaya, Raya, *Marx's "Capital" and Today's Global Crisis.* Detroit: News and Letters, 1978.

Dunayevskaya, Raya, *Marxism and Freedom, from 1776 until Today.* New York: Humanity Books, 2000.

Dunayevskaya, Raya, *The Marxist-Humanist Theory of State-Capitalism.* Chicago: News and Letters, 1992.

Dunayevskaya, Raya, *Nationalism, Communism, Marxist-Humanism and the Afro-Asian Revolutions.* Chicago: News and Letters, 1984.

Dunayevskaya, Raya, "New Developments in Stalin's Russia," *Labor Action*, October, 1946.

Dunayevskaya, Raya, *The Philosophic Moment of Marxist-Humanism: Two Historic-Philosophic Writings by Raya Dunayevskaya.* Chicago: News & Letters, 1989.

Dunayevskaya, Raya, *Philosophy and Revolution: From Hegel to Sartre and from Marx to Mao.* Lanham, Md.: Lexington Books, 2003.

Dunayevskaya, Raya, *Political Letters,* RDC, pp. 2906–3152, 1961–1966.

Dunayevskaya, Raya, "Post-Mao China: What Now?" in *New Essays.* Detroit: News & Letters, 1977.

Dunayevskaya, Raya, *The Power of Negativity: Selected Writings on the Dialectic in Hegel and Marx.* Lanham, Md.: Lexington Books, 2002.

Dunayevskaya, Raya, "Revision or Reaffirmation of Marxism," *American Economic Review*, Vol. 35, No. 4, September, 1945.

Dunayevskaya, Raya, *Rosa Luxemburg, Women's Liberation, and Marx's Philosophy of Revolution.* Urbana and Chicago: University of Illinois Press, 1991.

Dunayevskaya, Raya, *Russia: From Proletarian Revolution to State-Capitalist Counter-Revolution: Selected Writings by Raya Dunayevskaya.* Leiden: Brill, 2017.

Dunayevskaya, Raya, "Special Feature" (unsigned), *Correspondence,* April 30, 1953.

Dunayevskaya, Raya, "Stagnation of U.S. Economy," *News & Letters,* January 1960.

Dunayevskaya, Raya, "State Capitalism and the Bureaucrats," *Socialist Leader,* January 2, 1960.

Dunayevskaya, Raya, "Then and Now: 1920 and 1953," *Correspondence,* April 16, 1953.

Dunayevskaya, Raya, " 'True Rebirth' or Wholesale Revision of Marxism?" *News & Letters,* May and June–July, 1970.

Dunayevskaya, Raya, "Draft Perspectives, 1984–85: Where are the 1980s Going? The Imperative Need for a Totally New Direction in Uprooting Capitalism-Imperialism," *News & Letters,* May 1984.

Dunayevskaya, Raya, "Why Did Stalin Behave That Way?" (unsigned), *Correspondence,* March 19, 1953.

Dunayevskaya, Raya, *Women's Liberation and the Dialectics of Revolution: Reaching for the Future.* Detroit: Wayne State University Press, 1996.

Dunayevskaya, Raya, *The Year of Only Eight Months,* RDC, pp. 10690–10726.

Dunayevskaya, Raya and V.I. Lenin, *Philosophic Notes.* Detroit: News & Letters, 1956.

Dunayevskaya, Raya, Herbert Marcuse, and Erich Fromm, *The Dunayevskaya-Marcuse-Fromm Correspondence, 1954–1978: Dialogues on Hegel, Marx, and Critical Theory.* Lanham, Md.: Lexington Books, 2012.

Dunayevskaya, Raya, Harry McShane, Ivan Svitak, and X, *Czechoslovakia: Revolution and Counter Revolution* (Detroit: News and Letters, 1968).

Phillips, Andy, and Raya Dunayevskaya, *The Coal Miners' General Strike of 1949–50 and the Birth of Marxist-Humanism in the U.S.* Chicago: News and Letters, 1984.

Savio, Mario, Eugene Walker, and Raya Dunayevskaya, *The Free Speech Movement and the Negro Revolution.* Detroit: News & Letters, 1965.

Works by Karl Marx

Many works cited are included in the widely available Karl Marx, Frederick Engels *Collected Works* (MECW), 50 vols. New York: International Publishers, 1975–2004.

Marx, Karl, *Address to the Communist League, March 1850,* MECW 10, pp. 277–87.

Marx, Karl, *The American Journalism of Marx and Engels.* New York: The American Library, 1966.

Marx, Karl, *Capital,* Vol. l, trans. Samuel Moore and Edward Aveling. Chicago: Charles H. Kerr, 1909; reprinted New York: International Publishers, 1967.

Marx, Karl, *Capital,* Vol. I, trans. Ben Fowkes. London: Penguin Books, 1990.

Marx, Karl, *Capital,* Vol. II, trans. Ernest Untermann. Chicago: Charles H. Kerr, 1910.

Marx, Karl, *Capital,* Vol. II, trans. David Fernbach. London: Penguin Books, 1992.

Marx, Karl, *Capital,* Vol. III, trans. Ernest Untermann. Chicago: Charles H. Kerr, 1909.

Marx, Karl, *Capital,* Vol. III, trans. David Fernbach. London: Penguin Books, 1991.

Marx, Karl, *The Civil War in France,* MECW 22, pp. 307–59.

Marx, Karl, "Contribution to the Critique of Hegel's Philosophy of Law," MECW 3, pp. 3–130.

Marx, Karl, *A Contribution to the Critique of Political Economy.* Chicago: Charles H. Kerr, 1904.

Marx, Karl, *Critique of the Gotha Program,* MECW 24, pp. 74–99.

Marx, Karl, "Difference between the Democritean and Epicurean Philosophy of Nature," MECW 1, pp. 25–107.

Marx, Karl, *The Eighteenth Brumaire of Louis Bonaparte,* MECW 11, pp. 99–197.

Marx, Karl, *The Ethnological Notebooks of Karl Marx.* Assen, The Netherlands: Van Gorcum, 1972.

Marx, Karl, *Grundrisse.* London: Penguin Books, 1973.

Marx, Karl, "Inaugural Address of the Working Men's International Association," MECW 20, pp. 5–13.

Marx, Karl, *The Karl Marx Library Vol. VI: On Education, Women, and Children.* New York: McGraw-Hill Book Co., 1975.

Marx, Karl, "The Labor Question," MECW 12, pp. 460–63.

Marx, Karl, "Notebooks on Epicurean Philosophy," MECW 1, pp. 403–509.

Marx, Karl, "On the Jewish Question," MECW 3, pp. 146–74.

Marx, Karl, *On the First International.* New York: McGraw-Hill, 1973.

Marx, Karl, "The Opium Trade," in *On Colonialism.* Moscow: Foreign Languages Publishing House, 1960, pp. 185–88.

Marx, Karl, *Poverty of Philosophy.* Chicago: Charles H. Kerr, 1906.

Marx, Karl, *Pre-Capitalist Economic Formations*, with an Introduction by Eric J. Hobsbawm. New York: International Publishers, 1965.

Marx, Karl, "Provisional Rules of the Association," MECW 20, pp. 14–16.

Marx, Karl, *Texts on Method*, translated and edited by Terrell Carver. Oxford: Basil Blackwell, 1975.

Marx, Karl, *The Theories of Surplus Value.* London: Lawrence & Wishart, 1951.

Marx, Karl, and Frederick Engels, *Arkhiv Marksa y Engelsa*, Vol. 9, Leningrad: Marx-Engels-Lenin Institute, 1941.

Marx, Karl, and Frederick Engels, *The Civil War in the United States.* New York: International Publishers, 1970.

Marx, Karl, and Frederick Engels, *The Communist Manifesto*, MECW 6, pp. 477–519.

Marx, Karl, and Frederick Engels, *The Communist Manifesto,* preface to the 1882 Russian edition, MECW 24, pp. 425–26.

Marx, Karl, and Frederick Engels, *The German Ideology*, MECW 5, pp. 19–539.

Marx, Karl, and Frederick Engels, *The Holy Family*, MECW 4, pp. 5–211.

General Bibliography

Abahlali baseMjondolo, "South African activists slam Communist Party," *News & Letters,* November–December 2010.

Adorno, Theodor, *Hegel: Three Studies.* Cambridge, Mass.: MIT Press, 1993.

Adorno, Theodor, *Negative Dialectics.* New York: Seabury Press, 1973.

Albers, Patricia, and Beatrice Medicine, ed., *The Hidden Half: Studies of Plains Indian Women.* Washington, D.C.: University Press of America, 1983.

Althusser, Louis, *For Marx.* London: Penguin Press, 1969.

Althusser, Louis, *Lenin and Philosophy and Other Essays*, trans. Ben Brewster. London: New Left Books, 1971.

Anderson, Kevin, "The French Edition of *Capital,* 100 Years After." Paper presented at the Conference of the Eastern Sociological Society, Philadelphia, March 19, 1982.

Anderson, Kevin, "The 'Unknown' Marx's *Capital*, Vol. I: The French Edition of 1872–75, 100 Years Later," *Review of Radical Political Economics*, 15:4 (1983).

Arendt, Hannah, *The Human Condition*. Chicago: University of Chicago Press, 1958.

Automation and Technological Change, Hearings before Joint Commttee on the Economic Report, 84th Congress, Washington, D.C., 1955.

Baldan, Attilio, "Gramsci as an Historian of the 1930s," *Telos* No.31, Spring 1977.

Baran, Paul, "New Trends in Russian Economic Thinking," *American Ecnomic Review,* Vol. 34, No.4, December, 1944.

Barreno, Maria Isabel, Maria Teresa Horta, and Maria Vello da Costa, *The Three Marias: New Portuguese Letters*. Garden City, New York: Doubleday, 1975.

Barry, Kevin A., "The French Edition of *Capital,* 100 Years After," *News & Letters,* October 1981.

BBC report, "1983: Grenada's prime minister 'assassinated,'" October 20, 1983.

Bell, Daniel, *The End of Ideology: On the Exhaustion of Political Ideas in the 1950s.* Glencoe: Free Press, 1960.

Bell, Daniel, *Work and its discontents: The Cult of Efficiency in America*. Boston, Beacon Press, 1956.

Bendix, Reinhard, and Seymour Martin Lipset, ed., *Class, Status and Power: A Reader in Social Stratification*. Glencoe, Ill.: The Free Press, 1953.

Blackstock, Paul W., and Bert F. Hoselitz, ed., *The Russian Menace to Europe*. Glencoe, Illinois: Free Press, 1952.

Blake, William, "London," *Songs of Experience.*

"British Civilization on Trial," May–June, 1981, *Marxist-Humanism.*

Carver, Terrell, "Marx, Engels and Dialectics," *Political Studies*, Vol. 28, No.3, September 1980.

Carver, Terrell, *Marx and Engels: The Intellectual Relationship*. Bloomington: Indiana Univ. Press, 1983.

Carver, Terrell, "Marxism as Method," in *After Marx,* edited by T. Ball and J. Farr. Cambridge: Cambridge University Press, 1984.

Carver, Terrell, "Marx's Commodity Fetishism," *Inquiry,* 18, 1975, pp. 39–63.

Chapman, John J. *The Selected Writings of John Jay Chapman.* New York: Farrar, Strauss and Cudahy, 1957.

Chira, Susan, "Korea is Breeding a New College Radical," *The New York Times,* June 17, 1986.

Corey, Lewis, *The Decline of American Capitalism.* New York: Covici, Friede, 1934.

Coy, Peter, "Marx to Market," *Businessweek,* September 14, 2011.

Current, Richard N., "Lincoln and the Proclamation," *The Progressive*, December 1962.

Darnton, John, "Women Add a Certain Pizazz to Portugal's Politics," *The New York Times*, Feb. 24, 1984.

Day, Richard B., "The Theory of Long Waves: Kondratiev, Trotsky, Mandel," *New Left Review*, No. 99, September–October, 1976.

de Beauvoir, Simone, *The Second Sex*, trans. H.M. Parshley. New York: Bantam, 1961.

Denby, Charles, *Indignant Heart: A Black Worker's Journal*. Detroit: Wayne State University Press, 1989.

Denby, et al, *Workers Battle Automation*. Detroit: News and Letters, 1960.

Diamond, Stanley, "The Marxist Tradition as a Dialectical Anthropology," *Dialectical Anthropology*, Vol. 1, No. 1, January 1975.

Ding Ling, "Thoughts on March 8," in *I Myself Am a Woman: Selected Writings of Ding Ling*, edited by Tani E. Barlow with Gary J. Bjorge. Boston: Beacon Press, 2001.

Dollard, John, *Caste and Class in a Southern Town*. New York: Harper, 1937.

Draper, Hal, Foreword, in *Karl Marx and Friedrich Engels: Writings on the Paris Commune*. New York: Monthly Review Press, 1971.

Draper, Hal, *Karl Marx's Theory of Revolution*, 5 volumes. New York: Monthly Review Press, 1977–2005.

Draper, Hal, "Marx and Engels on Women's Liberation," *International Socialism*, July/August 1970.

Draper, Hal, *Marx-Engels Register*. New York: Schocken Books, 1985.

Drucker, Peter F., "The Changed World Economy," *Foreign Affairs*, Vol. 64, No. 4, Spring, 1986.

Drucker, Peter F., *The Landmarks of Tomorrow/* New York: Harper and Brothers, 1959.

Dupré, Louis, *Marx's Social Critique of Culture/* New Haven: Yale University Press, 1983.

Dupré, Louis, *The Philosophical Foundations of Marxism*. New York: Harcourt, Brace & World, Inc., 1966.

Economic and Social Implications of Automation: Abstracts of Recent Literature. East Lansing, Mich.:Michigan State University, 1958.

Engels, Frederick, *Herr Eugen Dühring's Revolution in Science [Anti-Dühring]*. New York: International Publishers, 1987 [MECW 25, pp. 5–309].

Engels, Frederick, *The Origin of the Family, Private Property and the State*. New York: International Publishers, 1972, 1975 [MECW 26, pp. 129–276].

Engels, Frederick, *The Peasant War in Germany*. New York: International Publishers, 1978 [MECW 10, pp. 397–482].

Engels, Frederick, Paul Lafargue and Laura Lafargue, *Correspondence*, Vol. I. Moscow: Foreign Languages Publishing House, 1959.

Fanon, Frantz Fanon, *The Wretched of the Earth*. New York: Grove Press, 1966.

Fejtö, François, *Behind the Rape of Hungary*. New York: David McKay Company, 1957.

Firth, Raymond, "The Sceptical Anthropologist? Social Anthropology and Marxist Views on Society," in *Marxist Analyses and Social Anthropology*. London: Malaby Press, 1975.

Foster, Peter, "West Germany: The Troubled Giant," *Financial Post*. Toronto, Sept. 17, 1977.

Fredericks, John [John Dwyer], "Oil and Labor," *Fourth International,* May 1958, August 1948, and September 1948.

Freymond, Jacques, ed., *La Première Internationale, Receuil et documents,* Vol. II. Geneva: Librairie Droz, 1962.

Fromm, Erich, *Marx's Concept of Man.* New York: Frederick Ungar Publishing Co., 1961.

Fromm, Erich, ed., *Socialist Humanism.* New York: Doubleday, 1965.

Galbraith, John Kenneth, *The Affluent Society.* Boston: Houghton Mifflin, 1958.

Garrison, Wendell Phillips, and Francis Jackson Garrison, *William Lloyd Garrison—The Story of His Life.* New York: Century Co., 1885–89.

Geras, Norman, *The Legacy of Rosa Luxemburg.* London: NLB, 1976.

Gilman-Opalsky, Richard, *Specters of Revolt: On the Intellect of Insurrection and Philosophy from Below.* London: Repeater Books, 2016.

Goldmann, Lucien, "The Dialectic Today," in *Cultural Creation in Modern Society.* Telos Press, 1976.

Gramsci, Antonio, *The Modern Prince and Other Writings.* London, New York: International Publishers, 1957.

Gramsci, Antonio *Selections from Political Writings, 1910–1920,* edited by Quintin Hoare, translated by John Mathews. London: Lawrence & Wishart, 1977.

Gramsci, Antonio, *Selections from the Prison Notebooks.* London: Lawrence & Wishart, 1971.

Graves, John Temple, "The Southern Negro and the War Crisis," *The Virginia Quarterly Review,* Vol. 18, No. 4, Autumn, 1942.

Guettel, Charnie, *Marxism and Feminism.* Toronto: The Women's Press, 1974.

Hacker, Louis M., *The Triumph of American Capitalism: The Development of Forces in American History to the End of the Nineteenth Century.* New York: Simon and Schuster, 1940.

Hamilton, Mary, Louise Inghram, et al, *Freedom Riders Speak for Themselves.* Detroit: News & Letters, 1961.

Harman, Chris, "Gramsci vs. Eurocommunism," *International Socialism,* No. 98, May 1977, and No. 99, June 1977.

Harrell, Bill J., "Marx and Critical Thought." *Paunch* No. 44–45, May 1976.

Hegel, G.W.F., *Hegel's Logic,* trans. William Wallace. Oxford: Oxford University Press, 1892.

Hegel, G.W.F., *Natural Law,* translated by T.M. Knox with an introduction by H.B. Acton. Philadelphia: University of Pennsylvania Press, 1975.

Hegel, G.W.F., *The Phenomenology of Mind,* translated by J.B. Baillie. New York: The MacMillan Co., 1931.

Hegel, G.W.F., *The Philosophy of History.* New York: Dover, 1956.

Hegel, G.W.F., *Philosophy of Mind,* translated by William Wallace. Oxford: Oxford University Press, 1892.

Hegel, G.W.F., *Science of Logic*, translated by A.V. Miller. N.Y., Humanities Press.

Hegel, G.W.F., *Science of Logic*, Vol. II, translated by W.H. Johnston and L.G. Struthers. New York: The MacMillan Co., 1951.

Henri-Lévy, Bernard, *Barbarism with a Human Face*, translated by George Holoch. New York: Harper & Row, 1979.

Hilferding, Rudolf, *Finance Capital*. London and New York: Routledge, 2006.

Hill, Robert A., ed., *The Marcus Garvey and Universal Negro Improvement Association Papers,* 10 volumes. Berkeley, Calif.: Univ. of. California Press, 1983–2006.

Hobsbawm, Eric J., ed., *The History of Marxism,* Vol. I. London: Indiana University Press and Harvester Press, 1982.

Jacobson, Howard B., and Joseph S. Roucek, eds., *Automation and Society.* New York: Philosophical Library, 1959.

James, C.L.R., *Mariners, Renegades and Castaways: The Story of Herman Melville and the World We Live In.* London: Allison & Busby, 1984.

James, C.L.R., *Notes on Dialectics: Hegel, Marx, Lenin.* Westport, Conn.: Lawrence Hill & Co., 1980.

James, C.L.R., *State Capitalism and World Revolution: Written in Collaboration with Raya Dunayevskaya and Grace Lee.* Oakland, Calif.: PM Press, 2013.

"The Japan They Don't Talk About," *NBC White Paper,* April 22, 1986.

Jonas, Norman, "The Hollow Corporation," *Businessweek*, March 3, 1986.

Joravsky, David, *Soviet Marxism and Natural Science, 1917–1932.* New York: Columbia University Press, 1961.

Kamenka, Eugene, *The Ethical Foundations of Marxism.* New York: Frederick A. Praeger, 1962.

Karpushin, V.A., "Marx's Working Out of the Materialist Dialectics in the Economic-Philosophic Manuscripts in the Year 1844," *Voprosy Filosofii* (*Questions of Philosophy*), No. 3/1955.

Kennan, George F., *American Diplomacy, 1900–1950*, by George F. Kennan. Chicago: University of Chicago Press, 1951.

Keynes, John Maynard, *General Theory of Employment, Interest and Money.* London: Stellar Classics, 2016.

Kolakowski, Leszek, *Toward a Marxist Humanism.* New York: Grove Press, 1969.

Kornhauser, William, *The Politics of Mass Society.* Glencoe, Ill.: The. Free Press. 1959.

Kosik, Karel, *Dialectics of the Concrete.* Dordrecht, Holland and Boston: D. Reidel Publishing Company, 1976.

Krader, Lawrence, "The Works of Marx and Engels in Ethnology Compared," *International Review of Social History*, Vol. XVIII, Part 2, 1973.

Krader, Lawrence, and M.M. Kovalevskiĭ. *The Asiatic Mode of Production: Sources, Development and Critique in the Writings of Karl Marx.* Assen: Van Gorcum, 1975.

Kronholz, June, "A Year after Marcos, Celebration is Quirky as Coup Itself Was," *The Wall Street Journal*, Feb. 26, 1987.

Kuznets, Simon, *Postwar Economic Growth*. Cambridge: Harvard University Press, 1964.

Leopold, Labedz, ed., *Revisionism*. New York: Frederick A. Praeger, 1962.

Lange, Oscar, *Political Economy*. New York: Macmillan, 1963.

Lasky, Melvin J., ed., *The Hungarian Revolution*. New York: Frederick A. Praeger, 1957.

Lenin, V.I., Abstract of Hegel's *Science of Logic*, in *Collected Works*, Vol. 38, pp. 85–238. Moscow: Foreign Languages Publishing House, 1961.

Lenin, V.I., *Collected Works*, 45 volumes. Moscow: Progress Publishers, 1960–70.

Lenin, V.I., "The Immediate Tasks of the Soviet Government," in *Collected Works*, Vol. 27, pp. 258–59.

Lenin, V.I., "Last Testament," in *Collected Works*, Vol, 36, pp. 593–611.

Lenin, V.I., "On the Significance of Militant Materialism," in *Collected Works*, Vol. 33, pp. 227–36.

Lenin, V.I., *One Step Forward, Two Steps Back*, in *Collected Works*, Vol. 7, pp. 203–425.

Lenin, V.I., "Preface to the collection *Twelve Years*," in Lenin, *Collected Works*, Vol. 13, pp. 94–113.

Lenin, V.I., "The Taylor System—Man's Enslavement by the Machine," in *Collected Works*, Vol. 20, pp. 152–54.

Lenin, V.I., *What Is to Be Done?* in *Collected Works*, Vol. 5, pp. 347–530.

Lichtheim, George, "Western Marxist Literature 1953–1963," *Survey*, No. 50, January 1964.

Lipset, Seymour Martin. *Political Man: The Social Bases of Politics*. Garden City, N.Y.: Doubleday & Co., 1960.

Lissner, Will, "Soviet Economics Stirs Debate Here," *New York Times*, Oct. 1, 1944.

Lomax, Louis L., *The Negro Revolt*. New York: Harper Collins Publishers, 1962.

Lukács, Georg, *History and Class Consciousness*. Cambridge, Mass.: MIT Press, 1971,

Lukács, Georg, *The Young Hegel*. Cambridge, Mass.: MIT Press, 1977.

Luxemburg, Rosa, *Accumulation of Capital*. New York: Monthly Review Press, 1968.

Luxemburg, Rosa, *The Crisis of German Social Democracy*, in *The Mass Strike, the Political Party and the Trade Unions; and the Junius Pamphlet*, pp. 95–222. New York: Harper Torchbooks, 1971.

Luxemburg, Rosa, "Lassalle and the Revolution." https://www.marxists.org/archive/luxemburg/1904/03/lassalle.html, accessed Nov. 27, 2017.

Luxemburg, Rosa, *The Letters of Rosa Luxemburg*, ed. Stephen Bronner. Boulder, Colo.: Westview Press, 1978.

Luxemburg, Rosa, *The Mass Strike, the Political Party, and the Trade Unions*, in *The Mass Strike, the Political Party and the Trade Unions; and the Junius Pamphlet*, pp. 9–92. New York: Harper Torchbooks, 1971.

Luxemburg, *Organizational Questions of Russian Social Democracy,* in *Selected Political Writings,* pp. 283–306. New York: Monthly Review Press, 1971.

Luxemburg, Rosa, "Our Morocco Leaflet," *Leipziger Volkszeitung,* August 26, 1911.

Luxemburg, Rosa, *The Rosa Luxemburg Reader,* edited by Peter Hudis & Kevin B. Anderson. New York: Monthly Review Press, 2004.

Luxemburg, Rosa, *The Russian Revolution and Leninism or Marxism?* with an introduction by Bertram D. Wolfe. Ann Arbor: University of Michigan Press, 1961.

Luxemburg, Rosa, *Selected Political Writings,* edited by Dick Howard. New York: Monthly Review Press, 1971.

Luxemburg, *Social Reform or Revolution,* in Dick Howard, *Selected Political Writings,* pp. 52–134. New York: Monthly Review Press, 1971.

Luxemburg, "What Next?" in *Rosa Luxemburg: Selected Political Writings,* edited by Robert Looker. New York: Grove Press, 1974.

Lynd, Robert S., and Helen Merrell Lynd, *Middletown: A Study in Contemporary American Culture.* New York: Harcourt, Brace and Company, 1929.

MacFarquhar, Roderick, *The Hundred Flowers Campaign and the Chinese Intellectuals.* New York: Frederick A. Praeger, 1960.

Magnus, George, "Give Karl Marx a Chance to Save the World Economy," *Businessweek,* August 28, 2011.

Mandel, Ernest, "A Hesitant, Uneven and Inflationary Upturn," *Intercontinental Press,* Nov. 29, 1976.

Mandel, Ernest, *Marxist Economic Theory.* New York: Monthly Review Press, 1970.

Mann, Floyd C., and L. Richard Hoffman, *Automation and the Worker: A Study of Social Change in Power Plants.* New York: Holt, 1960.

Marcuse, Herbert, *Eros and civilization: A philosophical inquiry into Freud.* New York: Vintage, 1962.

Marcuse, Herbert, "The Foundation of Historical Materialism," *Studies in Critical Philosophy.* London: New Left Books, 1972.

Marcuse, Herbert, *One-Dimensional Man: Studies in the Ideology of Advanced Industrial Society.* Boston: Beacon Press, 1964.

Marcuse, Herbert, *Reason and revolution: Hegel and the rise of social theory.* Amherst, New York: Humanity, 1999.

Mattick, Paul, *Marx and Keynes: The Limits of the Mixed Economy.* Boston: Extending Horizons Books, 1969.

Maupin, Joyce, *Labor Heroines.* Berkeley, Calif.: Union WAGE, 1974.

Maupin, Joyce, *Working Women and Their Organizations.* Berkeley, Calif.: Union WAGE, 1974.

Mayo, Elton, *The Human Problems of an Industrial Civilization.* New York: MacMillan, 1933.

Moon, Terry, and Ron Brokmeyer, *On the 100th Anniversary of the First General Strike in the U.S.* Detroit: News & Letters, 1977.

Moon, Terry, "Dunayevskaya, Raya," in *Women Building Chicago 1790–1990: A Biographical Dictionary,* edited by Rima Lunin Schultz and Adele Hast. Bloomington: Indiana University Press, 2001.

Moon, Terry, "Eleanor Marx in Chicago," *News & Letters*, March 1984.

Morgan, Lewis Henry, *Ancient Society.* Chicago: Charles H. Kerr Pub. Co., 1907.

Myrdal, Gunnar, with the assistance of Richard Sterner and Arnold Rose, *An American Dilemma: The Negro Problem and Modern Democracy,* 2 volumes. New York: Harper & Bros., 1944.

Nagy, Imre, *Imre Nagy on Communism.* New York: Frederick A. Praeger, 1957.

News and Letters Committees, *Constitution.* Detroit: News and Letters, 1983.

O'Brien, [John Dwyer], *Johnsonism: An Appraisal.* Detroit: News & Letters, 1956.

O'Malley, Joseph, ed., *Marx's Critique of Hegel's "Philosophy of Right."* Cambridge: Cambridge University Press, 1970.

Ollman, Bertell, *Alienation.* New York: Cambridge University Press, 1971.

Padover, Saul K., *Karl Marx: An Intimate Biography.* New York: McGraw-Hill, 1978.

Phillips, Wendell, *Speeches and Writings.* Boston: Lee and Shepard, 1872.

Physician Task Force on Hunger in America, *Hunger in America: the Growing Epidemic.* Middletown, Connecticut: Wesleyan UP, 1985.

Piccone, Paul, "Czech Marxism: Karel Kosik," *Critique,* No.8, 1977.

Record, Wilson, *The Negro and the Communist Party.* Chapel Hill: University of North Carolina Press, 1951.

Reed, Evelyn, *Woman's Evolution.* New York: Pathfinder Press, 1975.

Rich, Adrienne, "Living the Revolution," *The Women's Review of Books,* Vol. 3, No. 12, September 1986.

Rich, Adrienne, "Raya Dunayevskaya's Marx," in *Arts of the Possible: Essays and Conversations by Adrienne Rich.* New York: W.W. Norton & Company, 2001.

Riddell, John, ed., *Founding the Communist International.* New York, Anchor Foundation, 1987.

Riesman, David, *Individualism Reconsidered, and Other Essays.* Glencoe, Ill.: The Free Press, 1954.

Riesman, David, *The Lonely Crowd: A Study of the Changing American Character.* New Haven: Yale University Press, 1950.

Roberts, Michael, "David Harvey, monomaniacs and the rate of profit" on his blog, https://thenextrecession.wordpress.com/2014/12/17/david-harvey-monomaniacs-and-the-rate-of-profit/, accessed, Oct. 7, 2017.

Robinson, Joan, *Essay on Marxian Economics.* London: Macmillan, 1967.

Rosdolsky, Roman, *The Making of Marx's "Capital."* London: Pluto Press, 1977.

Rowbotham, Sheila, *Women, Resistance and Revolution*. New York: Vintage Books, 1974.

Rowbotham, Sheila, *Women's Liberation and Revolution*. Bristol, England: Falling Wall Press, March 1972, expanded in 1973.

Rubel, Maimilien, *Rubel on Karl Marx,* edited and translated by Joseph O'Malley and Keith Algozin. Cambridge University Press, 1981.

Ryazanov, David, "New data about the literary legacy of Marx and Engels (report of Comrade Ryazanov made to the Socialist Academy on Nov. 20, 1923)," *Bulletin of Socialist Academy*, book 6, October–December 1923. Moscow and Petrograd: State Publishing House, 1923.

Sartre, Jean-Paul, *Critique de la raison dialectique*. Paris: Librairie Gallimard, 1960.

Sartre, Jean-Paul, *Search for a Method*. New York: Alfred A. Knopf, 1965.

Schumpeter, Joseph, *A History of Economic Analysis*. Oxford: Oxford University Press, 1954.

Schumpeter, Joseph A., *Capitalism, Socialism and Democracy*. London and New York: Routledge, 1994.

Schwarz, Walter, "Despairing Voice of France's Lost Generation," *The Manchester Guardian,* June 26, 1977.

Sebestyen, Miklos, "My Experiences in the Central Workers' Council of Greater Budapest," *The Review*, Vol. III: 2, 1961.

Senghor, Léopold Sédar, *African Socialism* by Senghor. New York: American Society of African Culture, 1959.

Senghor, Léopold Sédar, *On African Socialism*. New York: Praeger, 1968.

Shanin, Teodor, ed., *Late Marx and the Russian Road: Marx and 'the Peripheries of Capitalism.'* New York: Monthly Review Press, 1983.

Sherwin, Oscar, *The Prophet of Liberty*. New York: Bookman Associates, 1958.

"The Siege of Cuba," editorial, *New Left Review*, 7, Jan–Feb. 1961.

Singer, Charles Joseph, ed., *A History of Technology*. Oxford: Clarendon Press, 1954.

Steffens, Lincoln, *The Autobiography of Lincoln Steffens*. New York: The Literary Guild, 1931.

Stein, Maurice R., *The Eclipse of Community: An Interpretation of American Studies*. Princeton, N.J.: Princeton University Press, 1960.

Stillman, Edmund O., ed., *Bitter Harvest*. New York: Frederick A. Praeger, 1959.

Studies in Soviet Thought, No. 4/1963.

Sue, Eugène, *Les Mystères de Paris*. Bruxelles: Haumann, 1843.

"Teaching of Economics in the Soviet Union."*American Economic Review*, Vol. 34, No. 3, September 1944.

Technology and Culture, Vol. I, No.1, Winter 1959.

Thomas, Edith, *The Women Incendiaries*. New York: George Braziller, 1966.

Thomas, W.I., and Florian Znaniecki, *The Polish Peasant in Europe and America: Monograph of an Immigrant Group*, 5 volumes. Boston: Badger, 1918–1920.

Toure, Sekou "Africa's Path in History," *Africa South*, Vol. 4, No. 3, April–June 1960.

Tristan, Flora, *Union Ouvrière*. Paris: Prévot, Rouanet, 1843.

Trotsky, Leon, *In Defense of Marxism: Against the Petty-Bourgeois Opposition*. New York: Pioneer Publishers, 1942.

Trotsky, Leon, *The Revolution Betrayed*, trans. Max Eastman. New York, Pathfinder, 1937.

Tucker, Robert, *Philosophy and Myth in Karl Marx*. Cambridge: Cambridge University Press, 1961.

Turner, Lou, and John Alan, *Frantz Fanon, Soweto and American Black Thought*. Chicago: News and Letters, 1986.

Van Allen, Judith, "Aba Riots or Igbo Women's War," *Ufahamu*, Vol. 6, No. 1, 1975.

Van Allen, Judith, " 'Aba Riots' or Igbo 'Women's War'? Ideology, Stratification, and the Invisibility of Women," in *Women in Africa: Studies in Social and Economic Change*, Nancy Hafkin and Edna Bay, eds. Stanford, Calif.: Stanford University Press, 1976.

Veit, Lawrence A., "Troubled World Economy," *Foreign Affairs*, Vol. 55, No. 2, January, 1977.

Vitkin, Michael, "The Asiatic Mode of Production," *Philosophy and Social Criticism*, Vol. 8, No. 1, 1981.

Vitkin, Michael, "Marx Between West and East," *Studies in Soviet Thought* 23, 1982.

Vitkin, Michael, "The Problem of the Universality of Social Relations in Classical Marxism," *Studies in Soviet Thought* 20, 1979.

Vitkin, Mikhail, *Vostok v Philosophico-Historicheskoi Kontseptsii K. Marksa y F. Engelsa*. Moscow, 1972.

Walker, Charles R.., *Toward the Automatic Factory: A Case Study of Men and Machines*. New Haven: Yale University Press, 1957.

Warner, Lloyd W., and Paul S. Lunt, *Yankee City*, 5 volumes. New Haven: Yale University Press, 1941–1959.

"What the Marxists See in the Recession," *Businessweek*, June 23, 1975.

Wirth, Louis, *The Ghetto*. Chicago: University of Chicago Press, 1928.

Index

www.ingramcontent.com/pod-product-compliance
Lightning Source LLC
Chambersburg PA
CBHW070900030426
42336CB00014BA/2272